THE AMERICAN CHILD

The American Child

A CULTURAL STUDIES READER

Edited by Caroline F. Levander and Carol J. Singley

RUTGERS UNIVERSITY PRESS
NEW BRUNSWICK, NEW JERSEY AND LONDON

Library of Congress Cataloging-in-Publication Data

The American child : a cultural studies reader / Edited by Caroline F. Levander and Carol J. Singley.

   p.   cm.

Includes bibliographical references (p.   ) and index.

   ISBN 0-8135-3222-1 (hardcover : alk. paper)—ISBN 0-8135-3223-x (pbk. : alk. paper)

   1. Children—United States—History.   2. Children—United States—Social conditions.

I. Levander, Caroline Field, 1964-   II. Singley, Carol J., 1951-

   HQ792.U5 A524 2003

   305.23'0973—dc21   2002156095

British Cataloging-in-Publication information is available from the British Library.

The essay "Child's Play," Gillian Brown, *differences* 11, no. 3 (2000): 76–106, is reprinted with permission of Indiana University Press.

The essay "Playing at Class," Karen Sánchez-Eppler, *English Literary History* 67 (2000): 819–842, is reprinted with permission of the copyright holder and original publisher, Johns Hopkins University Press.

Manufactured in the United States of America

For their love and support of us as children,
we dedicate this book to our parents:

CHARLES AND GERMAINE FIELD

GRACE L. BROWN AND CHARLES SINGLEY

CONTENTS

THE AMERICAN CHILD

Introduction

Caroline F. Levander and Carol J. Singley

Since Philippe Ariès's landmark study *Centuries of Childhood* was published in 1962, there has been increased critical interest in the child as a rich and varied site of cultural inscription. Scholars from a wide range of disciplines have turned their attention to the child in order to interrogate how it comes to represent, and often codify, the prevailing ideologies of a given culture or historical period. From a number of disciplinary perspectives, such work has asked, in short, What do ideas about children—as represented in the narratives, rituals, legislation, or common practices a society develops around the child—tell us about that culture? Answers to this question have revealed the numerous and unique ways that the child represents and then helps to disseminate the ideals governing various cultures. Some scholars—such as Lauren Berlant, Roger Cox, Lee Edelman, James Kincaid, Michael Moon, Jacqueline Rose, Carolyn Steedman, and Michael Warner, for example—have studied the child as a means of thinking in new ways about the adult self and the social, civic, and erotic elements that comprise it. Others—Gillian Avery, Karin Calvert, Hugh Cunningham, and Jacqueline Reiner, to name only a few—have been concerned with documenting the impact that the child's ideological work has on real children and have therefore assessed the material cultures surrounding children of diverse classes, races, and ethnicities in order to learn more about how they experience their lives. Yet despite their different emphases, all of these studies are a response to the idea, originally propounded by Ariès, that the child is not only born but made—not only a biological fact but a cultural construct that encodes the complex, ever-shifting logic of a given group and therefore reveals much about its inner workings. Approaching the child as a complex conceptual field, these studies have charted the diverse ways the child absorbs and helps to disseminate the divergent, sometimes contradictory ideologies that typify particular historical periods.

This collection of essays extends these ongoing inquiries into the cultural meanings of childhood, but from the distinct perspective of U.S. history, literature, and cultural studies. Such a book is particularly timely at this juncture in child studies because the American nation, since its inception, has been identified with and imagined as a child, yet the full significance of this alliance and its relevance to critical inquiries into the figure of the child have yet to be fully understood. Narratives of U.S. national identity are persistently configured in the language of family: national identity is implicated in shifting notions of childhood, from the first colonial separation from a punitive and authoritarian parent country and formal Declaration of Independence to the repeated figuring, in nineteenth-through late-twentieth-century American culture, of the child as a nostalgic symbol of lost innocence and youth. Whether it be Thomas Paine, who argued that "the infant state of the colonies" justifies their "separation from the corrupt parent" country of Great Britain, or Ralph Waldo Emerson, who contended in *Nature* that the child inevitably reminds Americans of their own lost "spirit of infancy," the child operates as a rich metaphor for U.S. writers and thinkers engaged in considering evolving notions of U.S. national identity. Furthermore, because the nation has variously attempted both to emulate the lines of blood and inheritance that define western European nations and to embrace the concept of independence that celebrates severance of the genealogical tree from its roots, the child operates as a particularly dense and contradictory site of meaning in a U.S. context. Thus, the broken genealogy that constitutes the nation and becomes a cornerstone of the American story makes U.S. cultural studies especially productive context in which to extend critical inquiry into the wealth of current analysis of the child.

U.S. literature is not, of course, unique in its representation of the child as the inspiration or embodiment of an authentic self that derives from nature as well as culture. Such romantic sensibilities abound in Western romantic literature. But the United States is distinctive in the ways that it has seized upon the image of the child in opposition to that which is constructed or institutionalized, and in the extent to which it has promoted the child as a force of resistance as well as innocent vulnerability. Such claims of potentiality and independence—and with them ongoing assertions of the right to self-invention; the entitlement to youthful, even reckless, adventure; and the pursuit of infinite possibility—align the nation with what is often taken for granted as the essence of childhood. Seen another way, the child signifies both a space and border between youth and maturity, between new world and old, wilderness and civilization, innocence and experience. This imagined opposition between child and adult has proved fertile ground for writers, from Anne Bradstreet to Don DeLillo, who figure their writing in terms of the child and also enlist the child to convey particular cultural preoccupations. The child is a compelling interpretive site precisely because it is so open and so vulnerable to competing, even opposing, claims. And in a U.S. context, the child functions as an empty or loaded cipher, a conscious or unconscious presence, or a provocative or inert force, with greater intensity and duration than it has in other cultural contexts.

Feminist, postcolonialist, and other postmodern scholarship has complicated optimistic, simplistic views of the child as emblematic of either nature's regenerative power or its opposite, the deviant or abnormal. Such scholarship has similarly expanded the notion of a defenseless child in need of adult protection in favor of a more complex, mutually reinforcing dynamic in which the child elicits adult responsiveness and in turn grants the adult legitimacy, protection, or even cover; and it has challenged the assumption of the generic child. Through the lens of race, class, and kinship, the pure or innocent child may be seen as a white, middle-class fantasy, a construction, as both Ariès and Ian Hacking note, that originated during the Enlightenment and has been employed to erase those events that disenfranchise certain children and their families. Just as the generic child is construed as "other" in relation to the adult, so too do poor, disabled, or orphaned children or children of color occupy marginalized positions in relation to more idealized versions of childhood. These contemporary critical lenses have—in useful ways—helped to complicate the simple equation of the child with innocence and nation. Yet because the child offers a new praxis along which to consider questions of difference, the full extent and versatility of its role in relations between self and other are only beginning to be understood. Sexuality studies and queer theory have begun to theorize the child's significance, but we have yet to investigate fully how the child helps to perpetuate and disrupt the complex social formations that produce particular racial, ethnic, class, sexual, gender, and national identities.

This collection represents current, ongoing work in these developing areas of inquiry and asks us to think in innovative ways about how the child engags in a wide range of social formations. The essays investigate childhood from diverse methodological perspectives and approaches. The volume is grounded in the literary but draws heavily on various other disciplines, making clear that literary representations of children and childhood are not isolated aesthetic artifacts but cultural productions that in turn affect the social climates around them. The essays explore configurations of childhood across centuries, regions, and literary and historical movements. They consider literature written about and sometimes for the child. In the former case, the child functions as the vehicle through which adult identity, behavior, and attitudes are constructed, manipulated, and reinforced. In the latter case, the child is a recipient of adult values and expectations; but even this literature, as Anne Scott MacLeod notes, says more about what adults want children to think, feel, or do than about what children themselves actually desire or understand. In sum, the essays herein view the child as an integral piece in the puzzle of identity that includes self, family, region, nation, and language.

The opening essay, "Child's Play," by Gillian Brown, exemplifies the collection's overarching concerns with material culture, representation, and cultural critique. Beginning with an analysis of the media images of children playing with guns that surrounded the Columbine High School and other American school shootings, Brown delineates how the representational materials of play within children's lives have activated concerns about the effects of culture on citizens. From the end of the eighteenth century to the present, child's play, as Brown shows, has offered a tableau of how Americans become absorbed in different objects and interests. Thus the space of children's play is one of the sacred spaces of modern American life precisely because children's absorption in the charged matter of playthings, on the one hand, reenacts past concerns about the unprecedented production and consumption of objects that typify American life and, on the other hand, acts as a rehearsal for how modern mass consumption will affect that life in the future.

Like Brown, Karen Sánchez-Eppler takes play as her subject. In "Playing at Class" she asks how play, in relation to work and working-class children, operates as a cultural marker for middle-class identity in the mid-nineteenth-century. Positing class as an identity to be "grown into" much like adulthood, Sánchez-Eppler explores how the figure of the street child complicates easy affiliations among play, leisure, labor, and class identity. Through juxtaposing literary depictions of street children by such writers as Lydia Maria Child, Louisa May Alcott, and Horatio Alger to the records and written documents that real street children have produced, Sánchez-Eppler is able to identify the important role of childhood play in the construction of class identity for both middle-class and working-class children.

Melanie Dawson, in "The Miniaturizing of Girlhood: Nineteenth-Century Playtime and Gendered Theories of Development," looks more particularly to nineteenth-century entertainment guidebooks, games, and play activities in order to consider how children's play practices schooled them in distinct gender identities. Through analysis of a wide range of instructive texts such as *Remarks on Children's Play, The Boy's Home Book of Sports,* and *Home Games for Little Girls,* Dawson identifies the uneven gender developmental models that structure and are disseminated through these leisure manuals throughout the nineteenth century. Encouraging girls to act out scenes of maturity and to develop self-monitoring skills and boys to indulge in a careless, unfettered escapism, the "rules" of play, as Dawson shows, reinforce social rules that align masculinity with childlike freedoms and sever girlhood from nondomestic activities. Thus, through the ideological economies promoted by nineteenth-century games, girls and women bear the double burden of being at once always childlike and preternaturally adult.

Interrogating racial rather than gender formations, Lesley Ginsberg, in "Of Babies, Beasts, and Bondage: Slavery and the Question of Citizenship in Antebellum American Children's Literature," examines how the repeated allusion to the seemingly innocent, loving bonds between humans and their pets becomes a medium through which to express one of the era's most pressing social concerns—that of slavery. Rereading the figure of the animal in a wide range of antebellum serial texts such as the *Juvenile Miscellany* and *McGuffey's Reader,* Ginsberg shows how it operates as a trope for slavery and domesticity on both sides of the slavery debate. The textual representations of people and pets that, as Ginsberg shows, abound in this literature obsessively pit black against white, domesticity against liberty, and slavery against freedom and in so doing represent the central conflicts that fired the antebellum imagination.

Kelly Hager's essay "Betsy and the Canon" considers how the question of what children read is foregrounded in much nineteenth-century writing and is connected to questions of canon formation as well as to successful child maturation. After tracking how nineteenth-century writers like Louisa May Alcott, Susan Warner, Kate Wiggin, and Lucy Montgomery represent in their fictions the idea that a precocious taste for the canonical is desirable, Hager charts how such a taste is gradually acquired by such fictional girl readers as Jo March and Betsy Ray. Furthermore, as Hager suggests, these idealized patterns of reading are presented as programs to be implemented by young female readers as well as by female characters. Yet if these novels of female literary education in turn produce reading lists that female readers use, they also, as Hager shows, suggest alternative programs of reading for both their heroines and their readers that undermine simple narratives of canon formation.

Shifting our attention from the broad cultural effects of a wide range of literary texts, Jane F. Thrailkill's "Traumatic Realism and the Wounded Child" reads the image of child death in Mark Twain's *The Adventures of Huckleberry Finn* in order to interrogate contemporary trauma theory's ongoing reliance on the body of the child. Suggesting that Twain offers his own "realist" antidote to sentimental excessiveness with Huck's account of Buck's death, Thrailkill delineates the potent association in trauma theory of the child, corporeal harm, and the irrefutably real. Charting how trauma theory's reliance on the child proceeds from the nineteenth-century sentimental tradition's attention to it, Thrailkill argues that the mutilated child becomes a symbolic figure for unmediated access to the real. In so doing it acts as an unacknowledged, deeply moralistic figure for innocence outraged, and the occasion for theorists and readers alike to cradle an abstraction to their bosom and feel more human in a world understood to be dominated by unreal images.

In "Constructing the Psychoanalytic Child: Freud's *From the History of an Infantile Neurosis*," Michelle A. Massé, like Thrailkill, is interested in the centrality of the child's place in theoretical models of identity formation. Massé, however, focuses on psychoanalytic narratives in order to determine how the child is constructed in, and undergirds, Freudian psychoanalytic practice. Taking the childhood case history of the "Wolf Man" as her subject, she suggests that Sigmund Freud gives us a superb demonstration of how a child's identity is created through adult narrative. If psychoanalysis demands the attention of those interested in the child because it makes up "perhaps the most culturally authorized fiction of voice-throwing," then extended attention to such pivotal cases as that of the Wolf Man in turn reveals the extent to which the reality of the child is less at stake than that of the adult—in particular in the practice of Freudian analysis. Although Freud offers, in "A Child Is Being Beaten," to raise "his voice on behalf of the claims of childhood," Massé concludes that such voicings of child reality inevitably tell us more about their authors than their subjects.

In "Black Babies, White Hysteria: The Dark Child in African-American Literature of the Harlem Renaissance," Laura Dawkins takes "black baby" fables—stories of "milk-white" infants being suddenly transformed into black babies—as her subject. While such fables in the nineteenth century typically recount the destruction of women found guilty of miscegenation or of "passing" for white, by the time of the Harlem Renaissance, the black baby becomes a sign of African-American strength and resilience. Living proof that the race had survived both enslavement and the genocidal violence following Reconstruction, the black baby not only represented the endurance of a people deemed "unfit" by social Darwinists at the turn of the century, but also signaled the newly emergent racial consciousness of the Harlem Renaissance. Dense with images of birth and rebirth—with, for example, images of infants springing immediately from birth to join the political struggle of their race—the Harlem Renaissance, as Dawkins shows, draws heavily on the black baby fable and reframes it as a cornerstone of a new cultural aesthetic.

Richard S. Lowry likewise explores the interplay of the political and the aesthetic in his essay about Hine's child-labor photographs of the 1920s, "Lewis Hine's Family Romance." Wishing to complicate the pervasive notions that Hine's images worked to humanize a victimized working class and that subjecting poor children to the camera's eye pathologizes them as entities to be cured, Lowry places Hine's work in the context of political reform, mass culture, and industrialized labor. In particular, he positions the question of "humanity" and "otherness" within progressive-era discourses about childrearing, education, and family life. Hine's photographs, following the narrative conventions of what Lowry terms an "industrial family romance," put children at the center of a developmental story in which young bodies were used as instruments in the production of adults even as experts sought in public discourse to remove children from the ravages of industrial production.

In his essay "On Boyhood and Public Swimming: Sidney Kingsley's *Dead End* and the Representations of Underclass Street Kids in American Cultural Production," Jeffrey Turner, like Lowry, explores the child's visual power; he takes the Depression-era Broadway musical success *Dead End* as his subject. Set in the tenement slums of Manhattan's East Side and documenting the consequences of environmentally wrought decay upon a group of young boys still innocent enough to dream of a better way of life, *Dead End,* in Turner's analysis, functioned as a powerful display of class difference for middle-class audiences anxious about their own potential economic downward mobility. Yet Turner contends that the unprecedented success of Kingsley's musical is explained not only by the images of economic difference the boy actors made palpable, but also by the erotic underpinnings that these images of street-boy culture held for their audiences.

Julia Mickenberg's "The Pedagogy of the Popular Front: 'Progressive Parenting' for a New Generation, 1918–1945" is interested in the ideological work that Depression-era formulations of children accomplish as well. She investigates the ways that 1930s democratic ideals were translated into a set of childbearing philosophies and practices. Although the slogan "Democracy Begins at Home" has garnered much critical attention, few scholars have examined the extent to which democratic efforts during this period were focused on children through an ongoing discourse of the "progressive parenting" that affected educational institutions, domestic practices, and children's literature. Antifascism, antiracism, prolaborism, and democratic Americanism and internationalism were translated into a willful attempt to shape future generations through a politically progressive parenting ideology. This effort, as

Mickenberg illustrates, left the child open to formation as well as malformation, resulting in practices that, while leftist overall, were both proactive and reactive.

Leslie Paris, in her essay "'Please Let Me Come Home': Homesickness and Family Ties at Early-Twentieth-Century Summer Camps," more particularly interrogates the ways that camp-life culture during the interwar years was imagined as a rich site for inculcating the social acculturation and good citizenship that would, in turn, transform the homes to which children subsequently returned. The children of immigrants, union activists, socialists and progressive educators, Jews, and Catholics all went to camp in record numbers during this period, and they were promised activities that, available only in a rural setting, would give them added strength, health, and social skillfulness. Thus these camps, as Paris demonstrates, promised that the nuclear family would be improved if it were temporarily dismantled and functioned as an important addition to the twentieth-century ideal of the loving, emotionally transformative family.

Catherine Ceniza Choy and Gregory Paul Choy, in "Transformative Terrains: Korean Adoptees and the Social Constructions of an American Childhood," shift our attention to the intersections of cultural and personal identities. They examine how Asian-American adoption narratives, such as Kari Smalkoski's, represent the complex, even contradictory, set of impulses toward both striving to assimilate and maintaining a sense of difference that often structure the adoptions of Korean children by American families. No longer barred from entering the United States, Asians in the last decades have immigrated in record numbers, but transracial adoption remains an understudied element of this new migration, as Choy and Choy show. Challenging canonical ideas of immigration, assimilation, and multiculturalism in American liberal ideologies, transracial adoption in an Asian-American context opens the field of inquiry into the child and provides multiple perspectives on identity formation.

The final essay, Manuel M. Martín-Rodríguez's "Reel Origins: Multiculturalism, History, and the American Children's Movie," returns us to the concerns with which this collection began. Taking, as does Gillian Brown, popular images of children as his subject, Martín-Rodríguez asks how popular Hollywood films created for children represent adults' fictions of nation formation even as they inculcate those ideals in their child audiences. Martín-Rodríguez turns to the Disney films *Pocahontas*, *The Road to El Dorado*, and *The Emperor's New Groove* to examine historical rewritings of such significant events as the arrival of the Anglo-European, the story of the Spanish conquistadors, and the scripting of an idyllic pre-European America. Popular Hollywood images created of and for children, like images of child's play, thus extend into contemporary culture anxious, contradictory accounts of national identity formation. And it is such accounts, scripted through the child, that undergird and continue to structure U.S. self-making.

As the range of essays in the volume demonstrate, American childhood is a dynamic rather than static analytical site, inviting examination from an ever evolving variety of critical perspectives. Inextricably linked to understanding of the self, the family, and the nation, the concept of childhood offers a unique lens through which to glimpse assumed, neglected, or hidden processes of cultural signification. The essays in the collection attest to the multiplicity of meanings inscribed in American childhood and, we hope, help to bring childhood studies into the center of literary and cultural studies.

BIBLIOGRAPHY

Ariès, Philippe. *Centuries of Childhood: A Social History of Family Life.* New York: Knopf, 1962.

Avery, Gillian. *Behold the Child: American Children and Their Books, 1621–1922.* Baltimore: Johns Hopkins University Press, 1994.

Berlant, Lauren. *The Queen of America Goes to Washington City: Essays on Sex and Citizenship.* Durham, N.C.: Duke University Press, 1997.

Calvert, Karin. *Children in the House: The Material Culture of Early Childhood, 1600–1900.* Boston: Northeastern University Press, 1992.

Cunningham, Hugh. *The Children of the Poor in England: Representations of Childhood since the Seventeenth Century.* Cambridge: Blackwell, 1991.

Cox, Roger. *Shaping Childhood: Themes of Uncertainity in the History of Adult-Child Relationships.* London: Routledge, 1996.

Edelman, Lee. "The Future is Kid Stuff: Queer Theory, Disidentification and the Death Drive." *Narrative* 6, no. 1 (1998): 18–30.

Emerson, Ralph Waldo. *Nature.* New York: Random House, 1929.

Hacking, Ian. "The Making and Molding of Child Abuse." *Critical Inquiry* 17 (1991): 253–288.

Kincaid, James. *Child-Loving: The Erotic Child in Victorian Culture.* New York: Routledge, 1992.

———. *Erotic Innocence: The Culture of Child Molesting.* Durham, N.C.: Duke University Press, 1998.

MacLeod, Anne Scott. *American Childhood: Essays on Children's Literature of the Nineteenth and Twentieth Centuries.* Athens: University of Georgia Press, 1994.

Moon, Michael. *A Small Boy and Others: Imitation and Initiation in American Culture from Henry James to Andy Warhol.* Durham, N.C.: Duke University Press, 1998.

Paine, Thomas. "The Crisis." In *The Political Writings of Thomas Paine.* 1837. Reprint Middletown, N.J.: George Evans, 1837.

Reiner, Jacqueline. *From Virtue to Character: American Childhood, 1775–1850.* New York: Twayne, 1996.

Rose, Jacqueline. *The Case of Peter Pan, or, the Impossibility of Children's Fiction.* Philadelphia: University of Pennsylvania Press, 1984.

Steedman, Carolyn. *Strange Dislocations: Childhood and the Idea of Human Interiority, 1780–1930*. Cambridge, Mass.: Harvard University Press, 1995.

Warner, Michael. "Zones of Privacy." In *What's Left of Theory? New Work on the Politics of Literary Theory*. Ed. Judith Butler, John Guillory, and Kendall Thomas. New York: Routledge, 2000.

1 Child's Play

Gillian Brown

A ten-year-old American boy vacationing in Ireland met an Irish boy of the same age. "Have you got a gun?" the Irish boy immediately asked.

"No, but I've got a stick," replied the American.

"Let's play!" said the Irish boy, and delighted with each other, the two boys spent the rest of the day together.[1]

Incidents like this one might signify the long-standing association of America with guns and violence or the universality of boys' interest in weapons. The most significant point of this encounter, however, is not that boys in a global culture dominated by American productions commonly desire gunplay, but that they readily see the possible identity of sticks with guns. In child's play, a stick can serve as gun; the instant convertibility of one thing into another is the very condition of play violence. Just as children pretend to kill and to be killed, they pretend toy guns are real guns, garden hoses are blasters, and whiffle bats are light sabers. Objects aren't even necessary: one can always point a finger as if it were a gun and emit shooting noises.

In the wake of the 1999 Columbine High School shootings in Littleton, Colorado—when the yearbook picture of Eric Harris and Dylan Klebold pointing their fingers in just this fashion appeared throughout American media—the connection between play and real violence immediately became the subject of conversation nationwide. Besides sparking renewed concern about gun control, the shootings at Columbine and other American schools sparked criticism of video games and spurred attacks on Hollywood for producing entertainment in which violence figures so prominently and relentlessly. Clearly, the picture of the boys suggested that play violence presages real violence. But the picture, when not cropped, as it often was, to focus on Klebold and Harris, included at least five other adolescent boys and girls in the same pose, shooting at the camera, which was shooting their photograph. If pretend violence prefaces and portends real violence, shouldn't we be worrying about when the other kids in the picture are going to act?

Of course, most parents do not worry that their children's play shooting is preparation for future killings. They don't worry even if they find this kind of play distasteful, because pretend shooting and toy guns are not actual shooting and guns. They assume that even though make-believe involves innumerable transformations, it does not translate into reality. The space of child's play is one of the sacred spaces of modern life, a realm rationalized and promoted by psychology, a domain celebrated and perpetuated by literature, a sphere served and stocked by innumerable products. Thus, it is now common to speak of the culture of childhood, and the recent school shootings and bombings inevitably have generated intense concern not just about the weaponry children may acquire but also about the representational materials within children's lives: the movies they see, the television and video they watch, the Internet and arcade games that they play. This concern about the effects of culture upon citizens of course is an ancient one, a form of criticism familiar since at least the time Plato articulated it in book 10 of his *Republic,* in which he banned poets from the perfect state because of their emotional appeal. For American society, the anxiety about cultural influence has been soldered to worries about modern mass consumption, the unprecedented production and consumerism of objects that accompanies the history of the United States since its institution at the end of the eighteenth century.

Many of the features that characterize the contemporary sense of American culture as dominated by consumerist technologies—in particular, by the communicative and representational media of video and computers—have been with the nation since the early nineteenth century. Transformations in transport and communications have proceeded in tandem with the growth of the United States, from the coming of the railroad to that of the automobile and eventually the airplane. Besides the train and car, the nineteenth century witnessed the advent of the light bulb, telegraph, telephone, camera, and phonograph—inventions as influential and transformative in their time as cell phones and computers were for the late twentieth century. According to Ann Douglas, whose landmark study *The Feminization of American Culture* rooted contemporary culture in the Victorian past, the nineteenth century introduced Americans to mass consumerism. Through popular fiction, then the predominant mode of leisure activity, Americans became accustomed to finding pleasure in emotional representations, representations that in Douglas's view were removed from the realities of the advancing capitalist economy producing them. By engrossing readers, fiction distracted citizen from contemporary problems. Ostensibly celebrating and promoting sentiment and sympathy for the sufferings of children, women, and slaves, nineteenth-century American popular fiction actually "provided the inevitable rationalization of the economic order" in which slavery, female subordination, and child labor operated. "Sentimentalism," Douglas notes, "asserts that the values a society's activity denies are precisely the ones it cherishes." Through this "dishonesty," sentimentalism "provides a way to protest a power to which one has already in part capitulated." [2]

For nineteenth-century popular fiction to sentimentalize American society in this fashion, it had to grip readers, to enthrall them as Plato thought the theater enthralled audiences. The power of such books as Harriet Beecher Stowe's *Uncle Tom's Cabin* and Martha Finley's *Elsie Dinsmore* to absorb readers motivates Douglas's project to discover a sociopolitical plot behind the production of these pleasurable artifacts—her hypothesis of an alliance between ministers and women writers to attain a new form of "influence" in the United States. Douglas herself attests to the power of sentimental fiction to enthrall readers: "Reading these stories, I first discovered the meaning of absorption: the pleasure and guilt of possessing a secret supply." [3] Douglas's striking description of literary absorption might aptly apply to a range of adolescent experiences, to sex or drugs or junk food or friendships or partying or even sleeping, to any form of immersion. In characterizing immersion in fiction as a secret, guilty pleasure, Douglas depicts the all-absorbing literary objects as a kind of contraband. Popular sentimental fiction appears as a harmful substance primarily because sentimental fiction absorbed and continues to absorb vast numbers of persons. Such books typify mass produced and consumed objects of absorption, which, in the refrain of cultural critique that Douglas joins and repeats, subject persons to certain beliefs. As Walter Benjamin put it, people in the age of mechanical reproduction operate as a "distracted mass." They passively absorb works of art instead of willingly being absorbed by them while actively concentrating on them. [4] Distracted absorption, unlike the active absorption that Benjamin believes is generated by individual, original works of art (for example, a painting), makes the public "absent-minded," and hence susceptible to manipulation, if not "mastery." [5] According to Douglas's similarly anxious narrative of sentimental absorption, readers take in and relay a false account of their society from stories that, in her reading, "obfuscate the visible dynamics of development," the industrial capitalism of nineteenth-century American life.[6]

From such twentieth-century critical perspectives, objects of absorption—sentimental fiction for Douglas, films for Benjamin—take on considerable prestige by virtue of their mass emotional or sensory appeal. Sentimental fiction, in Douglas's view, seems to produce a hypnotic state in which readers lose sight of the real conditions in which they live. The corollary to this image of popular literature as amnesia inducing is the image of cultural forms leading readers to apply aspects of their imaginative experience to their actual lives, for good or bad purposes. Events like school shootings can easily be put into this narrative of absorption, which furnishes a causality for seemingly senseless violent acts.

The crossover from imaginative to real spheres of activity is especially vivid in the case of children because it in fact entails *two* crossovers (and thus the permeability of two lines): the movement from an imaginative to an actual childhood, and the movement from child actuality to adult actuality. We think of childhood simultaneously as a sphere separated from adult experience and as a sphere that is itself divided into two realms. These two realms within childhood, the provinces of actuality and imagination, restage within the child the poles of adulthood and childhood. The child's imagination stands apart from the actuality in which the child lives, an actuality identified with and ratified by adults. In this geography of childhood experience, children appear simultaneously accessible and inaccessible to adults. Hence, thinking about childhood paradoxically proceeds by insisting upon both the fundamental likeness and absolute difference between children and adults, issuing in contradictory expectations about childhood.

Our cherished common sense of the distinctiveness of child life, as well as our habit of blurring the distinctions between children and adults, emerges in the nineteenth century, in part through sentimental fiction. The most salient aspect of Douglas's account of modern American culture is her identification of absorption with sentimentalism, and more specifically, with sentimental representations of childhood. From the nineteenth-century American discourse about children and absorption to which sentimental fiction significantly contributed, children emerge as emblems of both penetrability and impenetrability, figures for the states that absorption entails. Through Douglas's twentieth-century critical lens, absorptions with objects readily fit into cautionary narratives about the ill effects of consumerism. At the same time, however, Douglas's recognition of the nineteenth-century connection between absorption and sentimental portraits of childhood invokes a more extensive sense of absorption that includes but is not limited to the critical suspicion of absorption that now predominates.[7]

Since 1976, Douglas's characterization of sentimentalism has been persistently challenged and revised by feminist and cultural critics (such as Jane Tompkins, Nina Baym, Philip Fisher, and others) who proclaim the political and social value of the literary artifacts that Douglas deemed sentimental and feminine. Yet despite the reformulations of nineteenth-century popular literature and women's fiction, Douglas's fearful sense of consumerism in general and of literary commodities in particular remains prevalent in late-twentieth-century criticism. The critical imperative to find social protest and revision in women's writing, or in minority writing, proceeds not just from an effort to represent properly the hitherto underrepresented or misrepresented but also from the belief that representations decisively affect members of a culture. The different views of sentimentalism share a squeamishness about the relation of persons to objects, a concern that takes the form of questioning whether this relation produces sensitivity or insensitivity to social problems.[8] The feminist critique of Douglas rehabilitates the objects of sentimental absorption, declaring them sources of beneficent influence. Thus, Tompkins's critique of Douglas centered on a different reading of *Uncle Tom's Cabin* in which the novel was demonstrated to espouse an admirable politics, a progressive and revolutionary "sentimental power."[9] Through a few decades now of debates about sentimentalism, there endures an anxiety about the artifacts we experience, and, more than this, an anxiety about what we enjoy. As critics continue to debate the relation of sentimentalism to gender and race, they share and sustain Douglas's sense of the influence of absorbing objects.

To be sure, legitimate concerns about sexism and about racism have driven late-twentieth-century conversations about the nineteenth century, making gender and race and the perspectives advanced or denied through these categories crucial signposts in contemporary thinking. But contemporary criticism also continues to operate according to the guilt and discomfort driving Douglas—her initial sense of shame about our absorption in popular literature. As Douglas and her critics variously evaluate the political and social performance of a given book, they regard culture as a defining and ruling force. Thus sentimentalism figures for Lauren Berlant as a generic strategy and mode of containment developed by what she calls, borrowing from Theodor Adorno and Max Horkheimer, "the American female culture industry."[10] The current critical preoccupation with the moral and political importance of literary objects follows from an initial premise that literary objects dictate readers' attitudes. This same sense of consequences attending our absorption by objects informs current worries about the objects of children's play.

At the center of Douglas's negative portrait of absorption—what we might now call the modern tradition of critical distrust about absorption—is the figure of the child. As Douglas recounts her absorption in nineteenth-century fiction, she recalls her fondness for "the timid exploits of innumerable pale and pious heroines," epitomized by Stowe's Little Eva. Douglas confides that she "read with formative intensity" stories about girls such as Finley's Elsie Dinsmore in the series of that name.[11] The titles Douglas mentions belong to a long list of well-known nineteenth-century fictional pious young heroines, including Catharine Maria Sedgwick's Jane Elton and Ellen Bruce, Louisa May Alcott's Beth March, Susan Warner's Ellen Montgomery, and Susan Coolidge's Katy.[12] From this literary imagery of childhood virtue, Douglas derives her account of sentimentality and its connection to consumerism. What seems the distance of these figures from the market values of nineteenth-century American society leads Douglas to regard them as false ideals, all the more deceiving for their capacity to absorb the reader. This capacity stems from the very youth of the heroines, the frailty that their paleness illuminates. Compelling the sympathy of readers, these sentimental portraits of little girls too good for their world serve "the self-evasion of a society both committed to laissez-faire capitalism and disturbed by its consequences."[13]

Mooring her account of the rise of consumerist absorption in the mid-nineteenth-century sentimental imagery of childhood, Douglas astutely recognizes the crucial role of children in sentimentalism. Eva and Elsie exemplify a postromantic conception of children as inherently good. Their goodness sets them apart from the world they inhabit, and even from their parents. Eva differs from both her selfish mother and her indulgent father in her spiritualism and abolitionism; Elsie similarly holds deep religious beliefs (without political convictions) despite the religious indifference of the cold, strict father whom she is always trying to please. The remarkable character of these heroines lies not just in their goodness but in the fact that they maintain and manifest their virtues absolutely independently of their parents. In Elsie's case, her faith in God proceeds in dramatic opposition to her father. In the most disturbing instance of the often abusive treatment Elsie receives from her father, she suffers his wrath and punishment for refusing to play music for his guests on a Sunday. When Elsie tells her father that she cannot comply with his command because it conflicts with God's command to honor the Sabbath, Mr. Dinsmore orders her to sit at the piano without supper until she changes her mind. Though a guest calls Elsie's father "a brute" for coercing "a child into doing violence to its conscience," Mr. Dinsmore remains adamant about shaming and punishing Elsie for not submitting to his will.[14] Elsie eventually faints and falls against the piano, severely injuring her head and developing a dangerous fever. Her now repentant father regrets his harshness and begins to respect and value her religious devotion, as well as to treat her affectionately.

Such sentimental narratives of the ultimate triumph of the child's values, usually at the cost of her life or suffering, clearly express and celebrate the softer Christianity that was gaining ascendancy over Calvinism during the nineteenth century. Horace Bushnell's popular child-rearing guide *Christian Nurture* removed the mark of original sin from children, redefining them as "seeds" of goodness who just need the right conditions and care to realize "Christian sensibility." [15] As the children in sentimental fiction espouse and embody Christian virtues, they also exemplify the new importance of the child's nature and perspective that mid-nineteenth-century education theorists such as Elizabeth Peabody and Mary Mann were elaborating in their writings on kindergartens and schools. Following Friedrich Froebel's ideas of kindergarten training, Peabody proclaimed that the child is "not to be made by education a sensibility," but rather is "an infinite sensibility already." [16] Stories of saintly children forward this changing conception, this new regard for children as independent entities with their own interests and investments.

The sentimental stories that generate Douglas's argument about consumerist absorption are part of a new American fiction for and about children, which was furnishing increasingly varied representations of children. The imaginative psychological portraits of the child that begin to circulate in the 1850s and subsequent decades include not just the pious and saintly Little Eva and all her avatars, but the mischievous Topsy, the preternatural Pearl, the madcap Capitola and Jo March. Alongside these good and not-so-good girls emerges a panoply of good and not-so-good boys: the conscientious Rollo, the hardworking Horatio Alger heroes, the sweet and generous Little Lord Fauntleroy, the disobedient and fun-loving Tom Sawyer, and the numerous bad boys like him. [17]

These new representations show children absorbed in a range of activities and interests, including not only piety but play, work, worry, grief, anger, jealousy, fighting, friendships, and enmities. Written to appeal to children, this fiction also helped construct the separate province of childhood that became codified by various sciences over the course of the late nineteenth century. The broad scope of child life described in American fiction from the 1850s onward registers the recognition of children's interests that was emerging concurrently in literature and in the practices of education, medicine, and psychology. As children become objects of absorption for nineteenth-century America they also become types of absorption. From the recognition that children have their own interests, spiritual and material, emerges a lasting discourse about the pleasure children derive from objects. The nineteenth-century preoccupation with children's cares and pleasures manifested in sentimental fiction anticipates subsequent paradigms of human subjection to objects of absorption. Well before twentieth-century American society accepted and implemented Freud's concept of the hedonistic child, Americans already believed in the importance of children's pleasure. While Freud understood absorption in sexual terms (and thus registered and amplified the sense of shame and scandal attendant upon absorption), sentimental accounts of childhood focused on the material objects of absorption: Eva's Bible, Beth March's dolls, Jo March's plays, Ragged Dick's and Fauntleroy's clothes, Tom Sawyer's games.

The dynamics between children and objects presented in nineteenth-century American children's fiction suggest that children's engagements are a natural fact of their existence, a fact that can be useful to parents and educators. Initially described and understood as an effect of human immersion in divinity, absorption becomes a closely studied attribute of human activity. Children's play, then, offers a tableau of how absorption works. In studying this tableau, nineteenth-century Americans found a pattern for attaching persons to different objects and interests, illustrating the adaptability of the now recognized human instinct for absorption. Oscillating between admiration for and anxiety about children's absorptions, nineteenth-century American discourse about childhood instantiates the spectrum of concerns about independence and vulnerability that children continue to epitomize in American culture.

Children's Pleasure

As any visit to a museum of childhood immediately reveals, children have had toys for at least as long as people have been keeping track. The specific sense of play as a prerogative, characteristic, and necessity of childhood has a much less extensive history. Since the late seventeenth century, when John Locke noted the importance of children's pleasure, pedagogy and child rearing have recognized and attended to the central role of play in childhood.[18] While experts over the last three hundred years have differed on the nature, components, and effects of child's play, all regard it as a crucial feature of childhood. Locke's principle of pleasure informed and generated the new eighteenth-century business of publishing children's literature, a mass literature designed to please and suit children through its small size, illustrations, and simplified subject matter. In the nineteenth century, publishers produced more children's books and magazines, more elaborately designed and decorated for children's pleasure. In tandem with the expansive development of printed media for children came the proliferation of children's paraphernalia:

new kinds of dolls, automata, puppets, puzzles, games, and gymnastic equipment — new and more engrossing matter. At the same time that greater numbers of play and literary objects entered children's lives, pedagogical accounts of children stressed that "the human being comes into the world with an aesthetic nature" that seeks "objective embodiment."[19]

Not surprisingly, then, the recognition of the fundamental role of pleasure in the child's psyche permeates mid-nineteenth-century American child-rearing literature.[20] In *The American Woman's Home* (1869), Harriet Beecher Stowe and Catharine Beecher echoed the standard view of educators and physicians when they counseled mothers to exert "a constant effort to appreciate the value which [children] attach to their enjoyments and pursuits." Children retain these feelings about their pleasures even after they have become adults. The Beecher sisters cite the case of a woman acquaintance who has never forgotten "one of the most acute periods of suffering in her whole life," an occasion caused by her mother burning some milkweed silk with which the child had been playing. They write, "The child had found, for the first time, some of this shining and beautiful substance; was filled with delight at her discovery; was arranging it in parcels; planning its future use, and her pleasure in showing it to her companions—when her mother, finding it strewed over the carpet, hastily swept it into the fire, and that, too, with so indifferent an air, that the child fled away, almost distracted with grief and disappointment. The mother little realized the pain she had inflicted, but the child felt the unkindness so severely that for several days her mother was an object almost of aversion."[21]

This awareness of children's investment in their absorbing pleasures, and their attraction to and need for pleasurable absorptions, continues in more professionalized and scientific psychological and pedagogical writings later in the century. In *Talks to Teachers,* a series of lectures William James delivered to some Cambridge, Massachusetts, teachers in 1892, he stresses the now accepted fact that children will not learn if they are not interested, either natively (naturally) or artificially (by association with already interesting matters), in the subject presented to them. "The native interests of children," James observes, "lie altogether in the sphere of sensation."[22] Thus it was the sheen and beauty and novelty of the milkweed silk that made it so delightful to the child described by Beecher and Stowe. When deprived of the sensory pleasure of the milkweed silk, the girl understandably feels grief for the loss of not just her plaything but of the possibilities for play. Her mother unwittingly eliminated the entire relationship of play in which the girl had been engaged.

The recognition that objects with sensory appeal deeply absorb children becomes in James's view a very useful consideration for teachers in holding the attention of their students. "Novel things to look at or novel things to hear, especially when they involve the spectacle of action of a violent sort, will always divert the attention from abstract conceptions of objects verbally taken in." James thereby explains why such phenomena as "the grimace that Johnny is making, the spitballs that Tommy is ready to throw, the dog-fight in the street, or the distant fire-bells ringing" constitute strong "rivals with which the teacher's powers of being interesting incessantly have to cope." The objects that most directly appeal to the senses always elicit more attention than the objects presented through the mediations and abstractions of speech. When no immediate distractions arise to claim the attention of the child in the classroom, "the child will always attend more to what the teacher does than to what the same teacher says."[23] Teachers must beware of the possibility that they themselves present distractions that can become wholly absorbing. As James reports, "A lady told me that one day, during a lesson, she was delighted at having captured so completely the attention of one of her young charges. He did not remove his eyes from her face; but he said to her after the lesson was over, 'I looked at you all the time, and your upper jaw did not move once!' That was the only fact he had taken in."[24]

James concludes that "Living things, then, moving things, or things that savor of danger or of blood, that have a dramatic quality,—these are the objects that are natively interesting to children, to the exclusion of almost anything else."[25] What a teacher should do, therefore, is "keep in touch with her pupils by constant appeal to such matters. Instruction must be carried on objectively, experimentally, anecdotally" so that children will give the same attention to acquired or artificial interests as they do to native interests.[26] Acquired interests can connect with and resemble native interests through the principle of association, and "[a]ny object not interesting in itself may become interesting through becoming associated with an object in which interest already exists. The two associated objects grow, as it were, together: the interesting portion sheds its quality over the whole; and thus things not interesting in their own right borrow an interest which becomes as real and as strong as that of any natively interesting thing."[27]

Because "there is no limit to the various associations into which an interesting idea may enter," the teacher has an infinite number of connections upon which to draw between children's native interests and different objects of attention.[28] Teaching through association, as James defines it, assumes and respects the child's prior investments. The Jamesian child, like the little girl with the milkweed silk, lives a very absorbing life. She comes to encounters with adults and adult matters already preoccupied, already engaged with objects. Whatever the objects, their appeal to the child's mind "is a psychological affair," as John Dewey stressed. Like James, he recommended that pedagogy acknowledge and "give free and effective play to the connection already operating" between the child and objects in the world.[29] The naturalized conception of children's absorption thus becomes the foundation for methodologies of shaping and socializing the citizens whom children become. The educational principles espoused by Dewey and James translate Peabody's insistence on the child's "infinite sensibility" and Bushnell's endowment of children with "Christian sensibility" into psychological attributes, giving scientific underpinning to the Beecher-Stowe recommendation of "constant effort to appreciate the value" of children's attachments "to their enjoyments and pursuits."[30]

As pedagogical uses of the new child psychology credit and respect the activity of absorption, they also comprehend the variety and changeability of objects of absorption. Because, as Dewey observes, children's minds continually seek objects with "go, movement, the sense of use and operation," they are always ready to absorb new objects so long as the objects fit into a "story-form" or "psychical" organization, by which Dewey means "the holding together of a variety of persons, things, and incidents through a common idea that enlists feeling."[31] It is not objects themselves but their "go"—their circumstantial fit with individual feeling—that elicits children's attention.

For children in nineteenth-century America, pleasure appears the most common idea holding together objects that compel their attention. James's description of the distracted student and distracting objects like Johnny's grimaces and Tommy's spitballs follows the fashion of representing children's pleasurable preoccupations initiated and sustained by children's fiction. In addition to the pious commitments of Elsie and Eva, nineteenth-century readers encountered an array of childhood absorptions in the escapades of girls and boys, a detailed account of children's investments most vividly furnished by Mark Twain in *The Adventures of Tom Sawyer*. Twain's scenes of Tom playing with a beetle in church and doing everything and anything but his lessons at school stand as a prototype for the vagaries of children's attention that James and Dewey studied. Twain quite sympathetically shows Tom Sawyer engaged in behavior that might merit concern about how a child's interest distracts from interests imposed by teachers and parents and society. His representation of childhood absorption—a series of sketches in which Tom's activities regularly get interrupted, if not punished, by adults—thus conveys an acute awareness of the temporariness of both children's pleasure and the childhood state that harbors it. With the psychological realism that children's fiction produces and children's psychology codifies comes a concomitant protectiveness and nostalgia toward childhood. The inevitable evanescence of childhood, whether or not hastened by adult interference, inspires an elegiac response that, following *Tom Sawyer,* attaches the specialness of children's absorption to boys and their play.

Boyhood and the Romanticization of Childhood

From both nineteenth-century fiction and science emerges the belief in childhood as a special realm, a place to which adults can never return but which they can always remember. This composition of the unique space of childhood stresses the temporariness as well as particularity of childhood, a particularity articulated in gender terms, especially in the distinct character attributed to boyhood. Remembering his 1870s Kansas childhood, William Allen White lamented the impossibility of returning to the state he called "Boyville": "[I]f once the clanging gates of the town are shut upon a youth, he is banished forever. From afar he may peer over the walls at the games inside, but he may not be of them." [32] The irretrievability of childhood takes its most dramatic form in the singularity of boyhood so celebrated in late-nineteenth-century American memoirs and fiction about boys. If children inhabit their own world, boys seem to occupy their own satellite of that world. As B. P. Shillaber wrote in 1879, "The boy must not be judged by the standard of Childhood or Manhood. He has a sphere of his own; and all of his mischief, frolic, and general deucedness belongs to his condition." [33]

A poem in an 1859 number of the children's magazine *Merry's Museum* provides a characteristic description of boys at play:

Pell-mell, they run and jump, and leap
Tumbling in one promiscuous heap.
Until you wonder by what token
They scape with heads and limbs unbroken.
Bold, reckless, cunning, cool, or sly
What won't they try?

Boys emerge miraculously unscathed from their activities. The primary feature of the "mischief, frolic, and general deucedness" of boys is that it is just fun—it has no consequences. The poem then concludes that boys' play

Tis an epitome of life
Without its shades of cares and strife;
Each has its private joke and cracks it

Regardless how the other takes it.
And there's the point—boys take rough jokes
More pleasantly than older folks
Not heeding what's said or done
So they can have their fill of fun.[34]

This sense of actions devoid of any consequences other than pleasure becomes the hallmark of child's play for American culture, the mark of childhood's special status. As nineteenth-century accounts of boyhood advance the values of pleasure and carelessness in childhood, accounts of girlhood present another, now equally familiar, notion of childhood and child's play as preparation for adulthood. Whereas boys embody the radical difference and distance of childhood, girls embody the continuity between children and adults. Louisa May Alcott's girls, for example, strive to be "little women" as they emulate their mother's virtues and learn her housekeeping as well as temper-keeping skills.[35] Toys, games, and activities designed for girls stressed domestic concerns. Popular guides on leisure occupations for girls, like Lydia Maria Child's frequently reprinted *The Girl's Own Book,* included instructions on basket making and needlework amid information on games, riddles, and gymnastics because, as Child wrote, "Every girl should know how to be *useful.*"[36] This conception of play as mimesis of adult activities led to the production of gender-specific toys, such as increasingly lifelike dolls, the better to prepare girls for motherhood and childcare.[37]

Girls, however, in both the fictional and factual records of nineteenth-century American life, often played just like boys. Elizabeth Cady Stanton, for example, recalls her girlhood as filled with "all kinds of games, and practical jokes carried beyond all bounds of propriety. . . . These romps were conducted on a purely democratic basis, without regard to color, sex, or previous condition of servitude." Before Stanton married, she lamented leaving "a girlhood of freedom and enjoyment."[38] Jo March, probably the most memorable tomboy in American culture, likes and emulates "boys' games, and work, and manners." Her "disappointment in not being a boy" doesn't prevent her from playing "boyish tricks" whenever she can.[39] The gendering of play does not necessarily exclude girls from the reckless manner and spirit of play even as it links girlhood to adulthood. Nor does gendered play assure that children will learn the lessons that adults hope or intend play to impart. Jo leaves her doll "a wreck," after providing it with "a tempestuous life" like her own. Dolls fortunately do not suffer as real children do from rough treatment (though Beth persists in calling her older sister's doll a "poor dear"). In the play realm girls can fail at their lessons in their domestic role without inflicting damage. Even as gendered play aims to direct children, it is first and foremost an imaginary occupation, subject to the interests and whims of different children.

The sexual division of play simultaneously promotes two distinct but closely related ideals of play: play as reenactment of the past and play as rehearsal for the future. These two ideals, projected into different sexual and temporal spheres, reflect the nineteenth-century ambivalence toward children's absorption that issues in the paradoxically celebratory and anxious, or laissez-faire and watchful, attitudes toward children. These attitudes often bleed into one another, revealing how the two ideals sometimes work together to support specific programs of child's play. From the division of play into separate gender and time zones come functional narratives about absorption. In the ideal portrait of boys at play, absorption appears instinctive. Nineteenth-century Americans often characterized the sphere of boyhood, noted for its heedlessness and vitality, as a state of savagery. When Charles Dudley Warner declared, "Every boy who is good for anything is a natural savage," he articulated what became the typical phylogenetic account of childhood by the close of the century. "The scientists who want to study the primitive man, and have so much difficulty finding one in this sophisticated age," Warner recommended, "couldn't do better than to devote their attention to the common country-boy. He has the primal, vigorous instincts and impulses of the African savage, without any of the vices inherited from a civilization long decayed or developed in a barbaric society." [40] In this racist chronology of history, the white, American, middle-class country boy recapitulates human development from primitive times to "this sophisticated age." [41] The boy's future, needless to say, will not be the fate of Africans whose subordination is rationalized in this account; he will advance from his primitiveness directly to the modern man of the late nineteenth century. Boys at play thus restate the processes of human history, displaying both primitive energies and an increasingly accomplished use of those energies through their games and jokes.

From the vantage point of time, the aggression, imperviousness and "general deucedness" of boys can seem merely a phase whose disappearance indicates a process of advancement. When identified with ancient humanity, the strange and wild absorptions of boys acquire a progressive function. Yet boyhood interests gain a valid objective purpose only by going away. Boyhood's purpose is to end so that it can then look like a stage in development. Boyhood therefore retrospectively acquires the purposefulness associated with girlhood.

In the ideal portrait of girls at play, absorption appears effortful, adaptable, purposive. Girls at play also follow a recapitulative paradigm. Their play, though, represents not the ancient history of the race that can be invoked as the pedigree of the nation, but the history of the present that can be projected into the future. As girls play their versions of adult female roles, acting as little women, they prefigure the continuation of those roles. Educators recommended dolls and other domestic objects such as sewing kits and stoves for girls' play in order that girls from an early age might become absorbed with housekeeping. The prominence of objects in educational play signifies a hope that objects can hold and direct attention toward specific ends. Girls' play thus improves upon boys' play, supplying a much more direct and immediate example of progress. In this portrait of absorption, toys perform a crucial role, bringing purpose and particularity to the mobile and fantastical objects of children's absorption. Through toys, play ideally acquires an immediately manifest purpose.

Whether retrospective or prospective, play serves a narrative of progress. Thus, the two different ideals of play can resemble each other, despite the presence of toys to distinguish modern play. If boyhood inspires nostalgia by figuring the origins of human progress, girlhood generates an equally powerful though more difficult form of nostalgia: a longing for the present that projects it into the future condition when it will be the past, and like boyhood, part of the phylogenetic record.[42] While the girls' sphere of preparatory play would seem to stand firmly in the experience of nineteenth-century American life, it nonetheless attracted the same nostalgia accorded the exploits of boys. Interestingly, girlhood appeared endangered by the very objects defining it, by modern toys. Even as child-rearing professionals urged the notion of play as training, they worried that directing the play stripped it of its fun, imagination, spontaneity, and flexibility. Toys designed for teaching lessons, whether practical or moral ones, could fail to respect the natural propensities of children. Kate Douglas Wiggin, author and kindergarten teacher, noted with dismay the invention of an "altruistic doll" to which the child is supposed to ask "if she will have some candy." The doll then answers (after the child presses a button on it), "Give brother *big* piece; give me little piece!" Wiggin devoutly hopes that "the thing gets out of order," so that it will "return to a state of nature, and horrify the bystanders by remarking, Give me *big* piece! Give brother *little* piece!"[43]

Wiggin longs for the simpler dolls of the past whom "primitive children" surrounded with "halos of romance." "A doll had a personality in those times," she believes, a sense of character developed from the child's inspirations and machinations.[44] In this nostalgic account, Wiggin recapitulates the romance of play circulated in nineteenth-century literature about boys. Play appears in this romance as a primitive and pure activity, a natural and salutary human engagement that later cultural critics associate with preindustrial economy. Walter Benjamin thus finds Russian toys to be the best in the world because they display and recall the craft with which they were made. Such toys do not speak to him of industrial production and market exchange but of personal handicraft. Roland Barthes similarly celebrates the virtues of wooden toys over the predominantly plastic toys that became popular in the 1960s. Unlike the plastic toys that Barthes finds repellent because constructed of artificial materials and designed to replicate the economic and social character of adult experience, toys made from natural materials like wood supposedly exercise a greater appeal to the senses and the imagination, connecting children to a more natural relation to objects.[45]

The mythology of a past time of purer play and object relations begins to take its modern form in the discourse of late-nineteenth-century childhood theorists, who, like Wiggin, see play as a condition of life now threatened by industrialization. It is from this perspective that G. Stanley Hall observes the virtues of sandpiles for imaginative play and fondly remembers the rural pastimes of his own boyhood.[46] The nostalgic note increasingly sounded in the scientific and utilitarian accounts of child's play bespeaks the mixed response that new inventions always evoke: a concern that they destroy the familiar, or what stands as familiar, as they change the coordinates of everyday life. Criticisms of modern toys like the altruistic doll charge that the pedagogical methods and materials of play repress the child's desire for pleasure and exercise of imagination. Better to give children a sandpile, as Hall recommends, in which they may construct their object relations from scratch.

Lost in nostalgia, Hall disregards the fact that the children whom he observes at play in a sandpile build a virtual facsimile of contemporary American society, a town with increasingly complicated and altogether familiar economic relations.[47] Given the most basic, undesigned materials, children in this example reproduce the social practices that specialized toys would encourage. In Hall's sandpile the two ideals of play merge, as undirected children replicate the results that directed play seeks. Without coercion, play in the sandpile both respects and reproduces contemporary society. Yet children also can build other things from sandpiles.

If children's activities appear to adults as repetitions and anticipations, their mimetic practices still produce surprise—dramatic variables like Jo's tomboyishness, which prepares her to run not just a family but a boys' school, prepares her indeed to reconceive the nuclear middle-class family as a larger social institution embracing orphan, vagrant, and delinquent children. The imaginative scope and operation of child's play thus can have real effects, effects usually effaced by the ordering of play into different temporal sites, into museums of the past and future.

Wiggin's worry about the didactic modern toy disregards the possibility that children could ignore or abuse the altruistic doll, just as Jo mistreats her doll (or fails to use the doll in the prescribed maternal fashion). If, according to the mantra of progressive era child study, children are naturally imaginative, why should any toy exert particular authority over imaginative play? What gets denied in the portrait of the child constrained by the toy is the child's own capacity as an imaginative agent—the ways children see, move, and use toys. The fear that children's absorption in objects might be curtailed by the objects themselves displaces the fear of possibly unfamiliar interests and actions of children. So the nostalgia of the progressive child advocate for untrammeled play still registers as it represses anxieties about unchecked absorptions that might not fit recognizable patterns of development.

Tom Sawyer's Queer Enterprises

The predominant modern American narrative of childhood emerging from the nineteenth century thus oscillates between the conception of children's absorption meriting adult respect and the conception of children requiring adult protection from their objects of absorption. This narrative often doubles back upon itself so that the monitory and reverent attitudes toward children regularly coincide, such as when Wiggin and Hall simultaneously advocate the educational function of play and celebrate the independent imaginative play of children. The twists and turns in thinking about children most sharply stand out in children's fiction where the representational project is to enter the child's perspective, a desire Jacqueline Rose calls "the impossibility of children's fiction."[48] Mark Twain takes this impossibility as the condition of writing about anyone, making the omnipresence of adult perspectives operating in accounts of child life the subject of *The Adventures of Tom Sawyer*. In the preface to this novel, Twain writes that he intended this book not only "for the entertainment of boys and girls," but also "to try to pleasantly remind adults of what they once were themselves, and of how they felt and thought and talked, and what queer enterprises they sometimes engaged in."[49] Characterizing childhood as the prehistory of adulthood, Twain echoes nineteenth-century nostalgic accounts of childhood like William Allen White's memory of "Boyville."

One enterprise Tom Sawyer and his friends especially like to engage in is playing Robin Hood. This game is so satisfying to the boys that they declare that "they would rather be outlaws a year in Sherwood Forest than President of the United States forever" (69). Playing outlaws, the boys get the satisfactions of power and adventure without any effort or danger. Adam Phillips writes that "it is one of the most striking things about children that, in their play, good things can come easily." The immediacy with which children can gratify their desires in play suggests to Phillips that there is a type of child whom psychoanalysis has forgotten, "the child with an astonishing capacity for pleasure."[50] This description of the pleasure-loving and pleasure-seeking child recalls the nineteenth-century portraits of childhood as a haven of care-free activities, with no aim other than enjoyment. Tom Sawyer demonstrates this charmed aspect of play when he and his friends reenact the adventures of Robin Hood. After Tom as Robin kills Sir Guy (acted by Joe Harper), Joe demands "you got to let me kill you. That's fair" (68). Tom refuses, declaring that there is no precedent in the story for this turn of events. The boys nevertheless find a way to incorporate Joe's desire to be the victor into the narrative that they are following. Tom suggests to Joe that "you can be Friar Tuck, or Much the Miller's son and lam me with a Quarter-staff; or I'll be the Sheriff of Notttingham and you be Robin Hood for awhile and kill me" (68). Playing by the book does not preclude changing identities and returning from the dead. The boys follow Tom's suggestion and then "Tom became Robin Hood again, and was allowed by the treacherous nun to bleed his strength away from his neglected wound. And at last Joe, representing a whole tribe of weeping outlaws, dragged him sadly forth, gave his bow into his feeble hands, and Tom said, 'Where this arrow falls, there bury poor Robin Hood under the greenwood tree.' Then he shot the arrow and fell back and would have died but he lit on a nettle and sprang up too gaily for a corpse" (68). Of course, Tom really wouldn't have died even if he hadn't landed on the nettle. It is crucial that the boys can pretend to die in this game, again and again.

Indeed pretending to die turns out to be one of Tom's favorite pastimes. When Becky Thatcher spurns him, Tom takes refuge in imagining himself peacefully dead: "Ah, if only he could die *temporarily*," Twain writes (64). At this juncture, Tom finds greater pleasure in imagining other lives for himself, fantasizing his transformation into a soldier or an Indian chief or a pirate. But later Tom gets the pleasure of dying temporarily when, after he, Joe, and Huck Finn run away to a nearby island, the townspeople think them drowned in the river and hold a funeral for the boys. While Tom enjoys scenarios of pretend death and resurrection, his nonimaginary experience involves the all too real prospect of bodily harm and death. Twain presents Tom's adventures as a series of games and usual play being invaded by adult violence. When Tom pretends to be sick, Aunt Polly roughly pulls out his tooth. Her parental care includes forcing medicines down Tom even when he isn't pretending to be sick. Outside the house, other dangers pervade Tom's life. Out at night for fun, he and Huck witness a murder; on a ramble in the caves, he and Becky Thatcher get lost and nearly starve to death. Twain quite relentlessly shows how little security, fun, and carefreeness actually inhere in childhood. The boys' site for hanging out turns into a violent crime scene; as they fantasize encounters with ghosts, they get an even closer encounter with dead bodies. Instead of ghosts, Tom and Huck see an actual disinterred corpse. Then, as if that isn't a sufficient reminder of death, they see Injun Joe kill the doctor.

Though *The Adventures of Tom Sawyer* opens on a nostalgic note, the narrative quickly and continually undercuts this conventional tone in nineteenth-century childhood discourse with scenes of unpleasant or dangerous experiences. Twain, moreover, demonstrates that child's play itself, even before adults come on the scene to interfere with it or change the activity to chores or schoolwork or sleep, is already anxiety-ridden. Tom and Huck continually scare themselves with worries about ghosts and witches. When they are in the graveyard at night and a faint wind moans "through the trees," Tom fears "it might be the spirits of the dead complaining at being disturbed" (72). Fear is not the only constraint that they enthusiastically conjure in their play. They play Robin Hood or robbers or pirates according to strict rules. They subject themselves to all sorts of constraints in their games. As they play, they engage in the highly stressful activities of emulation, comparison, imitation, and experimentation that characterize adult experience. Twain finds in child's play a microcosm of adult life, whether the amusing account of romantic conventions that Tom and Becky display in their courtship or the shrewd conmanship with which Tom manipulates his friends.

In the famous whitewashing-of-the-fence episode, Tom transforms chore into play by pretending to have fun with the assigned task so that all his friends want to join in the activity. Tom successfully applies a psychology of desire to labor: "in order to make a man, or a boy, covet a thing, it is only necessary to make the thing difficult to attain" (16). Twain inserts here an adult elaboration of the incident, remarking, "If he had been a great and wise philosopher, like the writer of this book, he would now have comprehended that Work consists of whatever a body is obliged to do and that Play consists of whatever a body is not obliged to do. And this would help him understand why constructing artificial flowers or performing on a treadmill is work, while rolling ten-pins or climbing Mont Blanc is only amusement" (16). But this revelation of the operative distinction between work and play is not really to the point of Tom's enterprise, which converts work into play and reaps the benefits of both activities: fun and material profit.

While play may be "whatever a body is not obliged to do," it nevertheless incurs obligations—specific tasks or protocols—that a body chooses to accept. Like labor, which proceeds with the goal of production and reward, play, as Tom pursues it, results in wealth. By offering trade options for participation in his painting chore, Tom accrues an apple, a kite, "a dead cat, twelve marbles, part of a jewsharp, a piece of blue bottle-glass to look through, a spool cannon, a key that wouldn't unlock anything, a fragment of chalk, a glass stopper of a decanter, a tin soldier, a couple of tadpoles, six firecrackers, a kitten with only one eye, a brass door-knob, a dog collar—but no dog—the handle of a knife, four pieces of orange peel, and a dilapidated old window-sash" (15). This inventory of Tom's gain, a collection of curiosities, some conventional toys, animals, and tools, most in fragmentary or useless condition, signifies the profitability of activity that informs both work and play. Tom's adventures outside his own play realm likewise culminate with him taking possession of a treasure, though this monetary one immediately gets put under the supervision of adults, who put it into the bank for further investment.

Showing Tom getting what boys regard as a fortune through clever avoidance of his duty, Twain parodies the contemporary Horatio Alger narratives of good boys who amass fortunes, or at least financial security, through hard work.[51] Alger heroes such as Ragged Dick and Luke Larkin diligently apply themselves to work and study, but they rise from poverty only when these qualities are noticed, encouraged, and rewarded by prosperous citizens. Twain had already mocked this scenario of success by luck of the right connections or acquaintances in an unpublished short story called "The Good Little Boy Story," which ends with this improbable scenario: "Then the bank man took the little boy into partnership, and gave him half the profits and all the capital."[52] Tom's avoidance of work through canny delegation likewise makes a "substantial change" in "his worldly circumstances" (16), suggesting that concerted guile as well as sheer luck figure in economic success. Tom's success at making work into fun, like the Alger hero's rise from poverty to respectability, projects the same transformation of childhood occupations into adult activities that late-nineteenth-century educators envisioned through programs of pedagogical play.

While Twain thus satirizes accounts of child's play that make it resemble adult practices, he also invokes the nineteenth-century nostalgic reverence for child's play by distinguishing the wages of play from the wages of child or adult labor. In the work sphere, successful activity results in usable currency; in the play sphere, successful activity nets objects that hold value only in the select economy of childhood. The things that Tom amasses from play have value only for himself and his peers. From an adult perspective, such odd objects could operate as currency only in some remote or obsolete culture. Twain's list of peculiar things that boys trade in reads like a catalog of artifacts from a strange or ancient people. The objects that the boys treasure stand as tokens of a state to which adults no longer have access. Twain thus underscores the anthropological character of childhood for adults.

The queer enterprises of boys and girls, signifying an irretrievable past for adults, belong to the nineteenth-century romance of childhood. The divide between childhood and adulthood furnishes adults with a sense of a prior time in which they were, or might have been, free like boys, which is to say free to act without their actions having predictable consequences. Even as he elaborates and exploits this idealization of childhood, Twain undercuts it by making clear that Tom and his friends suffer plenty of consequences— whether beatings, other punishments, embarrassment, guilt, or melancholy. The effects that they experience, from both their own actions and the actions of others, show that their childhood is not the idyllic condition of Boyville. Far from being free of constraints, children in *The Adventures of Tom Sawyer* bear not only many of the same difficulties that plague adults, but also the burden of adult nostalgia.

Tom Sawyer, Model Boy

The adults of St. Petersburg can't seem to get enough opportunities to revere Tom's exploits. Aunt Polly, thinking Tom drowned when he, Joe, and Huck run away to Jackson's Island, mournfully remembers him as "the best-hearted boy that ever was." Rather than disobedient and bad, Tom in his absence now seems "only just, giddy and harum scarum. He warn't any more responsible than a colt" (116). In Polly's grief-stricken memory, Tom's behavior is purely natural and innocent, as in the customary romances of boyhood. In the village minister's eulogy, the "mischeevous" Tom and his friends apotheosize into saints: "The minister related many a touching incident in the lives of the departed which illustrated their sweet, generous natures, and the people could easily see, now, how beautiful those episodes were, and remembered with grief that at the time they occurred they had seemed rank rascalties, well deserving of the cowhide" (131). Tom, Joe, and Huck have the pleasure of hearing this encomium and then the enjoyment of being heroes to their peers for having run away and lived like pirates.

Tom and Huck later become heroes to the entire village after Tom and Becky survive being lost in the caves, Huck protects the Widow Douglas from robbers, and the two boys find the robbers' treasure. These adventures elevate the boys into living legends: "Wherever Tom and Huck appeared they were courted, admired, stared at . . . now their sayings were treasured and repeated; everything they did seemed somehow to be regarded as remarkable; they had evidently lost the power of doing and saying commonplace things; moreover, their past history was raked up and discovered to bear marks of conspicuous originality." Their escapades now belong to history, entering St. Petersburg's written as well as oral annals when "the village paper published biographical sketches of the boys" (254). Once again, boyhood transcends actual experience to signify social ideals.

From the village's admiring perspective, Tom's past acts acquire an even greater shine than they did in the minister's eulogy. Judge Thatcher places Tom in the tradition of great men typified by George Washington. When he learns from Becky about Tom's lying to save her from a whipping (which Tom then suffered), he declares "that it was a noble, a generous, a magnanimous lie—a lie that was worthy to hold up its head and march through history breast to breast with George Washington's lauded truth about the hatchet!" (255). Judge Thatcher's glorification of Tom's lie elevates it to national significance. The absurdity of such a hyperbolic claim reflects upon the silliness of mythologizing boyhood, and traces the genealogy of this practice to the nineteenth century's construction of national legends. The anecdote of Washington's admission that he chopped down his father's cherry tree comes out of the American mythology composed by Mason Weems's 1800 *The Life of Washington*.[53] Both Tom's noble lie and Washington's lauded truth here appear as the wishful thinking exercised by adults in their narratives of childhood.

All the mythologizing views of Tom's and Huck's adventures invoke and exaggerate contemporary idealizations of childhood. Once carefree, pleasure-seeking boys enter the pantheon of national heroes, they also enter adult society, as Huck learns to his dismay. Boyhood is no longer like boyhood as he formerly experienced it—private, independent, and wild—when he gets fame, respect, a bank account, and a steady income. At the moment when the boys least need adults, the Widow Douglas adopts Huck. As Tom and Huck's escapades get cast in the celebratory mythology of childhood, the boys find themselves living according to adult plans for their futures. In Twain's narrative arc, the boys move from the romance of boyhood to the characteristic girlhood experience of living a prospective adulthood. The widow invests Huck's money and starts socializing him; Judge Thatcher invests Tom's money and envisions Tom as "a great lawyer or a great soldier someday. He said he meant to look to it that Tom should be admitted to the national military academy, and afterwards trained in the best law school in the country, in order that he might be ready for either career or both" (255).

Huck's response to the new organization of his life is to run away and live in his former haunts until Tom convinces him to return to the widow's household by inviting him to join his robber gang. The prospect of this new game immediately engages Huck, and Twain then leaves Huck and Tom absorbed in the matters of initiation, oaths, secrets, coffins, and midnight meetings. Stopping this chronicle of boyhood here, Twain returns the boys to the same interests and activities with which all their adventures started. In order for the book to be "strictly the history of a *boy,*" Twain must remove Tom and Huck from the situation to which they have progressed (260). The history of a boy, however, Twain has just demonstrated, is finally the history of adult investments in childhood. As Twain leaves Tom and Huck absorbed in playing robbers, the boys continue to be boys in the face of all the evidence of this impossibility. Only in fictive space and time, where Tom need not age and might go on playing forever, can the romance of childhood pleasure endure. Twain, in this book and in the further adventures of Tom Sawyer (though not in *The Adventures of Huckleberry Finn*), simply decrees that the boys can still happily pursue their queer enterprises as if adults did not exist.[54]

When the objects of children's absorption become the objects with which adults desire children to be engaged, as when Tom's interests and escapades become the noteworthy materials of a model American life, play once again becomes the preeminent object of nostalgia. In Twain's exposition of the nineteenth-century paradoxical discourse about childhood, the persistent, if not insistent, nostalgia for child's play marks the hope that different objects of interest can continue to offer pleasurable distractions. Stressing children's capacity to keep discovering other interesting objects (such as Tom's new variant of the Robin Hood game), Twain suggests that the inevitability of change in child experience, like the restlessness of boys, might yield some fun. Put another way, absorption doesn't end with childhood, and the modern absorption with childhood might find other objects.

The nostalgic absorption in childhood is still so deep that, despite Twain's detailed report of the burial of childhood by a society intent upon building a glorious past for itself, Tom Sawyer remains to this day a quintessential figure of boyhood fun. Perhaps because Twain himself cannot resist the anthropological imperative toward childhood, the image of Tom, Joe, and Huck appearing at their own funeral continues to offer a reassurance that children will come through the dangers of life just fine. But the sad fact is that children very often do not survive childhood unscathed, or survive it at all. So long as child's play is purely play, an imaginative exercise conducted with harmless equipment, Robin Hood can forever expire and revive. Children and their lives, though, contain much more than child's play, just as play itself contains factors from outside the charmed circle drawn about play; and therein lies all the difference, all the factors that can cause children, like their elders, to kill and be killed.

In the narrative of child's play that I have unfolded here, the violence encountered by children appears just as vividly in the Beecher-Stowe example of the mother's indifference to her daughter's play and playthings as in *The Adventures of Tom Sawyer*. With a quick sweep of the broom, the mother denies and destroys her child's investments in the milkweed silk that she unthinkingly treats as trash. Child's play is thus as vulnerable to adult indifference as it is to the kinds of adult interference that Twain chronicles. The presence of adults—the effect of their movements upon children's imaginative as well as practical experience—means childhood can never be the impermeable zone that adults so persistently desire it to be. The difficulties facing children in nineteenth-century American popular literature by Twain, Alcott, Finley, Stowe, Wiggin, and many other writers suggest that child protagonists do not tempt readers to evade reality, as Douglas apologetically avers, but rather mark the impossibility of evading the world, a world ratified and sustained by adults. Douglas and other twentieth-century critics might usefully turn their anxiety about absorption from the propriety of objects to the contexts in which objects engross us. If children's absorptions are pervious to others' interest and indifference, the lesson of child's play is that absorption always entails playing with charged matter, which—depending upon the conditions and environment of play and upon the ways children use playthings—may or may not explode.

NOTES

1. Reported by Jennifer Hammett, Summer 1999. For their helpful responses to an earlier version of this essay, I thank Frances Ferguson, Phil Gould, Walter Michaels, Ronald Paulson, Len Tennenhouse, Irene Tucker, Judith Walkowitz, and the faculty and graduate students at Johns Hopkins University.
2. Ann Douglas, *The Feminization of American Culture* (New York: Knopf, 1976), 11–12.
3. Ibid., 1.
4. Benjamin's figure for active, concentrated absorption is a man walking into a painting. See Walter Benjamin, "The Work of Art in the Age of Mechanical Reproduction," in *Illuminations*, ed. Hannah Arendt, trans. Harry Zohn (New York: Schocken, 1969), 239.
5. Ibid., 241, 240.
6. Douglas, *The Feminization of American Culture*, 13.
7. Thus, as I am arguing that the Douglas thesis, following the contours of Benjamin's social critique, has shaped and limited critical thinking about nineteenth-century American culture, I am also noting that Douglas's own invaluable research furnishes grounds for different ways of thinking about absorption.
8. Elaine Scarry illuminates the modern suspicion of aesthetic objects by demonstrating how an incoherent conception of beauty aligns these objects with both incapacity and injustice. See Scarry, *On Beauty* (Princeton, N.J.: Princeton University Press, 1999), esp. 58–86.
9. Jane Tompkins, *Sensational Designs: The Cultural Work of American Fiction, 1790–1860* (New York: Oxford University Press, 1985), 122.
10. Lauren Berlant, "The Female Woman: Fanny Fern and the Form of Sentiment," in *The Culture of Sentiment: Race, Gender, and Sentimentality in Nineteenth-Century America*,

ed. Shirley Samuels (New York: Oxford University Press, 1992), 268. Writing within the critical register of the anxiety of absorption, Berlant also describes sentimentality as a "commoditized expression" that operates like "dreaming," offering a site of critical distance (even a "utopia") as well as "consoling pleasure." Berlant thus reiterates both Douglas's worry that readers find pleasure and distraction in the space of sentimental absorption and Tompkins's related hope that readers use sentimental absorption to criticize and reform, if not revolutionize, society. See Berlant, "Poor Eliza," *American Literature* 70, no. 3 (1998): 647.

11. Douglas, *The Feminization of American Culture*, 1.

12. These heroines appear in Catharine Maria Sedgwick, *A New England Tale* (1822) and *Redwood* (1827); Louisa May Alcott, *Little Women* (1868); Susan Warner, *The Wide, Wide World* (1850); and Susan Coolidge, *What Katy Did* (1872). Informative accounts of nineteenth-century fictional heroines can be found in Gillian Avery, "Homes and Heroines," in *Behold the Child: American Children and Their Books, 1621–1922* (Baltimore: Johns Hopkins University Press, 1994), 155–83; and Anne Scott MacLeod, "American Girlhood in the Nineteenth Century: Caddie Woodlawn's Sisters," in *American Childhood: Essays on Children's Literature of the Nineteenth and Twentieth Centuries* (Athens: University of Georgia Press, 1994), 3–29.

13. Douglas, *The Feminization of American Culture*, 12.

14. Martha Finley, *Elsie Dinsmore* (New York: M. W. Dodd, 1868), 243.

15. Horace Bushnell, *Christian Nurture* (1861; reprint Grand Rapids, Mich.: Baker, 1984), 12.

16. Elizabeth Peabody, *Lectures in the Training School for Kindergartners* (Boston: D. C. Heath, 1888), 197. Peabody's sister Mary Mann echoed Bushnell in calling the children in her school "cherubs." See Mann, *Moral Culture of Infancy and Kindergarten Guide* (New York: J. W. Schemerhorn, 1870). Peabody supplied the guide of kindergarten activities in this volume.

17. Capitola is the tomboy heroine of E. D. E. N. Southworth's *The Hidden Hand, or, Capitola the Mad-Cap* (New York: G. W. Dillingham, 1859). Rollo was the young hero of a series of books by Jacob C. Abbott, who also wrote popular child-rearing manuals. The vogue in fictional stories and memoirs about so-called bad boys, normal boys who frequently misbehaved, began with the 1869 publication of Thomas Bailey Aldrich's *The Story of a Bad Boy* in the Boston juvenile magazine *Our Young Folks* and included George W. Peck's *Peck's Bad Boy* series, William Dean Howells's *A Boy's Town* (1890), Edward Hale's *A New England Boyhood* (1893), and Hamlin Garland's *Boy Life on the Prairie* (1899). For informative discussions of this subgenre of nineteenth-century children's literature, see Alice M. Jordan, *From Rollo to Tom Sawyer* (Boston: Horn, 1948); and Gillian Avery, "Frank and Manly: Ideals of Boyhood," in *Behold the Child*, 184–210.

18. Locke advised that learning should never be "imposed on children as a *task*." Rather, the pedagogical practice should be to make the child "in love with the present business." See Locke, *Some Thoughts Concerning Education*, ed. Ruth W. Grant and Nathan Tarcov (Indianapolis: Hackett, 1996), 51–52.

19. Peabody, *Lectures*, 211.

20. The best history of nineteenth-century American ideas about child rearing is Bernard Wishy, *The Child and the Republic: The Dawn of Modern American Child Nurture* (Philadelphia: University of Pennsylvania Press, 1968).

21. Catharine Beecher and Harriet Beecher Stowe, *The American Woman's Home* (New York: J. B. Ford, 1869), 280.

22. William James, *Talks to Teachers* (New York: W. W. Norton, 1958), 73.

23. Ibid., 73.

24. Ibid.

25. Ibid.

26. Ibid.

27. Ibid., 74.

28. Ibid.

29. John Dewey, *The School and Society,* ed. Jo Ann Boydston (Carbondale: Southern Illinois University Press, 1980), 98, 99.

30. Beecher and Stowe, *The American Woman's Home,* 280.

31. Dewey, *The School and Society,* 97.

32. William Allen White, *The Court of Boyville* (1899; reprint Freeport, N. Y.: Books for Libraries Press, 1970), xviii.

33. B. P. Shillaber, cited in Gillian Avery, "Frank and Manly: Ideals of Boyhood," 202.

34. "After School," *Merry's Museum, Parley's Magazine, Woodworth's Cabinet, and The Schoolfellow* 38 (1859): 47.

35. Louisa May Alcott, *Little Women* (1868), ed. Elaine Showalter (New York: Penguin, 1989).

36. Lydia Maria Child, *The Girl's Own Book* (New York: Clark, Austin, 1833), iii; emphasis in the original. By contrast, William Clarke's *The Boy's Own Book* (Boston: Munroe and Francis, 1829), aims to furnish "everything that will amuse" youth (4).

37. On the gendering of children's play and toys, see Karin Calvert, *Children in the House: The Material Culture of Early Childhood, 1600–1900* (Boston: Northeastern University Press, 1992), 79–120. In an interesting study of nineteenth-century doll play, Miriam Formanek-Brunell argues that this activity did not limit development of girls to domestic and maternal concerns. Doll play instead encouraged a wide variety of imaginative explorations. See Formanek-Brunell, "Sugar and Spite: The Politics of Doll Play in Nineteenth-Century America," in *Small Worlds: Children and Adolescents in America, 1850–1950,* ed. Elliott West and Paula Petrik (Lawrence: University Press of Kansas, 1992), 107–24.

38. Elizabeth Cady Stanton, *Eighty Years and More: Reminiscences, 1815–1897* (1898; reprint New York: Schocken, 1971), 55, 71.

39. Alcott, *Little Women,* 3.

40. Charles Dudley Warner, *Being a Boy* (Boston: James R. Osgood, 1877), 198.

41. Ibid.

42. Late-nineteenth-century views of childhood often invoked the recapitulation theory of human life, in which ontogeny repeats phylogeny. For delineations of this theory as applied to childhood, see James Mark Baldwin, *The Story of the Mind* (New York: D. Appleton, 1902), 51–100; and Alexander Francis Chamberlain, *The Child: A Study in the Evolution of Man* (New York: Charles Scribner's Sons, 1900), esp. 213–354.

43. Kate Douglas Wiggin, *Children's Rights: A Book of Nursery Logic* (Boston: Houghton, Mifflin and Company, 1892), 61; emphasis in the original.

44. Ibid., 62.

45. Benjamin writes that "the entire process of [toys'] production . . . is alive for the child in the toy, and he naturally understands a primitively produced object much better than one deriving from a completed industrial process." See "Russian Toys," in *Moscow Diary,* trans. Richard Sieburth (Cambridge, Mass.: Harvard University Press, 1986), 123–24. Roland Barthes, "Toys," in *Mythologies,* trans. Annette Lavers (New York: Hill and Wang, 1972), 53–55.

46. G. Stanley Hall, "The Story of a Sand Pile" and "Boy Life in a Massachusetts Country Town Forty Years Ago," in *Aspects of Child Life and Education by G. Stanley Hall and Some of His Pupils,* ed. Theodate L. Smith (Boston: Ginn and Company, 1907), 142–56; 300–322.

47. For an elegant and insightful reading of the expositions (and naturalizations) of capitalist development operating in Hall's discourse of child study, see Bill Brown, "American Childhood and Stephen Crane's Toys," *American Literary History* 7, no. 3 (1995): 443–76. In my own reading, the children's transformation of the sandpile into a flourishing mercantile center unsurprisingly reflects their contemporary socioeconomic condition but their play town is only one form that their sandpile could take.

48. Rose writes, "Children's fiction is impossible, not in the sense that it cannot be written (that would be nonsense), but in that it hangs on an impossibility, one which it rarely ventures to speak. This is the impossible relation between adult and child." Jacqueline Rose, *The Case of Peter Pan, or The Impossibility of Children's Fiction* (Philadelphia: University of Pennsylvania Press, 1992), 1.

49. Mark Twain, *The Adventures of Tom Sawyer,* ed. John C. Gerber (Berkeley and Los Angeles: University of California Press, 1982), 33. Subsequent references are to this edition and appear parenthetically in the text.

50. Adam Phillips, *The Beast in the Nursery: On Curiosity and Other Appetites* (New York: Vintage, 1999), 18. Phillips further notes that psychoanalysis has institutionalized a notion of childhood as loss. For an interesting historical account of how Freudian psychoanalysis forwarded the idea of childhood as the lost past of the individual, see Carolyn Steedman, *Strange Dislocations: Childhood and the Idea of Human Interiority, 1780–1930* (Cambridge, Mass.: Harvard University Press, 1994).

51. Horatio Alger, *Ragged Dick and Struggling Upward,* ed. Carl Bode (New York: Penguin, 1986). *Ragged Dick* was first published in 1868 and *Struggling Upward, or Luke Larkin's Luck* was first published in 1890.

52. Gillian Avery reproduces a page of "The Good Little Boy" in *Behold the Child,* 196. The evolution of Tom Sawyer from this unpublished story is described in Albert E. Stone, *The Innocent Eye: Childhood in Mark Twain's Imagination* (Archon Books, 1970), 58–90. Michael Moon makes a fascinating and compelling case for the homoeroticism operating in Alger's stories, observing that the hero is always good-looking, attractive to the patron who befriends him. See Moon, "The Gentle Boy from the Dangerous Classes: Pederasty, Domesticity and Capitalism in Horatio Alger," *Representations* 19 (1987): 87–110.

53. Mason Weems, *The Life of Washington* (1800; reprint Cambridge, Mass.: Harvard University Press, 1997), 12.

54. Tom's adventures continue in *Tom Sawyer, Abroad* (1894) and *Tom Sawyer, Detective* (1896).

2 Playing at Class

Karen Sánchez-Eppler

Class and childhood are both highly visible yet often undertheorized features of nineteenth-century American identity, perhaps for the same reason: national ideologies of class promise that in the United States poverty, like childhood, is merely a stage to be outgrown. This essay will discuss class, conversely, as an identity to be grown into and childhood as a powerful site for such growth. That childhood is individually our most important period of identity formation has been a stable presumption of gender theory. I want to suggest that how childhood is imagined and inhabited similarly provides one of the most potent mechanisms of class formation, and one comparatively little explored.[1] Moreover, not only is class identity constructed in childhood, but in nineteenth-century America childhood itself is increasingly recognized as a sign of class status. The invention of childhood entailed the creation of a protracted period in which the child would ideally be protected from the difficulties and responsibilities of daily life—ultimately including the need to work. "For the history of children," Priscilla Clement explains, "the legacy of industrialization was the hardening of class lines," with middle-class families' exemption of their children from labor as one of the strongest markers of their difference from the lower classes.[2] Thus, to the extent that childhood means leisure, having a childhood is in itself one of the most decisive features of class formation. Yet since the "work" from which children were exempted never fully includes household labor, these general shifts in the definition of childhood function quite differently for girls than for boys.

Historians of leisure have charted the rising valuation of play throughout the nineteenth century while historians of the family have described the period's idealization of childhood.[3] My concern is with the links between these trends, as the same patterns of urbanization and industrialization that separate workplace from home, labor from leisure, simultaneously function to commodify leisure time and to idealize middle-class domesticity, especially that of childhood. "Play," explains Bronson Alcott in justification of his pedagogical proposals, "is the appointed dispensation of childhood." This wonderfully unplayful phrasing presents child's play as part of the created order of things. "Appointed dispensation" emphasizes in its very redundancy the guiding wisdom—divine and/or social—that regulates human affairs, and Alcott's discussion of children's play focuses on how teachers should use play to ready children for the "loftier claims" of "instruction" and "advancement."[4] Alcott, writing in 1830, was among the nation's earliest champions of children's play, and his defense of its "designed purpose" shows the marks of the culture's general view of leisure as a largely suspect activity and childhood as besmirched by infant depravity and original sin.[5] By the time Macy's opened the nation's first toy department in 1875 the merchandising of children's toys epitomized how leisure, not work, would drive the consumption patterns of mature industrial capitalism. The 1870 census would be the first to track children's employment, and it would also be in the 1870s that states would begin passing laws regulating child labor.[6] These are enormous and extremely swift shifts in the cultural understanding of childhood, work, and play. I will focus this exploration on the decades of the 1850s through 1870s—and on the figure of the working child, whose need to labor stands in potent opposition to the burgeoning idealization of childhood as a life stage appointed for play.[7]

This is not a simple story of playtime's haves and have-nots, for with remarkable consistency it is the working child who is seen to embody play, and hence who teaches the middle class about fun. By the end of the century, play—and the worlds of the imagination—would have become cultural markers for what was marvelous about childhood, and this culturally valuable play would be recognized as an attribute of middle-class affluence and leisure. Yet it is through depictions of working-class children that these middle-class ideals are first and most forcefully articulated.[8] In particular, this essay will focus on the paradigmatic example of the street child. With street trading one of the most visible forms of child employment in American cities, street traders figured largely in literary and reform discourses as the representative child laborer.

As children, street traders both embodied the chasm of class (since middle-class children would not occupy the streets in this way) and made that divide appear less frightening. For whatever New York's one-time chief of police George Mastell might say about the "idle and vicious children of both sexes, who infest our public thoroughfares," an infestation of children poses a largely future threat, while the adult poor appear far more immediately dangerous.[9] Street children, as children, accrued much of the charm that the middle-class associated with childhood, along with the pathos of lacking most of the material conditions that made such charming childhoods possible. For these reasons images of street children proved a popular means of representing and humanizing all that was troubling but attractive about urban spaces. These ambiguities express the instability, the cultural uncertainties, of the assignation of class identity to street children. Distributors, not producers, they are independent agents (however exploited); their labor is not characterized by the routinization of factory, office, or domestic work. Thus, despite their extreme poverty and the harshness of their work conditions, street children are nevertheless frequently evoked to represent a kind of liberty from the constraints and abjection of labor. Karl Marx counted "orphans and pauper children" among the "surplus-population," that "industrial reserve-army" required for the "free play" of capital.[10] His analysis suggests how these figurations of street trading as a form of play present a romance of the market, one that emphasizes the swirl of circulation and disregards the wasting of "surplus" lives. In a more conservative version of social critique, reformers like Charles Loring Brace (founder of New York's Children's Aid Society) would see in these children the clearest mark of social disintegration.[11] Wai Chee Dimock's observation that "leisure is class-inflected" not because "it is tied to one particular class" but because it is "variously nuanced and accented, when it is invoked as the salient characteristic for different groups" can thus be pressed one step further under the recognition that street traders are simultaneously seen to occupy a number of quite "different groups" with quite differently "accented" conceptions of leisure: they are workers, children, unproductive scamps, and entrepreneurs (or, as they were often called by apologists, "little merchants").[12]

Literary depictions of street children ricochet from spunky and resourceful (childhood insouciance simply taking the city and the labor it requires as conditions for a new kind of play) to vulnerable and exploited (childhood innocence abused by economic and urban circumstances). In both versions the association of these children with the streets, the ease with which their stories serve as potent figurations of urban life, conflicts with the traditionally domestic accents of childhood. Take, for example, the newsboy:

"Can you tell me, my lad, the way to Broadway?"
"Another insult by gorry," thought Bob, and quick as thought he

touched his thumb to the tip of his nose, and wheeling his fingers in the air answered, "no you don't, you don't come it over this child"; and he looked back and relieved himself of a great laugh, while the questioner remained standing and looking after him in utter amazement. "Just as if he didn't know he was in Broadway," thought Bob, and he gave an extra key to the compass of his voice to show his contempt for all fooling.[13]

A world where adults must ask the aid of children is a topsy-turvy place, one in which traditional models of deference, due to age or class, no longer hold. In a clash of cultures, Bob is as unwilling to recognize the depths of this gentleman's ignorance of the city, as the gentleman is incapable of recognizing Broadway or comprehending Bob's response to his question. Bob's insistence that "you don't come it over this child" rejects all middle-class notions of what a child should be—innocent, ignorant, and docile—and instead represents the child as the master of urban spaces; thumbing his nose at the very notion of deference, he is himself the champion of "fooling."

The alternative to Bob's jeering autonomy is sympathetic pain. "I had not gone far," writes Lydia Maria Child in one of her *Letters from New York*, "when I met a little ragged urchin, about four years old, with a heap of newspapers, 'more big as he could carry,' under his little arm, and another clenched in his small red fist. The sweet voice of childhood was prematurely cracked into shrillness, by screaming street cries at the top of his lungs; and he looked blue, cold, and disconsolate. . . . I stood looking after him as he went shivering along. Imagination followed him to the miserable cellar where he probably slept on dirty straw. . . . "[14] Child's *Letters* blend social criticism with rich accounts of the development of a moral and aesthetic imagination. They are thus simultaneously engaged in creating and elevating bourgeois subjectivity and in critiquing the social inequities that have historically made that subjectivity possible. Thus, this letter—in which Child invites her readers to follow her imagination as it fabricates a future of abuse and ultimate criminality for the newsboy—presses on to ask, "When, oh when, will men learn that society makes and cherishes the very crimes it so fiercely punishes and *in* punishing reproduces?"(84). The surprising word here is *cherishes*, a word that seems deeply descriptive of Child's own imaginative procedures, and unsettlingly perceptive of the ways society may foster crime. To be cherished is just what the nineteenth-century middle class had understood as the child's ideal, but necessary, role. The lisping child voice, with its awkward grammar that proclaims the pile of newspapers "more big as he could carry" is not, of course the newsboy's. It speaks in the third person; and besides, among the first things that Child notices about this newsboy is that he lacks "the sweet voice of childhood." By interpolating such a sweet voice into her letter, by the evident fondness with which she produces its little errors, Child demonstrates how a cherished childhood should sound.

One literary use of the newsboy is thus to define and value middle-class childhoods through the depiction of their antithesis. In Louisa May Alcott's "Our Little Newsboy" the possessive and the diminutive function to claim the newsboy for the middle-class home, and indeed the scene of the story is not Jo's encounter with the newsboy, but her retrospective telling of that meeting as a bedtime story.

> "If I saw that poor little boy, Aunt Jo, I'd love him lots!" said Freddy, with a world of pity in his beautiful child's eyes.
>
> And believing that others would be kind to little Jack and such as he I tell the story.
>
> When busy fathers hurry home at night I hope they'll buy their papers of the small boys. . . . For love of the little sons and daughters safe at home, say a kind word, buy a paper, even if you don't want it; and never pass by, leaving them to sleep forgotten in the streets at midnight, with no pillow but a stone.[15]

Here the middle-class child's response to the story of a homeless newsboy is itself definitive of a childlike vision—Freddy has "beautiful child's eyes"—and this vision urges charity from busy middle-class men. In this realm of middle-class benevolence, commercial interactions come to seem like moral attributes, and to buy "even if you don't want it" a mark of virtue. It is, after all, just as preposterous an imposition of possession for fathers to speak of "their papers" as it is for Aunt Jo to claim "our little newsboy," but middle-class identity is constituted in scenes like these so as to make the emotional traits of interest and concern indistinguishable from the economic processes of purchase and ownership. Read sentimentally, it is the middle-class child's compassion that marks him as a good child. It is the middle-class father's love of this child that affirms the father's class position and inaugurates the charitable social responsibilities of that position. Read commercially, middle-class affluence buys both comfort (material distance from need) and conscience (empathic proximity to need). Aunt Jo's bedtime terms—from Freddy's nursery to the newsboy's stone—resonate with the end of Child's letter, which finds her unable to sleep. The voices of street hawkers outside her window "proved too much for my overloaded sympathies. I hid my face in the pillow and wept; for 'my heart was almost breaking with the misery of my kind'" (86).

Class identity, it seems, is largely a question of pillows. Soft beds support sentimental suffering; they create a safe space for imaginative identification and so teach the comfortable virtues of feeling for someone else the very pain that this class position, this soft pillow, protects one from feeling in one's own person. As Child represents herself weeping into her pillow, the "confusing elision between sentimentality and domesticity" that June Howard incisively charges us to interrogate appears remarkably palpable, suggesting how very much the material conditions of middle-class households provide the contours and possibilities of sentimentality's imaginative form.[16] It is these comfortable and private spaces that enable reader and writer to luxuriate in feeling.

The hard beds of street children are perceived as teaching other lessons, but are just as certainly the source of class identities to be learned. "I known an old wagon, up an alley, where I can sleep like a top," Horatio Alger's bootblack Tim explains to Sam Barker, a greenhorn newly escaped to city life from the abundance and hard work of a New England farm. At day's end the boys climb into the wagon together: "There is everything in getting used to things, and that is where Tim had the advantage. He did not mind the hardness of his couch, while Sam, who had always been accustomed to a regular bed, did."[17] This lesson of hard beds produces a certain hardiness and resilience that Alger marks as an advantage. Clearly the recognition that "there is everything in getting used to things" proves a comfortable antidote to the tears brought on by "overloaded sympathies." But it is also true that such hardiness is one of the strongest attractions of Alger's fiction. Sam's sly resilience does, after all, keep him and the novel's plot "adrift in the streets"; his scams carry him and his readers humorously from one scrape to the next while Alger's anxious narrator "warn[s] my boy readers that I by no means recommend them to pattern after him" (84). Thus, as with Bob thumbing his nose, such stories of badly behaved boys celebrate the play of street life even as they press their young heroes toward softer beds and office jobs.

Novelistic images of the "child wage earner as an urban folk hero" and "seedling entrepreneur" run, of course, counter to the historical record: very few if any children actually prospered through street trading.[18] But to note the falsity of such images, or on the other hand to question the presumptions that underlie Lydia Maria Child's imaginings of the newsboys' dismal prospects, should initiate, not foreclose, explorations of the representational work done by street children. The simultaneous popularity of these two opposing images, in their very opposition, produces a middle space of exploitation and survival that may more accurately represent the noncontinuous manner in which class identity is lived. Thus, while these stock figures tell us a great deal about middle-class constructions of class identity, they do not end there, for as I will show, street children themselves learned how to move within and manipulate these stereotypes. The annual reports of the Children's Aid Society were bolstered with appendixes of miscellaneous documents, examples of newspaper coverage of the Society's work, reports and diary excerpts by visitors and staff detailing specific daily events, and—most remarkable of all—large collections of letters written by children who had been helped by the Society and by the families that took them in. These are obviously biased and mediated sources, but for all their limitations they provide a rich cache of documentation about the attitudes and experiences of particular, individual, nineteenth-century street children. The understandings of childhood work and play voiced by these children overlap with and diverge from the representations offered by philanthropists and novelists. Thus, the standard stories of street-child pathos or hardiness do not simply prove false, but rather provide a projected context that actual street children strove to use as best they could.

Critics of Alger's tales have pointed out not only the gap between his novels and the real conditions of street children in New York, but also the divergence between his novels and the rags-to-riches mythos that has grown out of them. Not only do Alger's heroes rarely achieve riches, settling rather for the humble rewards of office jobs, but even this small success is never dependent upon the skill and industry with which they work their street jobs. Rather, Alger's heroes get their chance at respectability through extraprofessional services rendered to the wealthy: it is the finding and rescuing of wallets and children that most often win Alger's street boys their patrons. This is not to say that work is irrelevant; the newsboy Rufus, for example, is called "Rough and Ready" because of his readiness in hawking papers, while Ragged Dick easily supports himself as a bootblack because he is "energetic and on the alert for business." [19] But Alger is not, in fact, so naive as to represent a change in work habits as able to do more than increase a boy's income within his street trade and indicate his capacity for success in other, more respectable, jobs once luck has intervened to move him there. Moreover, the new positions as clerks and office boys to which Alger's heroes rise are not represented as more richly remunerative than their street work. When Rufus quits newspaper selling to work for Mr. Turner, the businessman offers to pay his new clerk "the same you have been earning by selling papers, that is, eight dollars a week. It is nearly double what I have been accustomed to pay" (297). As Alger explains, the difference between clerk and street boy derives not from the difference in their earnings but from their different habits of expenditure. In the case of Ragged Dick,

There were not a few young clerks who employed Dick from time to time in his professional capacity, who scarcely earned as much as he, greatly as their style and dress exceeded his. Dick was careless of his earnings. Where they went he could hardly have told himself. However much he managed to earn during the day, all was generally spent before morning. He was fond of going to the Old Bowery Theater, and to Tony Pastor's, and if he had any money left afterwards, he would invite some of his friends in somewhere to have an oyster stew; so it seldom happened that he commenced the day with a penny. (43)

This is to say that Alger's project—the narrative of fitting street boys for the middle class—proves to be all about redirecting play rather than teaching work. In the process of these novels Alger's boys learn to save in newly opened bank accounts and to spend the cash they accrue not on swiftly consumed pleasures but on more lasting markers of status and domesticity: suits of clothes and regular beds.[20] Alger's heroes thus shed not only their rags but also their riches, if by riches we mean the luxuries of consumption, leisure, and play. If the audience for these books was primarily middle-class boys, might not such readers remember them as rags-to-riches stories precisely because in their renditions of street-boy excesses and pranks they offer such riches—teaching middle-class children to play and spend? Mr. Turner's son Walter envies Rufus his income from selling papers: "I only get fifty cents a week for spending money," he whines (262).[21]

There is some evidence that street children—at least those who relied upon Newsboys' Lodging Houses—read Alger's novels as well. In 1870 a New York Children's Aid Society table of statistics on the children who had stayed in the Lodging Houses in the previous year found only ten percent to be illiterate.[22] Alger advertises in his preface to *Fame and Fortune* that his publisher, A. K. Loring, would "send a gratuitous copy of the two volumes of the *Ragged Dick Series* already issued to any regularly organized Newsboy's Lodge within the United States," and some Lodging Houses appear to have taken him up on this offer. The preface notes, "The manager of the Newsboy's Home in St. Louis writes, 'when on East last year, I got a copy of *Ragged Dick*, and the boys have enjoyed it so much, that it will not last much longer, and are continually asking for the second volume. You will oblige us very much by sending us a copy of both *Ragged Dick* and *Fame and Fortune*."[23] I have no more further account of what it was about these books that the boys in St. Louis so enjoyed, but their consumption of Alger's stories attests to the ways that their self-making was in conscious dialogue with fictional images of street boys. Clearly, in the terms offered by the Lodging Houses (which quickly came to contain small libraries) and by Alger's fiction (where the decision to spend an evening reading rather than squandering earnings on oysters and vaudeville is one of the strong markers of a boy's rise), such enjoyment is itself a sign of reformation. But given the instability of riches and play in these books it is hard to be sure which pleasure is which.

When in the *Second Annual Report of the Children's Aid Society* Charles Loring Brace describes the sort of boys he hoped to reach through the founding of the Newsboys' Lodging Houses he emphasizes the nondomestic nature of their lives, and is evidently more troubled by their choices in play than by their exploitation in work. "The class of newsboys were then apparently the most wild and vicious set of lads in the city," he writes. "Many of them had no home, and slept under steps, in boxes, or in corners of the printing-house stairways. . . . Their money, which was easily earned, was more quickly spent in gambling, theaters and low pleasures, for which, though children, they had a man's aptitude" (1855: 13). Brace's use of the past tense suggests the possibility of reform. Indeed, he happily reports that since the founding of the Lodging House this "man's aptitude" for forms of play that strike him as inappropriate to childhood has been largely redirected; for example, "the game of chequers" was introduced into the Lodging House "as a check to gambling . . . serving to exercise harmlessly that incessant mental activity and love of venture peculiar to the class" (14). Of course, the Lodging House also provided regular beds and baths.[24] Yet despite such efforts to reshape the newsboys' leisure, and the sharp charge of viciousness, it remains clear that it is precisely the newsboys' peculiar love of venture that made this "class" such a potent embodiment of the play of entrepreneurial speculation, and similarly that made these street children so attractive to reformers.

Frederick Starr explains that at the Philadelphia Newsboys' Lodging House "pains is taken [*sic*] gradually to refine their tastes by entertaining lectures, readings, dramatic or otherwise, and innocent games."[25] Yet the lodging-house game he describes with greatest detail does not appear very likely to refine its players:

> A certain game, admitting of no euphemism in its suggestive title has possession of the floor. This is no other than "The Pile of Maggots," and its nature is that of a vortex, drawing in all appreciative spirits with an irresistible offer of fun. The rule is for all to "pile in," the best fellow keeping on top without injuring his competitors. Of course the party who supposes himself uppermost has but brief time for exaltation, soon finding himself at the bottom of the heap, and made thoroughly to *feel* his position. The struggle is generally of short duration, for as the fun grows fast and furious, the smaller boys shouting "Ouch! Get off uv me, you fellers," the superintendent taps a bell, and all is quiescent instanter.[26]

"The Pile of Maggots" does not appear in William Newell's *Games and Songs of American Children;* Newell, after all, holds that children's games "invariably came from above, from the intelligent class" and that while many games and songs "still common in our cities, judging from their incoherence and rudeness, might be inventions of 'Arabs of the streets'; these invariably prove to be mere corruptions of songs long familiar on American soil" and not immigrant made.[27] In Starr's telling, the game has the feel of a parable, but one in which Alger's stories of struggling upward are shown to require that others tumble downward.[28] Thus "The Pile of Maggots" plays at the inversion of the social order, and locates pleasure as much in the squirming and toppling as in any capacity to secure the "top." I find the language of Starr's account rather like the game itself in that his absurdly elevated phrasing vies for supremacy with the speech that he "quotes" from the boys, so that this description is itself a shifting pile of values and vocabularies. Starr's obvious falsifications in claiming that such a game could be played without injuring the boys below, or that one tap of a bell could reduce a heap of boys to "quiescence instanter" ultimately function to acknowledge the limits of staff control. If "The Pile of Maggots" indicates the boys' capacity to make squalor into play, and so impose a kind of imaginative control over the hardships of street life, Starr's narration of this game reveals a similar tendency among the philanthropists: a capacity to find "fun" and pleasure in boys' activities that they cannot manage to refine or reform.[29] The vision of the street boy playing offers a salve to middle-class consciences and a fantasy of the vicissitudes of the market as a game, even as images of the street boy's vulnerability helped form those consciences. After all, few in the middle class could say of themselves, as Alger can of Sam in *The Young Outlaw,* that without debts or assets they are "just even with the world" (251–52).

A Mr. Tracy, the superintendent of a Newsboys' Lodging House in New York, while claiming that the house is "working harmoniously . . . and its arrangements are popular with the boys," nevertheless recognizes the limitations of its appeal. "The temptations of a street life to such boys, and its excitements are so strong, that it is exceedingly difficult to get them in here, and induce them to stay," he reports (1857: 17). His accounts of the Lodging House are full of examples of such difficulties in reforming the street boys' models of pleasure and consumption:

> These boys always live well when they have the money. This evening, while a number of them were telling each other what they had for supper, I undertook to reason with them about their diet—that they should avoid some of the nice things which they had mentioned, and

live more upon plainer food, as that was healthier and cheaper. That they should allow their reason instead of their appetite to control them in the selection of their food, "Ah sir," said one boy, "when a feller is hungry and has a good diner smokin' before him, its no time to *reason;* and I have made up my mind that them ruffled shirt 'quills' (clerks) shant eat up all the good things, no how!" I concluded to let the matter drop for the present, and took another subject. (1855: 25)

This street boy understands himself to be engaged in a contest of status and pleasure with the city's other horde of working youth—"them ruffled shirt 'quills.'" Thus the boy is clear that Tracy's terms of reason versus appetite and the system of moral values they imply are an ethical gloss on what is in fact a class conflict. The boy knows that the issue is not one of learning to *control* desires but of who gets to have his desires fulfilled. Starr makes a joke of the Philadelphia newsboys, who upon learning that a Lodging House was to be opened in that city "made tours of the west end of the city, and brought back fantastic reports of several of the costly mansions there, which exactly met their lofty ideas." What they got instead were "plain, yet comfortable, lodging rooms in Pearl Street." [30] I suspect that in suggesting more illustrious addresses these boys were themselves jesting—pointing out the gap between the wealth of their benefactors (whose addresses appear in the subscription lists) and the modest nature of their grandly offered largess. Why is it that what is appropriate for one appears absurdly "lofty" for another? In these pranks the boys talk back to middle-class philanthropic presumptions; such responses suggest that the acceptance of these dinners and these beds does not necessarily mean concurrence in the process of reforming appetites nor gratitude for the beds and meals bestowed.

In an encounter with philanthropic visitors to a Newsboys' Lodging House in New York the newsboys' skill in balancing docility with provocation is even more apparent. After hearing their visitor speak, the newsboys were asked to treat him with a speech in return. Brace published an account of "Paddy's" speech in his *Annual Report* for 1861 noting that he had taken it "from the *Daily Times.*" Brace printed it again in his study *The Dangerous Classes of New York,* there identifying it as taken "from the journal of a visitor from the country." Presuming that both sources are true—that a visitor's journal entry was also published in the *Daily Times*—the disparity in attribution points to Brace's shifting sense of which kind of source gives more authority to his account: the prestige of newspaper coverage or the immediacy and authenticity of a diary. In all events, these multiple publications make it evident that Brace recognizes this scene as peculiarly useful advertising for the Lodging

House. It is thus remarkable how much of the newsboy's ironic relations to the charity offered by Brace and the Children's Aid Society remains legible through all of these beneficent publications:

> "Bummers," said he, "snoozers, and citizens, I've come down here among ye to talk to yer a little! Me and my friend Brace have come to see how ye'r gittin' along, and to advise yer. You fellers what stand at the shops with yer noses over the railin' smelling' ov the roast beef and hash—you fellers who's got no home—think of it how we are to encourage ye. [Derisive laughter, "Ha-ha's," and various ironical kinds of applause.] I say, bummers—for you're *all* bummers (in a tone of kind patronage)—*I was a bummer once* [great laughter]—I hate to see you spendin' your money on penny ice-creams and bad cigars. Why don't you save your money? You feller without no boots, how would you like a new pair, eh? [Laughter from all the boys but the one addressed.] Well, I hope you may get'em, but I rayther think you won't. I have hopes for you all. I want you to grow up to be rich men—citizens, Government men, lawyers, generals, and influence men."[31]

Paddy's speech cavorts in "the area between mimicry and mockery," as Homi Bhabha identifies it;[32] his performance for a philanthropic visitor permits him to imitate just such visitors, to play one of those "rich men" who can claim Brace as "my friend" and dole out advice and encouragement to hapless newsboys. What is so very funny about Paddy's identificatory claim "*I was a bummer once*" is the group's knowledge that the speaker had been a bummer—"roving about the streets of night without sleep"—in the recent past, and no doubt could soon be one again.[33]

Thus, it is in the gap between the actual present tense and this fictive past tense of progress and reform that Paddy's play doubles as critique. Paddy pleases both his audiences. The newsboys delight in this parody of their benefactors; with their "derisive laughter" and "ironical kinds of applause" they join in the game of mimicry, playing at being a good audience, and thus record the pleasures of ridiculing this oh-so-familiar good advice. But the visitor and Brace clearly appreciate the performance as well, hearing not mockery but intimacy in its capacity, teasingly, to reproduce their moral lessons. In a way that Bhabha's account does not quite recognize, it is clear that this mimicry is itself a mark of both inclusion and its limits: it is only in being part of this institution that Paddy can so knowingly mock it, and it is only to the extent that he remains outside its redemptive program that his words are funny. The appeal of Paddy's speech lies in the multiplicity of its targets, joking at the expense of the boy with no boots and the well-heeled philanthropist. The newsboys' famed capacity for play affectionately crosses class bounds, yet it is not without its barbs for both parties. As Paddy goes on to tell his life story of escapes from drunken and abusive parents, his audience grows ever more raucous:

> "Well, boys, I wint on till I kim to the 'Home' [great laughter among the boys], and they took me in [renewed laughter], and did for me, without a cap to me head or shoes to me feet, and thin I ran away, and here I am. Now boys [with mock solemnity], be good, mind yer manners, copy me, and see what you'll become."
>
> At this point the boys raised such a storm of hifalutin applause, and indulged in such characterizations of delight, that it was deemed best to stop the youthful Demosthenese, who jumped from his stool with a bound that would have done credit to a monkey. (111)

The visitor will write down his memories of this speech, and Brace will have them thrice published, yet (hiding the philanthropists' power within the passive voice) "it was deemed best to stop" the performance as the game of imitation becomes contagious and the newsboys' play at being a "hifalutin" audience threatens to turn into a "storm." If play makes the newsboy attractive to middle-class benefactors, it nevertheless remains precisely the characteristic that such philanthropies seek to contain. It may be the visitor's own penchant for irony that leads him to call Paddy "a youthful Demosthenese," but it is his anxiety about the incivility of such play that leads him to turn the classical orator into a monkey.

The stories Brace tells of street girls are quite different, and it is a difference of which he is himself acutely aware. He writes,

> A girl street rover is to my mind the most painful figure in all the unfortunate crowd of a big city. With a boy "Arab of the streets," one always has the consolation that, despite his ragged clothes and bed in a box or hay barge, he often has a rather good time of it, and enjoys many of the delicious pleasures of a child's roving life, and that a fortunate turn of events may at anytime make an honest, industrious, fellow of him. . . . With a girl vagrant it is different. She feels homelessness and friendlessness more; she has more of the feminine dependence on affection; the street-trades too are harder for her, and the return at night to some lonely cellar or tenement room, crowded with dirty people of all ages and sexes, is more dreary. . . . Then the strange and mysterious subject of sexual vice comes in.[34]

Even here, Brace cannot quite let himself imagine a street girl sleeping in a box. Homelessness, crowds, and dirt may offer boys "delicious pleasures," but they never offer such to girls. Femininity, in Brace's oft-repeated intensifier, requires "more." That is, for a street girl, Brace sees the loss of the accoutrements of domesticity without ambivalence, simply and purely as loss—pathos without play. Yet while the domesticity offered by Newsboys' Lodging Houses were imagined as refuge, that same domesticity clearly figures in the Lodging House for Homeless Girls as the product of their feminine labors. The house's matron complains of the girls' "foolish pride or prejudice against housework," but boasts that, under her administration, "[a]ll were taught that this Lodging House was merely a stepping-stone to getting on in the world [no long-term stays], and that nothing was so honorable as industrious *house-work*" (1863: 12–13). The sort of resistance that boys show through play and consumption appears among these girls as a more radical antipathy to domestic norms. The reports describe how "[a] young girl in our Lodging House was relating to us recently how she had been attracted to another young girl there by hearing her answer our Matron 'No, Ma'am! I don't know where my parents are. I don't care—*I hate them!*' This was at once a common bond of sympathy between the poor creatures!" (1858: 4). That the "bond of sympathy"—the emotional trait that underlies philanthropic labors like those of the Children's Aid Society—could be forged out of the hatred of parents threatens to explode the domestic ideals of these charitable *homes*. Brace's exclamation of pity ("poor creatures") insists on casting that bonding hatred as a mark of vulnerability and need, in a sentimental attempt to contain the reality that the family might be a site of animosity rather than a source of succor. After all, the entire structure of this charitable enterprise depends upon the presumption that domesticating these children will suture the social wounds of class.

Indeed, the Society's favorite project was not these temporary lodging houses but rather its placing-out system, which largely relied on its city charities to identify street children who could be relocated to work in rural families.[35] A highly innovative (and intrusive) program, the placing-out system was a self-conscious effort to invert the historical shifts in the practices and definitions of childhood. By transporting children who epitomized the new urban-based cultural patterns in order to provide agricultural labor in rural communities it recapitulated the time when it was normative for children's work to form a regular part of the middle-class household economy. Significantly, in many cases the labor of the transported children served to decrease the amount of work expected of other children in the family, and thus helped produce the ideal of middle-class childhood leisure even within these rural settings.[36] In a letter written by a child placed with a family in

Indiana, descriptions of the hired child's labor alternate with accounts of how the children of the family play: "I can saw and split wood for the fire. The little boy's father has given him a cannon." There is no rancor in this letter, but the child writing it is quite matter-of-fact about which children in the household have the leisure and material support for play; the writer is clear, too, about the ambivalent nature of his inclusion in this household, sometimes speaking of a familial "we" and yet referring to the members of the family with oddly distant nouns: "the lady," "the man," "the little baby" (1863: 62). In this way letters written to the Children's Aid Society by children who had been placed out powerfully document the children's own acute sense of class identities and differences, and the ways that they manifest themselves in daily patterns of intimacy, work, and play. These letters regularly detail the children's farm work and schooling, sometimes in pride ("I am busy now grafting our roots. Perhaps you would like to know something about gardening. I will tell you some kind of apples we have grafted" [1859: 49]) and sometimes in complaint ("Had to be up early to chop wood, fetch water and feed the pigs, and water the horse. . . . Hadn't I a time of it with that there horse—he used to kick up his heels so. I stayed one week there—couldn't stand the work" [1858: 53]).

Though deeply aware of how much their own days are structured by labor, the children who wrote these letters are remarkably consistent in the adamance with which they assert their need to play. Much like some children's unwillingness to "stand the work," constraints on play prove a significant rational for leaving placements. One child writes, "I have left Mr. S_____. Mrs. S_____ has been troubled with her head for about forty years, and she would not stand any noise, and I was very fond of singing, and sometimes I would sing, and not think anything about it, and she would scold me, and that was more than I could bear" (1863: 66). "Fun" appears in these letters as a defensible right in a way that seems to me quite unlike the attitudes toward play expressed in even the period's most permissive and celebratory texts of middle-class childhood. "They say I am a good girl, but too wild and daring, and will get me neck broke if I do not stop; but I must have some fun," one girl writes (1863: 75). "You know we can't be silent all the time, you know, so we must have a little fun once in a while," another child comments (1861: 59). In such letters the need to play figures as a powerful site of identity; the demand for at least a little fun is ardently claimed as a characteristic of self that survives these children's quite drastic geographic and class relocations. If these children understand play as a basic need for the maintenance of self, their letters are equally clear about how the difficulties of maintaining that need—the real limitations on their mode and time for play—change with their new environment.

Just as these letters defend the children's right to fun—to wildness, daring, and noise—against the expectations of the middle-class homes in which they now dwell, the remarks directed to the street children still living in Children's Aid Society Lodging Houses counter work-centered preconceptions of farm life and insist that fun is possible outside of New York: "I think there is as much fun as in New York for nuts and apples are free," one boy writes, though the letter goes on to suggest that less edible aspects of New York entertainment may be harder to find in Indiana: he asks whether "FATTY" could send him "pictorials to read, especially the *Newsboys Pictorial.* . . . I want something to read" (1860: 84–85). Another boy, while asking of news from the lodging house, vividly advertises the fun of horses and hunting. He writes, "Please let me know how the boys in the Eleventh Ward Lodging House are getting along. Tell them we are happy, and we hope they are also; if not, let them come out to see us, and we will make them happy. We will let them ride on our mustangs, or hunt with our double-barreled shot-guns, and we will go along with them and show them where there is lots of game, and then they will be happy. I bet" (1872: 58).

Clearly, one purpose of these correspondences was to help the Lodging Houses to "secure" (as the 1854 annual report put it) other children for the placing-out program (24). Children's letters speak often of the rewards of placing out that are consonant with the arguments mounted by the Society itself—testifying to their "good homes" (1861: 66), access to schooling, moral reform, and monetary success. But it is clear from letters like this one that the children also have an agenda of their own, and one as committed to preserving identity as it is to acculturation. In this boy's fantasy of leading a battalion of street children on a hunt, the one-upmanship of competition with city pleasures is speckled with nostalgia for the Lodging House community of boys: this boy locates his happiness in the imagined possibility of mingling in play the parts of his life that have been severed by his move west.

Because their labor in these new families is largely domestic in nature, the assertion of this need to play appears more disruptive and troubling in girls. In a long letter, a man in Peoria lays out the "*pro* and *con*" of keeping a girl named Elizabeth (1857: 51). The pros include her intelligence, "musical genius," physical weakness, and moral need; of the cons he writes,

> She is a very bad girl. I cannot say that she is *immoral*. I have had fears and suspicions, but she assures me that she is not guilty of indecency in speech or conduct. She is bad in the sense of impudent, stubborn, disobedient, hot tempered, and ungrateful. . . .
>
> And now, dear sir, when I tell you that I have young children, of whom it is necessary that Elizabeth should take charge, and that I am burdened with anxiety with regard to the influence such a girl must

exert on them, you will understand why I am not desirous to keep her. I say nothing of the peace of my family or the trouble the girl causes me; but the question is—*Is it my duty to risk the ruin of my children?* . . .

With regard to her position in my family, I have not adopted her as my child, but we wish to make her, and have her consider herself, as one of the family; not as a servant. And just in this particular, we have great difficulty with her; she persists in the closest intimacy with our kitchen servant, which for her own sake and for the sake of order in our household, we cannot allow.

With regard to my treatment of her . . . I have on two occasions, inflicted a slight punishment. . . . I would not treat a *servant* so; but my children often need and receive chastisement. (1857: 51–52)

Elizabeth is charged with care of the children but is not a servant; she is deemed one of the family but not adopted; this letter is riven by the contradictory nature of the girl's place in the household. How much clearer and freer to be a servant, permitted the intimacies of kitchen friendships and safe from the rod! As this letter makes abundantly clear there are no imaginative structures that can accommodate the wild play of the street into the proper domestic work of girls. Girls' impudence cannot be recuperated for a capitalist enterprise, but rather threatens to disrupt the order of the household and ruin the children.

An unusually indulgent Western family, with no children of their own, writes to the Children's Aid Society that the boy they have taken in "is full of fun and play; and seems to be as happy as the happiest." This letter recognizes and approves the child's sense of play and presents those traits in easy balance with the industriousness and piety that the family also prizes. The letter goes on to describe the boy's work habits, schooling, and church attendance, and concludes with the observation that "we feel that it is a great responsibility to train a child for the active duties of his life, but much more responsible for the never-ending ages of eternity" (1860; 75). The boy writes too, and his letter similarly juxtaposes work and play, his responsibilities for the cows, his successes at school, and his boastworthy collection of toys. "My large top will spin four minutes," we read. "I have got an India-rubber ball, and a boat that I made myself with a man on it, such as I used to see in New York. I have got a kite and a windmill, besides a good many other playthings. . . . I have got a large, nice sled—it is the nicest sled but H_____'s; you can't think what good times we had sliding down hill last winter on the snow" (1860: 76). The boy's toys are an interesting mix of the made and the bought, the rustic and the commercial. His attitudes toward play appear similarly double, as clearly for this boy the good times of sledding cannot be fully disentangled from the

KAREN SÁNCHEZ-EPPLER

consciousness of having one of the nicest sleds. If the play of the city street appears largely to be about expenditure of energy and resources, this rural play appears to be more about possession.

A family who has taken in "a daughter of a drunken mother," as Brace puts it in his introduction to their letter, appears similarly doting. The father writes, "Being a cabinet-maker myself, I have furnished her with a small bureau, bedstead, &c., and she has learned to take care of her own and her doll's clothes, and seems to take pride in keeping her things nice. We call her S_____A_____, and consider her our own" (1862: 48–49). This letter need not balance work and play, however, since for this girl play is itself a kind of domestic apprenticeship wherein she learns the household skills her "drunken" mother could not teach her. If the cabinetmaker and his wife have made of her a doll of their own, even to the extent of changing her name, this is only possible because the nondomestic family from which she comes can be so easily and thoroughly discounted.

Letters like these elaborate the ways in which play—which marked street identities—can also express incorporation into rural and middle-class values, and hence how conceptions of play themselves change with shifting class position. The letters these children sent back to their lodging houses thus participate to a surprising degree in the chiasmic imaginings of class and play that characterize middle-class discourses on childhood. The children recognize how their new lives within middle-class households gain them far greater access to material conditions that facilitate play (toys, horses, and the security of meals and homes) and yet find in these comfortable settings a far more anxious conception of what it means to play.

Through the philanthropic publication of their life stories and letters the children furnish a kind of real-life sentimental narration that allows middle-class readers to imagine and sympathize with the horrors of the street and to feel beneficent satisfaction over accounts of rescue and reform made possible by their contributions. The Children's Aid Society's 1857 annual report included, for example, a detailed vignette describing a twelve-year-old orphan's efforts to support herself "by selling wax-matches" and recounting her gratitude at being relocated by the Society to a "fine home" in Pennsylvania. The report ends with a touching letter from the girl that affirms the Society's reformist agenda; "I have got acquainted with good girls who do not say bad words. . . . I hope I will never see the bad girls of New York again," she writes (1857: 42–43). Yet in the 1858 annual report there is another letter "from the little match girl" that, although it certainly attests to her pleasures in her new life, nevertheless suggests this sentimental tale of reform might be read slightly differently by the children themselves: "[Mr. Jessup] gave me one of your reports. I could not help laughing when I saw my letter there. . . . I should be glad to have you send me some of your Reports, they are so interesting to me" (1858: 64). What accounts for her laughter? Is it amusement at her own younger self, delight in seeing her words in print, or a recognition — not unlike the laughter of the newsboys listening to Paddy's speech — of the ways in which her letters play along with the Society's program, knowingly producing the patterns of gratitude and reform that the situation requires? Even as her first letter affirms her separation from the "bad girls of New York," her interest in the reports indicates how these publications often functioned for the children as a kind of community newspaper, a means of preserving past relations and identities, a way to keep track, as one letter put it, of "how they are all in the City, and how times are there" (1859: 45).

"The Pile of Maggots," the oyster dinner, the child who "must have some fun," the children the Lodging Houses repeatedly failed to "secure" — all testify to the inability of reformist discourse to fully contain these unruly subjects, just as the girl's laugh intimates that the publication of these letters serves for her a different function than the reformist and sentimental harvest of donations and tears. Given the conditions of cultural production and preservation, it is hardly surprising that I have evidence for a far more detailed account of how the play of street children shapes middle-class identity than I do for how it matters to the children themselves. Images of the street child at play teach the middle class about the pleasures of circulation and expenditure and justify the "free play" of capital. Stories of street children's vulnerability and pathos elicit the generous sympathy of middle-class readers' distinguishing each caring individual from the exploitative system that produces such suffering. This is to say that these apparently opposing images functionally support each other in exonerating the middle class's increasing self-identification with childhood leisure. For street children, however, play serves not as a measure of leisure but as a mechanism of resistance, a means of claiming autonomy and pleasure on their own, nonproductive, terms — of thumbing their noses at the middle-class values that this same play nevertheless helps to install. And yet, in recognizing this resistance, we see as well the difference that is gender: how for girls — who have no imaginable place in the play of the market except in the terms of sexual vice at which Brace shudders — there is no way to figure work as a game.

NOTES

1. Considering the vast array of studies that have explored childhood as a site for the construction of gender or racial identity, it is striking how very little work has approached

class identity in this way, especially since the recognition that class is a social construction, and not a natural state, is far more widespread. Mary P. Ryan's historical analysis of the production of middle-class identities in the home in *Cradle of the Middle Class: The Family in Oneida County, New York, 1790–1865* (New York: Cambridge University Press, 1981) is an important exception here, acknowledging as it does the large role that changes in child-rearing practices made in the consolidation of middle-class values. See also Carolyn Kay Steedman, *Landscape for a Good Woman: A Story of Two Lives* (New Brunswick, N.J.: Rutgers University Press, 1987), for an account of how paying attention to class contests the psychoanalytic norms of ego formation in children.

2. Priscilla Ferguson Clement, *Growing Pains: Children in the Industrial Age, 1850–1890* (New York: Twayne, 1997), 7.

3. On shifting valuations of play, see Foster Rhea Dulles, *America Learns to Play: A History of Popular Recreation, 1607–1940* (New York: Peter Smith, 1952); David Nasaw, *Going Out: The Rise and Fall of Public Amusements* (New York: Basic Books, 1993); and Kathryn Grover, *Hard at Play: Leisure in America, 1840–1940* (Amherst: University of Massachusetts Press, 1992). Bill Brown, *The Material Unconscious: American Amusement, Stephen Crane, and the Economics of Play* (Cambridge, Mass.: Harvard University Press, 1996) and William A. Gleason, *The Leisure Ethic: Work and Play in American Literature, 1840–1940* (Stanford, Calif.: Stanford University Press, 1999) assess the manifestation of these changes on literary production. Philippe Ariès, *Centuries of Childhood: A Social History of Family Life,* trans. Robert Baldick (New York: Vintage, 1962), offers the classic account of the invention of childhood in Western culture. For accounts of the American version of these trends in addition to Ryan's *Cradle of the Middle Class* and Clement's *Growing Pains,* see Joseph Hawes and N. Ray Hiner, *America Childhood: A Research Guide and Historical Handbook* (Westport, Conn.: Greenwood Press, 1985) and their anthology of essays *Growing Up in America: Children in Historical Perspective* (Urbana: University of Illinois Press, 1985); see also Elliott West and Paula Petrik, eds., *Small Worlds: Children and Adolescents in America* (Lawrence: University Press of Kansas, 1992) and Henry Jenkins, ed., *The Children's Culture Reader* (New York: New York University Press, 1998). For the manifestation of these changes in material culture and hence childhood's links to consumerism see Karin Calvert, *Children in the House: The Material Culture of Early Childhood, 1600–1900* (Boston: Northeastern University Press, 1992); and Mary Lynn Stevens Heininger, Karin Calvert, Barbara Finkelstein, Kathy Vandell, Anne Scott MacLeod, and Harvey Green, *A Century of Childhood, 1820–1920* (Rochester, N.Y.: Margaret Woodbury Strong Museum, 1984).

4. Amos Bronson Alcott, "Observations on the Principles and Methods of Infant Instruction" (1830), in his *Essays on Education, 1830–1862* (Gainesville, Fla.: Scholars Facsimiles and Reprints, 1960), 5.

5. Ibid.

6. See Clement, *Growing Pains,* chap. 5; on the census, see 133. For a provocative account of how "the expulsion of children from the 'cash nexus' at the turn of the past century . . . was part of a cultural process of 'sacralization' of children's lives" in which emotional value comes to preclude economic utility, see Viviana A. Zelizer, *Pricing the Priceless Child: The Changing Social Value of Children* (New York: Basic Books, 1985), 11.

7. Daniel T. Roberts concludes his historical survey of nineteenth-century trends in middle-class child rearing with the observation that "what seems clearest about formal child shaping is the fact of repeated change." See Roberts, "Socializing Middle-Class Children: Institutions, Fables, and Work Values in Nineteenth-Century America," *Journal of Social History* 13 (1980): 364. Roberts divides the century roughly in thirds, with the first thirty years stressing obedience to authority, the middle decades devoted to

developing self-control, and the final decades of the century valuing imagination over systematization. What I find most valuable in his schema is his nuanced sense of the unevenness of transitions between these models so that in the disparate settings of home, storybook, and school widely differing ideals and expectations could be set upon the same child. In picking these decades I am focusing on the transition from self-control to imagination.

8. Melvin L. Kohn's influential mid-twentieth-century study of what values parents strive to inculcate in their children finds a significant divergence between working-and middle-class families: working-class parents emphasize "behavioral conformity" (obedience, cleanliness, and good behavior), while middle-class parents stress "internal process" (curiosity, happiness, and empathy). See Kohn, *Class and Conformity: A Study in Values, with a Reassessment, 1977* (Chicago: University of Chicago Press, 1977), 21. Clearly in the nineteenth century all classes would put more stress on conformity to authority than now; still it seems plausible that the tendencies that Kohn describes may well reflect on the class differentiated attitudes held within actual nineteenth-century families, even as literary representations would apportion obedience and curiosity quite differently, producing well-behaved middle-class children and playful working-class children.

9. George Mastell, quoted in Christine Stansell, *City of Women: Sex and Class in New York, 1789–1860* (New York: Alfred A. Knopf, 1986), 194.

10. Karl Marx, *Capital: A Critique of Political Economy* (1867; reprint New York: Modern Library, 1936), 697 ("orphans and pauper children"), 707 ("surplus population" and "industrial reserve-army"), and 696 ("free play").

11. *First Annual Report of the Children's Aid Society* (New York: Children's Aid Society, 1854), 6. In 1854 the Children's Aid Society was founded in the charitable hope of mitigating the social and individual dangers of child poverty and homelessness. It initiated a flurry of experimental programs: industrial workshops, Sunday meetings, schools, and clothing distribution. Its most famous programs, however, were those of a placing-out system that sent urban children to work in rural families, and a series of Newsboys' Lodging Houses, which provided cheap but clean room and board for children working on the streets of the city. The annual reports of the society were compiled under Brace's secretaryship, and much of the introductory and narrative materials appear to have been written by him, although the majority of each volume is made up of a collection of materials penned by others: treasury reports, excerpts from diaries, letters and reports by various staff, and letters by and about individual children aided by the Society. These volumes are one of my most important sources, and are hereafter cited parenthetically in the text with year of the report and relevant page number(s). I have worked from the complete run of these reports available at the New-York Historical Society, but the first ten reports are more readily available in a facsimile reprint, *Annual Reports of the Children's Aid Society: Nos. 1–10, February 1854–1863* (New York: Arno Press, 1971). These reports similarly underlie Brace's book-length summary of the Society's efforts, *The Dangerous Classes of New York and Twenty Years Working among Them* (1872; reprint Silver Springs Md.: National Association of Social Workers, 1973).

12. Wai Chee Dimock, "Class, Gender and a History of Metonymy," in *Rethinking Class: Literary Studies and Social Formations,* ed. Wai Chee Dimock and Michael T. Gilmore (New York: Columbia University Press, 1994), 84.

13. Elizabeth Oakes Smith, *The Newsboy* (New York: J. C. Derby, 1854), 36. Such stories of lost adults are standard features of Horatio Alger's street-boy series; see, for example the opening scene of *The Young Outlaw* (Boston: A. K. Loring, 1875), 9–12, where Sam Barker requests ten cents for directing to Canal Street a country deacon already standing on it.

14. Lydia Maria Child, "Letter XIV," dated 17 February 1842, in *Letters from New York* (New York: Charles S. Francis, 1843), 83; hereafter, page numbers are cited parenthetically in the text.

15. Louisa May Alcott, "Our Little Newsboy," in *Aunt Jo's Scrap Bag* (Boston: Roberts Brothers, 1872), 191–92.

16. June Howard, "What is Sentimentality?" *American Literary History* 11 (1999): 73.

17. Alger, *The Young Outlaw*, 158, 164; hereafter, page numbers are cited parenthetically in the text.

18. Adrienne Siegel, *The Image of the American City in Popular Literature, 1820–1870* (Port Washington, N.Y.: Kinnikat Press, 1981), 82, from which these phrases come, provides a useful survey of street-child stereotypes, and decries their inaccuracy. David E. Whisnant, "Selling the Gospel News, or: The Strange Career of Jimmy Brown the Newsboy," *Journal of Social History* 5 (1972): 269–309 goes further, arguing that this benign mythology of newsboy life actually functioned to exempt newsboys from child-labor protections well into the twentieth century.

19. Horatio Alger, *Rough and Ready* (1896, reprint Philadelphia: Porter and Coates, n.d.); and *Ragged Dick* (1868; reprint New York: Collier Books, 1962), 46.

20. The Newsboys' Lodging Houses shared this ethos, often providing the boys with better clothes; and by their second year of operation they were able to offer a makeshift savings bank, "a table in which each boy should have his own money-box numbered, where his earnings could be deposited. . . . This has given the first taste of the pleasure of saving" (1855: 14).

21. See Michael Moon, "'The Gentle Boy from the Dangerous Classes': Pederasty, Domesticity and Capitalism in Horatio Alger," *Representations* 19 (1987): 87–110. Moon writes about the ways in which Alger's narrative structures articulate the modest rewards and homoerotic bonds that impel corporate/capitalist culture. In this account the rags-to-riches formula speaks a truth about capitalism that is deeply consonant with the constructions of childhood and class identity at stake in my analysis here. In both cases the misreading of Alger's stories correctly asserts the sources of pleasure and attraction within them.

22. The statistics were cited as follows: "Number able to read and write 4,423; read only 2,371; unable to read and write 1,861; total 8,655 or 10% illiterate" (1870: 18). It is not clear whether it is Brace's math or his data that is off, but even a 20-percent illiteracy rate is not only impressive, but also convincing once one considers what a crucial survival skill literacy must have been for street traders, and especially for newsboys.

23. Horatio Alger, preface to *Fame and Fortune* (Boston: A. K. Loring, 1868), viii; and "At Our Desk," *Student and Schoolmate* 24 (1869): 530. Both passages are cited in Carol Nackenoff, *The Fictional Republic: Horatio Alger and American Political Discourse* (New York: Oxford University Press, 1994), 195.

24. The *First Annual Report* reads, "At the first opening of the Lodging House, it was made the condition of lodging that every boy should take a bath. To this there was great reluctance. Now it is prized as a priviledge" (1854: 14).

25. [F. Ratchford Starr], *John Ellard: The Newsboy* (Philadelphia: William S. and Alfred Martien, 1860), 39.

26. Ibid., 42.

27. William Wells Newell, *Games and Songs of American Children* (1883; reprint New York: Harper and Brothers, 1903), 7, 2. Newell does devote one chapter to "playing at work," but the games and dances he cites all imitate agricultural and artisan labor.

28. Horatio Alger, *Struggling Upward* (1890; reprint New York: Hurst, n.d.).

29. Vermin are a staple feature of the Society's annual reports. Long passages are devoted to detailing the process, for example, of removing lice from the head of a boy, "a sight sufficient to make the strongest nerves quiver. Every hair on his head was alive with vermin." But Mr. Macy, though, "nearly sickened at his task . . . persevered for about three hours with shears and comb, and soap and water" (1858: 54). Such passages record the quivering nerves of a middle-class sensibility, so as to mark the heroism of the Lodging House staff who must overcome such disgust in order to tend to these boys. In this context what are we to make of Lodging House games that blatantly play upon the aspects of street life that sicken the staff?

30. [Starr], *John Ellard*, 18. The Children's Aid Society's annual reports contain lists of benefactors and their gifts, making it clear that the Society drew many donations of clothing and gifts of $1 or less (the list of donations to the Newsboys' Lodging House in 1855 includes one dollar from "Lod the Newsboy"; in 1857 "Tillie and Winnie" gave fifty-six cents, and at separate times that year five cents and one penny were "found in box" and duly counted towards the year's total), as well as gifts like Mrs. J. J. Astor's annual $100–$150 for Sunday dinners or the nearly $4,000 that was left to the society by Mr. J. B. Barnard's estate.

31. "A Visit to the Newsboys" (1861: 74–75) excerpted in Brace, *The Dangerous Classes*, 110–11; hereafter page numbers are cited parenthetically in the text.

32. Homi K. Bhabha, "Of Mimicry and Man: The Ambivalence of Colonial Discourse," in *The Location of Culture* (New York: Routledge, 1994), 86.

33. This definition of *bumming* comes from the "Newsboys' Dictionary or Glossary" (1855: 26).

34. Brace, *The Dangerous Classes*, 114–15.

35. For fine historical accounts of this placing-out system see Marilyn Irvin Holt, *The Orphan Trains: Placing Out in America* (Lincoln: University of Nebraska Press, 1992); and Miriam Z. Langsam, *Children West: A History of the Placing-Out System of the New York Children's Aid Society, 1853–1890* (Madison: State Historical Society of Wisconsin, 1964).

36. See Clement, *Growing Pains*, 149, on how children in prosperous farm families benefited from the work of hired boys and girls.

3 The Miniaturizing of Girlhood

Nineteenth-Century Playtime
and Gendered Theories of Development

Melanie Dawson

There is one great defect in the present system of family education . . . we wish to call attention at present to the practice of obliging the girls of a family, in almost every instance in which self-denial is involved, to give way to the boys. "Remember he is your brother," is the appeal to tender little hearts, which, though swelling under a sense of injustice, naturally give way under this argument. This might be all very well, were the boys also taught reciprocity in this matter, but as this unfortunately is not often the case, a monstrous little tyrant is produced whose overbearing exactions and hourly selfishnesses are disgusting to witness.

—FANNY FERN, "A CHAPTER FOR PARENTS"

Fanny Fern's acerbic portrayals of nineteenth-century family life, although focused largely on adult interactions, hint at the root causes of the domestic infelicity that her fiction and newspaper columns satirized: vastly different behavioral expectations for the genders. Pointing to social constructions of boyhood and girlhood, Fern positions the conventional socialization of youth as a primary factor in perpetuating gendered stereotypes in mid-nineteenth-century America. In Fern's view, a specific unfairness to girls emerges from the valuation of nurturing activities that privilege family harmony over individual distinction. The disturbing corollary, Fern suggests, constructs boyhood as unfettered and self-invested.

Fern's critique partially exposes one problematic dimension of nineteenth-century representations of girlhood that I explore here, for the association of girlhood with domestic caretaking and "real life" experiences had a vast potential to inscribe gendered expectations about measuring maturity. Whereas boys' leisure was often cast as a private form of pleasure, girls were reminded of their specialized—and, the suggestion then follows, *necessary*—function as family caretakers. Through descriptions of leisurely pursuits, I argue, girls were denied the fantastical, self-selected, and competitive behaviors commonly associated with childhood itself, leaving unfettered youth aligned with male experiences. Guides to children's leisure activities portray girls' youth as a period that did not predict adult roles so much as embody them in miniature. Analyzing the social imperatives present in girls' play and attending to the social and familial roles that were represented during playtime enables us to see that play activities attributed to girls a mature notion of subjectivity. Encouraging girls to view themselves as socially conscious beings in constant negotiation with the expectations that surrounded them, play activities afforded little opportunity for girls to enjoy the kind of boisterous, rebellious activities encouraged among nineteenth-century boys.

The subjectivity assigned to girls, which infuses the materials surrounding playtime, calls attention to constructs similar to those typified by nineteenth-century behavioral guides for adults. As Nancy Armstrong has argued of conduct books, these texts "mapped out a field of knowledge that would produce a specifically female form of subjectivity."[1] Detailing the circular logic produced by conduct books and domestic novels, Armstrong explores the gendered "realities" produced by the attribution of subjectivity, which sought to inculcate qualities that were described as existing social norms. In children's culture, a similar circularity is at work, with texts about play assigning to girls the behaviors that they presumed to record. Among guidebooks on youthful recreations, as in the domestic fiction that Armstrong explores, the hegemonic relations inculcated during play produce a sense of social order that is rooted in unambiguous gender distinctions. In white, middle-class, nineteenth-century children's culture, these emphatically gendered configurations of growth reveal more than an impulse to represent childhood in popular entertainment materials; they visibly attempt to encourage specific behaviors, thereby ostensibly delighting and instructing, amusing and inculcating.

Ebullient Boys and Mature Little Ladies

Picturing rebellious, youthful boys and compliant, socialized girls, a *Harper's Bazaar* illustration from 1867 hints at the ways in which casual representations

3.1. *Social girls and ebullient boys. From* Harper's Bazaar, *7 December 1867.*

of leisure separated animated boys from domesticated girls. The boys who command the scene are much more active than the girls, dominating it with their energy and exhilaration, their possession of the hoop and whip (see fig. 3.1). While the three girls pictured are clearly participating peripherally in the amusement, their playfulness is much less evident, for their postures incline toward a sedate, social mode of interaction. As the girls gesture toward one another, they form an arc dividing the left side of the picture from the right, contrasting the composed female and the ebullient male, the mature girl and the childlike boy.

The illustration's depiction of male exuberance and female sociability takes on greater significance in light of a leisure culture's means of inscribing social values. Historians as diverse as Philippe Ariès, Norbert Elias, Jack Zipes, Ellen Seiter, and Miriam Formanek-Brunell have demonstrated that children's amusements perform exacting, lasting cultural work.[2] By setting up scenarios that refer to normative values and define acceptable boundaries of social interaction, the activities that constitute children's play inculcate distinct social patterns. Whether that play is communal, ceremonial, or personal, play activities, as Ariès, Elias, and Zipes have argued, have resulted in an increased attention to *civilité,* or the world of polite social customs, along with a growing tendency toward differentiated roles within families.[3] Entertainment guidebooks, which treat children's leisure time didactically, offer an important vehicle for assessing how expectations about gendered behavior were articulated for late-eighteenth- and nineteenth-century children.

Children's play and the conventions governing it, of course, are often imagined to exist apart from ideological, and, broadly put, "political" concerns. Yet the attribution of a subjectivity to female youth reveals the degree to which the supposedly innocent activities of childhood have the capacity to shelter pointedly ideological imperatives.[4] Because girls are encouraged to act out scenes of maturity, take on domestic duties, and develop self-monitoring skills, girlhood appears nearly indistinct from womanhood. Ironically, although girlhood was promoted as a unique developmental phase by a burgeoning market of entertainment books for girls (one sign of a growing attention to and production of childhood as a unique phase of development), girlhood nonetheless occupies the odd position of being characterized most completely by ideals that are inseparable from domestic womanhood. Nineteenth-century girlhood thus appears as troublingly indistinct, devoid of a set of characteristics and behaviors entirely its own.[5]

In late-eighteenth- and early nineteenth-century guidebooks on children's play, the gendered imperatives of leisure time, along with implied models of development, are especially evident when they are most vehemently belied. Even when texts that set forth the "rules" for play claim to dispense the same information to all children, there are signs that girls and boys constitute separate audiences, as in *A Little Pretty Pocket-Book*.[6]

Although the book begins with two letters, one to "Little Master Tommy" and another to "Pretty Miss Polly," these missives are actually the same; they direct children to be dutiful, to be "obedient to your Master, loving and kind to your Play-fellows, obliging to every Body."[7] Despite the similarity of the two letters, the need to separate boys and girls is so strong that there are two printings of the missive, a significant fact in an age when the printed text was both rare and expensive.

While insisting that play is beneficial to both sexes, children's recreational guidebooks point to an increasing preoccupation with producing gendered behaviors. *Youthful Recreations*, for example, which advocates play for reasons of health, insinuates that its broad rhetoric of healthfulness is more applicable to boys than girls, for the girls' games are noticeably less active.[8] Girl players are pictured as participants in "Have a ride in my chair," "Swinging," and "Blindman's Buff," but these games constitute only three of the fifteen activities pictured. Female participation, furthermore, is peripheral in two of these activities, where girls are pushed in a swing and given a ride in "my chair," thus constituting an appreciative audience rather than agents pursuing their own enjoyment. The entertainment guidebook *Remarks on Children's Play* similarly excludes girls from active play (such as playing with marbles or tops; sledding; and football).[9] Girls do appear in the illustrations of "Dressing the doll," "Blindman's Buff," "Swinging," "Jumping the rope," "Thread the needle," "Tossing the ball," "Hunt the slipper," and "Soap bubbles." By depicting girls' roles in such a limited repertoire of activities, the text does not, in any practical sense, prevent girls from playing more aggressive outdoor activities such as "Leap-frog" or "Flying the kite" or "Trundling the hoop," but it suggests that interactive and cooperative activities are more appropriate for girls than those that develop physical and competitive ones.

In contrast to the "noble" traditions of Greek and Roman leisure that *Remarks on Children's Play* links to boys' play and evokes in regard to activities such as "Trundling the hoop" and other competitive activities, recreations for female players are isolated from an impressive history of sport and leisure accomplishment. Instead of being linked to a fantastic, transhistorical trajectory of entertainment, girls' play is treated as most appropriate when unchallenging, a manifestation of a clear preference for a practical, familial set of leisure enterprises. A girls' game such as "Cup and Ball" is described as "easy" and is treated as "a trifling diversion, and may properly be called a pastime, as there seems not much to be gained by it on the score of exercise: it is a diversion only fit for girls to amuse themselves, and for them only in rainy weather, or on a very hot day."[10] These early-nineteenth-century texts suggest that while boys' games encouraged healthful and competitive behavior that prepared them for a future life of work, girls' games offered a different preparation for adult duty.[11] Believed to require no escape from the womanly duties of domestic management, adult women (before the advent of the twentieth century) were not expected to need to "work out" to relieve the tensions of daily life; for them, domestic labor was positioned as emotionally fulfilling, rendering release unnecessary. Because domestic womanhood serves as the model for girls' play, gaming texts therefore find it difficult to define leisure in terms of an escape from the social sphere.[12]

As Lynne Vallone has argued of nineteenth-century American fiction, girls are typically portrayed as though "they could not be trusted with the freedom of boy-life." Nor is the girl "believed to possess the ability to maintain" a boyish mode of freedom.[13] Similarly, an unresolved tension about the fantastic and unfettered aspects of girls' play appears in regard to the description of "Soap bubbles" in *Remarks on Children's Play*. While the narrative focuses on the necessity of engaging girls in safe activities, it also displays a deep ambivalence about the benefits of girls' entertainment:

It is an innocent and pleasing employment for little girls occasionally to be engaged in making air balloons, with the assistance of a pipe and some soap and water; their motions in the air, with their variegated colours delight the infant mind.

The ingenuity of man, in latter times, has invented balloons of such strength and size as to buoy up men, who have ascended to a great height in the air, and thus travelled as on the wings of the wind a great space in a little time; but some have lost their lives thereby.[14]

Even while depicting the activity as "innocent" and "pleasing," the text (which ascribes "infant" or undeveloped minds to girls) emphasizes boundaries of safe play. The text's suggestion of technology (via balloon travel) warns about the dangers of new inventions—and little girls' similarly inflated goals. Anticipating a future of mothering and caretaking for its female subjects, the text encourages young women to approach domestic play as "imitative." Girls are encouraged to view themselves as "imitative little creatures" who "exactly . . . copy their mother and nurse," by way of "qualifying themselves for more useful employment."[15] Severed from professional promises and competitive scenarios, girls' play appears diminutive in both scope and presumed inventiveness; in this sense, nineteenth-century girls' play was not inscribed *as play*—at least in the modern understanding—but was instead positioned as an exercise in adapting to adult responsibilities.

Womanhood in Miniature

As a sign of their overt socializing of young women, nineteenth-century texts about youth miniaturize girlhood, constructing the girl as an idealized woman in waiting. These texts position the girl as something other than a child despite her diminutive physical stature. Instead, girlhood is deeply indebted to an idealized version of womanhood. Such portrayals result in a construction of miniaturized womanhood with no obvious transition out of childhood and into adulthood.

The cultural work performed by miniaturization is fascinatingly complex, particularly given the equation of the miniature with the child. Susan Stewart has argued persuasively that nostalgia and the miniature are closely related, pointing out that the diminutive figures of children are frequently positioned as vehicles for reenacting past values.[16] The miniature, she suggests, allows for the compression of history onto an easily sentimentalized body, which is positioned as innocent while being invoked as a symbolic reference to past cultures. The relation between the nineteenth-century girl and the miniature has also been explored by Ellen Garvey, who argues that nineteenth- and early-twentieth-century advertisers sought to instill consumer loyalty in girls, creating the consumers for a future generation via materials such as advertising cards and contests. Colorful and decorated, these cards formed the material for elaborate displays in scrapbooks.[17] Garvey's account focuses on both the girl card collector and the adult female consumer, exploring the link that advertisers forged between girls at play and women at work, for the cards "offered girls a representation of both their own and their mothers' lives."[18] By attempting to create a new (and brand-loyal) generation of consumers, advertisers helped to construct a vision of girlhood that overlapped purposefully with the economics of domestic womanhood. Encouraging girls to identify with adults' consumer choices effectively disallowed girlhood an identity of its own.

Whereas girlhood in play texts appears as a compressed version of adulthood, boyhood is effectively severed from adult concerns. Ebenezer Landells's *The Boy's Own Toy-Maker* and its successor, *The Girl's Own Toy-Maker,* by Landells and his daughter Alice, present themselves as companion pieces, offering parallel portraits of boyhood and girlhood.[19] The preface to *The Boy's Own Toy-Maker* readily asserts a connection between boyhood and professional manhood by speaking of the merits of a "knowledge of common things," or the "useful" and "dignified" aspects of working with tools, or those emblems by which boys learn to shape their world, to carve out and construct the space that they will inhabit. Accordingly, the types of toys that boys are directed to make (namely, toys of territorial exploration) encourage boys to recognize the tangible benefits of colonizing and transforming their worlds. Throughout, the text claims that forms of play pave the way to manhood, linking practical play with the "manlier amusements" of the future.[20]

Landells also attempts to evoke hopes of future success as he mentions the discoveries of "great" men such as James Watt, Sir Isaac Newton, and George Stephenson, noting that "whoever would be a great inventor to the benefit of humanity must begin to learn common things in very early life."[21]

In play, then, boys are encouraged to imagine future successes and to envision themselves as agents in shaping their own destinies. As Landells argues, the boy "engaged in making a toy-house becomes half-architect in the knowledge acquired of the aims and uses of forms and materials which, without a model, he could hardly comprehend."[22] All the while, Landells carefully preserves a distinction between boyhood and manhood, positioning play as a site to explore individual abilities that may be developed later, upon the inheritance of economic and professional spheres.

The Girl's Own Toy-Maker, by contrast, establishes the expectation that girls serve cultural ideals such as propriety and familial duty.[23] The text encourages girls to form adult responsibilities, but not to develop their own ambitions. Most of the book works to sever the female subject from any agency over her activities, continually highlighting the pervasive expectations and external pressures governing her life. Indeed, the text's preface deconstructs its young readers' agency by addressing the mother rather than the child, unlike the preface of the boy's book, which speaks directly to young men. The book argues that it exists "to assist those, who have not the leisure or opportunity of leading the young mind into habits of thought and study, in a way that is most likely to benefit them."[24] This strangely admonitory introduction suggests that both girls at play *and* their mothers require corrective intervention in matters of leisure time. Girls' toys "get soon broken or destroyed, as their value is either not understood or properly felt," the text contends, treating the destruction of toys as a habit that is linked directly to the habits of "destructiveness" that, when "carelessly engendered . . . may ultimately have pernicious effect on the future character of the child."[25] Indicting what it presents as a mother-daughter lineage of carelessness, the text endows girls' play with a profound social imperative, for, as Landells continues, "when taught to construct toys" for themselves, toys "are more likely to be valued, and the habit of preserving them ought to be carefully encouraged and promoted."[26]

So conscious is the text of the impending duties of womanhood that it erases any reference to a transformation into womanhood, treating girlhood as encapsulated by womanhood. We read that "[n]othing is more becoming than to see a home neatly and tastefully embellished by the handiwork of its inmates; while the formation of habits of industry and usefulness are not only satisfactory, in enabling young ladies to decorate their own homes by employing their leisure hours profitably, but also in furnishing the means of making suitable presents to their friends, or of having the pleasing gratification of adding by their skill to the funds of some charitable or benevolent institution."[27] Intent on describing girls as little women rather than as children deserving recreation, the book attempts to inculcate in its young readers a recognition of the domestic industry characterizing women's roles, based on the gratification presumably surrounding women's work. The kinds of "toys" that the girl readers of *The Girl's Own Toy-Maker* are to make are thus not objects of their "own," but items for general domestic use; the pleasure for girls should lie in creating useful items, not in pursuing fantasies.

Girls' play, as depicted here, is miniature, domestic, and ornamental. Because girls are invited to venture no farther than the domestic exterior, their toys include fire aprons, mats, fans, fly-catchers, screens, bookmarks, woven baskets, pincushions, pen wipers, flower stands, sundials, lampshades, and doll clothing. Strikingly, a number of the functional items are constructed in the image of young women, including the spill holder that is made to resemble a fashion plate, along with a stylish pincushion and crinoline skirt. These objects illustrate how leisure practices include tools that socialize girls into a feminine ideal that is fashionable, domestic, and, above all, functional.[28]

Boys' toys, by contrast, include a range of paper and wooden toys, board games, and "apparatus" toys, as depicted in the frontispiece to *The Boy's Own*

Toy-Maker. Directions for making a cart, kite, balloon, and ship are contained within the book, as are guides to making horses, soldiers, forts, and other items that emphasize exploration and conquest. Alluding to adult activities such as traveling, sailing, inventing, and colonizing—the important preoccupations of the nineteenth-century Anglo-American male—these toys do not require boys to participate in the world as miniatures, but predict a full assumption of adult activities.

Indeed, for boys, escapist entertainment is upheld as a means of preserving youth. *Holiday Sports and Pastimes for Boys,* for example, situates boisterousness as preferable to an inappropriate worldliness. Adult concerns are equated with a corruption of innocence.[29] Like *Holiday Sports and Pastimes, The Sports and Pastimes of American Boys* presents outdoor amusements as a way to avoid the "viscious ways of fast men" and adult activities such as gambling, racing, and drinking.[30] Physical play, often described as vital and energized in entertainment guidebooks, is also suggested as a defense against encroaching adulthood.

A similar emphasis on boyish vigor also surfaces in *The Boy's Home Book of Sports, Games, Exercises, and Pursuits,* which, like other entertainment guides for boys, focuses on physical play as the primary form of male amusement.[31] The text positions "Blind Man's Buff" as a dangerous activity originally linked to the outdoors, contending that it "should be played with extreme caution in a room, as the sightless one is very liable to bruise himself against unexpected corners and projections, and to knock over articles that are more or less fragile. A better game for indoor play is 'Seated Blindman.'"[32] Despite such a warning, the book's illustration nonetheless encourages the more dangerous form of play, as it portrays boys taking part in "Blind Man's Buff"— indoors (see fig. 3.2). Even though one of the players appears ready to trip over a low footstool, the image is hardly cautionary as it encourages boys to regard the game's attending hint of danger as exciting. Along with other physical games for boys (among them dubious activities such as chomping down on brandy-drenched, flaming raisins—"Snap Dragon," it was called), pastimes for nineteenth-century boys take as a given that boys' physically and socially unfettered forms of play offered boys a privileged haven apart from adult cares.

Treatments of girls' play reveal neither a parallel boisterousness, nor the accompanying assumption that leisure time allowed for the suspension of ordinary social restrictions. Whereas boys in the nineteenth century are invited to explore their landscapes, girls are encouraged to experience the outdoors only vicariously. In *Home Games for Little Girls; Exciting to Play, No Trouble to Learn,* the text presents scenes of twelfth-century falconry, pearl diving in India, and eighteenth-century croquet—activities that are generally as inac-

BLIND MAN'S BUFF.

3.2. "Blind Man's Buff": Indoor play with a hint of danger. From The Boy's Home Book of Sports, Games, Exercises and Pursuits. *Philadelphia: Porter and Coates, 1875.*

cessible to girls as an afternoon of rustic fishing (also pictured in the text)—that players access only through board games.[33] For girls, fantastical sites of entertainment are to remain vicarious, and as a consequence, girls are encouraged to imagine their relation to the extradomestic world in the abstract.

Entertainment guidebooks for girls also reinforce ideals of propriety and moderation, often detailing alternative versions of the same games that boys play while pointing to the boundaries of playtime. Lydia Maria Child's *The Girl's Own Book* simultaneously encourages and admonishes girl players as it presents games such as "Shadow Buff" as "the best kind to play in winter's evenings," noting, "It is so safe and quiet that it disturbs no one: and good little girls will never play noisy games, without first ascertaining whether it will be pleasant to parents and friends. Thinking of the wishes and feelings of others, even in the most trifling things constitutes true politeness."[34] Eliza Leslie's *The American Girl's Book* similarly impresses on girl players the need for restraint.[35] "The Prussian Exercise" (similar to "The Huntsman") is presented as "rather a boisterous play," and participants are urged to play outdoors on the grass or in a field so as to prevent injuries and to preserve the sanctity of home.[36] In its narration of "Blindman's Buff," the text extols the dangers of play, mentioning that "no one must mischievously annoy the

BLINDMAN'S RING.

3.3. "Blindman's Ring": The safer girls' version of "Blind Man's Buff." From The American Girl's Book; or, Occupation for Play Hours. *New York: R. Worthington, 1879.*

blind-girl by pinching, pulling, or in any way teazing her. If she approaches any thing that may hurt her (the fire, for instance) her companions must immediately call out to apprize her of her danger." [37]

Leslie goes on to advocate the removal of rugs and the rearrangement of the fire fender in order to prevent injuries. The text's illustration of "Blindman's Ring" (advocated but not shown in *The Boy's Home Book*) accordingly directs girls to this more subdued version of "Blindman's Buff," where players are demurely seated in a circle, with polite postures and contemplative expressions (see fig. 3.3). Additionally, the illustration from the 1879 edition appears pointedly nostalgic, for the text (first issued in 1831) was in its sixteenth printing. As both cautionary and retrograde, *The American Girl's Book* demonstrates a larger difficulty with a nineteenth-century girls' culture as it was portrayed in popular materials, where ideals of girls' play encourage a return to older practices and ideals. To revise Philippe Ariès's observation that childhood has traditionally functioned as a "repository for abandoned customs," it can be argued that a nineteenth-century girls' culture functioned as such a collection site, remaining less active, less technological, and less invested in constructions of child development than its male counterpart. [38]

Linked to the promise of lucrative work in the future, boys' play pointed to the economic and professional frontiers that were to follow a period of childishness and self-indulgence. Whereas boys, with their expectations of professionalism and technological exploration, were encouraged to *reinvent* history, girls were to *reenact* it. The central paradox of a boys' culture—that boys required a state of innocent irresponsibility in order to reach maturity— is consolidated and naturalized through the presentation of boys' recreations. Girlhood, however, is much more uniform in conception, allowing for no internal contradiction, no ambiguousness, and no imagined trajectory of future development.

A Theory of Feminine Completeness

Just as a miniature represents completeness, but on a smaller scale, so has girlhood been understood in popular texts as a seed of womanhood, a construction promoted by both conduct and entertainment guides. In theory, the girl contains all the qualities that flower at maturity, a belief that robbed girlhood of the rebellion associated with those boisterous elements of male youth. In the words of Mrs. J. A. Graves, author of *Girlhood and Womanhood: Sketches of My Schoolmates,* it is possible to "read" the girl as an indicator of what the woman would be.[39] Graves's portraits of girlhood directly parallel sketches of adult women in, for example, "Anna Percival, or the Maniac Mother," "Emily Howard, or the Gentle Wife," and "Amelia Dorrington, or the Lost One." Graves contends that "if we had studied every opening character as it became unfolded beneath our watchful observation, carefully marked every indication of mental power, or mental weakness, rejoicing in the first rays of rising genius, or sadly brooding over the leaden clouds of dullness, then our vain fancies might have given place to a prophetic glance. When truth and a sound judgment are our basis, then we may venture to predict what will be, from what is."[40] Operating under the assumption that "[a]s the girl is, the woman will be, unless some powerful counteraction has intervened," Graves voices a popular conception of girlhood as the encapsulation and predictor of womanhood.[41]

Treated as compact women rather than as beings whose maturation demanded special behavioral privileges, girls in nineteenth-century development texts are frequently discussed through the organic metaphor of the seed. W. H. Davenport Adams, in *Woman's Work and Worth in Girlhood Maidenhood, and Wifehood,* argues that it "may not be always true that the boy makes the man, but it is always true that the maiden makes the woman"; "the female character is fixed and matured at an earlier age."[42] As late as 1916 Mary Eliza Moxcey, author of *Girlhood and Character,* describes girlhood as the seed of womanhood, contending that "[b]y putting your plant in a different soil, or by regulating the heat and moisture, you may get a larger or more richly colored blossom, but you will not change the kind of flower."[43] By suggesting that for girls the future is fixed, such texts assert that although external conditions affect growth, they can only enhance a being rather than transform it.[44] Such a theory—which the 1827 discovery of the female ovum, in the body from birth, could only have supported—perpetuates the assumption that even young girls could be held accountable for adult behaviors.

Manifesting itself through a reluctance to grant girls a developmental privilege comprised of youthful social immaturity and personally motivated (as opposed to familial) interests, the miniaturization theory of development has persisted into the twentieth century. Popular theories of growth, among them those promoted by G. Stanley Hall, associate social propriety with girlhood while accepting a necessary period of "savagery" for adolescent boys.[45] Hall portrays savagery in boys as an antidote to what he perceives as widespread overcivilization and effeminacy; according to Hall, these cultural maladies could be combated by encouraging adolescent boys to express their antisocial impulses, thus allowing boys to develop into civilized men who will lead the culture at large out of a developmental crisis. Via a "recapitulation" theory of development, Hall argues that in boys the history of the human race's development is encapsulated step by step, meaning that boys experience every stage of human evolution. Enacting primitive behaviors, according to Hall, offers boys a way to avoid troubling modern diseases such as neurasthenia and nerve dysfunction. Girls, however, are absent from Hall's paradigm. He sees young women as both mature and social—as lacking the savage impulses that justify the display of uncivilized, unsocial behaviors.[46] In Hall's emphatically gendered theory of development, boys' progress is indicative of radical change, encapsulated by the transition from a nascent state of unfettered, unsocialized childhood into the assumption of adult responsibilities.[47]

The consequences of such theories are apparent in inscriptions of girlhood that disallow rebellious and unsocial behavior in girls. When girls' leisure activities are described as scaled-down versions of women's work, they undercut the possibilities of seeing girls' development as transformative.[48] Louisa May Alcott's *Little Women* (1868), perhaps the definitive portrait of nineteenth-century girlhood, begins with the girls' dilemma about purchasing Christmas gifts for Marmee, detailing the economic sacrifices the girls make in order to procure presents; immediately after, the sisters give away their Christmas breakfast to a needy family.[49] By detailing these events at the beginning of the text, Alcott establishes that girls are expected to act as caretakers, selfless givers, and domestic managers. Similarly, other famous "girl stories" of the nineteenth century focus on the significant social and moral duties expected of young girls, with the figure of the child-woman offering a redemptive innocence to other characters. Little Eva, of Harriet Beecher Stowe's *Uncle Tom's Cabin* (1852), acts as the moral center of the novel, spiritually guiding the adults in her world. *St. Elmo,* Augusta Jane Evans's 1867 best-seller, depicts a young girl who experiences multiple personal disasters that lead her to become the moral caretaker of a dissipated adult male; orphaned and homeless, Edna Earl nonetheless provides a mature insight and religious spirit that is, for the rebellious central male character, redemptive. Susan Warner's *The Wide, Wide World* (1850) and Maria Susanna Cummins's *The Lamplighter* (1854) also trace the lives of orphaned girls who are forced to adapt to the hardships of a world that expects not only behavioral and spiritual maturity from them but also nurturing guidance. As these influential plots make a concentrated effort to present a girl's youth as signaling womanly control, they also rob girls of the rebellions that would signal radical change.[50]

The cautionary narratives surrounding girls' leisure experiences are particularly visible when compared to representations of boys' play. Various nineteenth- and twentieth-century fictions encourage boys to find the miniature worlds of their sisters limiting and, in some cases, threatening. Along with famous characters such as Huck Finn, whose fantastic experiences are predicated upon the need to escape a social sphere, numerous other boys resist a feminized, miniaturized realm of adult responsibilities. A quirky but striking tale of travel and adventure from an 1879 issue of *St. Nicholas* magazine, "Budsy, the Giant" suggests the horrors associated with male miniaturization. The tale's hero, Thomas Feathercap, undergoes a Gulliveresque adventure in a land of "giants." He first encounters a "monstrous and ponderous" giant wearing a velvet cap, a blue frock, and red shoes that are "badly stubbed at the toes."[51] What Thomas has encountered is not just a giant but a giant *baby,* a fact that both Thomas and the narrative refuse to acknowledge directly. Afraid that the "giant" will step on him, Thomas fires his gun at Budsy, "just by way of caution."[52] The shot produces some degree of social conditioning through the "giant's" astonishment, when with "a cry as loud as the whistle of a steam engine," the chubby, whimpering Budsy learns a healthy respect for Thomas, who proceeds to accompany Budsy on a tour of his home, until "our brave Yankee boy" escapes. Stealing away in one of Budsy's toy boats, Thomas leaves Budsy crying at the double loss of his miniature playmate and his toy boat. From this adventure, Thomas declares that he has learned that "'some giants are babies and can be handled,'" the first oblique acknowledgment that Budsy is in fact a child.[53]

Thomas's determined and aggressive resistance to Budsy can be read as a refutation of the nurturing and caretaking a child would require (and which a girl in his position would provide). Throughout, the narrative refers to Budsy as behaving "like a child in a fright," as possessing a "queer, toddling trot," and as being "simple" and "harmless." Never, until the story's end, does Budsy appear as a toddler, a recognition that would force Thomas to serve as a miniature adult ministering to a giant baby. Thomas instead chooses to live out his asocial, savage adolescence, brandishing his gun and attempting to hold Budsy to adult behavioral models so that he may retain his own independence. Disgusted by Budsy's prattling, lisping speech, by his lack of courage, by his tears at every mishap, Thomas repeatedly ridicules Budsy's baby ways. He abhors childish needs, particularly as Budsy reveals a sibling, "the most colossal infant that Thomas had ever seen, even in a nightmare." [54]

In rare cases such as the story of Budsy, where boys appear as miniaturized, their social stature is increased by an agency over the scenario, even while their childish resistance to social responsibilities is maintained. The young hero's horror, we might posit, lies in being drawn into a miniature scene that promises to domesticate and, by extension, feminize him. Dramatically illustrating the ways that a boy's culture resisted participation in the world of the miniature by refuting mature caretaking, the tale of Budsy serves as a powerful defense of a male youth's supposed "need" to cling to a period unmarked by adult social expectations. This privilege of resisting familial needs, however, is not extended to girls by nineteenth-century popular culture; for girls and female adolescents alike, duty is positioned as more significant than play.

The female heroine of "Ned and Norah," from Ellis A. Davidson's *The Happy Nursery,* acts out a typically mature girlhood by watching over a childish boy in the following poem:

Ned and Norah sat at home,
    On a rainy day.
Ned was Sulky, for mamma
    Wouldn't let him play
In the garden soft and wet
    With his bat and ball;
So he hid his sulky face,
    Turned it to the wall.
Then his sister Norah came,
    Took him by the hand,
Looking kindly in his face,
    Made him understand

3.4. *"Ned and Nora," a drama of boyish rebellion. From* The Happy Nursery, *1875. Courtesy Winterthur Library Printed Book and Periodical Collection.*

What a naughty thing it was
    Thus to be so rude,
When mamma had kept him in
    Only for his good.[55]

In a contest between childish play and beneficent caretaking, Norah (who cannot be much the elder of Ned, according to the illustration accompanying the poem [see fig. 3.4]) is pictured as the more mature, socialized character. Instead of indulging in childish play, Norah has accepted the duties of the domestic world that she is expected to inhabit, taking on her mother's prohibition and explaining it to the petulant Ned until he is "made" to understand the boundaries placed on playtime.

Even while the text praises Norah's understanding and caretaking, the accompanying illustration focuses on Ned, who occupies the center of the illustration and who rejects his mother's mandate and resists his sister's pleading; his sulky disappointment supplies the vignette's drama. Norah, who kneels on a small stool, implores Ned to understand the decisions made on his behalf. In a posture that transforms her into a diminutive figure of supplication, the more mature Norah is nonetheless rendered less pictorially interesting than Ned. Turned away, with her face half hidden, she becomes a figure of predicable girlhood, having cast off her childish role (along with her doll) out of concern for the real child beside her. For childish boys like Ned, however, there will be a moment of profound transformation into maturity, or so the text and illustrations imply. Through Ned, the distinction between childhood and adulthood takes on a dramatic potential, highlighting the importance of Ned's future development. Norah, however, is rendered not half as interesting as her brother, since she is devoid of any dramatic rebellion. As a conduit of absorbed, repeated information, Norah is too good to be interesting, too predictable to be unique, and ultimately, a girl who exemplifies the maturity of a miniature adult, a figure devoid of a transformative potential.

Like other representations of youthful development, that of Ned and Norah situates adolescent experimentation and rebellion as an exclusively male province, an argument that late-nineteenth-and early-twentieth-century leisure activities repeatedly suggested. F. Scott Fitzgerald's stories about youth, collected in *The Basil and Josephine Stories*, provide a problematic portrait of gendered developmental expectations for early-twentieth-century teens. Divided into separate groups of boys' and girls' stories, Fitzgerald's tales explore the experiences of two distinctively modern youth, Basil Lee and Josephine Perry.[56] There are startlingly different experiences of adolescence attributed to the two. Whereas Basil's life is treated in eight stories, Josephine's receives five. Additionally, Basil's experiences span the ages of fourteen to seventeen while Josephine appears as a "young woman" of sixteen in her stories, which follow her through to the age of seventeen. Because the stories implicitly promise to convey the symmetry of comparable experiences, such inequities are striking. In the resulting narrative, Basil's adventures allow him to mature over a longer span of time, which configures his development as more traceable than Josephine's. Even from the outset of her stories, Josephine appears locked into a narrower field of interest, which includes boys and marriage but little else. Portrayed as a mature predator, Josephine is able to bend the most settled of men to her will; yet at the outset of her adulthood, in the final story, she kisses a lover, only to find no emotion left inside her, only a "vast, tragic apathy."[57] There is no real youth for Josephine, who appears not a silly prankster like Basil, but a selfish, irretrievably spoiled young woman preying on war veterans and her sister's suitors.

Most significantly, the narrative voice allows no leniency for Josephine, no privilege of youth, for throughout her stories she is held to adult standards of behavior by the narrator, who encourages readers to view Josephine's actions as resulting in grave consequences—among them her disillusionment and purposelessness. Josephine repeatedly wishes she were dead and, at seventeen, believes that she is paying for her "past." These are not just Josephine's assertions; the narrator, who is less obviously present in Basil's stories, agrees, noting that "compared to a seventeen-year-old girl of today, [her friend] was an innocent; Josephine Perry, however, belonged to the ages."[58]

Positioning Josephine's maturity as the source of her despair, Fitzgerald's narrator upholds Basil's youthful vigor as a promise of his bright future. Even a character out of sympathy with Basil, in judging him "dispassionately," "felt, too—as even those who disliked him felt—that there was something else in his face—a mark, a hint of destiny, a persistency that was more than will, that was rather a necessity of pressing its own pattern on the world, of having its way."[59] Governed by "ambition, struggle, and glory," the still youthful Basil is excused from his missteps, whereas Josephine (no less ambitious, in her way) is soundly condemned.[60] Whereas Basil's moments of social deviance are associated with a moment of privileged development, Josephine's transgressions are cast as evidence of a deeper psychological dissolution—a sign that she is allowed no period of rebellion comparable to Basil's. While he is vital, energetic, and in transition to some greater, grander phase of life, she is fatally flawed, hardened, and molded for life.

Addressing what she presents as a pervasive cultural problem in 1899, Charlotte Perkins Gilman describes the consequences of expecting development in boys, but maturity in girls. She writes, "When our infant son bangs about, roars, and smashes things, we say proudly that he is 'a regular boy!' When our infant daughter coquettes with visitors, or wails in maternal agony because her brother has broken her doll, whose sawdust remains she nurses with piteous care, we say proudly that 'she is a perfect little mother already!' What business has a little girl with the instincts of maternity? No more than the little boy should have with the instincts of paternity. They are sex-instincts and should not appear till the period of adolescence."[61] As Gilman asserts, what is most startling about a gendered understanding of childhood is its suggestiveness for separate theories of development, including the ludicrous expectation that girls should naturally take to maternal activities.

Echoing the same sentiments Fanny Fern expressed some fifty years earlier, Gilman's recognition of the vastly different expectations infusing playtime reminds us of a pronounced reluctance to allow girls the experience of playful, boisterous childhood. In their pointed refusal to encourage girls to act out a modern version of carefree childhood, leisure activities reflect the larger culture's deep and pervasive understanding of girlhood as virtually indistinguishable from feminized nineteenth-century adulthood. As we see in the constructions of playtime circulated in nineteenth-century popular texts, accompanying the acceptance of separate forms of leisure for girls and boys are those expectations that leave a carefree childhood to the boys.

NOTES
Much of the material for this paper was collected during a short-term research grant at the Winterthur Museum and Library.

1. Nancy Armstrong, *Desire and Domestic Fiction: A Political History of the Novel* (New York: Oxford University Press, 1987), 14.
2. See Philippe Ariès, *Centuries of Childhood: A Social History of Family Life*, trans. Robert Baldick (New York: Vintage Books, 1962); Norbert Elias, *The Civilizing Process* (Cambridge, Mass.: Blackwell, 1994); Jack Zipes, *Fairy Tales and the Art of Subversion: The Classical Genre for Children and the Process of Civilization* (New York: Routledge, 1994); Ellen Seiter, *Sold Separately: Parents and Children in Consumer Culture* (New Brunswick, N.J.: Rutgers University Press, 1995); and Miriam Formanek-Brunell, *Made to Play House: Dolls and the Commercialization of American Girlhood, 1830–1930* (New Haven, Conn.: Yale University Press, 1993).
3. Zipes additionally claims that children's roles were so significant that many folktales were reinvented as fairy tales, which encouraged youngsters to adhere to notions of polite social interaction. As Zipes argues, "The fairy tales were cultivated to assure that young people would be properly groomed for their social functions." Bourgeois culture, according to Zipes, encouraged the perpetuation of existing social roles so as to ensure its own longevity, engendering among the young a sense of the behaviors that were expected in adulthood. See Zipes, *Fairy Tales*, 14.
4. See Armstrong, *Desire and Domestic Fiction;* Nancy Cott, *The Bonds of Womanhood: "Woman's Sphere" in New England, 1780–1835* (New Haven, Conn.: Yale University Press, 1977); Mary P. Ryan, *Cradle of the Middle Class: The Family in Oneida County, New York, 1790–1865* (New York: Cambridge University Press, 1981); and Barbara Welter, "The Cult of True Womanhood: 1820–1860," all in *The American Family in Socio-Historical Perspective*, 3d ed., ed. Michael Gordon (New York: St. Martin's Press, 1983). An examination of nineteenth-century guidebooks about leisure amusements—books directed toward the children of the evolving American middle class—reveals that gender was perceived as an essential aspect of middle-class status, an argument made persuasively by the above scholars.
5. See Joseph F. Kett, *Rites of Passage: Adolescence in America, 1790 to the Present* (New York: Basic Books, 1977). Kett situates the rise of a modern American construction of childhood from the late eighteenth and into the early nineteenth centuries.
6. *A Little Pretty Pocket-Book Intended for the Instruction and Amusement of Little Master Tommy and Pretty Miss Polly with Two Letters from Jack the Giant Killer* (Worcester, Mass.: Isaiah Thomas, 1787), 16.
7. *Ibid.*
8. *Youthful Recreations* (Philadelphia: J. Johnson, c. 1810).
9. *Remarks on Children's Play* (New York: Samuel Wood and Sons, 1819).
10. Ibid., 40.
11. See Harvey Green, *Fit for America; Health, Fitness, Sport, and American Society* (New York: Pantheon, 1986); and Michael Newbury, "Healthful Employment: Hawthorne, Thoreau, and Middle-Class Fitness," *American Quarterly* 47, no. 4 (1995): 681–714.
12. See Anne Scott MacLeod, "The Caddie Woodlawn Syndrome: American Girlhood in the Nineteenth Century," in Mary Lynn Stevens Heininger, Karin Calvert, Barbara Finkelstein, Kathy Vandell, Anne Scott MacLeod, and Harvey Green, *A Century of Childhood, 1820–1920* (Rochester, N.Y.: Margaret Woodbury Strong Museum, 1984). It is important to recall that the kinds of expectations discussed here are normative ones. Among actual nineteenth-century girls, MacLeod has argued, tomboys certainly existed. And advocates

of physical activity such as William James and Annie Payson Call were among those who spoke out about women's need for exercise to release tension. Various dress-reform advocates, particularly *Arena* editor B. O. Flower, also upheld the need for physical activity among healthy women.

13. Lynne Vallone, *Disciplines of Virtue: Girls' Culture in the Eighteenth and Nineteenth Centuries* (New Haven, Conn.: Yale University Press, 1995), 120.

14. *Remarks on Children's Play*, 41.

15. Ibid., 4.

16. Susan Stewart, *On Longing: Narratives of the Miniature, the Gigantic, the Souvenir, the Collection* (Baltimore: Johns Hopkins University Press, 1984).

17. Ellen Gruber Garvey, *The Adman in the Parlor; Magazines and the Gendering of Consumer Culture, 1880s to 1910s* (New York: Oxford University Press, 1996).

18. Ibid., 43. Garvey also writes that nineteenth-century advertisers relied on contests for children that would "impress" brand consciousness onto future consumers under the belief that children would purchase what their parents did. The effect, Garvey argues, is that "[c]hildhood became a repository of a commercial unconscious, where early habits left their untraceable mark on adult behavior" (53).

19. Ebenezer Landells, *The Boy's Own Toy-Maker: A Practical Illustrated Guide to the Useful Employment of Leisure Hours* (Boston: Shepard, Clark and Brown, 1859) and Ebenezer Landells and Alice Landells, *The Girl's Own Toy-Maker and Book of Recreation* (London: Griffith and Farran, 1860). Portions of *The Girl's Own Toy-Maker* were also published as *Ornamental Toys and How to Make Them*, which bore Landells's name, and in *Godey's Lady's Book* of 1861 (in what appears to be a pirated replication). The positioning of girls' play in a women's magazine further suggests the "natural" link between such play and the adult female world.

20. Landells, *The Boy's Own Toy-Maker*, v.

21. Ibid., vi–viii.

22. Ibid., vii.

23. See Ruth Schwartz Cowan, *More Work for Mother* (New York: Basic Books, 1986); and Dolores Hayden, *Redesigning the American Dream: The Future of Housing, Work, and Family Life* (New York: W. W. Norton, 1984). Historically speaking, the reasons for the differing treatment of girls and boys are comprehensible in that many middle-class young women married at an earlier age than did their male counterparts. In addition, the gendering of adult work allotted to women the management of household resources rather than the gathering or constructing of them, a construction of women's work as repetitive and inherited, or as unchanging, even in an age of rapidly advancing technologies.

24. Landells and Landells, *The Girl's Own Toy-Maker*, v.

25. Ibid.

26. Ibid. Many entertainment guides for girls assume that girls are developing badly, that their imperfections need to be corrected quickly. See Gillian Avery with Angela Bull, *Nineteenth-Century Children: Heroes and Heroines in English Children's Stories, 1780–1900* (London: Hoddern and Stoughton, 1965). In regard to nineteenth-century English fiction, Avery and Bull argue that "[t]he writers of juvenile literature recognized at an early state that in the boy they had an entirely different animal. Girls were malleable, suggestible, sensitive to correction; it was possible to reform them and improve them through their reading. But boys would not stomach much of this sort, and from early days were allowed to go their own way" (138–39).

27. Landells and Landells, *The Girl's Own Toy-Maker*, vi.

28. See Deborah Gorham, *The Victorian Girl and the Feminine Ideal* (Bloomington: Indiana University Press, 1982) and Miriam Formanek-Brunell, *Made to Play House; Dolls and the*

Commercialization of American Girlhood, 1830–1930 (New Haven, Conn.: Yale University Press, 1993). Gorham argues that dolls allowed girls to "rehearse their future maternal role," noting that most Victorian dolls came without wardrobes and that girls were expected to dress them by making clothing (75). Formanek-Brunell also argues that nineteenth- and early twentieth-century dolls provided girls with a sense of agency over their lives, suggesting that dolls could be used to act out countercultural urges as well as promote some sense of feminist activism.

29. H. D. Richardson, *Holiday Sports and Pastimes for Boys* (London: W. S. Orr, 1848).

30. Henry Chadwick, *The Sports and Pastimes of American Boys* (New York: George Routledge and Sons, 1884), 9.

31. *The Boy's Home Book of Sports, Games, Exercises and Pursuits* (Philadelphia: Porter and Coates, 1875).

32. Ibid., 10.

33. *Home Games for Little Girls; Exciting to Play; No Trouble to Learn,* Aunt Louisa's Big Picture Series (New York: McLoughlin Brothers, 1870).

34. Lydia Maria Child, *The Girl's Own Book* (1833; reprint Bedford, Mass.: Applewood Books, 1992), 58.

35. Eliza Leslie, *The American Girl's Book; or, Occupation for Play Hours,* 16th ed. (New York: R. Worthington, 1879).

36. Ibid., 65–66.

37. Ibid., 60.

38. Ariès, *Centuries of Childhood,* 71.

39. Mrs. A. J. Graves, *Girlhood and Womanhood; Sketches of My Schoolmates* (Boston: T. H. Carter, 1844).

40. Ibid., iv.

41. Ibid.

42. W. H. Davenport Adams, *Woman's Work and Worth in Girlhood, Maidenhood, and Wifehood* (London: J. Hogg, 1880), 91–92.

43. Mary Eliza Moxcey, *Girlhood and Character* (New York: Abington Press, 1916), 27.

44. Moxcey mentions the single-cell theory of development as part of her proof that a girl's development can be traced to some original state. The text makes no mention of the fact that all creatures, male and female, begin from a single cell.

45. G. Stanley Hall, *Adolescence; Its Psychology and Its Relations to Physiology, Anthropology, Sociology, Sex, Crime, Religion, and Education* (New York: Appleton, 1904).

46. See Gail Bederman, *Manliness and Civilization; A Cultural History of Gender and Race in the U.S., 1880–1917* (Chicago: University of Chicago Press, 1995), 97, for a discussion of Hall's failure to include female adolescence in his paradigm.

47. Although nineteenth-century guidebooks on leisure suggest widespread denial of any transformation from girlhood into adulthood, later fictional narratives envisioned a model of girlhood more congruent with transformative boyhood. See Anne Scott MacLeod's discussion of Carol Ryrie Brink's 1935 novel *Caddie Woodlawn.* Focusing on Caddie's punishment for teasing her very feminine visiting cousin, MacLeod assigns the term "the Caddie Woodlawn syndrome" to textual moments when girls are confined to home and its womanly duties after a period of tomboyish freedom outdoors. Relying on diaries and autobiographies, MacLeod also relates the portrayal of Brink's heroine to the lived experiences of nineteenth-century women.

48. Ellen Seiter notes that over the last fifty years, ads for girls' toys have remained stable in their emphasis on depicting girls' play as "a miniature version of their mothers' domestic work." She also contends that girls' play continues to be characterized through work, which is positioned as more gratifying to girls than play. See Seiter, *Sold Separately,* 74, 76.

49. See Vallone, *Disciplines of Virtue,* chapter 5, "The Daughters of the New Republic," for her reading of the entertainments in *Little Women,* which she argues are recuperated under the auspices of domestic womanhood and its practical goals.

50. See Mary Lynn Stevens Heininger, "Children, Childhood, and Change in America, 1820–1920," in Mary Lynn Stevens Heininger, Karin Calvert, Barbara Finkelstein, Kathy Vandell, Anne Scott MacLeod, and Harvey Green, *A Century of Childhood, 1820–1920* (Rochester, N.Y.: Margaret Woodbury Strong Museum, 1984). Heininger writes that at around 1850 Americans were urged to adopt a more tolerant attitude toward their children, one that encompassed leisure time. "If instruction too much and too early would be the death of young children," Heininger contends, "then play should give them life. Approval of amusement for its own sake was growing, and technological innovations and increases in expendable income were channelled toward the young as never before" (16). In this context, the separation of gender norms appears as part of a larger interest in consolidating behavior via class and age boundaries as well.

51. J. W. De Forest, "Budsy, The Giant," *St. Nicholas* 7 (1879): 103.

52. Ibid., 104.

53. Ibid., 108.

54. Ibid., 106.

55. Ellis A. Davidson, *The Happy Nursery, a Book for Mothers, Governesses and Nurses* (London and New York: Cassell, Petter, and Galpin, 1875), 46.

56. F. Scott Fitzgerald, *The Basil and Josephine Stories* (New York: Scribner's, 1997).

57. Ibid., 326.

58. Ibid., 310.

59. Ibid., 209.

60. Ibid., 222.

61. Charlotte Perkins Gilman, *Women and Economics* (1899; reprint New York: Harper and Row, 1966), 56.

4 Of Babies, Beasts, and Bondage

Slavery and the Question of Citizenship
in Antebellum American Children's Literature

Lesley Ginsberg

The most recognizable antislavery iconography of the antebellum era is familiar and direct: the image of the kneeling slave, naked to the waist, with enchained arms prayerfully up-raised was popularized in the early 1800s by Josiah Wedgwood as part of the British antislavery movement and was soon adopted by the American campaign. Often accompanied by the question "Am I not a man, and a brother?" (or if the figure was female, as she often was in the first few decades of the nineteenth century in America, "Am I not a woman, and a sister?"), this famous antislavery icon graced all manner of productions, from books and pamphlets to pincushions and pen wipers made by Northern women to benefit the antislavery cause.[1] It also appeared in various permutations in the children's antislavery periodical *The Slave's Friend,* which sustained a three-year run beginning in 1836. In 1836 alone, versions of this abolitionist icon appeared five times in the magazine's run of that year, supplied with captions that occasionally emphasized the figure's putative maternal role ("O my great massa in heaven, / Pity me, and bless my children" declares the chained supplicant on the cover of the magazine's second issue). In one of its most striking appearances, the familiar image of the kneeling African woman in chains was entitled "The Afflicted Mother," and when aimed at the child reader, this famous emblem unabashedly invites the child to harness his or her fears of parental abandonment in the service of abolitionism: "See that afflicted mother! She is almost broken-hearted. Her husband and children have been

THE AFFLICTED MOTHER.

4.1. "The Afflicted Mother," The Slave's Friend 1, no. 2 (1836): 1. Courtesy American Antiquarian Society.

torn from her; and her wrists and ancles [*sic*] are fastened with a chain" (see fig. 4.1).[2] Yet there are many other images that appear repeatedly throughout *The Slave's Friend* that, at first glance, seem to have little to do with the antislavery cause, and many that were also printed in decidedly more conventional juvenile books and pamphlets. Consider an image of a well-dressed white child seated in a garden, with a butterfly hovering above her outstretched hand (see fig. 4.2). This woodcut appeared three times in the magazine's three-year run, as did a woodcut by the well-known American illustrator Alexander Anderson that shows a young boy, outside his home, with an empty birdcage to his left. In his open and outstretched right hand rests a bird, whose wings are raised, depicted in a moment just before flight (see fig. 4.3). While the repetition of images in *The Slave's Friend* was no doubt a money-saving strategy, abolitionists were well aware of the power of such images and used them self-consciously to promote the antislavery cause, to the extent that Senator John C. Calhoun introduced legislation intended to prohibit newspapers that included "pictorial representations" of

TO A BUTTERFLY ON GIVING IT LIBERTY.

4.2. Untitled illustration, accompanying "To a Butterfly on Giving It Liberty." The Slave's Friend *1, no. 4 (1836): 14. Courtesy American Antiquarian Society.*

slavery from circulating through the U.S. mail. Abolitionist William Lloyd Garrison's biographer Henry Mayer asserts that "many young readers remembered the pictorial headings of *The Liberator* . . . as their introduction to abolitionist ideas."[3] In this essay I will argue that not only does abolitionist rhetoric allow us to understand how these more conventional images may have been linked to controversies over slavery and the question of citizenship, but I will also suggest that images such as "The Favoured Captives" from a 1844 issue of *Graham's* magazine (see fig. 4.4) can be read as retreats from demands for full citizenship, as odes to female subordination, and as apologies for slavery.

I begin with an anomaly: in 1831, the abolitionist-leaning children's periodical *Juvenile Miscellany* offered the child reader a story called "The Prisoners Set Free," in which the Elsworth children decide to liberate their beloved caged pets. Authored by Hannah Flagg Gould, whose poetry appeared in

4.3. *Untitled illustration, accompanying "The Pretty Robin."* The Slave's Friend *2, no. 9 (1837): 16. Courtesy American Antiquarian Society.*

4.4. *"The Favoured Captives."* Graham's, May 1844, frontispiece. Courtesy American Antiquarian Society.

periodicals and gift books throughout the 1830s and 1840s, "The Prisoners Set Free" self-consciously radicalizes the genre of antebellum children's literature. Unlike the typical children's story of this period, which so often equivocates over its relation to the civic battleground of adult discourses, this story firmly situates itself in the contemporary political landscape: as the fictional Mrs. Elsworth affirms, there is "no doubt" that her children's former pets "longed for freedom as much as the poor Africans do, who have to live and die in bondage to white men."[4] As Mrs. Elsworth applauds her children's decision to abdicate the pleasures of owning living creatures with the hope that "by the time you are grown up . . . you will understand the injustice of keeping slaves in a free country like ours," the reformed pet holders assure their friends that "if they had any animal shut up and deprived of its liberty, they might depend upon it, that if they would only let them go free, they would experience more real satisfaction . . . than all they had [felt] during its captivity." If this story represents the forcible domestication of animals as an explicit metaphor for the master/slave relationship, it also invites us to re-read the figure of the animal in literature for and about children as a mirror for adult anxieties over the borders and boundaries of citizenship in antebellum America.

While proslavery advocates were quick to sentimentalize slavery by repeated allusions to the loving bonds between humans and their pets ("slave children are pets in the house," soothes the popular and prolific antebellum writer Joseph Holt Ingraham in his 1835 travelogue *The South-West, By a Yankee*), and while abolitionists sought to dramatize the horror of slavery with repeated references to its desecration of the boundary between human and animal, the animal in antebellum American children's literature also became a figure through which the period's most pressing social issues were articulated. The relationship of human to animal was understood by antebellum Americans as a trope for both slavery and domestic inequality; further, the scene of animal abuse that haunts antebellum domestic manuals and children's literature can be read as an emblem of the tensions that marked the divisive social politics of the 1830s and '40s, tensions that resurfaced in the seemingly apolitical discourses of domesticity and childhood. By reading the figure of the animal in antebellum children's literature against both sides of the slavery debate, and by juxtaposing this figure to images of animal ownership reproduced throughout the period we can see the debate over the question of citizenship in antebellum American children's literature emerge.

In a romanticization of dependency whose tenets permeated American literary culture, justifications of slavery promulgated during the antebellum period were predicated on an increasingly literal analogy between the peculiar institution and the more familiar pattern of subordinations upon which the antebellum family was built. According to William Drayton's vitriolic *The South Vindicated* (1836), the condition of dependency means that slaves are merely children by another name: "the negro is a child in his nature, and the white man is to him as a father."[5] As George Fitzhugh—one of the slavery's most notorious defenders—puts it by way of comparison, "We do not set women and children free because they are not capable of taking care of themselves. . . . To set them free would be to give the lamb to the wolf to take care of. . . . If the children . . . were remitted to all the rights of person and property which men enjoy, all can perceive how soon ruin and penury would overtake them. But half of mankind are but grown-up children, and liberty is as fatal to them as it would be to children."[6]

In Mary Schoolcraft's glowing memoirs of growing up as the privileged daughter of a South Carolina plantation owner (1852), slavery is nothing more than benign paternalism: "How I do love to recall the patriarchal responsibility, and tenderness, my father felt for his poor, ignorant, dependent slaves." Like trusting juveniles, slaves "confide in their master," and like guilty, remorseful children, slaves "feel no enmity towards their master when he is forced to punish them. . . . When the slave commits a crime, his master switches him, with the same impulse that he switches his own child. The slave does not hate him for thus punishing him, any more than the child does; and an hour afterwards he is as merry, perhaps, as if no chastisement had been inflicted upon him."[7]

Yet if Southerners tried to smooth over the hard edges of slavery by painting the peculiar institution as just another version of the familiar inequalities of the antebellum family, many prominent Northerners were also reluctant to extend the democratic ideal to the familial sphere. In 1843, *Robert Merry's Museum*—one of the North's best-known children's periodicals—reprinted an excerpt from a new children's book by the popular and prolific Samuel Griswold Goodrich (who was also the editor of *Merry's Museum*). In "Something about Government," lifted from Goodrich's *The Young American, or, the Book of Government and Law* (c. 1842), Goodrich asserts that "*absolute equality*" is "impossible." As Goodrich elaborates in an example that reifies the inequalities upon which the antebellum family was built, "Females . . . are never placed on an equality with men before the law. . . . They are excluded from all share in the government, by the stronger sex, who proceed to make such laws as they please; and in all countries these laws exclude women from political power."

Disenfranchisement from the antebellum political and social order, however, was hardly the exclusive burden of the female sex. Lest the young male reader use Goodrich's claims to arrogate to himself an undeserved appreciation of his own privilege, Goodrich reminds the child reader that children, like slaves, are non-citizens under the paternal eye of the law: "If we take no account of slaves, still the children of white persons are not born free; they are under the control of their parents till they are twenty-one years old." In the simple woodcut that accompanies the excerpt, a dwarfish male leaning on a cane is juxtaposed to a tall, well-proportioned adult; this image reads as an illustration of Goodrich's claim that despite the Declaration of Independence, "mankind are not born free and equal."[8] Yet antebellum children's literature is aimed at an audience that is categorically excluded from the realm of American independence. In other words, just as the child is invited to identify with the small figure whose motor skills are only partly developed, the paradox of antebellum American children's literature is that didactic tales of equality and justice are presented to readers who are at least temporarily if not permanently excluded from the exclusive precincts of antebellum political citizenship.

I cite this moment in antebellum children's publishing to show that the realm of childhood was drafted into an undeclared war over the limits of citizenship. Yet the literatures of the child are just beginning to be included in scholarly attempts to reconstruct the textual and ideological terrain of antebellum America. Though nineteenth-century children's literature has been studied for its moral and socializing effects, and the profusion of child-rearing manuals and pedagogical tracts have been treated in terms of their relation to the liberalization of American Calvinism and the humanistic paradigms of John Locke and Jean-Jacques Rousseau, nineteenth-century American literatures of the child must be contextualized within the period's most compelling debates—especially the debates over slavery and female subordination.[9]

Just as proslavery rhetoric invariably dehumanized African Americans, abolitionists consistently exploited the horror of slavery's tendency to collapse the boundaries between human and animal. As David Walker charges in his incendiary 1829 *Appeal to the Coloured Citizens of the World,* slaveholding ideology routinely classed those of African descent as "a tribe of TALKING APES."[10] Lydia Maria Child's 1835 *Anti-Slavery Catechism* charges that under Southern slave codes, "poor human brutes" are defined as beasts of burden, in statutes that with a brutal, unconscious metonymy link slaves with "working beasts, animals, &c."[11] In an expert revision of abolitionist codes, Frederick Douglass's 1845 autobiographical *Narrative* explicitly highlights the terrors of a system in which an orchard is an irresistible temptation to "hungry swarms of boys," who later devour their inadequate rations "like so many pigs." Douglass poignantly recounts moments of mental agony during which the slave system made him despise his own humanity: "I have often wished myself a beast."[12] In a discussion entitled "Selling Slaves by the Pound," the abolitionist children's magazine *The Slave's Friend* uses the same analogy to condemn the peculiar institution: "What, sell boys and girls, like Julia and me, as they do so pigs and fish! Is it so, father? . . . It is indeed true, my son."[13]

Additionally, taking abolitionist rhetoric to its logical extreme, *The Slave's Friend* asserts that animals may well have it better than the slave, noting, "It is a blessed thing to be free. So thought Michael, as he was at work very hard in the field for a cruel master. He . . . saw the birds and animals all free, and . . . thought, 'but I am a poor slave!' The ducks dabbled in the pond . . . the chickens roamed at liberty . . . the old gray horse grazed contentedly in the pasture. Michael sighed, and said to himself, 'and yet I am a man; and while all other creatures are free, I am a poor slave!'"

The Slave's Friend visually emphasizes the horror of slavery with obsessively recurring woodcuts sprinkled throughout the magazine's three-year run, including an illustration of a coffle-yoke, which is suspiciously like an oxen's yoke. In the narrative that accompanies the appearance of this illustration in the 1837 edition, *The Slave's Friend* explicitly links the horror of slavery to the devolution from animal to human, as well as to the "hypocrisy" of American rhetorics of liberty:

> *Ellen.* Did you ever, papa, see a coffle of slaves?
> *Mr. Murray.* Yes, my dear, I once saw the shocking sight. I was seated at the front window of a hotel in the city of Washington, and saw a large number of slaves, chained together by the wrists, two and two, driven by two men on horseback. They held whips in their hands, which they were snapping very loud, and the poor creatures were driven at what they called a *dog-trot,* that is as fast as a dog usually runs.
> *Ellen.* In the city of Washington, father! where Congress sits! Is it possible?
> *Mr. Murray.* Yes—it was even so; and I remember that the national flag, with its stars and stripes, was waving at the same time at the top of the Capitol, where Congress was in session. The sight was enough to make any one's heartache [*sic*], and to make an American blush.
> *Ellen.* The *stripes* in the national flag make me think of the stripes the poor slaves suffer. Wont the rest of the world ridicule us, dear father, for having such a flag?
> *Mr. Murray.* Yes, child; they do begin to ridicule us. They call us hypocrites, because we boast of our liberty, and yet enslave our fellow men.[14]

The magazine also regularly featured a woodcut of one of the most charged antebellum symbols of cringing dependency and the lack of full citizenship: the whip. In an essay on the horrors of the "cart-whip" *The Slave's Friend* teaches, "Dumb beasts have thick hides, covered with hair, to defend them. . . . But think how tender our bodies are—how thin our skin is—how quick we feel the pain of a blow.[15]

Finally, following Gould's paradigm for abolitionist children's literature, in 1837 *The Slave's Friend* opened an issue with what at first appears to be a conventional story featuring two boys who indulge in the "cruel sport" of "bird-nesting." James is the instigator, while John lapses into paternalistic rationalizations for baby-bird stealing: "[A]s the little things could not take care of themselves, we thought it would be better to bring them home, put them in a cage, and feed them every day." The birds, separated from their parents and deprived of their native freedom, are dead within "a few days." Yet at the very moment of contrition when a more familiar admonitory tale might end, the narrator interjects a moral that compels us to reread the story as an explicit metaphor for both the problem of slavery and the inequalities of citizenship played out within the dependencies of the antebellum family: "James acted as the slaveholders do. They seize men as James seized the birds . . . [while men] like John, look on, and either help to commit the robbery, or offer all manner of excuses for the robbers. They say, as John did, 'if I should let the birds go, they cannot take care of themselves.'"[16] What makes abolitionist children's literature compelling is in part its willingness to enlist children—those human creatures judged unable to "take care of themselves"—in the service of freeing others in radically like positions. Though antislavery juvenile writing proffers gross simplifications of complex problems, it nevertheless invites the child reader to play out the process of reform within the familial sphere.[17]

If slave-owning ideology rested heavily on the supposed brutish and animal-like nature of black people, and if abolitionists exploited such rhetoric for their own ends, proslavery advocates were quick to sentimentalize the relationship of master and slave through repeated allusions to the cloying imagery of the affectionate bonds between humans and their domesticated animals. In his defense of slavery, William Harper explains that "The relation of master and slave . . . is, as the experience of all the world declares, naturally one of kindness. . . . Is it not natural that a man should be attached to that which is *his own,* and which has contributed to his convenience, his enjoyment, or his vanity? This is felt even toward animals." At the center of the proslavery argument was the claim that the chains of slavery were equivalent to the affective bonds that link the unequal members of the antebellum family. And in a stunning passage that conflates slavery and family life, Drayton declares, "We are all, in early life, slaves. . . . The child is the slave of his father. . . . The laws of every community justify a certain state of domestic bondage." [18]

Yet Northerners also represented family government on the antidemocratic model of master and slave. As Francis Wayland counsels in his enormously popular *Elements of Moral Science* (1835), the state of dependency necessitates absolute subordination. "[T]he child," he notes, "is bound to obey the parent so long as he remains . . . dependent upon his parent." [19] In a chapter depicting the proper exercise of authority in the family, John S. C. Abbott's *The Mother at Home* offers a scene that reads as a Lacanian parable of parental power. When young John refuses to pronounce the letter *A* during a reading lesson at home, his father resolves to punish him until he does so. Three times his father beats him, each time more severely than the first, yet young John refuses to yield. Though his father regrets the beatings, "exceedingly . . . [he] knew the question was now to be settled who should be the master." But just after John's father threatens a fourth beating, the child relents. As Abbott glosses, "John learnt a lesson which he never forgot. . . . He learnt that it was the safest and happiest course for him to obey" his "master." [20] These sentiments are echoed fifteen years later in America's first school desegregation case, *Roberts v. The City of Boston* (1849). In the words of then Supreme Court Chief Justice Lemuel Shaw, "the great principle" that "all persons . . . are equal before the law" is the sort of principle that may legitimately appear "in a declaration of rights." However, this declaration must never be applied to those who are legally classed as being in a temporary or perpetual state of nonage, since "when this great principle comes to be applied to the actual and various conditions of persons in society, it will not warrant the assertion that men and women are legally clothed with the same civil and political powers, and that children and adults are legally to have the same functions . . . but only that the rights of all . . . are equally entitled to the paternal consideration and protection of the law, for their maintenance and security." [21] In other words, as Wayland, Abbott, and Shaw have suggested, the condition of childhood is by definition the opposite of that of full citizenship.

Like other Northern writers who published for the children's literature market, Goodrich regularly condemned slavery as a "bad system"—though never in terms that hurt his phenomenal popularity (he was one of the most successful American publishers of children's literatures in the 1830s and '40s). If Goodrich seems at times to repeat the tenets of proslavery domestic ideology, however, he also warns that absolute power is easily abused. In *Fireside Education* Goodrich reports a version of that scene of animal abuse so familiar to antebellum child rearing guides—in this case an episode lifted from

Catharine Maria Sedgwick's *Home.* In a fit of anger, young Wallace Barclay plunges his sister's kitten into a vat of boiling water. Guilty of "murderous cruelty to an innocent animal," Wallace redeems himself by learning to wield his power wisely.[22] As Sedgwick notes in *A Love Token for Children,* children who take advantage of their power over brute creation are likely to trample on the rights of their human friends: "those children who are in the habit of pulling off flies' wings, throwing stones at birds, beating dogs, and kicking horses, are never loved; such children cannot be, for those that are cruel to animals will not care for the feelings of their companions."[23] Or, as the abolitionist Eliza Cabot Follen muses in an essay entitled "Animals" that appeared in her children's magazine *The Child's Friend,* "I believe we seldom do animals justice. We have unquestioned power over them, and we ungenerously abuse it."[24] In a collection entitled *True Stories About Dogs and Cats* (1856), Follen would later analogize that "we have made cats our slaves. We have taken them from the woods, that we may have them to catch our rats and our mice. We make them do just as we please, and ought we not to make them as comfortable and as happy as we can?"[25]

Using the model of abolitionist children's literature exemplified by Hannah Flagg Gould's didactic offerings, *The Slave's Friend* continued to link pet keeping with slavery. As shown in the aforementioned figure 4.2, a little girl sits in a patch of flowers while a butterfly floats freely above her. The 1836 appearance of this illustration is accompanied by a poem entitled "To a Butterfly on Giving it Liberty," lifted from Ann and Jane Taylor's *Original Poems for Infant Minds* (1804). The speaker muses,

Why should my tyrant will suspend
A life by wisdom giv'n
Or sooner bid thy being end
Than was designed by heaven?

In a reappearance of the same illustration in 1837, the picture is followed by a caption that reads,

Go pretty butterfly
Wing away in the sun
Enjoy sweet liberty
Till thy little life's done.

An essay called "The Butterfly" makes the link between the desire to catch a living creature and the mechanics of slavery explicit when a boy is trying to catch and "to kill the poor harmless insects." As the narrator admonishes,

"I was pained to see so much cruelty. I fear that boy, if he lives to grow up, will be a wicked man. Poor slaves, when they escape from bondage, are chased just so. Like the butterfly they love freedom, and those who are stronger than they knock them down."[26] The caption to *The Slave's Friend*'s 1837 reprinting of the aforementioned Alexander Anderson woodcut (see fig. 4.3) narrates a scene of liberation that would make Gould proud: "Go little bird! Take thy liberty. I will emancipate you, Robin-redbreast. I'll turn you loose into the open air. I dare say you can take care of yourself. There! Good-by to you, my little fellow. I am sorry I ever shut you up in this cage." The appearance of the same illustration in the previous year is paired with "The Pretty Robin" (titled "The Robin" in the Taylor sisters' *Original Poems*), in which the speaker renounces the pleasures of captivity: "But then t'would be cruel to keep thee, I know/So stretch out thy wings, little robin, and go." Yet in one of the glaring ironies that surround abolitionist attempts to remake antebellum juvenile literatures, this British poem was apparently innocuous enough to be reprinted in *The Confederate First Reader*.[27]

It may be that the spirit of protest that wafts through these vignettes of liberation did not attract Southern displeasure because these works echo (if American editors or publishers did not explicitly reprint) the more familiar work of British Romantic-era writers who wrote for the juvenile Anglo-American middle-class reading public of the previous generation. Yet this tradition could be invoked (as well as reprinted) with a peculiarly American slant. For example, take Anne Taylor's companion pieces, "The Little Bird's Complaint to His Mistress" and "The Mistress's Reply to Her Little Bird," which first appeared in *Original Poems*. In the first poem, the captive speaker pleads for liberty in tones that would be at home in abolitionist children's literature; pining away in his "wiry prison," the animal chides, "Why was I taken from the waving nest" . . . Torn from my mother's downy breast, / In this sad prison-house to die unseen?" The poem ends with a plaint that easily translates into an abolitionist call to redemption:

Kind mistress, come, with gentle, pitying hand,
Unbar that curious grate, and set me free;
Then . . . I'll . . .
. . . sing sweet songs to freedom and to thee.

Indeed, "The Little Bird's Complaint" appears in slightly truncated form in William Lloyd Garrison's *Juvenile Poems, for the Use of Free American Children, of Every Complexion* (1835), and in *The Slave's Friend* of 1836. The inclusion of this poem in Garrison's collection suggests that it had been selected specifically for the edification of "Free American Children." However, Taylor's "Reply" is conspicuously omitted from these American antislavery collections. In the "Reply," the bird's "kind mistress" reminds her captive that he is ill-equipped to survive in the wild; true humanity requires resignation to the captive state:

> Then do not pine, my favourite, to be free,
> Plume up thy wings, and clear that sullen eye;
> . . . But now 'twould kill thee soon, to let thee fly.

The omission of the "Reply" reads as a deliberate Americanization of the British romantic child as well as a transformation of this tradition in the service of antebellum American aims.[28]

Other Northern children's publications included warnings against forcible domestication whose terms recall the dynamic between master and slave. In 1833, Goodrich's *Parley's* magazine printed a poem called "The Captive Bluebird" in which a recently caged bird pleads with her "sweet little mistress" to "let me go": "Blessings on thee, my mistress dear," says the bird as she receives her liberty. Gould's "The Escape of the Doves" (which appeared without attribution in that magazine in 1835) also incorporates another highly charged term from slavery's lexicon when it opens with a plaint addressed to runaway pets: "'Come back, you fugitive things!'" The "fugitive" pets do not return; nor do they seem to miss their "old master." In "The Lost Nestlings," another of Gould's poems to appear anonymously in *Parley's,* a "mother robin" searches for her "darling" progeny, until "a little wanton boy" admits that "was I, that had the pleasure/your nestlings to destroy." When the mother bird articulates her anguish and the boy becomes aware of her subjective pain he is shamed into contrition and vows never to harm another nestling.[29]

The drama of "The Lost Nestlings" echoes that melancholy scene that antislavery literature would exploit throughout the antebellum period—the forcible separation of families on the auction block. "I have seen the slaves weep as though their hearts would break, for fear that some of them might be sold and separated from their families," admits a young Southerner in the 1856 abolitionist children's story *Gertrude Lee; Or, The Northern Cousin.*[30] Theodore Dwight Weld's encyclopedic indictment of slavery, *American Slavery As It Is,* includes what could be called a stock scene in the literature of abolition: "I saw a mother with eight children sold at auction. I watched their emotions closely—they were to be separated, probably forever—the scene cause[d] tears, and I was not ashamed to give vent to them."[31] Just as Weld's *Slavery As It Is* invites the reader to cry with the slave, *Robert Merry's Museum* admonishes its young readers to identify with the birds whose nests they would steal: "Would not your father and mother be sorry, if any cruel person should come and destroy their house? Why then shall girls and boys destroy the houses of pretty birds?" [32] *The Child's Friend* offers the parable of an angelic African-American boy who puts young birds back into their nests; this boy goes so far as to "step aside, lest he should tread on an ant-hill, and thus destroy the industrious little creatures' habitation." [33] In Lydia Sigourney's "The Prisoner Bird," published in *Parley's,* the speaker offers to liberate the caged animal: "Twould be a great pleasure, / Sweet bird! to me," to hear the bird sing "The song of the free." [34] And if Sigourney's poem attempts to teach children the stoic satisfactions of liberating what one loves, Hannah Gould's "The Bird Set Free," published in *Parley's* in 1838, takes Sigourney's poem a step further when the only direct speech in her piece is that of the liberated bird: though the bird's "keeper" is "kind," the newly emancipated, speaking bird recalls "los[ing] my voice and forget[ting] my song"; like the unlettered slave, captivity renders the bird literally "shut up," silently pining for freedom "the whole day long."

Though *Parley's* published such odes to independence as Gould's "The Bird Set Free," representations of freedom that explicitly included children were far more equivocal. An essay on the Fourth of July reminds the child reader of the ease with which liberty becomes libertinism: "I was talking of the Fourth of July. It is a sorrowful consideration, that the day is too often disgraced by the sins of gambling and intoxication." [35] And in a description of a "Juvenile Celebration of Independence [Day]" published in *Parley's* for 1836, children are cautioned that though there may be "a great many sorts of freedom," the most "important" is that freedom of which "the Bible so often speaks"—"FREEDOM FROM SIN." [36] Finally, in 1838 *Parley's* featured the "Story of Edward and the Parrot," in which young Edward finds a runaway parrot still bearing the traces of forcible captivity; he "had round his neck half a broken chain, which he had evidently snapped at to get his liberty." Edward recaptures the parrot and takes it home; he even indulges the animal with occasional outings, since the bird craves "a little liberty." In a gesture that highlights the political iconography of the broken chain and the desire for liberty, Edward's mother identifies the bird as "a very valuable species . . . an African parrot." And in an echo of proslavery ideology, the parrot learns to love his benevolent "master," while "Edward's affection for him knew no bounds." When the parrot turns out to be the escaped property of Lady Lovepet, Edward reluctantly returns the bird. Yet we soon discover that the chains of affection are the strongest of all; for Lady Lovepet hears the story and decides to make Edward a gift of the bird, who chirps "I love Edward!" and voluntarily perches on "the wrist of his young master." [37]

In 1832, Caroline Gilman, an early contributor to the *Juvenile Miscellany* who broke with Child in part over the issue of slavery, inaugurated a new children's periodical, the *Southern Rose Bud*.[38] If Northern periodicals charged their child readers to resist the temptation to make pets out of formerly wild animals, the *Rose Bud* generally concurred—though the paper also acknowledged the emotional satisfactions of pet keeping, pleasures the *Miscellany* often stigmatized. The *Rose Bud* confounds the pious homilies of writers like Gould when it offers "Frank, To His Rabbit," an ode to childish affection as well as to the pleasures of bondage:

> No doubt your little heart did beat,
> While aunt Flora tied your feet,
> . . . Little Rabbit! Young and bright,
> You are *now* my heart's delight!

And in terms whose emphasis on valuation implicitly recall slavery's commodification of human worth, the poem's juvenile speaker sentimentally affirms, "I cannot wish you to be *free/* You're worth a *diadem* to me!!"[39]

Though Gilman kept the *Southern Rose* free from those very literal proslavery rants that would soon be found, for example, in the *Southern Literary Messenger,* Gilman's sympathies are not undetectable. In her "New Books" column for 1833, she recommends a children's publication entitled *Cuffy's Description of the Progress of Cotton.* Offering a brief eight-line poem for each phase of the production of cotton (including sowing, picking, ginning, weaving, and bleaching), *Cuffy's Description* neatly divides King Cotton into a series of interlocking parts that nevertheless reinforce the racial inequalities built into the smooth-running system it purports to describe. As Cuffy puts it under his description of picking,

> When the blossoms fade
> Comes the cotton wool
> This from day to day
> We poor negroes pull
> Take it to the store
> Throw it in a pile
> And the [white] overseer
> Watches all the while.

But like the slaveholder's fiction of the happy slave, Cuffy doesn't allow himself to wallow in self-pity. In his description of the cotton gin, Cuffy explains,

I suppose you know
In the wool the seed is
And to get it out
There the greatest need is
This the *gin* must do
And, when that is over
Negroes go to sleep
Bathe, or live in clover.[40]

Here it is worth noting that Noah Webster's 1828 dictionary includes the phrase "to live in clover" in its definition of the word *clover*. Webster asserts that *"To live in clover* is to live luxuriously, or in abundance; a phrase borrowed from the luxuriant growth of clover," and, in an attribution that is perhaps even more telling, from "the feeding of cattle in clover."[41]

Yet when read alongside explicitly antislavery children's literature, Gilman's politics are revealed in the most seemingly innocuous of literary scenes. Consider, for example, a scene from her last novel, *Love's Progress,* in which the ingenuous Ruth Raymond is forced to confront the limits of an exaggerated sensibility. Like the encounters between girl and butterfly that reappear throughout the pages of *The Slave's Friend,* circumstances dictate that Ruth must judge whether the treatment of a butterfly is really an allegory for the treatment of human beings. When a German naturalist stays with the family, Ruth is at first appalled by his butterfly catching until she learns to surrender to the patriarchal rod:

> Ruth burst into the doctor's room on one occasion, when he was about to impale a butterfly . . . Ruth soon sided with the weaker party. . . . Too intent on his prize . . . he saw not the tears gathering in her eyes as the needle was inserted . . . Ruth . . . rushed from the spot . . . [and] flew to her mother. . . .
>
> "An old, dirty, snuff-taking onion eater!" said she; "I wish he may be stuck on a needle as thick as our spit, and six yards long!"
>
> "Ruth, Ruth," said her mother sternly, "you forget that you are as cruel now as you think Dr. Gesner to be."

Soon Ruth encounters Dr. Gesner in the act of catching another butterfly outside. She attempts to save it, but in so doing she falls into a stream. Our naturalist lets go the butterfly in order to rescue Ruth, and injures himself in the attempt. We read, "It was many days before he was restored to entire consciousness. Ruth sat by his bedside with a pitying look . . . and when he recovered, her arms were round his neck . . . unsettled thoughts of justice, undefined and disturbing, oppressed her [that evening] as she nestled on her pillow. She pitied the butterflies, but she loved the good doctor who saved her life, and the morning sun awoke her to a knowledge of good and evil."[42] In contrast to the abolitionist/feminist pieties of *The Slave's Friend* and the *Juvenile Miscellany,* Gilman suggests that social, political, and gendered inequalities can be reified in much the same way that the difference between human and animal is naturalized in her novel. Ruth's portentous awakening to "a knowledge of good and evil" situates her newfound adult sensibilities in terms of the more familiar antebellum romance of female subordination.

If the relationship of pet to pet owner was understood by antebellum Americans as a trope for both slavery and domesticity, in the 1840s *Graham's* magazine was saturated with the sentimental iconography of this bond.[43] In May of 1844 *Graham's* offered an engraving that forms an ironic counterpoint to "The Prisoners Set Free" and the genre of abolitionist children's literature it spawned, though in this picture of the pleasures of captivity, aimed at adults, our heroine is inextricably linked to the caged bird just outside her window (see fig. 4.4). In "The Favoured Captives," the arched window that frames the woman mirrors the curved birdcage, while an iron grating completes the visual link between the captive bird and her captivated owner. In *Graham's* the image proffers the subtle joys of mutual dependency; in the poem that accompanies the engraving, a male viewer pines for the snares of love: "Ah! Could I be as fondly loved [as her caged bird],/Content, her captive I would rest!"

While here *Graham's* used the notion of pet keeping to promote a conservative domestic ideology, two months after the 1848 Women's Rights Convention in Seneca Falls, New York, issued a feminist declaration of independence, *Graham's* included an image that highlighted the insecurities of freedom and the dangers inherent in the break away from domestic confinement. In "The Lost Pet" (fig. 4.5), a runaway bird is not only lost but killed, borne off in the jaws of a homely predator. The cage's open door implicates the bird's hapless owner in her pet's demise, and highlights her childish lack of foresight. More ominously, the poem that accompanies the engraving conflates child and bird: the girl who roves "bird-like, here and there, / Amid her flower[s] dear" may risk straying too far from the fenced-in security of home. As the story of "Edward and the Parrot" suggests, for antebellum dependents, the desire for a little liberty could well be a dangerous thing.[44]

The relation of human to animal in antebellum American children's literature reads as a version of the culture's more pressing debates over the boundaries and borders of citizenship. Yet antebellum children themselves were

4.5. *"The Lost Pet."* Frontispiece, Graham's, *September 1848, 152. Courtesy American Antiquarian Society.*

noncitizens by definition, a category of the disenfranchised like women, slaves, and animals, who could only trust in the "paternal" arm of the law to guarantee what rights the law deemed worthy to bestow upon them. I conclude then by suggesting that it is precisely because of the paradox that any children's story about inequality is aimed at a reader who is inherently unequal that children's literature provides one of the most crucial texts for understanding the debate over the limits of citizenship in antebellum America.

NOTES

Research for this essay was funded by an American Antiquarian Society/National Endowment for the Humanities Grant and a grant from the Committee on Research and Creative Works, University of Colorado at Colorado Springs.

1. Jean Fagan Yellin, *Women and Sisters: The Antislavery Feminists in American Culture* (New Haven, Conn: Yale University Press, 1989), 3–26.
2. *The Slave's Friend* 1, no. 2 (1836): 1; *The Slave's Friend* 1, no. 8 (1836): 1.
3. Yellin, *Women and Sisters,* 3–5, and 180, nn. 2–3; Henry Mayer, *All on Fire: William Lloyd Garrison and the Abolition of Slavery* (New York: St. Martin's Press, 1998), 124; see also the caption to tipped-in illustration following 232.

4. Hannah F. Gould, "The Prisoners Set Free," *Juvenile Miscellany* May/June 1831; 201–10.

5. William Drayton, *The South Vindicated from the Treason and Fanaticism of Northern Abolitionists* (1836; reprint New York: Negro Universities Press, 1969), 304.

6. George Fitzhugh, *Sociology for the South, or the Failure of Free Society* (1854); in *Slavery Defended: The Views of the Old South,* ed. Eric L. McKitrick (Englewood Cliffs, N.J.: Prentice-Hall, 1963), 37–38.

7. [Mary Schoolcraft], *Letters on the Condition of the African Race in the United States. By a Southern Lady* (Philadelphia: Collins, 1852), 11, 14, 18.

8. [Samuel Griswold Goodrich], "Something about Government," *Robert Merry's Museum,* January 1843, 37–38.

9. Bernard Wishy, *The Child and the Republic: The Dawn of Modern American Child Nurture* (Philadelphia: University of Pennsylvania Press, 1968). See also Anne Scott MacLeod, *A Moral Tale: Children's Fiction and American Culture, 1820–1860* (Hamden, Conn.: Archon, 1975); Gillian Avery, *Behold the Child: American Children and Their Books, 1621–1922* (London: Bodley Head, 1994). Other useful studies include John C. Crandall, "Patriotism and Humanitarian Reform in Children's Literature, 1825–1860," *American Quarterly* 21 (1969): 3–22; Anne Tropp Trensky, "The Saintly Child in Nineteenth-Century American Fiction," *Prospects* 1 (1975): 388–413; Nancy F. Cott, "Notes Toward an Interpretation of Antebellum Childrearing," *Psychohistory Review* 7 (1978): 4–20; Barbara Finkelstein, "Casting Networks of Good Influence: The Reconstruction of Childhood in the United States, 1790–1870," 111–52, and Anne M. Boylan, "Growing Up Female in Young America, 1800–1860," 153–84, both in *American Childhood,* ed. Joseph M. Hawes and N. Ray Hiner (Westport, Conn.: Greenwood, 1985); Karen Sánchez-Eppler, "Raising Empires Like Children: Race, Nation, and Religious Education," *American Literary History* 8 (1996): 399–425; and Etsuko Taketani, "The 'Omnipresent Aunt' and the Social Child: Lydia Maria Child's *The Juvenile Miscellany,*" *Children's Literature* 27 (1999): 22–39. My study is especially indebted to Richard Brodhead's groundbreaking essay, "Sparing the Rod: Discipline and Fiction in Antebellum America," *Representations* 21 (1988): 67–96.

10. David Walker, *Appeal to the Coloured Citizens of the World, but in particular, and very expressly, to those of the United States of America* (1829), ed. Sean Wilentz (New York: Hill and Wang, 1995), 61.

11. Lydia Maria Child, *Anti-Slavery Catechism* (1835; 2nd ed. Newburyport, Mass.: Charles Whipple, 1839), 10, 11.

12. Frederick Douglass, *Narrative of the Life of Frederick Douglass, An American Slave* (1845), ed. Benjamin Quarles (Cambridge, Mass.: Belknap Press, 1982), 39, 52, 37, 67.

13. "Selling Slaves by the Pound," *The Slave's Friend* 1, no. 1 (1836): 3.

14. "The Coffle-Yoke," *The Slave's Friend* 2, no. 2 (1837): 1–4; this tale is strikingly reminiscent of the scene that forms the April 1831 version of *The Liberator's* masthead. See Mayer, *All On Fire,* 124, and the tipped-in illustration following 232.

15. "The Cart-Whip," *The Slave's Friend* 2, no. 2 (1837): 11–12.

16. "Bird-Nesting," *The Slave's Friend* 2, no. 7 (1837): 1–4.

17. As Holly Keller puts it, abolitionist children's literature often posed "a clear challenge to the moral authority of adults." Holly Keller, "Juvenile Antislavery Narrative and Notions of Childhood," *Children's Literature* 24 (1996): 87.

18. Drayton, *The South Vindicated,* 82, 87.

19. Francis Wayland, *The Elements of Moral Science* (1835; reprint Boston: Gould and Lincoln, 1853), 327.

20. John S. C. Abbott, *The Mother At Home; Or, The Principles of Maternal Duty Familiarly Illustrated* (1834; reprint New York: Arno, 1972), 38–40.

21. *Roberts v. The City of Boston*, 5 Cush. (59 Mass.) 198 (1849), quoted in Kermit L. Hall, William M. Weicek, and Paul Finkelman, eds., *American Legal History: Cases and Materials* (New York: Oxford University Press, 1991), 247.

22. Samuel Griswold Goodrich, *Fireside Education* (1838; 6th ed. London: William Smith, 1841), 26–27; Catharine Maria Sedgwick, *Home*, 15th ed. (Boston: James Munroe, 1841), 14–27.

23. [Catharine Maria Sedgwick], *Love Token for Children* (New York: Harpers, 1838), 50.

24. "On Animals—The Dog," *The Child's Friend*, June 1846, 97.

25. [Eliza Cabot Follen], *True Stories about Dogs and Cats. By Mrs. Follen. With Illustrations by Billings* (Boston: Whittemore, Niles and Hall, 1856), 42.

26. "To a Butterfly on Giving It Liberty," *The Slave's Friend* 1, no. 4 (1836): no. 4 (1836): 14; "Go Pretty Butterfly," *The Slave's Friend* 2, no. 3 (1837): back cover; "The Butterfly," *The Slave's Friend* 1, no. 5 (1836): 8.

27. See *The Slave's Friend* 2, no. 4 (1837): back cover; *The Slave's Friend* 1, no. 8 (1836): 10; see also *The Slave's Friend* 2, no. 9 (1837): 16; "The Robin," in R. M. Smith, *The Confederate First Reader* (Richmond, Va.: G. L. Bidgood, 1864); "Pieces in Poetry," digitized by the University of North Carolina in "Documenting the American South," online at <http://docsouth.unc.edu/imls/smith/smith.html#confed13>.

28. Ann Taylor, "The Little Bird's Complaint to His Mistress" and "The Mistress's Reply to Her Little Bird," in *British Women Poets of the Romantic Era*, ed. Paula R. Feldman (Baltimore: Johns Hopkins University Press, 1997): 736–38; "Little Bird's Complaint," *Juvenile Poems, for the Use of Free American Children, of Every Complexion*, ed. William Lloyd Garrison (Boston: Garrison and Knapp, 1835), back page; "Little Bird's Complaint," *The Slave's Friend* 1, no. 4 (1836), 17.

29. "The Captive Bluebird," *Parley's* 1 (1833): 157; "The Escape of the Doves," *Parley's* 3 (1835): 103, reprinted in Hannah Flagg Gould, *The Golden Vase: A Gift for the Young* (Boston: Benjamin B. Mussey, 1843), 157–58; "The Lost Nestlings," *Parley's* 2 (1834): 53–54, reprinted in Hannah Flagg Gould, *The Youth's Coronal* (New York: Appleton, 1851): 162–64.

30. M. A. F. *Gertrude Lee; Or, The Northern Cousin* (Cincinnati: American Reform Tract and Book Society, 1856), 94.

31. Theodore Dwight Weld, *Slavery As It Is* (1839; reprint New York: Arno Press, 1968), 167.

32. "The Bird's Nest," *Robert Merry's Museum*, April 1843, 128.

33. "The Melancholy Boy," *The Child's Friend*, May 1844, 37.

34. L[ydia] H. S[igourney], "The Prisoner Bird," *Parley's* 4 (1836): 48.

35. "The Fourth of July," *Parley's* 1 (1833–34): 135–36.

36. "Juvenile Celebration of Independence," *Parley's* 4 (1836): 250–51.

37. "Story of Edward and the Parrot," *Parley's* 6 (1838): 363–68.

38. Carolyn L. Karcher, *The First Woman in the Republic: A Cultural Biography of Lydia Maria Child* (Durham, N.C.: Duke University Press, 1994), 630, n. 3. Jan Bakker also mentions Gilman's "pro-slave stand" in "Another Dilemma of an Intellectual in the Old South: Caroline Gilman, the Peculiar Institution, and Greater Rights for Women in the Rose Magazines," *Southern Literary Journal* 17, no. 1 (1984): 13.

39. "Frank, To His Rabbit," *The Rose Bud* 1, no. 46 (1833): 182.

40. *Cuffy's Description of the Progress of Cotton* (Boston: Lilly, Wait, Colman and Holden, 1833).

41. "Clover," in Noah Webster, *An American Dictionary of the English Language* (1828; reprint, New York: Johnson Reprint, 1970), n.p.

42. [Caroline Howard Gilman], *Love's Progress* (New York: Harper and Brothers, 1840), 18–22.

43. While *Graham's* published abolitionist sympathizers like Henry Wadsworth Longfellow and Catharine Maria Sedgwick, it also featured well-known Southern advocates like James Kirke Paulding, and as a result embodied a meeting ground for these opposing forces.

44. Lydia H. Sigourney, "The Lost Pet," *Graham's*, September 1848, 152.

5 Betsy and the Canon

Kelly Hager

In *Betsy and Tacy Go Downtown,* twelve-year-old Betsy Ray is indoctrinated into the rules and rigidities of the canon. After her parents discover that she has been reading the hired girl's dime novels (*Lady Audley's Secret* in particular), they exhort her to read "Good books. Great books. The classics," instead.[1] Accordingly, she goes to the library and announces to Miss Sparrow, the librarian, "I want to read the classics. . . . All of them"(84). Taking Betsy's request seriously, Miss Sparrow proceeds to show Betsy exactly what the classics are:

> She went back to the shelves and returned with an armful of books. She handed them to Betsy one by one.
> "*Tales from Shakespeare,* by Charles and Mary Lamb. Classic. *Don Quixote,* by Miguel de Cervantes. Classic. *Gulliver's Travels,* by Jonathan Swift. Classic. *Tom Sawyer,* by Mark Twain. Classic, going-to-be."(85)

There is much to be said about Miss Sparrow's selections and about her pronouncement that *Tom Sawyer* is "going-to-be" a classic (the year is 1904), but what interests me most about this scene of instruction is the conviction with which Miss Sparrow can nominate each of these books as a classic, and the way in which her certainty echoes the literary judgment that has brought Betsy to the library in the first place.

To go back to that first, shameful scene of reading, Betsy has been so influenced by the hired girl's novels that she herself has been writing what we might call juvenile sensation fiction. When the novel opens, Betsy is starting to work on *The Repentance of Lady Clinton,* having already written several other novels with lurid titles like *Her Secret Marriage* and *Lady Gwendolyn's Sin.* Impressed with Betsy's diligence (but unaware of what her daughter is writing), her mother decides to create a special writing corner for her, complete with an old trunk that she outfits as a desk. But as she brings the notebooks that contain her novels to her new desk, Betsy is suddenly ashamed of her writing and afraid that her mother will learn, from the titles she has given to her works, that she has been borrowing novels from Rena, the hired girl. Of course, Betsy's mother does learn the shameful secret of Betsy's reading habits and counsels her accordingly: "Betsy, it's a mistake for you to read that stuff. There's no great harm in it, but if you're going to be a writer you need to read good books. They train you to write, build up your mind. We have good books in the bookcase downstairs. Why don't you read them?" Betsy's reply, "I've read them all," gives her mother pause and leads to the family meeting at which her father exhorts her to read "the classics" and to take advantage of the newly opened Carnegie Library, where Miss Sparrow is so unerringly sure about what those classics are (75). But before Betsy goes to the library, in preparation for her new habits of reading, she comes to a decision. As she looks out her bedroom window that night, she imagines her future as a writer:

> All the stories she had told Tacy and Tib seemed to be dancing in those trees, along with all the stories she planned to write some day and all the stories she would read at the library. Good stories. Great stories. The classics. Not like Rena's novels.
>
> She . . . opened her desk. She took out the pile of little tablets and ran with them down to the kitchen and lifted the lid of the stove and shoved them in. Then she walked into the back parlor, dusting off her hands. (79–80)

As in the case of Jo March in Louisa May Alcott's *Little Women,* Betsy's first efforts at writing are burned. But there is a crucial difference, for Jo's first stories are burned by her sister Amy in a fit of jealousy, whereas Betsy burns her own stories in a moment of conscience that is depicted as a realization of her ambition and her talent. It is also important to note that Jo's first creations are fairy tales, stories that are universally approved of and admired by her family, while Betsy's stories are imitations of cheap sensation fiction. The more exact parallel between Betsy Ray and Jo March is found later in *Little Women,* when Jo's rather fatherly suitor, Professor Bhaer, expresses his distaste for sensation fiction in terms much stronger than Mrs. Ray's. As opposed to Betsy's mother's concession that "there's no great harm in it," the professor talks about this kind of writing as "poison in the sugarplum" and compares its dangers to those of whiskey.[2] After the professor's condemnation, Jo, like Betsy, burns her sensation stories. True, there seems relatively little harm in Betsy's juvenilia, whereas Jo's stories ("A Phantom Hand," "The Curse of the Coventrys") have been published and, according to the professor, pose such a danger to their readers that he declares "good young girls" should not even see them, and "I would more rather give my boys gunpowder to play with than this bad trash" (355). But parental censorship is the cause of both scenes of book burning, and the real targets of this judgment are not so much Jo's and Betsy's fiction as writers like Mary Elizabeth Braddon and E.D.E.N. Southworth, whose writing so influences these characters and whose work is none-too-subtly judged and found wanting by Louisa May Alcott and Maud Hart Lovelace. In their place Alcott valorizes the pious and sentimental novels of Charlotte Mary Yonge and Susan Warner, along with Charles Dickens and Sir Walter Scott, while Lovelace recommends that her characters read the usual suspects—William Shakespeare, Dickens, and Scott—along with Americans like Nathaniel Hawthorne, Mark Twain, and Harriet Beecher Stowe.

This scene from *Betsy and Tacy Go Downtown* raises a number of issues ranging from the canon debate, to the status of sensation fiction, to the question of what children (and, particularly, young girls) should be allowed to read; in this essay I explore the reasons these issues cluster together like this so often, and why they so often take center stage in children's literature, especially in novels for young girls. From Louisa May Alcott's *Little Women* (1868–69), *Eight Cousins* (1875), and *Rose in Bloom* (1876) and Kate Douglas Wiggin's *Rebecca of Sunnybrook Farm* (1903) to Lucy Maud Montgomery's *Anne of Green Gables* books (1908–39) and Maud Hart Lovelace's Betsy-Tacy series (1940–55), the questions of what young girls should read and like to read is linked to the emergence of a set of culturally hallowed texts, what we now gesture toward as the canon. Indeed, we find the literary heroines Jo March, Rose Campbell, Rebecca Randall, Anne Shirley, and Betsy Ray are all encouraged to read the same list of classics and forbidden to read the same kinds of novels (although the girls secretly read "this bad trash" nevertheless).[3] The issue of what is appropriate for young girls to read is thus inextricably tied up with the question of what constitutes a "classic." By looking at these concerns as they are manifested in such apparently benign works as *Betsy and Tacy Go Downtown* we can, I hope, start to learn something about what we read, why we read, and how these reading habits were shaped by our parents, librarians, and teachers—and by our reading itself. That is, what we read as children has some rather surprising and largely ignored ramifications for the present debates over the canon. Whatever our position in the debate, at some level we all believe, along with Betsy's father, that we should read the "classics" because the books we read as we were growing up told us to do so.

This essay departs from those studies that focus on how a girl's reading disciplines and educates her to move beyond a tomboyish girlhood into a more markedly feminized adolescence.[4] Instead of thinking about how *Little Women* encourages its young readers to be "good wives," I am interested in how the novel makes its audience into good readers. In order to probe the kind of intellectual norming performed in and by novels for young girls, I combine the antebellum theory of maternal, affectionate child rearing with John Guillory's work on canon formation. This method of child rearing, emerging in the early decades of the nineteenth century and opposed to the belief in infant depravity, has been articulated by Richard Brodhead, in his critical account of "disciplinary intimacy," and by historians Mary P. Ryan, in her investigation of the American family around the turn of the century, and Bernard Wishy, in his study of "the nurture reformers." Ryan's identification of the move to "maternal socialization" and Wishy's focus on "kindness, love, and tender care by a mother" point to a project of discipline marked by affection and engendered by a mother on her impressionable child in the private domestic space of the home.[5] Brodhead derives his account of the move from flogging and will breaking to a more affectionate, albeit emotionally manipulative, program of child rearing from Michel Foucault's account of the transformation of punishment from torture to discipline and imprisonment. And my account of the canonical discipline enacted by novels for young girls is, no doubt, as marked by my reading of Foucault's *Discipline and Punish* as it is by the Betsy-Tacy books.

My approach is also indebted to Guillory's *Cultural Capital* in that, like Guillory, I am more interested in how the canon is formed than in what it is formed of. Guillory asks us to turn our attention away from the question of inclusion and exclusion and think instead about how the school is involved in the process of controlling cultural capital. I expand on his notion of the school as the agent of cultural capital by examining the way that popular, sentimental, domestic literature participates in the formation of a canon from which it is excluded and aids the school (from which it is also, by and large, excluded) in "regulating access" and establishing—and, ultimately, valorizing—the canon.[6] Guillory views "literary works" as "the vector of ideological notions which do not inhere in the works themselves but in the context of their institutional presentation, or more simply, in the way in which they are taught," a perspective that helps us see that it is by virtue of the "institutional presentation" of, say, *Ivanhoe,* in *Betsy in Spite of Herself,* that readers of Lovelace are taught to read and to perceive Sir Walter Scott as literature, while what they are reading as they are taught this canonical lesson goes unmarked (ix).

Perhaps even more important is my debt to Guillory for providing me with the right questions to ask. Defining literacy "not simply as the capacity to read but as the *systematic regulation of reading and writing,*" he goes on to describe it as "a complex social phenomenon corresponding to the following set of questions: Who reads? What do they read? How do they read? In what social and institutional circumstances?" (18). It is relatively easy to find the answers to Guillory's questions in novels for young girls since, as the scene from *Betsy and Tacy Go Downtown* with which I open this essay suggests, the reading list is a recurrent element in these novels. What is more, there is a striking uniformity to the reading lists we find in Alcott, Wiggin, Montgomery, and Lovelace, not only in the way they are transmitted, but also in their contents.

There are a number of correspondences among the lists in each of these novels, not only in terms of the kinds of reading these girls are discouraged from and the ways in which their tastes are similarly normed, but also in terms of specific writers and novels. For instance, Jo, Anne, and Betsy are all markedly influenced by the same three Shakespeare plays—*Macbeth, Hamlet,* and *The Merchant of Venice.* Similarly, Jo, Rebecca, and Betsy have all read *Uncle Tom's Cabin* (several times, it appears, given the facility with which they quote from it), and Rebecca and Betsy can act out scenes from Stowe's novel on cue. Perhaps most striking is the prominence of Dickens in these novels; all of these heroines (and their siblings, friends, and boyfriends) read his novels and read them widely (both Jo and Anne have read *Martin Chuzzlewit,* for instance). And while each of the girls has read many Dickens novels, it is not unimportant that the one novel they all have in common is *David Copperfield*—a novel that is probably the urnovel for this study of the disciplining of taste and its role in the education of a writer, and another novel in which we are presented with the hero's reading list.[7] By the same token, Scott is a universal favorite: Mrs. March reads his works to her girls, Rose's cousins act out scenes from the novels, Rebecca Rowena Randall is named for both heroines of *Ivanhoe,* and Betsy seems to know that novel by heart.

The sheer number of these scattered correspondences suggests not only the degree to which these novels are all engaged in regulating the tastes of their heroines and thus of their readers, but also the degree to which that taste is regulated in precisely the same fashion and toward the same standard. Both Anne and Betsy are so taken with Alfred, Lord Tennyson's "Lancelot and Elaine" that they fancy themselves Elaine—Anne going so far as to act out the poem as she floats down the pond on a raft. Both Rebecca and Anne recite William Wordsworth's "Lament of Mary, Queen of Scots," and they both know Caroline Norton's poem "Bingen on the Rhine." Henry Wadsworth Longfellow's "Hiawatha" and John Greenleaf Whittier's "Barbara Fritchie" are among Rebecca's and Betsy's favorite poems, while *Vanity Fair* is a favorite with Anne and Betsy, and they both get in trouble for reading *Ben Hur.* These correspondences, numerous and random as they are, suggest a concerted program of standardization. That we find such similar patterns, such striking recurrences in texts that span almost one hundred years suggests a program at work in the culture and a shared system of belief that has to do both with the nature of childhood and with the proprieties of taste. That we can find such a coherent manifestation of a canon just by looking at what these girls read is telling; the community of taste suggested by their reading lists adds to our sense that what is being done through the agency of these novels is a striking instance of what Foucault identifies as the standardizing and coercive "power of the Norm."[8]

I am by no means arguing that the reading lists in these novels are uniform or even that they are uniformly received. But the difference in tastes among these characters and the varying specifics of their reading lists are less striking than the similarities, and the "power of the Norm" overwhelms the differences that are present. The discrepancies among lists suggest that the idea of a canon acquires a power that dwarfs the significance of its contents; these differences serve to highlight the predominant pattern of reading at work in all these novels. At the same time, the texts on these lists are, as I have suggested above, just consistent enough to substantiate a sense of cultural values as unchanging. In her essay "A Theory of Resonance," Wai Chee Dimock suggests that "the literary might refer to that which resonates for readers past, present, and future" and asserts that "canonicity is the prize won by an assertive linguistic object that, fortifying itself against the burden of time, can claim a time-proof integrity."[9] Similarly, Frank Kermode finds that "the books we call classics possess intrinsic qualities that endure, but possess also an openness to accommodation which keeps them alive under endlessly varying dispositions."[10]

I am arguing, in other words, for an overarching pattern and a cultural program of taste so consistent that sometimes even the books excluded from a canon share characteristics. Indeed, one of the most striking recurrences on these heroines' reading lists, especially in the context of an argument about canon formation, is the prevalence of what we tend to think of as the noncanonical: sensation fiction, sentimental religious novels, and best-sellers. These girls are fascinated with sensation fiction: Jo is wrapped up in reading and writing E. D. E. N. Southworth-like tales, Anne feverishly reads *The Lurid Mystery of the Haunted Hall,* and Betsy and her friends read *Lady Audley's*

Secret. These girls are also inordinately fond of sentimental religious fiction; they read *The Wide, Wide World, The Heir of Redclyffe,* the Pansy books, and even *Elsie Dinsmore.* They are drawn toward cliff-hangers and tearjerkers, and a taste for the classics must be instilled in them just as it must be imposed upon the reader herself. While the authors strive to give the impression that their heroines naturally grow out of their taste for the sensational, the sentimental, and the popular, the fact is that these are not tastes that they give up as they mature but are instead habits of reading they are scolded out of, cajoled away from, and made ashamed of. While I would not define the canonical as genuinely distinct from cliff-hangers or tearjerkers, the reading lessons contained in these novels suggest that it is. Accordingly, I want to look at the ways in which these novels suggest an alternative (and conservative) program of reading for their heroines and for their readers.

The methods by which Jo, Rose, Rebecca, Anne, and Betsy are encouraged to give up their inappropriate reading habits and replace them with more canonical programs of reading reflect the antebellum strategy of maternal, affectionate child rearing. But while historians of the antebellum family focus on the effect of the loving mother imprinting her beliefs and values on the child (and while Foucault points to the panopticonic exercise of power that operates by "increasing its own points of contact"), in the scenes I will analyze, both a novel and a guardian figure provide the loving guidance (or, to use Foucault's terms, both novel and parent figure are "so subtly present" in the very system they seek to discipline)—and we as readers absorb the novel's lessons just as its own heroine does. Just as the group Wishy calls "the nurture reformers" posit that a child absorbs a parent's ethics along with her love, these scenes of disciplined reading suggest that a child also internalizes the standards and norms of a cherished book.[11] In *Cradle of the Middle Class,* Ryan argues that "all the gentle admonitions and sly manipulations of maternal socialization conspired to equip children with sensitive consciences. This faculty would operate as a kind of portable parent that could stay with the child long after he left his mother's side and journeyed beyond the private sphere out onto the streets and into the public world" (161). Whether my heroines are subtly encouraged to reject the sensational for the moral, as is the case with Jo March, or made to feel ashamed of their absorption in French novels, as is Rose Campbell, or forbidden to read ghost stories, like Anne Shirley, or lovingly encouraged (one might even say bribed) to eschew the sensational for the venerable old classics, as is Betsy Ray, in these novels we see both the installation of that conscience and its operation independent of the parent who installed it. We are treated to scenes of discipline, of renunciation, and of a transformation of taste so complete that it is ultimately enforced by the girls themselves. Because it is Jo who forces herself to burn her sensation stories and Rose who will not allow herself to finish her French novel, because we see our heroines impose these standards upon themselves, we as readers are all the more willing to do the same, to subscribe to what we, like these heroines, have come to believe are our own standards. In this vein, it is important to go back and look at these scenes of discipline in order to remind ourselves that the discipline is not, as it seems, self-imposed; rather, it is imposed from above. In the scenes of discipline I read below, I want to emphasize three things: the original agent of the canonical; the way in which a taste for the canonical is internalized (that is, the ease with which the original agent of discipline is effaced); and the ways in which this self-discipline is presented as a pattern for the reader. The discipline enacted in and by these novels for young girls works both to set a norm for these literary heroines' taste and to effect a similar kind of discipline upon the reader. We as readers accept this discipline almost unconsciously, assuming that our identification with Jo and Betsy is simply the result of our shared tastes, when in fact these shared tastes are themselves the results of our desire to be like the girls we read about and our willingness to regulate our reading accordingly.

When Jo meets Professor Bhaer, the father figure she will eventually marry, she is immediately struck by his library, which consists of "a fine Shakespeare . . . his German Bible, Plato, Homer, and Milton." He inaugurates their friendship by lending her books. What is more, for Christmas he gives her his "fine Shakespeare," along with a bit of advice: "Read him well, and he will help you much; for the study of character in this book will help you to read it in the world, and paint it with your pen" (343). This advice seems innocent enough at first, not even really advice, but simply the sort of thing one says about Shakespeare. But if we consider these words in the context of Jo's current literary labors in New York, when we compare reading Shakespeare "for the study of character" to the kind of research Jo thinks necessary to write her sensation stories ("police records and lunatic asylums had to be ransacked for the purpose"), then the counsel the professor offers along with his gift begins to seem both more pointed and disciplinary (349). The contrast becomes especially clear when the narrator darkly suggests that Jo's research, unlike the reading of Shakespeare, "was beginning to desecrate some of the womanliest attributes of a woman's character. She was living in bad society; and, imaginary though it was, its influence affected her, for she was feeding heart and fancy on dangerous and unsubstantial food, and was fast brushing the innocent bloom from her nature by a premature acquaintance with the darker side of life" (349). The narrator's bleak forecast also helps us to characterize Professor Bhaer's contribution more precisely; the contrast between "Read him well" and the desecration of womanliness makes clear the distinction between affectionate guidance and dire warning. The professor practices a positive kind of discipline by offering a more effective method by which Jo can pursue her writing, whereas the narrator threatens, offering not so much discipline as punishment.

Yet perhaps the most important aspect of this first scene of disciplinary intimacy between the professor and Jo has to do with what Brodhead calls "a purposeful sentimentalization of the disciplinary relation: a strategic relocation of authority relations in the realm of emotion, and a conscious intensification of the emotional bond between the authority-figure and its charge." [12] By including his advice along with a gift, the professor invests the occasion with sentimental significance, all the more so because this is the first gift the professor has given Jo. And the nature of the gift both adds to its emotional value and helps ensure that Jo will not reject the lesson that accompanies it. As Jo writes to her family, the volume of Shakespeare the professor gives her "is one he values much, and I've often admired it, set up in the place of honor . . . so you may imagine how I felt when he brought it down . . . and showed me my name in it, 'from my friend Friedrich Bhaer'" (343). Thus, this occasion "intensifi[es] the emotional bond between the authority-figure and its charge," and it marks the beginning of a relationship of what Brodhead calls "love-power" (19).

But this is only the beginning of the professor's influence on Jo, and his advice and his Shakespeare are only the opening moves in his program of taste.[13] Once he realizes the extent to which Jo needs his moral and intellectual guidance—that is to say, once he realizes that she is writing sensation stories—he sets out to rescue her. The language in which the narrator describes his mission is important to unpack, for it suggests that such interference is both as right and natural as it is motivated by a love that is maternal in its affection: "Now it occurred to him that she was doing what she was ashamed to own, and it troubled him. He did not say to himself, 'It is none of my business; I've no right to say anything,' as many people would have done; he only remembered that she was young and poor, a girl far away from mother's love and father's care; and he was moved to help her with an impulse as quick and natural as that which would prompt him to put out his hand to save a baby from a puddle" (354). This passage has much to do with the almost universal outcry against the marriage of Jo and the professor, for it reveals that their relationship is initially constructed as one of parent and child and that the professor's regard for Jo is a combination of material love and paternal care. This may not be the stuff of romantic fantasy, but it is precisely the kind of "constant, monitory, and affectionate parental guidance" that is, according to Ryan, so effectively exercised "in the privacy of the home" where "parents formed the cradle" of character formation (99). The fact that the professor's discipline is sentimental and parental, then, is what makes it such a successful mode of instruction.

After coming to the realization that he needs "to put out his hand to save" Jo, the professor makes a series of explicit and autocratic pronouncements against sensation fiction: he declares that "good young girls" should not even see it, that "I would more rather give my boys gunpowder to play with than this bad trash" (355). These are the judgments that lead Jo to burn her stories. But I want to bring to the fore what happens in between the professor's pronouncements and Jo's decision to burn her sensation stories because that part of *Little Women's* plot so paradigmatically represents the fruition of the program of discipline through love. As Brodhead describes this program, the goal is to reach a point at which the subject "internalize[s] such expectations as an inwardly felt obligation" (39). In Foucault's formulation, the subject "assumes responsibility for the constraints of power; he makes them play spontaneously upon himself; he inscribes in himself the power relation . . . he becomes the principle of his own subjection" (202–3). The internalization of the authority's expectations is spelled out so bluntly by Alcott in this chapter of *Little Women* (a chapter rather evasively titled "Friend") that it provides a blueprint for the subsequent scenes of discipline I will be reading.

After hearing Professor Bhaer's condemnation of sensation fiction, Jo reads over her own stories in a way that makes it plain that his standards are becoming her own:

> Being a little short-sighted, Mr. Bhaer sometimes used eye-glasses, and Jo had tried them once, smiling to see how they magnified the fine print of her book; now she seemed to have got on the Professor's mental or moral spectacles also, for the faults of these poor stories glared at her dreadfully, and filled her with dismay.
>
> "They are trash. . . . I can't read this stuff in sober earnest without being horribly ashamed of it; and *what should* I do if they were seen at home, or Mr. Bhaer got hold of them?" (355–56)

Seeing her writing through the professor's eyes, then, Jo learns to judge her literary efforts in his terms. His evaluation becomes hers—her recognition that "they are trash" so precisely echoes his epithet "this bad trash"—and his actions (burning the newspaper that contains the sensation stories) provide a model for hers (and for Betsy's and all the other literary heroines who are heirs of Jo's literary standards and practices).[14]

The next scene of discipline I want to examine is also one enacted by a father figure on a young woman old enough to know better. In this scene, from

Alcott's *Rose in Bloom,* the contraband book is a French novel, the undisciplined reader is Rose, and the forbidding authority is her guardian, Uncle Alec. This scene is especially interesting because it shows that while Rose understands the literary and moral norms she has been steeped in, and even the wisdom and logic behind those standards, she is still, at the age of twenty, a slightly recalcitrant pupil. While she has, like the child in Mary Ryan's example, "left [her] mother's side and journeyed beyond the private sphere out onto the streets" (though she is not out on the street as literally as Jo is), she is still in need of some parental guidance. In this regard she anticipates Lovelace's Betsy Ray. Betsy's journals are filled with resolutions to reform her reading habits, and throughout the series we see her constant struggle to put down the best-sellers she loves and concentrate instead on "the classics." Like Betsy, then, Rose knows she should not be reading this French novel, but she cannot resist. Learning, once she is halfway through the novel, that her uncle first "read it to see if it was fit for me" and "decided that it was not, I suppose; since [he] never gave it to me," Rose obediently says, "Then I won't finish it." [15] But the very next words out of her mouth, "But, uncle, I don't see why I should not," suggest that the lure of the story may be stronger than her better judgment. Uncle Alec, then, must remind her that the standard of taste she is trying to thwart is one she has internalized and thus cannot escape. In reply to Rose's half-defiant "But I don't see why I should not," he "gravely" asks, "You may not *see,* but don't you *feel* why not?" (189). This question forces her to admit that she knows "something must be wrong" about the novel since she "blushed and started" when her uncle found her reading it (189). But even this reminder of her own standards and her own accurate sense of propriety is not enough to convince Rose, thus providing Alcott with the occasion for another scene of the affectionate norming that is her hallmark.

After Rose admits that the book is one that makes her blush (bringing to mind the Dickens character Podsnap's "cheek of the young person" and his similarly rigid standards for what a young girl can be safely exposed to), she backslides into a further defense of the novel—"It is by a famous author, wonderfully well written as you know"—both indicting her uncle for having read it and pointing to its literary merits (189). The danger this defense portends can be seen in her subsequent reasoning: "But I really don't see any harm in the book so far," she insists. "I have read French novels before, and you gave them to me. Not many to be sure, but the best; so I think I know what is good, and shouldn't like this if it was harmful" (189). Rose's claim that she "shouldn't like this if it was harmful" stands in direct opposition to the fact that hearing her uncle's step "made her hastily drop the book, and look up with very much the expression she used to wear when caught in mischief years ago" (188). Rose is, in fact, behaving like a guilty child. Not only does she make a concerted effort to ignore her conscience, but she also invokes the system of education her uncle has put her through in a way that perverts the standards she has learned and calls that whole system of taste into question.

Such behavior is, for an Alcott heroine, evidence of the need for serious discipline. Of course, that discipline will be loving, and it will be characterized by the attempt to make the proper standards—that is, those of the authority figure, more firmly her own. So just as Jo was compelled to read her sensation stories through the professor's eyes, to put on his "moral spectacles," Uncle Alec leads Rose to read the French novel to him, translating as she goes. This exercise makes it plain to Rose that she cannot read the novel aloud to her uncle without blushing, and after a few pages she breaks down entirely. But she is still what we might call an undisciplined subject, for she rationalizes her discomfort by insisting that the problem is one of translation, rather than one of propriety: "Some phrases are untranslatable, and it only spoils them to try. They are not amiss in French, but sound coarse and bad in our blunt English" (190). Rose is forced to admit that she not only sees but also shares her uncle's standards; however, she has not willingly made them her own, nor can she accept the lesson as one of love. In order to complete the lesson, her uncle must give her a chance to internalize those standards and to discipline herself. So he ends the task of translation by saying, "Finish it if you choose," and leaves Rose to her own conscience (190). That she acquits herself honorably should go without saying, but the manner in which she does—as well as the way in which her uncle takes his victory—deserves our attention.

After an unspecified period of time, during which Uncle Alec tries to concentrate on a "learned article" in the "Quarterly Review" and Rose's young cousin Jamie is lost in *Twenty Thousand Leagues under the Sea* (it is not unimportant that, during this entire scene of discipline, Jamie has been absorbed in Jules Verne, a novel deemed appropriate reading in comparison to the Oliver Optic novels his older brothers used to be so fond of), Uncle Alec hears the bell in the hall, and discovers the French novel all wrapped up and ready for Jamie to return on his way home (191). What is more, Uncle Alec finds Rose asleep and "various old favorites with which [he assumes] she had tried to solace herself" on the table beside her (191). Not only does Rose give up the offending reading material, but she also tries to reinforce her newly refreshed standards by turning to old, approved books. Because this scene is a textbook example of disciplinary intimacy, Uncle Alec's response to the success of his lesson is to cap it off with a reward. While Rose is sleeping he goes out and gets a novel that he knows she has been wanting to read. Not only is Rose encouraged in her right behavior by this treat, but Uncle Alec's tactics insure that his benevolent reproof will not leave a bad taste in her mouth. The result of this lesson is, as her uncle characterizes the novel he gives Rose as a reward, "all pure sugar; the sort that sweetens the heart as well as the tongue, and leaves no bad taste behind" (192)—no bad taste, no resentment, and most important, no association of discipline with deprivation or of Uncle Alec with an imposed authority. Rather, the end of the chapter entitled "Small Temptations" leaves Rose feeling loved, indulged, and approved of. Perhaps best of all, it leaves her with a new book, one that she been longing to read and, what is more, one that she can read with a clear conscience. And for girls like Rose and her readers, this is not only the best treat of all, but the most effective way to ensure our taste for the kind of "simple, wholesome story" that Rose has before her and that we are in the midst of reading (191). Part of what is being redeemed here, then, is the assurance that aesthetics and ethical standards can be held together; they get detached by the French author, but the "simple, wholesome story" that Rose has been "longing" to read brings them back together and shores up the reader's moral and intellectual values.

The example of Anne Shirley, the heroine of Montgomery's *Anne of Green Gables* books, helps us see the ways in which novels for young girls make use of that "longing" to read in disciplining the enormous and indiscriminate appetite for books that these heroines share. For these readers and the girls who read about them, the love of reading is both symptom and cure. It is both the root of the problem (because they so love to read, they have a very hard time disciplining their reading in terms of kind or amount) and the key to the solution (since they are such avid readers, they are, like most of us, eager for advice about what to read). Anne is perhaps the best example of this two-in-one approach to norming because Anne so loves to read that she has to lock up "the new book that Jane Andrews had lent her" until she is done with her homework.[16] The narrator tells us that "Anne's fingers tingled to reach out for it," and Anne confesses to her guardian Marilla that "'it's a terrible temptation. Even when I turn my back on it I can see it there just as plain . . . I think I'll carry that book into the sitting-room and lock it in the jam closet and give you the key. And you must *not* give it to me Matthew, until my lessons are done, not even if I implore you on bended knees'" (200, 202). A few chapters later we see her give in to a similar temptation; she confesses to Marilla that "'Miss Stacy caught me reading *Ben Hur* in school yesterday afternoon when I should have been studying my Canadian history. . . . I spread the history open on my desk-lid and then tucked *Ben Hur* between the desk and my knee. It just looked as if I were studying Canadian history, you know, while all the while I was revelling in *Ben Hur*'" (316–17). When she is caught, the most serious penance she can think of is to "'never so much as look at *Ben*

Hur for a whole week, not even to see how the chariot-race turned out'"—a punishment that points to reading as an appropriate mode, as well as the necessary site, of discipline (317).

This discipline intersects with the project of canon formation when it is undertaken by what Guillory would call an institution. For instance, while Marilla and her best friend, the interfering but goodhearted Rachel Lynde, constantly criticize Anne for reading too much, their disapproval is ineffective. As we see when the schoolteacher takes Anne to task, the real question to be considered is what she is reading rather than how much she reads. At the end of her *Ben Hur* confession, Anne reveals that "'I never read ANY book now unless either Miss Stacy or Mrs. Allan [the minister's wife] thinks it is a proper book for a girl thirteen and three-quarters to read. Miss Stacy made me promise that. She found me reading a book one day called *The Lurid Mystery of the Haunted Hall*. . . . [O]h, Marilla, it was so fascinating and creepy. . . . But Miss Stacy said it was a very silly unwholesome book, and she asked me not to read any more of it or any like it. I didn't mind promising not to read any more like it, but it was *agonizing* to give back that book without knowing how it turned out. But my love for Miss Stacy stood the test and I did'" (317–18). Anne's breathless speech here reveals the ways in which the project of disciplinary intimacy (Miss Stacy asks, rather than tells; Anne's love for Miss Stacy is what enables her "'to give back that book without knowing how it turned out'") coincides with the norming of literary taste. Guillory's assertion that "judgments with canonical force are institutionally located" and his insistence that "an individual's judgment that a work is great does nothing in itself to preserve that work, unless that judgment is made in a certain institutional context, a setting in which it is possible to insure the *reproduction* of that work, its continual reintroduction to generations of readers" help us see that it is precisely because Miss Stacy is speaking as a teacher that her standards carry weight for Anne. This scene has an even more important implication, however, for here we see the program of disciplinary intimacy carried out by a book; we see the way in which the institution of the *Anne of Green Gables* series functions as an effective means of disseminating the lessons of the canon it imparts. Because Miss Stacy is a beloved teacher in a beloved novel for children that has been a best-seller for over ninety years and that young girls (and the adults they grow up to be) read over and over again, *Anne of Green Gables* exemplifies the kind of institutional context Guillory describes. It is "a setting in which it is possible to insure the reproduction of the [recommended] work [or works, or category of works], its continual reintroduction to generations of readers." In other words, Miss Stacy's status as teacher ensures that her judgments will be reproduced, whereas the status of the books as beloved best-sellers guarantees that their standards of taste will be continually reintroduced to what the book jackets celebrate as "millions of readers."

Similarly, Lovelace's Betsy-Tacy books are best-sellers that have, since 1940, contributed to the preservation, reproduction, and dissemination of standards of literary taste for young readers (a cultural function assisted by the fact that Harper Collins recently reissued all ten novels). Like the two Alcott novels that chronicle the coming-of-age of Rose Campbell, the Betsy-Tacy series is all about disciplining Betsy, about educating her taste and curbing her desire for the frivolous (marked in these books by her desire to be pretty and popular as much and in the same way as her taste for the sensational and the popular in literature). Not surprisingly, this disciplinary project begins at adolescence. And, it is important to note, like all programs of affectionate nurture, it begins with her parents.

Betsy does not just take herself off to the library because her father tells her to read "the classics." Rather, going to the library is her mother's idea, and it is part of what she calls "a splendid plan," a plan her parents devise to remedy Betsy's developing taste for the sordid, to inculcate a taste for "the classics," and to ensure that she will come to associate "great books" with their love for her and their pride in her abilities, as well as with the pleasures of appetite (76). This is that "splendid plan":

> "After the library opens, why don't you start going down . . . every other Saturday, say . . . and get some books? And don't hurry home. Stay a while. Browse around among the books. Every time you go, you can take fifteen cents. At noon go over to Bierbauer's Bakery for a sandwich and milk and ice cream. Would you like that?"
>
> "Oh, papa!" said Betsy. She could hardly speak. She thought of the library, so shining white and new; the rows and rows of unread books; the bliss of unhurried sojourns there and of going out to a restaurant, alone, to eat. "I'd like it," she said in a choked voice. "I'd like it a lot." (78)

In 1836, the Reverend Beriah Green advocated a new method of rearing children by pointing out that "the young home-bound child was nestled 'amid circumstances and relations which naturally lead to such exercises of mind and of heart, as give his parents high advantages for instructing and impressing him respecting his relations, duties, and prospects.'"[17] Citing Horace Bushnell's *Christian Nurture* (1848), Brodhead similarly emphasizes that under this kind of a disciplinary system, the "child is not surrounded with rules but bathed in what Bushnell calls 'genial warmth and love': the authority around him or her expresses its power not as authority but as affection, through an intensification of affectional warmth" (19). This seems a perfect description of what is going on at the Ray house, and this scene is characteristic of the way in which the Rays make use of that "high advantage for instructing" Betsy, "nestled" as she is in their loving home.

It is also a scene that makes literal its metaphors. The scene of supervised reading at the library is followed by a lunch that consists of "a sandwich and *milk*" (emphasis added): not only is milk a traditional and powerful symbol of a mother's love, but it is also the vehicle in the metaphor "the milk of human kindness," suggesting that the discipline Betsy is undergoing is benevolent and should be associated with the ultimate (and original) scene of maternal nurture. This scene is also quite literal in its application of the metaphor of sweetness to reading. While Alcott describes novels approved for young girls as "all pure sugar, the sort that sweetens the heart as well as the tongue, and leaves no bad taste behind," Lovelace gives Betsy an actual serving of sugar ("ice cream for dessert") and thus ensures that Betsy's association of "good books" with pleasurable sensations will be reinforced by the sweet treat it is meant to represent. Taken as a whole, then, Betsy's afternoon of consumption suggests that a parent's love is transmitted with (and is inseparable from) milk, ice cream, and the canon.[18]

When Betsy's behavior is disciplined in a harsher fashion, it happens not at home, but at school. And even there the discipline is not really what we would call harsh, and it does not come from her teachers. Rather, in a pattern much like the one at work between Jo and the professor in *Little Women,* Betsy is pushed toward more literary tastes by the boy she will eventually marry. Joe Willard appears throughout the Betsy-Tacy series to keep Betsy from backsliding by helping her see herself through his eyes. Betsy often seems perfectly content to read novels like *Beverly of Graustark,* curl her hair, make fudge, and hang out with "the Crowd."[19] But Joe, an orphan who is putting himself through school, has no time for such diversions and takes his education more seriously. And while the narrator stresses the degree to which they are alike because they both love to read and want to be writers, Betsy is constantly made aware of the degree to which she falls short in comparison to Joe, since he is not afraid to remind her of her inferior tastes and tendencies; meeting Betsy on the library steps, for example, he "unceremoniously" seizes her books and examines the titles. "'I'm surprised,' he says, '"I thought you'd be reading Robert W. Chambers.'"[20]

Joe is not completely wrong in assuming that Betsy is reading the lowbrow romances of Chambers. She is as fond of popular novels as she is of the "good books" on her parents' bookshelf and "the classics" Miss Sparrow recommends. But as she gets older and more concerned about conforming to her friends' standards, she becomes less and less willing to admit that she likes to read what her teachers assign, that what her friends regard as burdensome and unpalatable she reads for pleasure. At the beginning of her sophomore year, in *Betsy In Spite of Herself,* she is torn between her love for *Ivanhoe,* the novel assigned as summer reading, and her desire to fit in with her friends and grumble along with them about the onerous assignment. One moment she brags that she "read *Ivanhoe* in the cradle practically," while the next she insists that it was "beastly" of her teacher to assign it (3, 9). At one point she insists that she "just happened to read it when I was a child. Had a sore throat or something," while a few chapters later she admits to her friends that "it's a perfectly grand book" (21, 36). The reason she ultimately admits that she loves "Scott's masterpiece" is that Joe shames her into living up to her own literary standards. Flirting with him on the first day of school, Betsy blushes and flippantly asks if he has read *Ivanhoe,* to which he answers,

> "Of course. Why?" He sounded puzzled.
> "Don't you remember? Gaston told us to read it over the summer. None of the kids have read it. They're having fits."
> "You've read it, haven't you?"
> "Yes. But I'm not admitting it."
> He looked at her keenly. "You wouldn't!" he said.
> Now what did he mean by that? Betsy wondered, blushing again. Did he know she was so dissatisfied with herself that she was always pretending to be different? Probably he did, and despised her for it. (30)

The most important thing about this exchange is that it begins and ends with Betsy blushing. That is, because Betsy is so attracted to Joe, the lessons he provides are ones she is eager to learn. And they are ones that she has come to believe in, to internalize, and to try to apply on her own. Not only does Betsy act on Joe's implicit advice in the very next chapter, when she insists to her friends that "you couldn't read [*Ivanhoe*] without liking it," but she has been trying since the novel opened to admit her canonical values. The goal of the project of discipline is that the child will move from obedience to self-policing; because these lessons are inextricably connected with feelings of love (and in Betsy's case, with pride and respect, not to mention pleasure, for she likes school and enjoys what she calls "improving literature"), they become, according to Brodhead, a part of "the ground of [her] emerging selfhood"; they "establish an agency, within [her] nature" (20). That Betsy has adopted this mode of discipline becomes strikingly clear when we see her turn once again to Miss Sparrow, this time for reinforcement: "I wish you'd give me a list of novels to read" (71).

The reading list is, as I suggested at the outset, a topos in these books for girls, one that is crucial to the way in which these novels participate in canon formation. John Guillory insists—correctly, I would argue—that "the canon is never other than an imaginary list; it never appears as a complete and uncontested list in any particular time and place." He continues, "What does have a concrete location as a list . . . is not the canon but the syllabus, the list of works one reads in a given class, or the curriculum, the list of works one reads in a program of study" (30). Given this formulation, we can see Miss Sparrow's reading list as a syllabus of sorts, as "the list of works" we as young girls were told to read in that "program of study" that was our childhood reading. And because in these novels we are presented with the topos of the reading list, it makes sense to treat that list as a prescription for what we as readers of these novels should be reading. Given that we admire Jo March and Anne Shirley to such an extent that we frequently reread (and re-reread) *Little Women* and *Anne of Green Gables,* it stands to reason that we would want to model our own reading practices on theirs, which is why the beloved children's book functions so successfully as an agent of discipline. As a child I read and reread all these novels because I identified with their heroines and tried to pattern myself after them. As Foucault would have it, I understood that norming myself after them would guarantee my "membership" in that "homogeneous social body" of girls who read (184). I wanted to think of myself as a girl like Betsy—a girl who loved to read, who wanted to be a writer, who was smart and a heroine. I was deeply invested in what I saw as my sorority with the literary heroines I grew up with and on. And if they liked the classics, then I was sure I would, too.

If we think of our childhood reading as a school of sorts, as a kind of "standardized education," it becomes clear that children's literature works to form, at an early age, our ideas about the canon because in transmitting values, standards, and lists, it is, in essence, forming a kind of canon. According to Guillory, "every construction of a syllabus *institutes* once again the process of canon formation" (31). Every reading list that Betsy is given serves as an example young readers will take to heart. I close this essay with two syllabi, two reading lists from two rather different novels for young girls, both of which function as recommended reading, as lists that readers of these novels take quite seriously and try to make their own. The first is from Roald Dahl's *Matilda,* a novel in which the extraordinarily intelligent (and telekinetic) heroine learns to read at the age of three and at the age of four discovers the public library. The librarian, Mrs. Phelps, guides Matilda's reading, and "under Mrs. Phelps's watchful and compassionate eye," Matilda reads the following books:

Nicholas Nickleby by Charles Dickens
Oliver Twist by Charles Dickens
Jane Eyre by Charlotte Brontë
Pride and Prejudice by Jane Austen
Tess of the D'Urbervilles by Thomas Hardy
Gone to Earth by Mary Webb
Kim by Rudyard Kipling
The Invisible Man by H. G. Wells
The Old Man and the Sea by Ernest Hemingway
The Sound and the Fury by William Faulkner
The Grapes of Wrath by John Steinbeck
The Good Companions by J. B. Priestley
Brighton Rock by Graham Greene
Animal Farm by George Orwell

"It was," the narrator comments, "a formidable list."[21] And in *Rebecca of Sunnybrook Farm,* this list comes from Rebecca herself:

> "Oh, I've read lots of books," answered Rebecca casually.
> "Father's and Miss Ross's and all the dif'rent school teacher's, and all in the Sunday school library. I've read *The Lamplighter,* and *Scottish Chiefs,* and *Ivanhoe,* and *The Heir of Redclyffe,* and *Cora,* the *Doctor's Wife,* and *David Copperfield,* and *The Gold of Chickaree,* and *Plutarch's Lives,* and *Thaddeus of Warsaw,* and *Pilgrim's Progress,* and lots more.— What have you read?"[22]

NOTES
Versions of this essay were presented to the faculty of the expository writing program at Harvard University, to the Eighteenth- and Nineteenth-Century Colloquium of the Department of English at Yale University, on a panel organized by the Society for the Study of American Women Writers at the 2001 annual meeting of the American Literature Association, and on a panel organized by the Children's Literature Association at the 2001 annual conference of the Modern Language Association. My thanks to my audiences there, and especially to Jill Campbell, Diana Chlebek, Shanna Cleveland, Laura Green, Sharon Harris, Deidre Lynch, Rhonda Rockwell, and Nancy Sommers. Many thanks also to Caroline Levander and Carol Singley for their support of and enthusiasm for this project.

1. Maud Hart Lovelace, *Betsy and Tacy Go Downtown* (New York: Harper Trophy, 1979), 78; hereafter, page numbers are cited parenthetically in the text. *Betsy and Tacy Go Downtown* is the fourth book in the Betsy-Tacy series. Lovelace wrote the series (ten novels that take Betsy from the age of five through her first year of marriage) in the 1940s and '50s, and its appeal endures. There are Maud Hart Lovelace and Betsy-Tacy homepages on the World Wide Web; the children's bookstore owner played by Meg Ryan in the Nora

Ephron movie *You've Got Mail* recommends the Betsy-Tacy books to her customers; and Elaine Showalter, in a piece in *Vogue* on fashion and academia, reveals that when she was a little girl, she designed her own paper dolls, "copied from the heroines of my favorite children's books—Betsy, Tacy, and Tib." See Showalter, "The Professor Wore Prada," *Vogue*, December 1997, 80, 86, 92.

2. Louisa May Alcott, *Little Women,* ed. Elaine Showalter (New York: Penguin, 1989), 355; hereafter, page numbers are cited parenthetically in the text.

3. I take the term *literary heroine* from T. D. MacLulich, who reads L. M. Montgomery's Anne in the context of Alcott's Jo and Wiggin's Rebecca. The context of MacLulich's argument also brings up the matter of nationality. While my essay is about a kind of discipline that developed in the United States in the nineteenth century and an attitude toward education that is particularly American, I include the Canadian Anne in this study because, as MacLulich's essay suggests, she is strikingly similar to Jo, Rose, Rebecca, and Betsy. Further, in creating such a similar character and in disseminating parallel messages about the canon and education, Montgomery not only participates in a genre inaugurated by Alcott—one that is thus quite thoroughly American—but she also creates another chapter in the history of American girlhood. In fact, Montgomery seems deliberately to echo her American models, for not only is *Anne of Green Gables* remarkably like *Rebecca of Sunnybrook Farm* (and is in fact often criticized for its similarity to Wiggin's novel), but the pattern of intellectual education she imposes on Anne is much like the pattern I identify in Alcott, Wiggin, and Lovelace. See T. D. MacLulich, "L. M. Montgomery and the Literary Heroine: Jo, Rebecca, Anne, and Emily," *Canadian Children's Literature* 37 (1985): 5–17.

4. See, for instance, Deborah Gorham, "The Ideology of Femininity and Reading for Girls, 1850–1914," in *Lessons for Life: The Schooling of Girls and Women, 1850–1950,* ed. Felicity Hunt (Oxford: Basil Blackwell, 1987), 39–59; Kimberley Reynolds, "A Literature of Their Own? Or What Girls Read," in *Girls Only? Gender and Popular Children's Fiction in Britain: 1880–1910* (New York: Harvester Wheatsheaf, 1990), 91–110; and Elizabeth Segel, "'As the Twig is Bent . . .': Gender and Childhood Reading," in *Gender and Reading: Essays on Readers, Texts, and Contexts,* ed. Elizabeth A. Flynn and Patrocinio P. Schweickart (Baltimore: Johns Hopkins University Press, 1986), 165–86.

5. Mary P. Ryan, *Cradle of the Middle Class: The Family in Oneida County, New York, 1790–1865* (Cambridge: Cambridge University Press, 1981); Bernard Wishy, *The Child and the Republic: The Dawn of Modern American Child Nurture* (Philadelphia: University of Pennsylvania Press, 1968), 23. Hereafter, page numbers for these works will be cited parenthetically in the text.

6. John Guillory, *Cultural Capital: The Problem of Literary Canon Formation* (Chicago: University of Chicago Press, 1993), vii; hereafter, page numbers will be cited parenthetically in the text.

7. David's reading list appears in chapter 4 of *David Copperfield,* and he relates it to the reader as he remembers his younger self, "sitting on my bed, reading as if for life": "From that blessed little room, Roderick Random, Peregrine Pickle, Humphrey Clinker, Tom Jones, The Vicar of Wakefield, Don Quixote, Gil Blas, and Robinson Crusoe, came out, a glorious host, to keep me company." See Charles Dickens, *David Copperfield,* ed. Nina Burgis (Oxford: Oxford University Press, 1983), 44.

8. Michel Foucault, *Discipline and Punish: The Birth of the Prison,* trans. Alan Sheridan (New York: Vintage, 1979), 18; hereafter, page numbers will be cited parenthetically in the text.

9. Wai Chee Dimock, "A Theory of Resonance," *PMLA* 112 (1997): 1064, 1062.

10. Frank Kermode, *The Classic: Literary Images of Permanence and Change* (Cambridge, Mass.: Harvard University Press, 1983), 44.

11. The distinction I make here between parents and books as purveyors of reading values is a significant one. While it is true that books for children are written by adults and often chosen for children by adults, children do not always read what they are given or listen to what they are read. The books I am talking about here are perennial favorites, beloved books that children (and adults) read over and over again.

Catharine Stimpson accounts for the effect of a beloved children's book in a slightly different manner. She argues for a "paracanon" of works that includes "the lovable" as well as "the good"; the "rereadings that maintain a children's canon," Stimpson argues, "rehearse the rereadings that buttress an adult paracanon" (971). I would argue, however, that "the rereadings that maintain a children's canon" form, rather than "rehearse" or "buttress," both our general ideas about the adult canon and the specific texts that make up that canon. See Stimpson, "Reading for Love: Canon, Paracanons, and Whistling Jo March," *New Literary History* 21 (1990): 957–76.

12. Richard H. Brodhead, "Sparing the Rod: Discipline and Fiction in Antebellum America," in *Cultures of Letters: Scenes of Reading and Writing in Nineteenth-Century America* (Chicago: University of Chicago Press, 1993), 19; hereafter, page numbers will be cited parenthetically in the text.

13. This scene is also an example of the dissemination of the canon. As Stimpson points out, by "rebuking [Jo] for her popular writing" and "making her feel guilty about her professional talents, he upholds the canon." Alcott, the author of a good deal of sensation fiction herself, "labels her own worth counterfeit and banks instead with a masculinized canon." See Stimpson, "Reading for Love," 971.

14. Book burning occurs throughout these novels for young girls. There are three instances in *Little Women* alone (Amy burns Jo's fairy tales; Jo burns her sensation stories; and Mr. Davis burns the novels he confiscates from his pupils, Amy's classmates), while Aunt Jessie burns the Oliver Optic books Will and Geordie read in *Eight Cousins*. L. M. Montgomery also gives us a scene of book burning: in *Anne of the Island*, Anne burns her sensation story that won the Rollings Reliable Baking Powder Company fiction contest. The most famous instance of book burning in literature comes from Miguel de Cervantes's *Don Quixote;* Quixote's friends burn his books in an effort to protect him from himself, specifically from his inability to differentiate between the imaginary and the actual. But unlike Quixote, these literary heroines are learning to discipline their reading themselves; they burn their own books.

15. Louisa May Alcott, *Rose in Bloom* (New York: A. L. Burt, 1918), 189; hereafter, page numbers will be cited parenthetically in the text.

16. L. M. Montgomery, *The Annotated Anne of Green Gables*, ed. Wendy E. Barry, Margaret Anne Doody, and Mary E. Doody Jones (New York: Oxford University Press, 1997), 200; hereafter, page numbers will be cited parenthetically in the text.

17. Reverend Beriah Green, quoted in Ryan, *Cradle of the Middle Class*, 99.

18. For a suggestive and insightful account of the association of reading with eating, see Steven Mailloux's "The Rhetorical Use and Abuse of Fiction: Eating Books in Late Nineteenth-Century America," *boundary* 2, no. 17 (1990): 133–57.

19. George Barr McCutcheon's Graustark books, written around the turn of the century, are rather lowbrow best-sellers about the fictional land of Graustark, its political intrigues, and the love that visiting Americans find with the titled Graustarkians.

20. Maud Hart Lovelace, *Betsy in Spite of Herself* (New York: Harper Trophy, 1980), 71–72; hereafter, page numbers will be cited parenthetically in the text. Robert W. Chambers wrote pseudohistorical romances around the turn of the century; they have much in common with the Graustark books Betsy is so fond of.

21. Roald Dahl, *Matilda* (New York: Puffin, 1990), 17–18.

22. Kate Douglas Wiggin, *Rebecca of Sunnybrook Farm* (Boston: Houghton Mifflin, 1904), 18. *The Gold of Chickaree* was written by Susan and Anna Warner, while *Cora, the Doctor's Wife* is probably *Cora and the Doctor, or, Revelations of a Physician's Wife* by Madeline Leslie; both are didactic, sentimental novels. *Scottish Chiefs* and *Thaddeus of Warsaw* were written by Jane Porter; she bears the kind of relation to Scott that Barbara Pym does to Jane Austen.

6 Traumatic Realism and the Wounded Child

Jane F. Thrailkill

Bessel A. van der Kolk, a professor in the Department of Psychiatry at Boston University Medical School, has designated the central concern of trauma in pithy terms. "Unlike other forms of psychological disorders," he writes, "the core issue in trauma is reality."[1] Central to this reality, for many theorists of trauma, is its resistance both to cognition and representation. The physician Judith Herman has noted that "traumatic memories lack verbal narrative and context," and that "people who have survived atrocities often tell their stories in a highly emotional, contradictory, and fragmented manner."[2] Taking this empirical observation further, literary critic Cathy Caruth has asserted that the problem of representation entailed by trauma is not a matter of finding the right words or getting one's story straight. In *Unclaimed Experience: Trauma, Narrative, and History,* Caruth asserts that an experience is catastrophic or traumatic precisely in its ability to elude cognitive containment by the person undergoing the experience. As Ruth Leys has written in her *Trauma: A Genealogy,* for Caruth the "truth of the trauma [is] defined as an incomprehensible event that defies all representation."[3] A traumatic event is associated with the horribly, irrefutably real insofar as it shuts down the human capacity to express it; instead of remembering trauma, Caruth argues, survivors relive it. The work of van der Kolk on post-traumatic stress disorder seeks to designate the physiological register of this process, in which a person's limbic system is reactivated, plunging one biochemically back into the traumatic experience.[4] To borrow a chapter title from van der Kolk and colleagues' *Traumatic Stress,* "The Body Keeps the Score."

Given this understanding of trauma's resistance to representation, why is it that theorists of human suffering like medical anthropologist Arthur Kleinman, literary critic Cathy Caruth, and critical historian Ruth Leys all represent a wounded child at key moments in their arguments? Psychoanalyst Serge Leclaire's assertion (in the context of dream interpretation) that "the representation of a mangled child, even if it is veiled, disguised, or displaced, is to be taken as a clue not to be overlooked"[5] is richly suggestive for trauma theory's reliance on the child. Indeed, Leclaire extends an irresistible invitation to investigate the work done by the figure of the wounded child in recent influential critical treatments of the concept of trauma. In this essay I consider how the questions about reality and representation raised by trauma theory play out in the writings of the theorists themselves, and indeed how they *replay* a familiar debate from the nineteenth century over the epistemological and ethical status of literary realism and sentimentalism.

More particularly, I show how, in his *Illness Narratives: Suffering, Healing, and the Human Condition,* Kleinman employs representational conventions that partake of both the realist and sentimental traditions (indeed, marking the imbrication of the two) in making his case for the centrality of narrative to the experience and amelioration of suffering. Caruth's conception of trauma as a unique, unrecoverable, shattering experience, in sharp contrast to the work of Kleinman, leads her to a radical claim about the inadequacies of representation. However, in her account of the dream of the burning child from Sigmund Freud's *The Interpretation of Dreams,* Caruth implicitly depends on a certain moral and affective authority that representations of the wounded child have, as I explain in section 1, long made available. Moreover, even Leys, a theorist whose unsentimental critique of Caruth's theory of language—in particular its implication that writing about trauma inevitably "injures or 'murders' the historical record"—does not avoid employing the figure of the wounded child as a means of securing her own account of the reality of trauma.[6] While Leys points to the current "literary-critical fascination" with trauma, I would suggest that it is not just the concept of "the unspeakable" (16) that draws theorists to the topic, but perhaps the unacknowledged opportunity it provides, in the unlikely context of critical theory, for enlisting affect—something, I conclude, that is certainly worth talking about.

1

A brief and necessarily limited excursion into literary history will help to set the stage for the investigation of contemporary trauma theory. The association of the suffering child and literary realism has a rich and contradictory history dating back to the nineteenth century, when a number of (largely male) authors sought to produce realism as a representational mode in opposition to sentimentalism.[7] It is instructive here to consider the character of Mark Twain's *Huckleberry Finn,* later elevated into the sentimental exemplum of American boyhood by a wide array of twentieth-century readers, who serves as the ironic mouthpiece for Twain's scathing censure of what historian Ann Douglas has called "the domestication of death."[8] Douglas locates this domestication in the "almost countless obituary poems" (243) and narrative depictions of children "too good to live" (241) that circulated in nineteenth-century America, written by authors who took "heaven as [their] fictional specialty" (268). The paradox of the cultural placement of *Adventures of Huckleberry Finn*—an ostensibly antisentimental text that has provided an unplummable resource for fetishizing childhood—is, I hope to suggest, a useful vantage point from which to examine the centrality of the wounded child to recent scholarship on trauma theory.[9] Gregg Camfield has argued that Twain's writings embody the "intellectual tension between his sentimental leanings and his energetic efforts to believe in antisentimental versions of realism," and that they have bequeathed "to the twentieth century . . . sentimental ideas packaged in an anti-sentimental rhetoric."[10] Trauma theory, in the exemplary practice of Cathy Caruth, is one twentieth-century venue in which we can see the reemergence of this particular formulation.

I would first like to examine Twain's novel for its send-up of sentimental excessiveness in the maudlin verse of the character Emmeline Grangerford, who "could rattle off poetry like nothing."[11] In her "Ode to Stephen Dowling Bots, Dec.," the young poet (now deceased herself) had rattled off a series of rhetorical questions, articulating the standard preliminaries to the literary apotheosis of the dying child ("And did young Stephen sicken, and did young Stephen die? / And did the sad hearts thicken, and did the mourners cry?" [113]) before revealing the less-than-poetic final trajectory of the young body: "His soul did from this cold world fly, / By falling down a well" (114). In the rhetorical whiplash engendered by Emmeline's image—the boy's soul ascending to heaven, while his body plummets down a well—Twain marks the failure of sentimental representations of corporeal harm and death that, for all their verbiage, are nonetheless inadequate to lift the irreducible human body into language. Twain turns a sardonic eye on the sentimental problem posed by young Bots, who, by being a boy and by unceremoniously falling down a well, troubles the standard apotheosis of Harriet Beecher Stowe's Little Eva or Charles Dickens's Little Nell. (Stephen's last name, one might add, tries his eulogizer's capacity for rhyme, as she strives for pathos with words like "spots" and "knots.") Douglas has described the sentimental tableau in which the "reader is reminded from the outset that the memorialized is going to die—perhaps young, certainly well" (241). In contrast to Emmeline's sentimental ability to "slap down a line" and "to write about anything you choose to give her to write about, just so it was sadful" (114), Bessel van der Kolk notes that the dominant semantic mode of trauma is "speechless terror," which "leav[es] emotions to be mutely expressed by dysfunction of the body."[12] Huck Finn's own attempt to compose a "tribute" to Emmeline, appropriately, results in failure: "I tried to sweat out a verse or two myself, but I couldn't seem to make it go, somehow" (115).[13] The human body, rather than language, itself becomes the most eloquent (and the only adequate) testimony to the reality of what has transpired: this is what I take van der Kolk to be saying when he states: "history is written in blood."[14]

Twain in *Huckleberry Finn* offers a "realist" antidote that seeks to manage the rhetorical and affective excesses of the sentimental apotheosis of the broken body of the child. Huck's exceptional circumspection in describing the violent death of his friend Buck in the chapter following Emmeline's poem inaugurates what I wish to explore: the potent association in trauma theory of the child, corporeal harm, and the irrefutably real. It is worth revisiting the world-famous death of Little Eva as a point of contrast: Stowe takes a few chapters to set the scene of the girl's demise, which climaxes as follows: "On the face of the child, however, there was no ghastly imprint,— only a high and almost sublime expression,— the overshadowing presence of spiritual natures, the dawning of immortal life in that childish soul. . . . A bright, a glorious smile passed over her face, and she said, brokenly,—'O! love,—joy,— peace!' gave one sigh and passed from death unto life!"[15] Here is what Huck says of Buck's death: "I an't agoing to tell *all* that happened—it would make me sick again if I was to do that. I wished I hadn't ever come ashore that night, to see such things. I ain't ever going to get shut of them—lots of times I dream about them" (127). Whereas sentimental depictions of children's deaths are notable for their poetic flights, Huck's remarks are distinguished by their terseness. Deathbed scenes such as Eva's emphasize spiritual transcendence and ignore the experience of the physical body, but Twain focuses on Huck's nausea. Far from spiritualized, the grim reality of Buck's broken body is indicated by the novel's fractured storyline, and the elided details of his murder are replayed in the body and mind of the observer Huck, who, unable to "get shut of them—lots of times . . . dream[s] about them." The physical trauma experienced by Buck is translated into the psychic trauma of Huck, who sees the scene of violence unfold below the tree in which he takes refuge.

We can, then, articulate the series of oppositions through which Twain worked to distinguish the paradigmatic realist moment from the exemplary sentimental one: the "body's fall" versus the "soul's flight"; death materialized versus death abstracted; the prosaic body versus the poetic figure; the unspeakably private versus the excessively public. Whereas the sentimental impulse involved the movement from a particular scene—Eva's deathbed, say—to a transcendent truth, the realist imperative sought to remain doggedly at the bedside, to stick with the particulars, to record the specific corporeal aftereffects of death and to represent the failure of representation: "I an't agoing to tell *all* that happened." However, a comparison of Twain's child in the well with the still-memorable national focus on the eighteen-month-old who fell down a Midland, Texas, well in 1987 suggests that a century later the uneasy sentimental/realist dichotomy has undergone revision. In the case of Jessica McClure, details about the intimate physical exigencies of a child— the prosaic, material body, with its array of symptoms and secretions, with the technicalities of its entrapment and retrieval—became the occasion for an unprecedented outflow of both news reports and affect (not to mention money: a trust fund holds one million dollars or more in gifts sent to the girl, to be released when she is twenty-five). A news article marking the ten-year anniversary of the girl's accident and subsequent rescue states, "In a poll taken by The Pew Research Center for the People and the Press measuring coverage of Princess Diana's death found that in the last decade, only Jessica's rescue rivaled the Paris car accident in worldwide attention." [16] The story of the girl down the well, and her subsequent rescue, became the topic of a television movie titled *Jessica: Everyone's Baby*. The title expresses the alignment of two modes that Twain sought to distinguish, the realist (Jessica) and the sentimental (Everyone's Baby); here, the particular body exists unproblematically with a distinctly modern form of transcendence, the endlessly circulating sound bite.

In her study *Pricing the Priceless Child: The Changing Social Value of Children* sociologist Viviana Zelizer helps to place in context the sentimental failure of Stephen Dowling Bots, and the stunning sentimental success of Jessica McClure. Beginning in the 1870s, a range of cultural domains, from medicine and health reform to insurance companies and child labor legislation, began to translate the literary figure of the suffering and dying child—with its emphasis on the spirit, the transcendent, and the sublime—into an active concern with the physical welfare of wounded children. Zelizer notes, "By the 1920s, social response to the accidental death of children had changed dramatically. A child killed by an automobile was more than an isolated neighborhood tragedy or a catchy news-item; children's accidental death emerged as a 'serious, fundamental national problem.'" [17] Concurrent with the emergence of literary realism in the United States, with its commitment to managing excessive sentiment, politicians, businesses, and reformers elevated what Zelizer calls the "'sacralization' of children's lives" (11) to the level of public policy. In a dual move, the transcendent or symbolic power of the child became installed in the national psyche through a reformist discourse that traded in—even as it sought redress for—the battered bodies of children maimed in factories, mutilated in accidents, and ravaged by childhood diseases.

Today the figure of the brutalized child is a staple of the news media. No longer sublime stories of spiritual transition, our contemporary updates on this late-nineteenth-century phenomenon include stories of mothers drowning children, priests raping altar boys, children assaulting and killing other children. The sentimental has, it would seem, given way to the traumatic. The proliferation of news stories about wounded children has, according to Laurence Lerner, been matched by a shift in literary representation. In concluding his study of nineteenth-century representations of dying children, Lerner observes, "Children die in twentieth century fiction too—less often, and in a very different way. In the first place, they die of meningitis [rather than the more "sublime" tuberculosis]; a peculiarly horrible death." [18] If, as van der Kolk writes, "Experiencing trauma is an essential part of being human," [19] it would appear that our current media obsession with representing the wounded child might literally be a matter of sensationalism: a way of catalyzing an affective response, and thus reminding us (or confirming) that we really are human.

For Twain, the sentimental might enlist our emotions, but the sleep of reason also enabled the feud between two neighboring families, the Shepherdsons and the Grangerfords; indeed, Twain draws a direct narrative line between sentimental excess and the murder of Huck's friend Buck at the hands of adults. Huck gives the reader an inkling that Emmeline Grangerford's poetic and pictorial renderings of dead and dying children are more than humorously innocuous when he comments on the "spidery" look of one anemic wraith in a half-finished portrait (the young artist having died before choosing which expressive pair of arms to "scratch out" [113]). More significant, however, the chapter depicting Emmeline's talents is followed by scenes of intensified feuding between the two families, whose sentimental commitment to images of child morbidity are starkly juxtaposed with Huck's description of Buck and his young cousin being hunted down by a group of murderous Shepherdsons: "The boys jumped for the river—both of them hurt—and as they swum down the current the men run along the bank shooting at them and singing out, 'Kill them, kill them!'" (125–26). Sentimental piety (along with religious rhetoric and romantic codes of honor) is for Twain the enabling cover for viciousness.

James Baldwin, in his famous indictment of the sentimental mode, therefore merely codified what Twain half a century earlier had already implied: "Sentimentality, the ostentatious parading of excessive and spurious emotion, is the mark of dishonesty, the inability to feel; . . . it is always, therefore, the signal of secret and violent inhumanity, the mask of cruelty."[20] Writing of the apotheosized portrayals of child sickness and death, Ann Douglas echoes Twain (and Baldwin) in raising suspicion about adult uses of the scene of the suffering child. "Death," she writes, "province of minister and mother, instead of marking the end of power, had becomes its source" (249). This power, as Douglas describes it, is then leveraged into an undisputed expertise over the liminal realms of human experience—most vividly, death. For the nineteenth-century mother or minister, Douglas asserts, "Heaven [a nether realm that defied representation] was apparently as real, as concrete, as Texas . . . the writers of consolation literature established contact with the next world through prayers and hymns; then, like modern television reporters, they purveyed news of the heavenly realm back to earthly audiences. The authors of such accounts had enormous authority, for who could question their reports?" (257). By forming mystical (and mystified) "channels of communication to the other world" and by speaking for the ultimately voiceless (257), those whom Douglas critiqued acquired an obvious epistemological and a more encrypted moral unassailability.

2

It is my suspicion that there are some analogies to be drawn between Douglas's account of what we could term "sentimental experts," and the trauma expert Cathy Caruth. It may seem odd to designate trauma a "heavenly realm," but insofar as trauma articulates a space of purity—a moment outside of linear time, resilient to the framing artifice of narrative or human construction, embodying the shock of the real—it might, from a phenomenological point of view, be construed as a "little heaven." Serge Leclaire has referred to the figure of the child as a "'heavenly sign,'" a narcissistic vision of wholeness and immunity from death. "In the transparent reality of the child," he writes, "the Real of all our desires can be seen, almost without a veil."[21] The sublime clarity and pathos of the wounded child figures a world without mediation. As I will explain, Caruth articulates an understanding of trauma that conceives, as does sentimentalism, that one might "experience . . . vicariously someone else's emotions."[22] In *Unclaimed Experience*, trauma is imagined to act as a conduit between people, passing on the experience of a catastrophic event, and, strangely, providing a point of contact or "transmission" between the dead and the living; the theorist of trauma, then, might be said to act as Virgilian guide to this realm. For Caruth, a crucial figure in this transmission is the figure of the wounded child. Moreover, there is an active moral valence to Caruth's account of trauma and the failure of representation; the witness of trauma, she concludes, is caught up in "the story of an urgent responsibility, or what Lacan defines . . . as an *ethical* relation to the real" (102; emphasis in the original).[23]

I would now like to turn to three precise moments, in the work of Kleinman, Caruth, and Leys, at which the wounded child is invoked as a catalyst to a certain kind of literary-ethical attitude. My ultimate assertion is that certain invocations, and the theorizing they engender, do not propel us forward into a new understanding of the work—and limits—of representation (remember that van der Kolk asserted that the "core issue in trauma is reality"), but instead point us backward into the mystified sentimental terrain exemplified in Mark Twain's struggle to achieve an antisentimental version of realism. Eve Kosofsky Sedgwick and Adam Frank have recently commented on what they perceive as "the prevailing moralism of current theoretical writing," with its reliance on a bipolar analytic framework that savors the "good dog/bad dog rhetoric of puppy obedience school."[24] While Sedgwick and Frank are speaking of the tendency of contemporary theorists and critics to moralize the categories of *subversive* (approved) or *hegemonic* (censured), their pithy remark does speak to work being done in the field of trauma theory, where the epistemological adequacy of analytical stances are at moments subject to an implicit moral valuation.

Arthur Kleinman's early work on the centrality of storytelling to the medical encounter, while predating the critical focus on trauma theory in the late 1990s, nonetheless presents a moment that explicitly engages with trauma as both physical injury and psychic wound; he also appears to depict the sort of transfer of power Douglas describes. Kleinman prefaces his book *The Illness Narratives* with an anecdote drawn from his medical training. The patient involved was

> a pathetic seven-year-old girl who had been badly burned over most of her body. She had to undergo a daily ordeal of a whirlpool bath during which the burnt flesh was tweezered away from her raw, open wounds. This experience was horribly painful to her. She screamed and moaned and begged the medical team, whose efforts she stubbornly fought off, not to hurt her anymore. My job as a neophyte clinical student was to hold her uninjured hand, as much to reassure and calm her as to enable the surgical resident to quickly pull away the dead, infected tissue in the pool of swirling water, which rapidly turned pinkish, then bloody red.

Clumsily, with a beginner's uncertainty of how to proceed, I tried to distract this little patient from her traumatic daily confrontation with terrible pain. I tried talking to her about her home, her family, her school—almost anything that might draw her vigilant attention away from her suffering. I could barely tolerate the daily horror: her screams, dead tissue floating in the blood-stained water, the peeling flesh, the oozing wounds, the battles over cleaning and bandaging. Then one day, I made contact. At wit's end, angered at my own ignorance and impotence, uncertain what to do besides clutching the small hand, and in despair over her unrelenting anguish, I found myself asking her to tell me how she tolerated it, what the feeling was like of being so badly burned and having to experience the awful surgical ritual, day after day after day. She stopped, quite surprised, and looked at me from a face so disfigured it was difficult to read the expression; then, in terms direct and simple, she told me. While she spoke, she grasped my hand harder and neither screamed nor fought off the surgeon or the nurse. Each day from then on, her trust established, she tried to give me a feeling of what she was experiencing. By the time my training took me off this rehabilitation unit, the little burned patient seemed noticeably better able to tolerate the debridement. But whatever effect I had had on her, her effect on me was greater. She taught me a grand lesson in patient care: that it is possible to talk with patients, even those who are most distressed, about the actual experience of illness, and that witnessing and helping to order that experience can be of therapeutic value.[25]

Kleinman, as author, does not appear to speak the language of spiritual transcendence, but instead casts his narrative in a more limited clinical rhetoric, emphasizing "surgical ritual," infected tissue, the management of pain: "the little burned patient seemed noticeably better able to tolerate the debridement." Although detailed about the nature of the procedure, Kleinman is reticent, however, to quote the girls' actual words, in which she describes her experience of suffering, instead stating *that* she spoke, that "in terms direct and simple, she told me." The connection and subsequent transmission that took place between the girl and Kleinman is, as he describes it, as much corporeal as it is semantic: "While she spoke, she grasped my hand harder. . . . She tried to give me a feeling of what she was experiencing." Not only is the girl's anguish translated into a narrative form that helps assuage *her* pain, it clearly has a similar effect for Kleinman ("whatever effect I had had on her, her effect on me was greater"). The physician also finds his voice, and in *The Illness Narratives* the girl's suffering speaks across the divide installed in modern medicine, between "the patient's experience of illness and the doctor's attention to disease" (xii). And despite the unrelenting focus on the girl's terrible wounds, Kleinman's business is not just with therapy in the limited sense, but with a certain version of transcendence: "the study of the experience of illness," he writes, "has something fundamental to teach each of us about the human condition, with its universal suffering and death" (xiii).

In emphasizing that "empathic witnessing is a moral act, not a technical procedure" (154), and in calling attention throughout *The Illness Narratives* to his own emotional responses to his patients ("I felt a deep sadness break like a wave. I think my eyes teared; I may well have cried with him" [169]), Kleinman does not neatly eschew the sentimental in favor of the clinical, but instead imagines that affect is at the center of the therapeutic encounter and even the physiological experience of pain itself. And while Kleinman's anecdote springs from a perception of the inadequacy of words to the experience of suffering, it concludes by evoking the soothing, even healing effects of human expression. This insight, of course, provides the conceptual foundation for *The Illness Narratives,* one that argues passionately for the diagnostic and therapeutic centrality of a patient's story of sickness, while cautioning that a physician must beware of the "over-literal interpretation of accounts best understood metaphorically" (52). In this comment, Kleinman cautions that it is a mistake to construe diagnosis as the unmediated engagement with either the human body or a patient's illness narrative. Not just representation, but also the complicated act of reading, is understood to be at the center of the doctor-patient encounter.[26]

Whereas Kleinman, a doctor, begins his text with a narrative of transmission that inaugurates healing, Cathy Caruth, a critic, ends hers with a transmission that would appear to preclude the possibility of healing, for the passage she focuses on takes place between a dead child and a father. For Caruth, it is not a child but the burning corpse of a child that becomes the occasion for her argument that traumatic experience necessarily eludes representation and instead must be passed on from one person to another as a quasi-corporeal experience rather than symbolic expression. Caruth traces how the words of a dead child, which are heard in the child's father's dream, migrate not just between family members, but from Freud's *Interpretations of Dreams,* through the work of Jacques Lacan, into Caruth's own text.[27] As reported by Freud, a father is awakened while dreaming the child's words— "'Father, can't you see I am burning?'"—only to find that the child's corpse, lying in state, had been burned by the sacramental candles that surrounded it. For Caruth, the dream words signify the belatedness or failure of representation, for they appear after the child is dead, and indeed after the body has begun to burn, once both child and corpse are beyond assistance. The child's impossible words, conveying an impossible request, can only haunt the living with their own failure—just as the father could not save the child, and just as Freud, Lacan, and Caruth could not, so Caruth's readers cannot. Instead of adequately conveying the experience of the child's death, these words, Caruth argues, traumatize the father and all subsequent hearers of the tale: "what is passed on, finally, is not just the meaning of the words but their performance" (111).

Yet how precisely does this performance work? Because of "the curious resistance of trauma to symbolism" (140, n. 6), Caruth suggests that trauma works directly on the body, by engaging the sympathetic nervous system. Drawing on the biopsychology of van der Kolk, Caruth imagines that the trauma involves "the Engraving of Memory" (141, n. 8), whereby the child's traumatic death is first encrypted in the child's impossible words and then passed on to the father in quasi-corporeal form: not as "a fiction . . . nor a direct representation, but a repetition" (100; emphasis in the original). Caruth's point, that "trauma is not locatable in the simple violent or original event in an individual's past, but rather in the way that its very unassimilated nature— the way it was precisely *not known* in the first instance—returns to haunt the survivor later on" (4; emphasis in the original), indicates that the words pass on, rather than represent, the child's trauma to the father. As such, the individual child's death is understood to be both irreducible and to express the (universalizable) structure of trauma.[28] As Leys interprets it in *Trauma: A Genealogy,* Caruth has a "primary commitment to making victimhood unlocatable in any particular person or place, thereby permitting it to migrate or spread contagiously. In this case, the primary importance of the contagion is that it allows her to imagine how the reader might be implicated in the trauma of others" (296). Trauma becomes for Caruth the exemplary instance in which words can convey not meanings, but the thing itself—or, as Caruth might actually inscribe it, *the thing itself.* (One thinks of her italicizing *repetition* in the passage quoted above. This choice would appear to underscore Caruth's point that traumatic experience must be received rather than precisely interpreted; it is as if the italicized word on the page is less a representation of an idea than a miniature typographical assault on the reader).

Like Douglas's hymn-singing and praying "sentimental experts" who monitor the unmediated channels of communication from the other side, Caruth suggests that contemporary theory-reading "trauma experts" have the following role: to take the traumatic death of the child and see that it is "transformed into the imperative of a speaking that awakens others" (108). This speaking is, as Caruth explains, "the passing on of psychoanalytic writing," which is intriguingly cast as something more akin to inspiration than interpretation: "The transmission of the psychoanalytic theory of trauma, the story of dreams and of dying children, cannot be reduced, that is, to a simple mastery of facts, and cannot be located in a simple knowledge or cognition" (111). Theory in this account becomes a means of transcendence, and would appear to fulfill a psychoanalytic critic's dream: direct correspondence with Freud.

The final page of *Unclaimed Experience* supports the idea that, for Caruth, "transmission" implies something more like apostolic succession than literary critical influence. In lieu of an analytical conclusion, Caruth quotes the passage from Lacan, in which the French psychoanalyst quotes and glosses Freud's earlier account of the dead burning child's words (it is probably worth remembering that these words, not unlike a work of fiction, were dreamed rather than spoken, and came to Freud from a patient who heard it in a lecture). The passage quoted by Caruth contains the intermingling of Freud's German and Lacan's French, with Caruth supplying an English translation in a footnote. Like the italicized word *repetition,* the foreign languages are meant to give the reader the real thing, not just the symbol of the original (in this case) critical event, but the event itself.[29] Caruth then concludes the book with these words: "The passing on of the child's words transmits not simply a reality that can be grasped in these words' representation, but the ethical imperative of an awakening that has yet to occur" (112). Writers of trauma theory, and by extension, their audience of committed readers, are clearly designated as the keepers of the flame, the memorializers of not just this particular dead child, but of what that figure embodies and indeed etches on the body of the receptive reader (tellingly, Caruth tends to employ the term *witness* rather than *reader,* emphasizing the you-are-there effect): the catastrophic inability of language to adequately convey human suffering.

It is my sense, however, that Caruth's distinction—between representations that are mediated by the mind, and traumatic experience that gets inscribed directly on the body—is belied by her unacknowledged appeal to the sentimental, in the figure of the speaking, burning child; for what lingers on is the pathos of the child who cannot be saved, whose death catalyzes a series of adult accounts of its meaning and who "speaks from beyond the grave" first in Freud's text, then in Lacan's, and then in Caruth's—potentially ad infinitum. The performance Caruth mystifies in deconstructive language is, I think, the performance of sentiment familiar from "countless" nineteenth-century depictions, updated and sensationalized by the media in the twentieth century, and now invoked by theorists of trauma. The figure of the wounded child becomes the occasion for the assertion of a theoretical authority that is deeply moralized. For Caruth, I would suggest, the "self-evident" pathos elicited by the figure of the wounded child becomes in her account the foundation for the pathos of representation itself and then the source of its redemption. For even if they are never able to understand, prevent, or ameliorate the suffering of others, readers of critical theory can absorb and then pass on the trauma, thereby fulfilling, perhaps, the terms of their "urgent responsibility." While the resistance to representation aligns trauma theory with the realist imperative I isolated in the scene from *Huckleberry Finn,* this last move secures a connection to the tradition of sentimentalism, for it reprises Harriet Beecher Stowe's earlier injunction to her readers that "*they feel right . . .* [for] the man or woman who *feels* strongly, healthily, and justly, on the great interests of humanity, is a constant benefactor to the human race"[30]

I proceed toward a conclusion by way of Ruth Leys, who is deeply critical of Caruth, both for what Leys believes is her misreading of Freud and for her desire to link trauma to an external event that is inscribed in the body without symbolic mediation.[31] What interests me here, however, is the fact that Leys, in her highly successful effort to place the concept of trauma within its complex institutional and discursive history (and, thereby, to wrest the concept from critical theorists who use it as a convenient vehicle to support a performative theory of language) herself makes use of the figure of the wounded child to draw a line between real and debased trauma. Leys begins *Trauma: A Genealogy* by contrasting two stories: that of a group of kidnapped Ugandan children (as told in a 1998 *New Yorker* article) who were sent to a trauma center after they had been forced by a guerilla group to participate in atrocities, and that of Paula Jones, the woman who brought a sexual harassment case against President Bill Clinton to court, and whose lawyers argued she suffered from post-traumatic stress. The purpose of Leys's coupling is to point up, as she explains, the difference between the "absolute[ly] indispensib[le]" use of the concept of trauma to understand "the psychic harms associated with certain central experiences of the twentieth century," and its misuse at the hands of opportunists or charlatans: "it is hard not to feel that the concept of trauma has become debased currency when it is applied both to truly horrible events *and* to something as dubious as the long-term harm to Paula Jones" (2).

It is important to note that the coupling of the two anecdotes is somewhat uneven, for the Ugandan episode is described as including a good deal of physical battery, including the rape of the children, their being forced to fight the Ugandan army, and beatings if they refused to cooperate in "hacking to death, with hoes, axes, and branches, a recently kidnapped girl who had been caught escaping" (1). By contrast, the sketch of Paula Jones's suit against Clinton offers no depiction of the event that led to the case and instead refers only to "alleged sexual harassment" (2). The use of "alleged" here puts into question the actuality of the events, while sexual harassment as a category of offense invokes cultural uncertainty about the corporeal reality of the initial harm or wounding.

In tracing the history of the idea of trauma from the mid-nineteenth to the late twentieth centuries, Leys is at pains to critique the privileging of physical wounds over psychic ones—a negative assessment, as I have mentioned, that she extends to Caruth's ideas about the corporeal register of trauma. Those nineteenth-century neurologists who presumed a corporeal seat for nervous shock, as well as recent critics who conceive of trauma as a literal inscription on a primitive, precognitive part of the human brain, are vigorously censured for their presuming that psychic trauma is "uncontaminated by subjective meaning, personal cognitive schemes, psychosocial factors, or unconscious symbolic elaboration" (7). In short, the distinction between real wounds, which are of the body, and merely psychical ones, which involve the mind's meaning-making processes, is dismissed as naive. And indeed, in the paired stories of Leys's introduction, what is at stake appears to be the distinction between two sorts of *psychic* harm: one that is valid, by virtue of being linked to a "central experience of the twentieth century" (i.e., genocide), and one that is "debased" or unfounded. As already noted, however, Leys does not examine the foundation for Jones's claim, which might have illuminated for readers the difference, in terms of psychic harm, between being exposed to a politician's penis and being exposed to genocide. Instead, the case is presented as absurd on its face. To repeat Leys's formulation, "*it is hard not to feel* that the concept of trauma has become debased currency when it is applied both to truly horrible events *and* to something as dubious as the long-term harm to Paula Jones" (emphasis added). Later, she refers to "the attribution of trauma . . . by lawyerly fiat" in the Jones case (8), but this statement obviously begs the question, assuming the illegitimacy of the claim at the outset.

Perhaps one might conclude from the Ugandan children/Paula Jones coupling that the distinguishing mark between valid and invalid psychic trauma resides in the proximity to physical danger. But the anecdote does not assess whether Jones was in danger, or felt herself to be. It would appear, then, that the crucial distinction between the children and Paula Jones is twofold: first of all, the Ugandan children were subject to the ravages of war (emblematized in the body of the brutalized girl), not the dubious depredations of a lecher, which are assumed rather than argued to be invalid; second, the victims of war were children, and as such had unassailable moral standing (even in the appalling case described, in which the girls and boys were themselves made the agents of another child's mutilation). The crucial difference between the two cases, in other words, finally rests on a volatile combination of sentimentalist discourse and the very positivist tradition of distinguishing real from fictitious wounds that Leys is otherwise at pains to interrogate. Paula Jones, a physically intact and sexually active woman, had to depend on "lawyerly fiat" to make her trauma real; the Ugandan children, though at least some may have escaped physical harm, were metonymically linked to the (spectacularly harmed) murdered girl. Indeed, this anecdote appears not merely as an example of trauma, but—perhaps inadvertently—as a sort of primal scene for *Trauma: A Genealogy:* a shocking contemporary atrocity that compels the wordless and perhaps relieved assent of readers that yes, in the cynical, postmodern, theory-laden world of contemporary criticism, here, at least, is the real thing.

The prominence of the wounded child in critical work that is overtly theoretical in focus would seem to mark a latent yet unacknowledged sentimentalism structuring current debates about the capacity of language to be adequate to experience. The child who falls down a well, is burned, or hacked to pieces becomes not just a symbolic figure for unmediated access to the real (note the irony), but a deeply moralistic figure for innocence outraged. "The language of shame, the scenario of the pure and vulnerable child, the fantasy of an undifferentiated community standard": these, Michael Warner has insisted, are the dubious tools of a disciplinary society (which, in Warner's piece, is a society committed to keeping sex private, heterosexual, and normative).[32] This figure provides the occasion for theorists and readers alike, like the consumers of the television movie *Jessica: Everyone's Baby,* to embrace a representation and yet invoke an idea central to trauma theory, that of the unmediated access to the real—and perhaps to feel more human in a world understood to be dominated by unreal images.[33] As Elizabeth Barnes has argued of sentimentalism in *Uncle Tom's Cabin,* scenes of cruelty and the affect they produce may be "necessary for the reader to *feel* alive. Stowe's emphasis on identificatory pain . . . becomes vital to substantiating not only the character's humanity, but the reader's humanity, as well."[34] The figure of the wounded child is invoked for its affective power, its self-evidence, its ability to compel one's assent, and perhaps for its ability to lend a certain moral authority to the position being advanced—for precisely the reasons, as Ann Douglas argues, that nineteenth-century mothers and ministers made use of the figure of the child.

Furthermore, the Ugandan children/Paula Jones dichotomy, in arguing for what Leys calls the "absolute indispensability" of the concept of trauma, not only "borrows" (to use Elaine Scarry's terms) "the sheer material factualness of the human body" to give "the aura of a 'realness' and 'certainty'" to the notion of a psychic wound;[35] it also, and more dangerously, trades in skepticism about sexual harassment as a valid harm, and precisely for the epistemological difficulties that so vexed the nineteenth-century investigators Leys studies (difficulties that have, in slightly altered form, followed rape victims in the twenty-first century). Where, researchers such as Jean-Martin Charcot puzzled, can one physiologically (i.e., *really*) discern the exact location of the wound to one's psyche?

In the case of Caruth, smuggled-in sentimentalism may lead to the mistaken sense that a critical intervention might occupy the same register of efficacy as social activism or indeed medical care. "The notion of trauma," Caruth concludes, "also acknowledges that perhaps it is not possible for the witnessing of the trauma to occur within the individual at all, that it may only be in future generations that 'cure' or at least witnessing can take place" (136, n. 21). While the notion that reading about atrocities can produce intense affect in readers is certainly uncontroversial, the implication that some sort of "transmission" of another's experience takes place, and that the reader's reception of this event might effect some sort of retroactive cure, imparts a curious grandiosity to the activity of reading. Amy Hungerford has persuasively traced the logic of Caruth's and Shoshana Felman's theories to reveal even more radical claims about the nature of the reader's role: through the mechanism of sympathetic identification, in which readers are understood to "experience trauma by listening to testimony about trauma," Hungerford argues that trauma theory implies that "those who bear witness to suffering reverse death." [36] While Caruth would seem to freight literary criticism with an almost alchemical power to channel the dead and heal their wounds, I would suggest that Arthur Kleinman's work as both anthropologist and physician, and Michael Warner's work as critical theorist and gay activist, provide examples of how the registers of representation and reform might fruitfully interact without being conflated as precisely identical.

Finally, to revisit van der Kolk's formulation of trauma, one might question why the body, understood in its most material sense as isolated from the mind's meaning-making processes, alone must "keep the score." Isn't the mind, with its cognitive as well as affective capacities, itself a part of the body? In Kleinman's terms, stories of suffering needn't simply "miss" the reality of a catastrophic injury; instead he argues that such narratives are critical for defining the experience of illness as well as an instrumental part of healing. What is still missing from much critical theory is, on the one hand, an acknowledgement of how the big questions ("the core issue in trauma is reality") are shot through with sentimental investments and invocations; and, on the other hand, an adequate phenomenology of affect. I think the work of Marianne Noble, and the responses it has elicited from critics such as Michelle Massé and Elizabeth Barnes, points fruitfully in these directions, as does Sedgwick's recent writing on the twentieth-century psychologist Silvan Tompkins. Glenn Hendler has also begun to do some of this work when he argues for "a conceptualization of sentimental experience that doesn't rely on such a dichotomy between affect and language."[37] It is my sense that sub-rosa appeals to sentiment not only unwittingly reprise the dubious, century-old project of disentangling realism from the snares of sentimentalism, but also pose other, more important problems—not the least of which is the implicit devaluation of the realm of affect as a legitimate object of study, mode of judgment, and impetus to critical engagement.

NOTES

1. Bessel van der Kolk, "The Black Hole of Trauma," in *Traumatic Stress: The Effects of Overwhelming Experience on Mind, Body, and Society*, ed. Bessel A. van der Kolk, Alexander C. McFarlane, and Lars Weisaeth (New York: Guilford Press, 1996), 6. Van der Kolk's webpage reports that he is the clinical director of the Trauma Center at Human Resources Institute Hospital in Brookline, Massachusetts, and past resident of the International Society for Traumatic Stress Studies.

2. Judith Herman, *Trauma and Recovery* (New York: Basic Books, 1997),

3. Cathy Caruth, *Unclaimed Experience: Trauma, Narrative, and History* (Baltimore: Johns Hopkins University Press, 1996), 4–5; Ruth Leys, *Trauma: A Genealogy* (Chicago: University of Chicago Press, 2000), 269.

4. In "Trauma and Memory" (chap. 12 of *Traumatic Stress*), van der Kolk refers to cerebral imaging studies to argue that the brains of persons confronted with an overwhelming experiences follow a precise procedure: "Broca's area—the part of the left hemisphere responsible for translating personal experiences into communicable language—[is] turned off," while the amygdala, the part of the brain that "translates sensory stimuli into emotional and hormonal signals," becomes excessively active (293–94). In short, "during activation of traumatic memory, the brain is 'having' its experience: The person may feel, see, or hear the sensory elements of the traumatic experience. He or she may also be physiologically prevented from translating this experience into communicable language." See van der Kolk, "The Body Keeps the Score: Approaches to the Psychobiology of Posttraumatic Stress Disorder," in van der Kolk, McFarlane, and Weisaeth, eds., *Traumatic Stress*, 234.

5. Serge Leclaire, *A Child Is Being Killed: On Primary Narcissism and the Death Drive*, trans. Marie-Claude Hays (Stanford, Calif.: Stanford University Press, 1998), 8.

6. Ruth Leys, "The Pathos of the Literal," in *Trauma: A Genealogy* (Chicago: University of Chicago Press, 2000), 16; hereafter, page numbers will be cited parenthetically in the text.

7. Through a reading of *Huckleberry Finn* I try to show how Twain tries to produce a distinction between these two modes by distinguishing between excessive, proliferating speech and the imperative of speechlessness, and that the inciting moment for the performance of this distinction is for Twain the figure of the wounded child—a figure split between Buck, who is shot (physiological trauma), and Huck, who is not (psychological trauma). For a useful account of how the major promoters of literary realism (e.g., William Dean Howells) sought to protect the tenuous masculinity of the male artist by professionalizing literary production, see Michael Davitt Bell, *The Problem of American*

Realism (Chicago: University of Chicago Press, 1993); see also Amy Kaplan, *The Social Construction of American Realism* (Chicago: University of Chicago Press, 1988). A selective list of works for readers who wish to explore the literary-critical dimension of scholarship on sentimentalism would begin with the debate between Ann Douglas and Jane Tompkins. See Douglas, *The Feminization of American Culture* (New York: Avon Books, 1977) and Tompkins, *Sensational Designs: The Cultural Work of American Fiction, 1790–1860* (New York: Oxford University Press, 1985); esp. each book's discussion of Harriet Beecher Stowe's *Uncle Tom's Cabin*. For an excellent array of contemporary updates on the Douglas-Tompkins debate, readers should consult Shirley Samuels, ed., *The Culture of Sentiment: Race, Gender, and Sentimentality in Nineteenth-Century America* (New York: Oxford University Press, 1992). Recently, Glenn Hendler has interrogated the gendered nature of much work on sentimentalism; see Hendler, *Sentimental Men: Masculinity and the Politics of Affect in American Culture,* ed. Mary Chapman and Glenn Hendler (Berkeley and Los Angeles: University of California Press, 1999). Similarly, Lora Romero questions the dichotomies that subtend much scholarship on sentimentalism from the 1970s and 1980s (e.g., between masculine and feminine epistemologies, public and private spheres, white bourgeois and African-American cultures); see Romero, *Home Fronts: Domesticity and Its Critics in the Antebellum United States* (Durham, N.C.: Duke University Press, 1997). For more overtly theoretical accounts of how sentimentalism engages the reader affectively, see Philip Fisher, *Hard Facts: Setting and Form in the American Novel* (New York: Oxford University Press, 1987); Karen Sánchez-Eppler, *Touching Liberty: Abolition, Feminism, and the Politics of the Body* (Berkeley and Los Angeles: University of California Press, 1993); and Marianne Noble, *The Masochistic Pleasures of Sentimental Literature* (Princeton, N.J.: Princeton University Press, 2000).

8. Douglas, *The Feminization of American Culture,* 240; hereafter, page numbers will be cited parenthetically in the text.

9. For a useful account of the historical reception of Twain's text, with an emphasis on its canonization (and subsequent demonization), see Jonathan Arac, *Huckleberry Finn As Idol and Target: The Functions of Criticism in Our Time* (Madison: University of Wisconsin Press, 1997).

10. Gregg Camfield, *Sentimental Twain: Samuel Clemens in the Maze of Moral Philosophy* (Philadelphia: University of Pennsylvania Press, 1994), xi. Camfield notes that, judging from the range of contemporary critical reactions to *Huckleberry Finn*—that it envisions interracial harmony (sentimental) or that it embodies a grim racism (realist)—readers of Twain today participate in the realist/sentimental oscillation apparent in the writings themselves. "The moral and literary tensions that drove Twain's works," Camfield concludes, "have persisted . . . because they are part of the fundamental paradoxes of the modern world" (21).

11. Mark Twain, *The Adventures of Huckleberry Finn* (New York: Penguin Books, 1985), 114; hereafter, page numbers will be cited parenthetically in the text.

12. Bessel van der Kolk, "The Complexity of Adaptation to Trauma: Self-Regulation, Stimulus Discrimination, and Characterological Development," in van der Kolk, McFarlane, and Weisaeth, eds., *Traumatic Stress,* 193.

13. My thanks to Jack Kerkering for making this point.

14. Van der Kolk, "The Black Hole of Trauma," 3.

15. Harriet Beecher Stowe, *Uncle Tom's Cabin, or, Life among the Lowly* (New York: Penguin Books, 1986), 426, 428.

16. Mark Babinek, "Baby Jessica's Family Stays Low-Key Ten Years After Water Well Drama," *Abilene Reporter-News,* 14 October 1997, online at <http://www.reporter-news.com>.

17. Viviana A. Zelizer, *Pricing the Priceless Child: The Changing Social Value of Children* (New York: Basic Books, 1981), 37; hereafter, page numbers will be cited parenthetically in the text.

18. Laurence Lerner, *Angels and Absences: Child Death in the Nineteenth Century* (Nashville: Vanderbilt University Press, 1997), 162.

19. Van der Kolk, "The Black Hole of Trauma," 3.

20. James Baldwin, "Everybody's Protest Novel," *Partisan Review* 16 (1949): 579.

21. Leclaire, *A Child Is Being Killed,* 10, 3.

22. Camfield, *Sentimental Twain,* 7.

23. The notion of urgency (as in this passage) is central to Caruth's account. In "The Insistence of Reference," her introduction to a collection of essays titled *Critical Encounters: Reference and Responsibility in Deconstructive Writing* (New Brunswick, N.J.: Rutgers University Press, 1995), 1, 2, Caruth in consecutive paragraphs refers to the "urgent task" of reading "stories of rape or childhood abuse" for "those realities" that escape representation, and the "urgent claim" that these texts pose. This notion speaks to what Elaine Scarry has termed the "quite astonishing and immodest project" of some theoretically engaged contemporary criticism, which operates as if "retroactively, the historical persons and events temporally adjacent to that literature" are "capable . . . of being healed." See Scarry, introduction to *Literature and the Body: Essays on Populations and Persons,* ed. Elaine Scarry (Baltimore: Johns Hopkins University Press, 1988), xxiii. In Caruth's work, the urgency appears to arise from the affect enlisted by the representation, while the sense of moral responsibility emerges from the notion that "stories of rape or childhood abuse" are not merely representations. The critic, affectively refashioned as rescuer, feels motivated to act swiftly to assist the "person" in need. Amy Hungerford has examined how Caruth's work has contributed to the notion that we might have ethical responsibilities to texts comparable to our obligations to actual human beings; see Hungerford, "Memorizing Memory," *Yale Journal of Criticism* 14, no. 1 (2001): 67–92; and "Surviving Rego Park: Holocaust Theory from Art Spiegelman to Berel Lang," in *The Americanization of the Holocaust,* ed. Hilene Flanzbaum (Baltimore: Johns Hopkins University Press, 1999).

24. Eve Kosofsky Sedgwick and Adam Frank, "Shame in the Cybernetic Fold: Reading Silvan Tompkins," in *Shame and Its Sisters: A Silvan Tompkins Reader,* ed. Eve Kosofsky Sedgwick and Adam Frank (Durham, N.C.: Duke University Press, 1995), 5.

25. Arthur Kleinman, *The Illness Narratives: Suffering, Healing, and the Human Condition* (New York: Basic Books, 1988), xi–xii; hereafter, page numbers will be cited parenthetically in the text.

26. Kleinman is here attempting to rewrite the epistemological assumptions inherent in what Michel Foucault has termed the clinical gaze, which "refrains from intervening: it is silent and gestureless." See Foucault, *The Birth of the Clinic: An Archaeology of Medical Perception,* trans. A. M. Sheridan Smith (York: Vintage, 1994), 107. Whereas the gaze that Foucault describes is predicated on a normative model of disease entities, the transparency of corporeal symptoms, and the excision of meaning and value from clinical diagnosis, Kleinman's much more interactive, emotive gaze involves him in what he seeks to know. Moreover, his emphasis on the narrative component of illness necessitates the patient's spoken contribution, and his assertion that "illness has meaning" (8) recasts bodily symptoms as representations that gesture beyond solely corporeal etiological explanations (e.g., a virus).

27. Freud reports the case at the beginning of a chapter in *The Interpretation of Dreams:* "It was told to me by a woman patient who had herself heard it in a lecture on dreams: its actual source is still unknown to me. Its content made an impression on the lady, however, and she proceeded to 're-dream' it." See Freud, *The Interpretation of Dreams,* trans.

and ed. James Strachey (New York: Avon Books, 1965), 547. Lacan revisits the dream in "Touché and Automaton," in *The Four Fundamental Concepts of Psychoanalysis,* ed. Jacques-Alain Miller, trans. Alan Sheridan (New York: W. W. Norton, 1981): 53–64.

28. This implication is made even more explicit in Caruth's *Unclaimed Experience,* in the biographical discussion of Freud and Lacan, each of whom "would survive the death of his own child" (111). The supremely particular experience of losing a child, in Caruth's analysis, becomes something that is repeatable by someone else: "Indeed, in his theoretical and autobiographical repetition of Freud's story, Lacan could not possibly have known that his text on trauma, like Freud's, in effect anticipated his own crucial loss and trauma: . . . Quite uncannily, Lacan's life will repeat Freud's loss of his own daughter Sophie" (110–11). Moreover, the pathos attached to the idea that Lacan "could not possibly have known" of his impending loss, and the fact that the death of Sophie was "the unknown future" (111) of the then unsuspecting Freud, suggests that both men "missed" an experience that lay in their future—an assertion that, to my mind, takes the idea of trauma as "missed" experience to the point of absurdity.

29. In making this point, I am influenced by Walter Benn Michaels's analysis of dialect in realist writing at the end of the nineteenth century—in particular his argument that authors of local-color novels employed italics and foreign languages in an attempt to move beyond literary convention and "instead to present the reader with the real thing." See Michaels, "Local Colors," *Modern Language News* 113, no. 4 (1998): 734–36 (quote here from 735).

30. Stowe, *Uncle Tom's Cabin,* 624. Marianne Noble makes explicit the link between trauma theory and nineteenth-century sentimentalist discourse, both of which were committed to "getting at" the experiential reality of persons by means of suffering. She argues that Stowe sought to bypass the normal symbolic processes of readers by not representing scenes of violence and thereby eliciting a "sentimental wound" that, by producing "in the reader's body a gut feeling of pain," attempted to achieve " 'real presence,' " which in turn would "redress the cognitive failure of abstract analysis that women like Stowe believed had led the nation into its great moral crisis." See Noble, "The Ecstasies of Sentimental Wounding in *Uncle Tom's Cabin,*" *Yale Journal of Criticism* 10, no. 2 (1997): 295, 302, 296. According to Noble, Stowe compared the "fusion" that readers could achieve to "the reunion of a child with its mother" (306). Noble also highlights the dangers that lurk in the attempt to bypass the intellect and representation in order to achieve something more like affective communion with another: "it may turn the observer inward, compensating with a self-satisfying *illusion* of humanitarian altruism that may well not be acted upon at all" (313).

31. Leys makes an important contribution to the study of trauma, both in her attention to the complicated, uneven, multidisciplinary history of the idea and in her excavation of a tension in the conceptualization of trauma that persists from the nineteenth century to the present. Theorists of trauma, she argues, oscillate between a "mimetic" account, in which the subject of trauma is understood to be so shattered by a catastrophic occurrence that the distinction between person and event is disabled, thereby implicating the subject in the trauma and rendering the experience unavailable to memory; and an "antimimetic" account, which affirms the distinction between person and event, construing the subject of trauma as passive and securing the separate identity (and authority) of the therapist/physician. Caruth, in Leys's account, replicates both positions in their most deplorable forms. In imagining that traumatic experience eludes representation and elides the difference between victim and therapist (insofar as traumatic experience can pass from one to the other), Caruth offers "an inadvertent parody . . . of the mimetic theory" (17); she adopts a version of the antimimetic position, however, when she asserts that

symptoms produced by trauma, especially traumatic dreams and flashbacks, can be traced directly and literally to external events—"an etiological model for psychic trauma," Leys points out, "that Freud rejected from the start" (272).

32. Michael Warner, "Zones of Privacy," in *What's Left of Theory: New Work on the Politics of Literary Theory*, ed. Judith Butler, John Guillory, and Kendall Thomas (New York: Routledge, 2000), 100. In this article Warner criticizes the project of ex-mayor Rudolph Giuliani to eradicate public sex culture in New York City, arguing instead for the sorts of recognition and transmission of sexual knowledges made possible by places like Christopher Street. It is interesting to note that even Warner's argument is inflected with the pathos of the damaged child, though with a twist: one of his concluding points is that "[t]he sexual culture of New York City serves people around the world, even if only as the distant reference point of queer kids growing up in North Carolina or Idaho, who know that somewhere things are different" (107).

33. David Rothberg makes a version of this point in his *Traumatic Realism: The Demands of the Holocaust* (Minneapolis: University of Minnesota Press, 2000). "A potential risk of trauma theory," he writes, "based on Lacan's rereading of Freud is the collapse of distinction between the real and the traumatic—the notion . . . of 'the real understood as traumatic'" (137). Rothberg's analysis affirms what he terms a "traumatic realism" that preserves a commitment to representation—the search "for a form commensurate with the Holocaust's destruction of already existing forms"—while foregrounding "the mediations inherent in its acts of representation" (263). I am using the term *traumatic realism* in a different sense in the title of this essay, to indicate the tendency of trauma theorists such as Cathy Caruth to invoke the figure of the wounded child to construe a "real" that is "beyond words" yet is produced through standard realist conventions (as seen in Twain) of description and elision coupled with standard sentimental strategies (as seen in Stowe) for eliciting affect.

34. Elizabeth Barnes, "The Epistemology of the 'Real': A Response to Marianne Noble," *Yale Journal of Criticism* 10, no. 2 (1997): 323.

35. Elaine Scarry, *The Body in Pain: The Making and Unmaking of the World* (New York: Oxford University Press, 1985), 14.

36. Hungerford, "Memorizing Memory," 74, 73, 78. In this article, Hungerford excavates the radical account of language that underpins trauma theory, in which texts (especially survivor accounts of the Holocaust) are imagined not as representations of their author's experiences, to which a reader might have intellectual and emotional access, but as embodiments (and transmitters) of that experience. Hungerford argues that Caruth and Felman, influenced by deconstruction's notion of the materiality of the signifier, end up conflating writing and persons and thereby invest texts with "the pathos of life and death" (88) that properly belong to embodied individuals.

37. Glenn Hendler, "Further Responses to Marianne Noble on Stowe, Sentiment, and Masochism," *Yale Journal of Criticism* 12, no. 1 (1999): 150.

7 Constructing the Psychoanalytic Child

Freud's *From the History of an Infantile Neurosis*

Michelle A. Massé

In 1918, Sigmund Freud wrote the last of his five major case histories, *From the History of an Infantile Neurosis,* better known as the "Wolf Man" case because of the patient's childhood dream about wolves.[1] Freud saw Sergei Pankejeff as a patient from 1910 to 1914, and again from 1919 to 1920. In the years in between, the world changed cataclysmically. Those years also marked another major, if less noted, turning point: the ascendency of the child in psychoanalysis, literature, and American culture. In considering the enthusiastic adoption of the Freudian child by the United States, I want to explore how Freud's case history is decisive in establishing the significance of childhood for adult identity, so decisive that it is hard for us to imagine a time when there was not a psychoanalytic child. *From the History of an Infantile Neurosis,* itself a story about the childhood of psychoanalysis, both explains and creates the child of the twentieth century and beyond.[2]

The emergence of the "psychoanalytic child" and of "children's literature" are almost coterminous: in the latter half of the nineteenth century, both deliver the newly created "child" to an industrial world in need of docile subjects in order to run smoothly. As the span that constitutes "childhood" lengthens and the roles possible within that span multiply, the stories we tell ourselves about children through history, psychoanalysis, and literature multiply as well. Which of the narratives seen through these different lenses, however, is the one that can show us what identity could—or should—be in a postwar industrial world? The romantic child, father to the man, establishes the link between youth and age, but children no longer seem to be trailing clouds of glory. The model Victorian child surely shows a primal energy and an earnest attempt at conscious self-improvement, but the moral opprobrium attached to that energy seems stodgy, the lessons inculcated by rote of little use as guides in a new age. The swing of the historical pendulum from id to superego, and back to id again, slows as the ego, the "I" that can (potentially) tell its own story, becomes the weighty concern of a period in which another young creature—the United States—reaches its own ascendancy.

New lessons are needed, lessons culled from the books children read as well as from the books adults read to understand children. And children now have to be understood. No longer empty vessels, they are instead interesting, complicated beings fueled by libidinal urges, entangled in fascinating "complexes," and subject to phobias and neuroses." U.S. pragmatism and individualism accordingly rework psychoanalysis because, as Nathan Hale asserts in *Freud and the Americans,* emphasizing "correct child raising [is] the surest guarantee of progress."[3] Surefooted progress, and not the seemingly aimless ramblings of what later came to be known as "French Freud," was what the Americans wanted.

This thumbnail history of "the" American child's manifest destiny doesn't mark a change in ontological reality, of course. What it does point to, though, is the malleability of the construct we name "the child," a construct we continue to insist is natural and essential even while we scrutinize the other cultural imperatives once considered "natural," such as race and gender. As James Kincaid astutely maintains in *Child-Loving,* "What a child *is,* in other words, changes to fit different situations and different needs. . . . Any image, body, or being we can hollow out, purify, exalt, abuse, and locate sneakily in a field of desire will do for us as a 'child'. . . . "[4]

Whether that "child" is a physical child before us or the ghost we recognize as our younger selves, we weave narratives to clothe it or borrow ready-made outfits when necessary. In his essay "The Relation of the Poet to Day-Dreaming," Freud famously declares that "every child at play behaves like an imaginative writer, in that he creates a world of his own or, more truly, he rearranges the things of his world and orders it in a way that pleases him better." As adults we are still at play, but now it is "at play with history" (a phrase Dominick LaCapra uses in a somewhat different context)—an individual and collective history that explains who we are and what the world around us means.[5] That two young systems, the United States and psychoanalysis, narrated much of their stories through the structure of childhood development overdetermines those cultural stories.

William Kerrigan asserts that the twentieth century heralds "the culture of the child" and avers that "psychoanalysis is the science of the new culture."[6] I think that Kerrigan's general point is right, although I also think the causality less one-way and the U.S. penchant for "science" more pronounced than he indicates, insofar as psychoanalysis fought valiantly to be seen as a science and not just a fiction about emotions. I would add, however, that the equally new genre of children's literature also shed as much Arnoldian light as it did sweetness upon the child: both psychoanalysis and literature provide explanatory as well as prescriptive models.

Such models were much sought in the United States both before and after World War I. Some of Pankejeff's last words are "Give me some advice!" (WMCFP 247). The exclamation establishes him as a child of his age, but can also serve as a refrain for both the literature and science of the child in the United States during the twentieth century. Freud set the tone during his wildly successful lectures at Clark University in 1909, delivered at a time when, as Hale notes, "symptoms of crisis and change were coming to the surface in those aspects of American cultural and professional life that psychoanalysis touched most deeply."[7] After Freud's visit to the United States in 1909, psychoanalysis became all the rage. For scholars, avant-garde Greenwich Village socialites, and authors such as Sherwood Anderson, Theodore Dreiser, and F. Scott Fitzgerald, psychoanalysis also became a sort of parlor game, as people eagerly identified "slips," "complexes," or nodded knowingly when a behavior was announced to be "Freudian." By 1930, even the conservative *Ladies' Home Journal* was willing to pay for an advice column by the psychoanalyst Karl Menninger, in which he responded to readers' inquiries about child rearing, among other issues.[8]

Both psychoanalysis and children's literature, advisory genres of paramount importance in the modern United States, seek to represent the child as a "rounded" individual with a complete, if not yet fully shaped, identity. No longer romantic angel or Victorian demon, the modern child in fiction and case history is, as Peter Coveney maintains in *The Image of Childhood*, "conveyed as a child, with his awareness conveyed as it was experienced, from within."[9] The pedagogical goal of such reading (or therapy) also eschews the too-facile oppositions of rosy optimism or stygian gloom. Instead, as Kerrigan wisely states, what the best of our culture's psychoanalytic and fictional stories can offer is a reality tempered by hope: "But at its most sublime, good wishes for children merge with hostile suspicion of their brief paradise to engender an authentic literature of hope, which may be defined psychoanalytically as a wish that has internalized the possibility of its failure. From the best of their culture children may learn both to mourn, shedding illusion, and to want, shedding despair" (xvi). Not all are happy endings, then, but they are nonetheless endings in which a child can achieve the goals of psychoanalytic development: to work and to love.

Whether our adult good wishes are finally blessings or curses depends not only upon our adult selves, of course. Therapy is, in part, the attempt to integrate the less reasoning, archaic—childlike—forms of psychic identity and memory within the purview of the conscious, adult self. This attempt at integration often does not work for the therapist, the author, or the adult, let alone the patient. Consciously or unconsciously, the adult can all too easily create the child as a narcissistic extension. As Michael Goldman notes, "figures of adult power and sexual intensity have hovered over children, concerned to draw meaning, energy, and radical satisfaction from them." [10]

Among the cast composed of the female "grand neurotics" who occupy center stage in Freudian case histories, the servants and working class who fill the scene and serve as sin-eaters for those better able to afford transgression, and the briefly glimpsed ethnic and racial "others," there is another, slighter, and more silent figure so often on the psychoanalytic stage that commentary almost seems superfluous: the child, who is the first term in what Lionel Trilling notes as the mutual preoccupation of Freudian psychoanalysis and literature such as the bildungsroman "with children, women, peasants, and savages." [11] Strangely enough, however, the figure of the child, so central to the premises of analysis, and so manifestly constructed through hierarchical relationships with adults, nonetheless remains the preserve of "natural" subordination.

To speak "for" patients—even when they are "women, peasants, and savages"—rather than allowing them to speak for themselves is now quickly recognized as an appropriation of voice and agency. But contemporary analysts, like many adults, are almost as likely as Freud to helpfully supplement a child's faltering voice, sure that they have heard correctly and can translate accurately. As adults, we can easily tell ourselves that we speak "for," or in the place of, the child, because of our laudable advocacy "for," or on behalf of, the child. And we are all too often willing to listen to other adults' ventriloquist acts, unwittingly following what Michel Foucault calls "the rule of continual variations," still part of "the nineteenth-century grouping made up of the father, the mother, the educator, and the doctor, around the child and his sex" (99). And whereas almost every other matrix of subordination has emphatic boundary markers, childhood does not, for we are all authorities—we have all been children. When, weary of the adult patient, who already speaks "loudly enough," Freud instead offers to raise his voice "on behalf of the claims of childhood" and to narrate its story in "A Child Is Being Beaten" and elsewhere, we, such skeptical listeners in every other regard, are soothed by the old familiar tale of subordination when a child is the principal.[12] Surely there can be no harm in infantilizing the infant.

What I am suggesting here is that the construction of the child—and of the adult/analyst—within psychoanalysis demands our attention as perhaps *the* most culturally authorized fiction of voice throwing. Within the child's case history (or novel), the adult analyst (or author) can play his own fort/da game of consciousness and voice. The injunction to the child is "Thou Shalt Not Be Aware" (as Alice Miller's book title indicates); his state of nonknowing means that the analyst can, as Freud and others do, speak for the child's awareness in a way they can't for any other (nonpsychotic) group. Certainly, no other group presents so minimal a chance of contradiction and is so unlikely to launch a challenge that might topple the authority of the inquisitor. In addition, the very core of analysis—transference and countertransference—lends itself to the adult patient, and even the analyst, assuming the child's position.

Still, we do have our sentimental foibles about children, if not about patients. Just as we need to preserve the category of "good women" in order to create and maintain their debased opposites, so too do we split the image of the child within psychoanalytic discussion into "His Majesty the Baby" and the child dispossessed of identity, voice, and credibility. Freud readily identifies the pole of exaltation and overvaluation; somehow, its complement of depreciation and erasure is never addressed. The child thus joins the company of the subordinated that Freud assembles to explain the blind spots of the indulgent dominant in *Studies on Hysteria:* "I was afflicted by that blindness of the seeing eye which is so astonishing in the attitude of mothers to their daughters, husbands to their wives, and rulers to their favourites."[13] As well, what parents and adults see in children is a mirrored projection of their own sterling qualities, whether wishful or actual. In "On Narcissism," Freud assures us that parental "feeling, as is well known, is characterized by overestimation, that sure indication of a narcissistic feature in object-choice. . . . Parental love, which is so touching and at bottom so childish, is nothing but parental narcissism born again."[14] When stripped of the "perfections" and "cultural acquirements" doting adults project upon her, the child is ready for examination.

In traditional psychoanalysis, the child (whether actual or the reconstructed child of adult analysis), unable to distinguish fantasy from reality and communicatively impoverished, is seen scarcely to be a fit witness and certainly no interpreter. Paradoxically, Freud himself warns us that "too many words and thoughts have to be lent to the child" by the analyst (HIN 475)—if not in fact given. The overvaluing parents are also incapable of just assessment and, indeed, their spurious claim of authority can set itself against that of the analyst. "[I]t may seem tempting to take the easy course of filling up the gaps in a patient's memory by making enquiries from the older members of his family," Freud writes, "but I cannot advise too strongly against such a technique. Any stories that may be told by relatives in reply to enquiries and requests are at the mercy of every critical misgiving that can come into play. One invariably regrets having made oneself dependent upon such information . . . " (HIN 481–82, n. 2). As Freud fastidiously notes, the regrets of dependency ought not to be those of the analyst.

According to Freud, then, neither the experiencing child nor the adults around her can narrate the child's story. As adult, she is still effectively mute because not only is interpretation beyond her ken, but so too is the determination of what was actuality and what fantasy.[15] Only the analyst is able to decipher the "distortion and refurbishing" with which the narrating adult shapes the child's experience; only the analyst can do the "certain work of interpretation" that assures that the significance of childhood memories that seem "indifferent, worthless even," can "be appreciated," Freud asserts in "Poetry and Language." That "certain work . . . would either show how their content must be replaced by some other, or would reveal their connection with some other unmistakably important experiences, for which they were appearing as so-called 'screen memories.' "[16] Only by becoming like a child can one enter the kingdom of psychoanalysis, and whether, upon leaving, the story one tells about children is revelation or myth remains a mystery.

The publication of "Screen Memories" in 1899 marks, according to Carolyn Steedman, a radical, new "interiorized time coming into being in a child's body." In *Freud and the Culture of Psychoanalysis*, Steven Marcus suggests the 1905 *Three Essays* (which contained "Infantile Sexuality") as the crucial marker for "bringing to a close that epoch of cultural innocence in which infancy and childhood were regarded as themselves innocent."[17] Both publications indeed mark techtonic shifts, but it is the publication of *From the History of an Infantile Neurosis* in 1918 that keeps the earlier work from being washed away like so much else during the war years. By insisting upon the child's experience, hidden by "screen memory" and then revealed by the analyst, as central to knowledge, Freud assured the survival of the psychoanalytic child.

The case history of the "Wolf Man," based upon the four-year analysis of Sergei Pankejeff, a man in his middle twenties, is a superb demonstration of how the child's identity is created through the adult analyst's written narrative. By using a point of view ascribed to the child, an "unmistakably important experience" for psychoanalysis, the primal scene, was constructed.[18] In *From the History of an Infantile Neurosis,* Freud tells us that "we have rated the powers of children too low and that there is no knowing what they cannot be given credit for" (HIN 584). At the same time, however, the child is pointed to as a transparent spectacle and receptacle for the astute interpreter: "the life of a child under school age is easily observable, and we can examine it to see whether any 'problems' are to be found in it" (HIN 528). Finally, the power and "credit" to which Freud refers accrue to the adult analyst and not to the once-upon-a-time child who, in this case, displays an "obliging apathy" as an adult (HIN 477). Freud nonetheless assures us as earnestly as might a docudrama's narrator that "no construction or simulation on the part of the physician played any part" in the story we are eventually told (HIN 595), and he asks us to endorse his account, for "either the analysis based upon the neurosis in his childhood is all a piece of nonsense from start to finish, or everything took place just as I have described it above" (HIN 530).

What is at stake here is not only the child's reality, but that of Freud and of analysis itself.[19] As usual, though, Freud deconstructs Freud. While asking for full allegiance to his analysis and to his authority as analyst, he also reports his repeated attempts to "convince" and "force upon the patient" certain interpretations (HIN 536, 575). While insisting upon the "indisputable reality" of the child's seduction and introduction to castration anxiety by sister, nurse, governess, and servants as the "real" agents, for instance (HIN 577), he also notes the father's "affectionate abuse" (HIN 502).

Most conspicuously, Freud plaintively evokes his "powers in the art of exposition" (HIN 585), which have been amply demonstrated in the structure of the case history and through which he secures our narrative trust in conclusions and closures based on evidence "just as I have described it." In later revisions, however, he undercuts his adamant either/or, which demands full assent to a very detailed account or entire repudiation of analysis, to suggest that perhaps he as analyst could not, after all, distinguish what was fantasy, what reality. The reader, like the child, glimpses new possibilities when the seeming omniscience of the narrator crumbles with the admission that the painstaking specificity of the primal scene was not *quite* right and that, after all, "there remains the possibility of yet another interpretation" (HIN 531).[20]

The case history's contrasts are noteworthy on several fronts, as Patrick Mahony notes in *Cries of the Wolf Man*. Some of these tensions he ascribes to the account's historical function in establishing the authority of psychoanalysis and its biographical import for Freud's own authority at the time of composition. The case history also, however, displays a newly developing rhetoric of authorship, through which both authorities are articulated, with one providing a "further contrast between a writer in a new active phase and his clinical discussion of a remarkably passive personality" (75), a contrast that is of course underscored by their roles as adult/analyst, child/patient.

I would also note that Freud's and Pankejeff's complementary modes of response and roles obscure their common traits and interests. Each feels himself to be the child of destiny, signaled by birth with a caul;[21] both identify childhood nurses as their introduction to sexuality; both spend a remarkable amount of time worrying about their noses. More significantly, however, each is trying to excavate a "bygone era," as Freud's repeated invocation of his own favorite metaphor of investigation—the archaeological—indicates, and to lift away a veil that obscures some hidden truth. During his first course of analysis with Freud, Pankejeff's "principal subject of complaint was that for him the world was hidden in a veil, or that he was cut off from the world by a veil. This veil was torn only at one moment—after an enema" (HIN 551). In dreams "not possible to interpret completely," "it was as though . . . after her bath . . . he had tried . . . to undress his sister . . . to tear off her coverings . . . or veils—and so on" (HIN 486). These fantasies, Freud tells us, are sops to Pankejeff's "masculine self-esteem," and "corresponded exactly to the legends by means of which a nation that has become great and proud tries to conceal the insignificance and failure of its beginnings" (HIN 488).

From the History of an Infantile Neurosis is itself a major chapter in the "great and proud" history of analysis. For, while Pankejeff's attempts to conceal his ignominious history were futile, those of psychoanalysis are not, as Freud asserts in "Resistances to Psycho-Analysis": "to adults their prehistory seems so inglorious that they refuse to allow themselves to be reminded of it: they were infuriated when psychoanalysis tried to lift the veil of amnesia from their years of childhood."[22] Psychoanalysis, then, must have the means to accomplish what Pankejeff could not: it can itself unveil and interpret its own beginning and the auguries of future greatness. This case history—and outcome for this particular patient—*cannot* be "inglorious," "insignificant," or a "failure." Dora walks out, and Anna O. repudiates psychoanalysis; the "Wolf Man" must be a success.

The family history of Pankejeff when he begins analysis with Freud at twenty-three presents as startling a plot and set of characters, as does Dora's case history, *Fragment of an Analysis of a Case of Hysteria.* Born into an extremely wealthy Russian family, Pankejeff has one sister, Anna, who is two and a half years his senior. His father, perhaps a manic-depressive, goes to a sanatorium every few years; besides the penchant for "affectionate abuse" mentioned above, he engages in a bizarrely named game with his son, "Don't Get Angry, Man" (WM 8), and dies, probably a suicide, at forty-nine while away from home. His mother, characterized by Freud as cold, overly religious, and hypochondriacal, gives to her son the motto "I cannot go on living like this" when, at four and a half, he hears her lamenting her pains and hemorrhages (HIN 553). His grandmother kills herself; his grandfather competes with his son for a woman; his uncle Peter becomes an utter recluse whose death is announced in a tabloid as "A Millionaire Gnawed by Rats" (WM 81); a cousin is institutionalized for paranoia. And his sister Anna, a girl of "brilliant intellectual development [who] distinguished herself by her acute and realistic powers of mind" (HIN 488–89), kills herself at age twenty-two, tormented by not being "good looking enough" (HIN 489). As Pankejeff later tells the journalist Karin Obholzer in *The Wolf Man: Conversations with Freud's Patient Sixty Years Later,* she remained as envious of maids as when she ran away to become one as a child, because " 'being a maid is really the best profession. You do your work and the rest of the time is your own' " (WMCFP 80).

Deeply depressed by having contracted gonorrhea at age eighteen, Pan-kejeff, like his father, begins a series of visits to doctors and sanitaria that reads like a compendium of turn-of-the-century theories and treatments such as physical therapy, hydrotherapy, and electrical shock. In the five years between the ages of eighteen and twenty-three he consults with, or is treated by, seven therapists in Berlin, Moscow, Munich, St. Petersburg, and Odessa, until one suggests consulting Freud as someone who has some interesting new ideas. The young Pankejeff, then, already has something of a career as a patient: without job or school, his world is that of the clinic. Indeed, he falls instantly in love with his future wife, Therese, when he first glimpses her at the sanitarium where she is a nurse.

Pankejeff reports in "My Recollections of Sigmund Freud" that he finds in Freud a man whose appearance "was such as to win my confidence immedi-ately . . . I had the feeling of encountering a great personality" (WM 137). In Pankejeff, with his "obliging apathy" and receptivity, Freud finds the perfect patient through whom he can, with a "bold face" (HIN 585), establish the sig-nificance of infantile neurosis, the importance of the primal scene, the fore-grounding of the father in early childhood development, and the efficacy of analysis itself. The adult Pankejeff reports a recurrent dream that began at age four:

> I dreamt that it was night and that I was lying in my bed. (My bed stood with its foot towards the window; in front of the window there was a row of old walnut trees. I know it was winter when I had the dream, and night-time.) Suddenly the window opened of its own accord, and I was terrified to see that some white wolves were sitting on the big walnut tree in front of the window. There were six or seven of them. The wolves were quite white, and looked more like foxes or sheep-dogs, for they had big tails like foxes and they had their ears pricked like dogs when they pay attention to something. In great terror, evidently of being eaten up by the wolves, I screamed and woke up. (HIN 498)

In Freud's extraordinarily detailed revision, the dream refers to a still earlier experience in which the eighteen-month-old child awakens at five in the afternoon during an attack of malaria and then witnesses his parents having intercourse *a tergo* three times.[23] Although the primal scene makes no sense to the baby, according to Freud, it is allegedly invoked and reworked by the four-year-old in his dream after his "seduction" by his six-year-old sister, Anna. After Anna suggested that they "'show our bottoms,'" and her informing him that Nanya, his beloved nurse, did that and more with the gardener, he displays himself to Nanya. Her reprimand, as well as the indignation of the wicked witch/governess, Miss Oven, who comes upon the scene, cuts off the chance of any repeat offense. Little Sergei, in fear for his own "tail," displays acute castration anxiety and develops a religious obsessional neurosis.

Whereas Herr K., a would-be seducer, emerges relatively blameless in the case history of *Dora*—it is Dora's desires, after all, that are represented as the issue—the women in *History* are indubitably seductresses and the agents of castration in Freud's account, as the heading for section 3, "The Seduction," indicates. In order to "prove" that Pankejeff's "seduction by his sister was certainly not a phantasy," Freud suspends his prior injunction against accounts by relatives and reports Pankejeff's hearsay account of an older cousin telling him that "he very well remembered what a forward and sensual little thing she had been: once, when she was a child of four or five, she had sat on his lap and opened his trousers to take hold of his member" (HIN 488). It is she, the six-year-old child, who inflicts the trauma that "forced him [Pankejeff] into a passive role, and had given him a passive sexual aim" (HIN 496), and she, with the "merciless display of superiority" that secures her father's "unmistakable preference" for her (HIN 489, 485), who assures that that path will be followed. His adult tendency to "debase his love object," seen in his behavior and in his choice of partners of lower rank, is "to be explained as a reaction against pressure from the sister who was so much his superior" (HIN 573).

Following a somewhat strained line of linguistic reasoning, Nicolas Abraham and Maria Torok suggest, in *The Wolf Man's Magic Word*, that there is indeed a seduction in *From the History of an Infantile Neurosis*, but it is the one Jacques Derrida identifies in the foreword to their book as that of "his sister as seduced by the father and trying to repeat the same scene with her brother."[24] In their reading, the mother denies the son's account of paternal abuse, relayed by the subsequently dismissed English governess. Thus, as Barbara Johnson points out in her introduction to Abraham and Torok's text, their interpretation builds, and is built upon, "a dialogue—not an event," "a kind of lawsuit, investigating the real or fictional status of an event" (xlii). The young Pankejeff "was summoned to be the sole witness for the prosecution *and was at the same time* disqualified as such by the defense" (lviii).

Not surprisingly, he later obsessively identifies with Christ, who—also unacknowledged by the multitudes or courts—was sacrificed by his father. In such a scenario, I would suggest that it is not implausible that those five well-endowed wolves Pankejeff later draws, who stare so intently at the child in the bed, are the central adults in the household, as well as his sister Anna, all of whom seem to have the activity and potency from which he is excluded.

Within Freud's construction of this infantile neurosis, the categories *passive, feminine, child,* and *homosexual* mutually reinforce one another.[25] Pankejeff's sister, Anna, who "ought to have been . . . the boy" (HIN 482), is represented as having a masculine intelligence as keen as that of another Anna, Freud's daughter. Pankejeff, however, is akin to the "feminine" Anna Freud, because he, like the unnamed patient in "A Child Is Being Beaten" (actually, Anna Freud), fantasizes himself, from about five on, as "the heir to the throne being shut up in a narrow room and beaten" (HIN 494–95). Pankejeff's docility is noted by every analyst with whom he came in contact. What is less noted, however, are his sporadic lycanthropic reversals of these tendencies, during which he attempts to establish masculine heterosexual identity through aggression.

As a child, he raged against his Nanya and "took offence at every possible occasion, and then flew into a rage and screamed like a savage" (HIN 482); as an adolescent, he propositioned Anna; as a young man, he verbally attacked his mother and his sister. The "breakthrough to the woman," which Freud tells him is Pankejeff's "greatest achievement" (WM 56), begins with a break-in to the room of a nurse, Therese, to demand an assignation. Freud notes Pankejeff's sadism toward animals (HIN 483–84, 494), but no oddity in what Ruth Mack Brunswick (herself an analysand of Freud's, and Pankejeff's analyst sporadically from 1926 to 1938) later casually characterizes as his being "domineering with women, especially his wife and mother" (WM 282). Indeed, after noting Pankejeff's attraction to servants, Freud rather oddly comments that Pankejeff's looking at Freud "uncomprehendingly and a little contemptuously" when the topic is broached is enough to prevent "our overestimating the significance of his intention to debase women" (HIN 575). Brunswick's ear might be more keenly attuned, of course, particularly when Pankejeff's fantasies included shooting her and Freud; "and somehow those threats sounded less empty than those which one is accustomed to hear" (WM 290). Freud, on the other hand, dismisses Pankejeff's aggression in relation to himself, linking it to the father's "affectionate abuse": "he used to threaten me with eating me up and later with all kinds of other ill-treatment—all of which was merely an expression of affection" (HIN 588).

Mahony asks, "Between 1910 and 1914, whose thoughts, words, and fantasies dominated in that primal scene interminable?" (107). Mahony's reference to the title of Freud's essay "Analysis Terminable and Interminable" is appropriate, for neither analyst nor analysand could call a close to this analysis. It is interminable indeed, since Pankejeff remains the Wolf Man for the rest of his ninety-two years. Freud labored to convince his patient and the psychoanalytic community of the veracity and importance of the primal scene; the "Wolf Man" labored to become a man with an identity other than that bestowed upon him by his therapist. In a brief subsequent analysis with Freud; in his four-month treatment with Brunswick to clear up an unruly bit of transference; and in his extensive contacts with analysts throughout the rest of the sixty-five years after the termination of his first analysis with Freud, Sergei Pankejeff both represents himself and is seen as a child whose "thoughts, words, and fantasies" are known to most only through Freud's representation in the *History*.

Neither Pankejeff's analysts, the Freud Archives, or Karin Obholzer, the journalist who was his last savior, thought the man ill-served. Brunswick, startled at Pankejeff's vehemence against Freud and his attempt to hide his possession of the literal family jewels from Freud, helps, like his mother, to defuse his anger, happy to have fulfilled her own "almost negligible" role, in which she "acted purely as mediator between the patient and Freud" (WM 306). In Brunswick's account, neither the father idealized by him nor the Freud idealized by her can be to blame—only his own passive and infantile desires, to which he is redirected.

Pankejeff's interest in money and complaints about adequacy of support, which Brunswick and Obholzer comment upon, is noted by Freud years earlier only in relation to Pankejeff's mother and sister, whom Pankejeff accuses of trying to gain "sole control" of what he believes is rightfully his (HIN 550). He later launches financial accusations against Freud and other analysts, but this possibility isn't evident in the case history, where Pankejeff is represented as having an erratic and childlike attitude toward finances: "But he had no idea how much he possessed, what his expenditure was, or what balance was left over" (HIN 549). No "man of means," like Dora's father, despite actual familial wealth before emigration, he receives his income as a boy does his allowance. His questions about whether he has gotten as much as he has given remain as a puzzling symptom, nothing more.

In his interviews with Obholzer, the elderly Pankejeff remembers that, as a child "I sometimes wished that I would get sick, to be able to enjoy my mother's being with me and looking after me" (WMCFP 9). As an adult, his wish was granted: he always had an analyst to "look after him." The secondary gains of illness that accrued to Pankejeff as a patient assured the continuation of his "problems." Pankejeff worked as an insurance agent for thirty years, but psychoanalysts took up collections for six years to help support him and his wife after his emigration from Russia; as Obholzer discovered, he relied extensively upon royalty payments and a stipend from the Freud Archives in his old age.

Pankejeff's grandiose fantasies of being destiny's favorite came ironically closest to fulfillment, then, in being the psychoanalytic world's most famous patient, corresponded with and sought after. In referring to his financial support, Pankejeff adds, "And I receive free treatment. A whole number of dependencies arise, and that's harmful, of course. It harms the ego, I'd say . . . [Kurt] Eissler [the Director of the Freud Archives] wants to keep track of the case that has become so famous—Freud's most famous case—and see how it ends" (WMCFP 126).

In musing about not just "how it ends," but how it began, Pankejeff repeatedly mentions transference, which he feels encouraged infantilization. Transference, the patient's use of the therapist as a parental surrogate is, in his understanding, "a dangerous thing," "really like being hypnotized," "a falsification of reality" that leaves you "no longer able to make your own decisions" (WMCFP 31, 38, 50, 59). At one point he states that "transference is a positive relationship," but quickly adds, "I believe that psychoanalysis takes you back to childhood, and that you then react more or less like a child" (WMCFP 48); as an adult, "one gets used to living according to another person's guidance . . . [and] submits to authority" (WMCFP 139).

Abraham and Torok pose a "cui bono" question about psychoanalytic theories that appear to be clinically inadequate but which persevere: "What sustains these notions if it is not their contribution to theory? If the patient does not benefit from them, who does?" [26] And, in this context, I would emphasize that "these notions" are sustained by invoking the subject who cannot know: the child. In his interviews with Obholzer, Pankejeff suspects that it is psychoanalysis that did and does benefit, not the patient: "I wrote my memoirs and my case really became a propaganda piece for psychoanalysis" (WMCFP 185). "The disciples of psychoanalysis should not have laid hold of me after Freud. [They should have left me alone] because I would have acted more independently. This outside interference has not had a good effect" (WMCFP 137). Nonetheless, psychoanalysis was the life support to which he clung.

For Sergei Pankejeff, psychoanalysis never let go, as his grotesquely humorous last recorded words suggest: Obholzer reports that, during the last months of his life, "He holds on to me as if I could keep him alive. 'Give me some advice! Help me!' He keeps gasping the same phrases. . . . When I have to leave at the end of visiting hours, he won't let me go. 'Give me some advice!' he calls after me" (WMCFP 247). No adult intervened; the best-advised man-child in the history of psychoanalysis died.

In briefly sketching some of the ways in which Sergei Pankejeff remained what Freud called "our little boy" (HIN 558) and in which that status served the interests of Freud, his early followers, and the establishment of psychoanalysis itself, I am not suggesting that psychoanalysis, as a system of thought and therapeutic practice, is thereby discredited. My interest, rather, is in coming to understand how analysis's own insights can be brought to bear upon the historical and cultural forces that shape its very articulation and implementation in the United States. By questioning the development of the therapist as well as that of the patient, by scrutinizing the traces of counter-transference as well as transference, we address the asymmetry of authority in this most intimate of relationships and in larger cultural constellations. We, like Freud, all too often issue the paradoxical command Stanley Fish summarizes, in *Withholding the Missing Portion,* as "Be independent, rely entirely on me" in our personal and national fictions (158).

Pankejeff, with his "lack of independence and his incapacity for dealing with life" (HIN 549), was undoubtedly predisposed to find in analysis, as he had earlier found in his family and in his religious obsession, a structure that would support and maintain his passivity. His suspicion that he "might have acted more independently" without this "outside interference," however, is not without grounds. In minimizing Pankejeff's aggression and agency while emphasizing his "dominant masochistic aims" (HIN 594), "over-powerful homosexuality" (HIN 546), passivity, and "feminine" identification (HIN 518), Freud subtly assures the outcome he needs at this particular historical moment for himself and for what would become Freudianism. The headstrong child of a feudal world becomes the infantilized patient and bureaucrat of an industrial one.

We are all Freudians now: the "psychoanalytic" in "psychoanalytic child" almost seems a redundancy, so thoroughly have its concepts been naturalized. The constructed child is the cornerstone of psychoanalysis's foundation, the child who will figure in thousands of subsequent case histories and novels. The assumptions of analysis in turn become the authorization for a host of social, legal, and educational measures that shape children individually and collectively. At this time in our country's history, who will speak for the child is the focus of intense national debate. Domestic policies deny education, medical care, and food to children with the ostensible goal of fostering independent development; international conflict is sanctified by invoking the well-being of other countries' children (and women). Our basic presuppositions about a de facto infantilized group demand renewed critical attention; our good intentions must always be paired with self-conscious skepticism about the consolidation of authority through any cultural system. And Freud sets forth the key issues of our own dilemma brilliantly in *From the History of an Infantile Neurosis.*

NOTES
My thanks to James Catano, Irene DiMaio, Katharine Jensen, and Anna Nardo for their comments on versions of this essay.

1. Sigmund Freud, *From the History of an Infantile Neurosis,* in *Collected Papers,* vol. 3 (1918), ed. Ernest Jones, trans. under supervision of Joan Riviere (New York: Basic Books, 1959).

2. There are three texts central to this discussion: Freud's case history, *From the History of an Infantile Neurosis;* Pankejeff's anonymous autobiography, *The Wolf-Man by the Wolf-Man: The Double Story of Freud's Most Famous Case* (with "The Case of the Wolf-Man," by Sigmund Freud, and "A Supplement," by Ruth Mack Brunswick), ed. Muriel Gardiner (New York: Basic Books, 1971); and *The Wolf-Man: Conversations with Freud's Patient Sixty Years Later,* a series of interviews conducted by Karin Obholzer, a journalist, and trans. Michael Shaw (New York: Continuum, 1982). Hereafter the case history is referred to as HIN, the autobiography as WM, and the interviews as WMCFP, and page numbers will be cited parenthetically in the text.

3. Nathan Hale, *Freud and the Americans: The Beginnings of Psychoanalysis in the United States, 1876–1917* (New York: Oxford University Press, 1971), 366.

4. James Kincaid, *Child-Loving: The Erotic Child and Victorian Literature* (New York: Routledge, 1992), 5. The concept of the child as floating signifier can seem as implausible as that of the child with angelic wings until we think of the way in which common phrases such as "But she's only a child" can be the focal point of lively debate about acts committed at two or at twenty. See also Leslie Fiedler, "Good Good Girls and Good Bad Boys: Clarissa as a Juvenile" in his classic *Love and Death in the American Novel* (New York: Stein and Day, 1975), 259–90; Virginia Blum, *The Child between Psychoanalysis and Fiction* (Urbana: University of Illinois Press, 1995); Laura Berry, *The Child, the State, and the Victorian Novel* (Charlottesville: University Press of Virginia, 1999); and Carolyn Steedman, *Childhood, Culture and Class in Britain: Margaret McMillan, 1860–1931* (New Brunswick, N.J.: Rutgers University Press, 1990) for cogent analyses about the cultural uses of the child and various intersections of literary, educational, psychological, medical, and legal understandings.

5. Sigmund Freud, "The Relation of the Poet to Day-Dreaming," in *Collected Papers,* vol. 4 (1903), 174. See Dominick LaCapra's "History and Psychoanalysis," in *The Trial(s) of Psychoanalysis,* ed. Françoise Meltzer, *Critical Inquiry* 13, no. 2 (1987): 222–51.

6. Willian Kerrigan, introduction to *Opening Texts; Psychoanalysis and the Culture of the Child,* ed. Joseph H. Smith and William Kerrigan (Baltimore: Johns Hopkins University Press, 1985), xii; hereafter, page numbers will be cited parenthetically in the text.

7. Hale, *Freud and the Americans,* 17. Freud was originally nearly euphoric about the United States because the Americans lavished upon him the recognition he was refused in Europe. America's equally fervent embracing of C. G. Jung, penchant for experimental psychology, and emphasis upon controlled outcome (and hence depreciation of the unconscious) eventually cooled his ardor. Startled by the puritanism of the United States, Freud, as Murray Sherman observes, "was particularly distressed at the tendency in American psychiatry merely to incorporate psychoanalysis as one component in a cover-all eclecticism." See Sherman, *Psychoanalysis in America: Historical Perspectives* (Springfield, Ill.: Charles C. Thomas, 1966), 4.

8. In addition to Hale and Sherman, see Frederick Hoffman, "The Spread of Freud's Theory," in *Freudianism and the Literary Mind*, 2d ed. (Baton Rouge: Louisiana State University Press, 1967), 146–221, for a fine overview of U.S. reception. The information about Menninger's eighteen-month stint as an advice columnist is part of a current project by Jessamyn Hatcher based upon materials in the Menninger archives, tentatively titled *Psychoanalysis and Everyday Life: The Popularization of Psychoanalysis in the United States, 1909–35*. For descriptions of the premises and goals of earlier advice modes, see the U.S. Victorian examples cited by Peter Gay in *The Education of the Senses*, vol. 1 of *The Bourgeois Experience: Victoria to Freud* (New York: Oxford University Press, 1984), 323–25. See also Michel Foucault's discussion about the "pedagogization of children's sex," which simultaneously presented it as "natural" and "contrary to nature"; Foucault, *The History of Sexuality*, trans. Robert Hurley (New York: Pantheon, 1978), 104; hereafter, page numbers will be cited parenthetically in the text. See Alice Miller, "Sexual Abuse of the Child: The Story of the Wolf-Man," in *Thou Shalt Not Be Aware* (New York: Farrar, Straus and Giroux, 1987), 158–72; in this chapter Miller forcefully argues that what she elsewhere in her book calls "poisonous pedagogy" (26) is still integral to much of contemporary psychotherapy.

9. Peter Coveney, *The Image of Childhood: The Individual and Society: A Study of the Theme in English Literature*. (New York: Penguin, 1967), 306.

10. Michael Goldman, "Eyolf's Eyes: Ibsen and the Cultural Meanings of Child Abuse" *American Imago* 51, no. 3 (1994): 279–305. Kincaid describes memory as "itself a storytelling agency, a collection of narratives we can call on for various purposes"; see *Child-Loving*, 22. In discussing the latter decades of the nineteenth century, Coveney identifies what is still one of the most powerful of those purposes, "to create a barrier of nostalgia and regret between childhood and the potential responses of adult life. The child indeed becomes a means of escape from the pressures of adult adjustment, a means of regression towards the irresponsibility of youth, childhood, infancy, and ultimately nescience itself"; see Coveney, *The Image of Childhood*, 240. Anne MacLeod, like Coveney, notes that adults can use children—and their images—to withdraw from responsibility. See MacLeod, "An End to Innocence: The Transformation of Childhood in Twentieth-Century Children's Literature," in Smith and Kerrigan, eds., *Opening Texts*, 110–17. What Coveney sees as a risk, however, MacLeod sees as a reality. Because adults refuse "to accept the burden of responsibility" that creates the moratorium we call childhood, the realistic literature of divorce, disappointment, and disenfranchisement "is fundamentally anti-child" (115).

11. Lionel Trilling, "Freud and Literature," in *The Liberal Imagination* (New York: Doubleday/Anchor, 1950), 35.

12. Sigmund Freud, "A Child Is Being Beaten: A Contribution to the Study of the Origin of Sexual Perversions," in *Collected Papers*, vol. 2 (1919), 184.

13. Sigmund Freud and Josef Bruer, *Studies in Hysteria*, in *The Standard Edition of the Complete Psychological Works of Sigmund Freud*, vol. 2 (1893–95), trans. and ed. James Strachey et al. (London: Hogarth Press, 1974), 117, n. 1.

14. Sigmund Freud, "On Narcissism: An Introduction," in *Collected Papers*, vol. 4 (1914), 48.

15. The ongoing debate about whether and why Freud shifted his emphasis on actual abuse to fantasy, and the contemporary storm centering on "recovered memory," are beyond the scope of this essay, although they obviously bear upon it. For an excellent overview of contemporary ramifications, see Janice Doane and Devon Hodges, *Telling Incest: Narratives of Dangerous Remembering from Stein To Sapphire* (Ann Arbor: University of Michigan Press, 2001). Jeffrey Masson, *The Assault on Truth: Freud's Suppression of the Seduction Theory* is the most emphatic accusation of Freud (New York: Penguin, 1985). Kin-

caid is one of many authors who provide a more nuanced account, ceding the relocation of "the origin of the story away from a material scene," but also arguing for a necessary recognition of memory as "infinitely complicated, corrupted," "highly charged and devious." See Kincaid, *Child-Loving,* 248. In specific discussion of the adult/therapist misusing or abusing the child/patient in *From the History of an Infantile Neurosis,* Stanley Fish states, in reference to Pankejeff's thoughts upon first meeting Freud, that "this man is a Jewish swindler, he wants to use me from behind and shit on my head. This paper is dedicated to the proposition that the Wolf-Man got it right." See Fish, "Withholding the Missing Portion: Power, Meaning and Persuasion in Freud's *The History of an Infantile Neurosis,*" in *The Linguistics of Writing: Arguments between Language and Literature,* ed. Nigel Fabb, Derek Attridge, Colin MacCabe, and Alan Durant (New York: Methuen, 1987), 156. Nicolas Abraham and Maria Torok also assert that as "[w]itness to a *real* event, the child is told that it was all a dream, illusion, and fiction." See Abraham and Torok, *The Wolf Man's Magic Word: A Cryptonymy,* trans. Nicholas Rand (Minneapolis: University of Minnesota Press, 1986), 99. This is a point Michael Goldman also develops in "Eyolf's Eyes." Miller sadly cites the case as an instance of "the way a great innovator, laboring under the burden of the pedagogical principles he has internalized, pits his own intellect against what he knows to be true"; see Miller, "Sexual Abuse," 158.

16. Freud, "Poetry and Language," in *Collected Papers,* vol. 4 (1917), 359.

17. Carolyn Steedman, *Strange Dislocations: Childhood and the Idea of Human Interiority, 1780–1930* (Cambridge, Mass.: Harvard University Press, 1995), 88. Steven Marcus, *Freud and the Culture of Psychoanalysis: Studies in the Transition from Victorian Humanism to Modernity* (New York: W. W. Norton, 1984), 23.

18. Various clinicians have suggested that Pankejeff's problems were far greater than those identified by "infantile neurosis" and have offered alternative diagnoses ranging from obsessive-compulsive disorder, through generalized mood disorders, to borderline personality or pre-oedipal problems. For the most current bibliography on literature relating specifically to Pankejeff, see Whitney Davis, *Drawing the Dream of the Wolves: Homosexuality, Interpretation, and Freud's "Wolf Man"* (Bloomington: Indiana University Press, 1995), 241–56.

19. Carl Schorske notes the period preceding Pankejeff's analysis (and the outbreak of World War I) as a time of professional, political, and personal crises ranging from attacks upon psychoanalysis, through increasing anti-Semitism, to the death of his father. See Schorske, *Fin-de-Siècle Vienna: Politics and Culture* (New York: Knopf, 183–207). Sander Gilman makes some of the same points, particularly in relation to Freud's Jewishness, in *The Case of Sigmund Freud: Medicine and Identity at the Fin de Siècle* (Baltimore: Johns Hopkins University Press, 1993), 11–68. Lesley Dickson's videotape for therapists in training on this case history includes a fascinating dramatization of the "inner circle's" workshop discussion about the validity of Freud's interpretation, as well as about the weight he was placing upon screen memory. It also includes a vivid depiction of the Wolf Man, clad in a flowing poet's shirt, as well as voice-over narrating Freud's letter to Sandor Ferenczi, in which he insists upon the importance of this case—and its successful outcome—for the future of psychoanalysis. See Dickson, "What Means the Dream?" two videocassettes (Lexington, Ky.: Department of Psychiatry, University of Kentucky College of Medicine, 1993).

20. The process of being encouraged to speak out, and then being told that there was no event, or that the event was not what one thought it was, is of course repeated within the analytic frame, where the analyst is both another man that Pankejeff does not want to make angry and the court of appeal for the damages wrought by the first man, his father. And yet the analyst, too, is testifying, in this instance to the epistemological authority of

trauma. In his account, as in the patient's, there is the potential for merging fantasy and reality. If indeed the case history of Sergei Pankejeff is one in which the central puzzle is linguistic and the best translator wins, then there is indeed always the "possibility of yet another interpretation," yet another authoritative analysis. This possibility is embodied by the organization of Abraham and Torok's *The Wolf Man's Magic Word,* in which their analysis is framed by that of Jacques Derrida's "Fors," which is framed in turn by Barbara Johnson's "Foreword." The concatenation of interpretation presented by the golden-goose chain—Pankejeff, Freud, Abraham and Torok, Derrida, Johnson, and other inter-preters, and ourselves as readers—creates a rhetorical funhouse of possibilities.

21. See Carlo Ginzburg's discussion of the caul's significance, as well as of the crucial allusions during analysis to fairy tales that Freud would not have known, in "Freud, the Wolf-Man, and the Werewolves," in *Clues, Myths, and the Historical Method,* trans. John and Anne C. Tedeschi (Baltimore: Johns Hopkins University Press, 1992), 147–48, 149.

22. Sigmund Freud, "Resistances to Psycho-Analysis," in *Collected Papers,* vol. 5 (1925), 172.

23. Mahony notes that it is only in 1977 that a commentator makes the "obvious demurral" about the child Sergei's ability to recognize that his mother had no penis if his father was mounting from behind. See Mahony, *Cries of the Wolf Man* (New York: International Universities Press, 1984), 52; hereafter, page numbers will be cited parenthetically in the text. Janine Chasseguet-Smirgel makes the same point in "A Re-Reading of 'The Wolf Man,'" in *Creativity and Perversion* (New York: W. W. Norton, 1984), 44. I have not found any commentary on what seems to me an equally incredible claim in the reconstruction: intercourse three times in a half hour.

24. Derrida, "Fors," in Abraham and Torok, *The Wolf Man's Magic Word,* xv. Derrida's essay, like Johnson's "Foreword" to the same study, views the case as a linguistic conundrum, a "cryptograph" whose link to the "crypt" is more metaphoric than actual ("Fors," n. 20; Johnson's "Foreword" hereafter cited parenthetically in the text). Fish's exegesis also em-phasizes language's role, as does Lila Kalinich in "Where is Thy Sting? Some Reflections on the Wolf-man," in *Lacan and the Subject of Language,* ed. Ellie Ragland-Sullivan and March Bracher (New York: Routledge, 1991), 167–87.

25. In the case history, Pankejeff is constituted as an upper-class, masculine—and hetero-sexual—male through his droit-du-seigneur intercourse with maids, his aggression against all women and, least persuasively, his heterosexual "breakthrough to the woman" after a period of impotence. For a detailed and wide-ranging analysis of the last, see Davis's outstanding *Drawing the Dream of the Wolves,* as well as Miller's brief comments in "Sexual Abuse," 167.

26. Abraham and Torok, *The Wolf Man's Magic Word,* 85.

8 Black Babies, White Hysteria

The Dark Child in African-American Literature
of the Harlem Renaissance

Laura Dawkins

In a collection of horror stories for children, *More Short and Shivery: Thirty Terrifying Tales,* Robert D. San Souci retells an old New Orleans folktale about a young wife whose longing for a baby remains unfulfilled until she discovers an orphan in the woods—a "handsome" infant boy "swaddled in sky-blue cloth, with skin as white as milk." But the woman's joy at this unexpected answer to her prayers is short-lived, for when she picks up the crying baby, a shocking metamorphosis takes place: "No perfect infant with milk-white skin was in her arms. Instead she was holding something that was all black and shiny and ugly—like some beetle. . . . Poor Odette was so frightened she nearly died on the spot." Dropping the "black thing," who gives "a yell like forty devils," Odette flees the woods forever. Entitled "The Thing in the Woods," this "scary" story for children, in which the object of horror is a "perfect" white baby who suddenly becomes black (and simultaneously demonic) is presented without preface or apology; indeed, the author apparently revives the early twentieth-century Southern folktale because of its ability to inspire terror.[1]

It is not difficult to find disturbing connections between San Souci's tale of a "milk-white" infant transformed into a "black thing" (and subsequently rejected), and Patricia Williams's account in *The Alchemy of Race and Rights* of an American white woman who—declaring that her "insemination became a tragedy and her life a nightmare"—claimed damages from her sperm bank when she gave birth to a black child. Reflecting on "this case about the nightmare of giving birth to a black child," Williams states, "It is interesting to examine the image it evokes, the vision of white mothers rushing to remedy the depreciation of their offspring in suits about the lost properties of their children's bodies."[2] Continuing her meditation on "depreciated children" in *The Rooster's Egg*, Williams notes that the fee scales of some adoption agencies vary considerably, depending upon the racial designation of the child requested—thus establishing a "sickening . . . price system for 'goods,' a sale for chattel, linked not to services but to the imagined quality of the 'things' exchanged." Conceding "this system was devised to provide 'economic incentives' for the adoption of 'less-requested' children," Williams maintains that, nevertheless, "in our shopping-mall world it had all the earmarks of a two-for-one sale." She concludes that "the market valuation of children is reiterated at every level of social and legal thinking," and wonders, "what is the escape route to the future for 'cheap' black bodies, for those whose existence is continually devalued?"[3]

Accounts of black bodies being devalued or demonized within American culture have been well documented by historians such as Winthrop Jordan, George Frederickson, and Joel Williamson.[4] Less familiar, however, is a startlingly large group of folktales, stories, and anecdotes (such as the original version of San Souci's tale) that focus specifically on the black baby as an emblem of horror, disruption, or simply imperfection—the antithesis of "perfect" milk-white babies. Emerging during the late nineteenth and early twentieth centuries, "black baby" tales reflected (and fueled) the racial hysteria of a period now acknowledged as the lowest point of black-white relations in the United States.[5] Judith Berzon has described how white supremacists at the turn of the century promoted "Negrophobia" by adopting and distorting Darwin's concept of "reversion"—the principle "by which long-lost dormant structures are called back into existence." According to Berzon, white racists (particularly the "Radicalists" of the American South)[6] embraced a "pseudo-scientific concept of 'atavism'"—the notion that the Negro or mulatto, despite "[his] veneer of white civilization," can unexpectedly "'revert' to the savage, primitivistic behavior of the jungle."[7] Spawning a number of apocryphal accounts of black sexual marauders, the ideology of "atavism" also inspired several cautionary fables about coal-black babies born to white (or nearly white) mothers. Chiefly designed to warn injudicious white women against the dangers of mates without pedigrees, "black baby" fables played upon white racists' fears that an "invisible drop of Negro blood" in a parent—as the protagonist of radicalist Thomas Dixon's *The Leopard's Spots* authoritatively declares—can produce infant "reversions to type": "I happen to know the important fact that a man or woman of Negro ancestry, though a century removed, will suddenly breed back to a pure Negro child, thick-lipped, kinky-headed, flat-nosed, black-skinned."[8]

"Black baby" fables typically recount the downfall of women found guilty either of miscegenation or of "passing." In her autobiography, Ida B. Wells relates a widely circulated "piece of propaganda" that was "intended to keep white women from letting colored women join their clubs." Entitled "The Rushing In of Fools," this "news item" (published in the General Federation of Women's Clubs newsletter in 1900) describes how the integration of a women's club in "a certain city" led to the social interaction, and eventual marriage, of the white club president's daughter and a nearly white club member's son. Called to her daughter's home after the birth of the couple's first child, the club president discovers that her daughter has given birth to a "jet-black" baby, and has consequently "passed away": "The shock was so great that the young mother turned her face to the wall and died."[9] Similarly punished for an incautious union, a white woman in Southern novelist Robert Lee Durham's *The Call of the South* descends into madness when her secret marriage to an "all-but-white" mulatto produces a baby "the color of Ethiopia . . . a recession below the father's type!" The mother is committed to an insane asylum and spends her days in suicidal despair, "violently clawing at herself as she shrieks, 'kill me. . . . *Save* me! My baby was black, black!'"[10] In another white-authored "black baby" tale—Gertrude Atherton's *Senator North*—the fear of producing a dark child haunts a "passing" mulatto, who sinks for a moment into a death-like stupor when her white cousin tells her ("A terrible thing to have to say—but I must") that a child of her marriage to a white man might turn out "coal-black"; the mulatto ultimately drowns herself.[11] These sensationalistic pieces of fiction, clearly dramatizing the hysterical racial climate of the era, slipped into obscurity with the demise of radicalism and the rise of the "new Negro" of the Harlem Renaissance.

Yet several tales by Harlem Renaissance writers are eerily reminiscent of the white-authored "black baby" fables. Eloise Bibb Thompson's "Masks," for example, describes a light-skinned mulatto who "screams" in "horror" and collapses when she is presented with her "chocolate-colored" newborn infant; the inscription on her tombstone reads, "She died at the sight of her own babe's face."[12] Similarly, a "semi-white" mother in Wallace Thurman's *The Blacker the Berry*, "abysmally stunned" by the blackness of her newborn daughter, shuns her child as an "alien," a "tragic mistake which could not be stamped out or eradicated."[13] In Jessie Fauset's *Comedy American Style*, a light-skinned African-American woman initially denies her biological tie to her dark-skinned infant son ("That's not my baby!") and later tries to "forget he was hers"; the rejected son ultimately commits suicide.[14] Finally, in Marita Bonner's short story "On the Altar," an almost-white mother, discovering her pale daughter's secret marriage to a dark-brown man, conspires with a doctor to abort the couple's unborn child: "I won't be the grandmother of any black bastard!" [15]

Such tales of cataclysmic births are clearly more than meditations on the perils of "passing" or satires of "white fever" among light-skinned African Americans. Probing not only the self-alienation of the mulatto whose indoctrination into "white" ideology is so complete that she turns away from the reflection of blackness that her dark child gives back to her, Harlem Renaissance writers also examine racism as an all-pervasive societal disease—one capable of destroying deep filial connections. Frenzied attempts to submerge or repress blackness within light-skinned African-American families recall the larger society's maniacal attempts to contain "the rising tide of color" during the years after Reconstruction. Indeed, as Hazel Carby has pointed out, many black writers in the late nineteenth and early twentieth centuries used the figure of the mulatto as a "narrative device of mediation," a "vehicle for the exploration of the relationship between the races" within an increasingly segregated American society.[16] As a more accessible subject than the white Negrophobe, then, the "color-struck" mulatto implicitly functions as the fictional representative of the (absent) white world, while her "dark child" represents the repudiated American "new citizen"—the object of racist hatred and fear. Although Williamson, in *The Crucible of Race,* has contended that a "necessary" forgetfulness of the "depth of racism in those turn-of-the-century years" (321) characterized the following decades, black-authored dark child tales reflect a continuing sense of racial crisis among Harlem Renaissance writers. Certainly, their apparent mimicry of white-authored "black baby" stories indicates a self-conscious attempt both to burlesque and to anatomize American racial hysteria. The hopeful birth of the "new Negro," these writers suggest, is fraught with peril.

The Negrophobia that Harlem Renaissance writers parody or deplore in dark child tales emerges in mainstream fiction even before the Civil War. Perhaps the first white-authored "black baby" story is "Stealing a Baby," by Southwest humorist Henry Clay Lewis. In this slapstick tale, a medical student appropriates the body of a black baby from the school's morgue—a "subject" to "dissect" in his "private room"—only to have the "infernal imp of darkness" roll out of his cloak in the presence of his fiancée and her father. The dead black baby, who seems to come alive as it "burst[s]" out of "its envelope," disrupts the young man's life: the horrified father and daughter depart, the engagement is broken off, and the student is nearly expelled from medical school. Establishing ownership over his "subject," Lewis's "scientist," intent upon "anatomizing" the passive black body, is ultimately undone by a dead baby who becomes a decidedly active agent.[17]

Metaphorically invoking white Southerners' anxieties about their ability to maintain control over a potentially disruptive black population, Lewis's antebellum tale reflects race issues that would increasingly dominate the writings of Southern politicians and social scientists during the latter part of the nineteenth century. Indeed, literal black babies were the focus of much white racist concern during this period. In *The Black Image in the White Mind*, Frederickson reports that the census of 1880, which "appeared to demonstrate that the rate of increase of Southern Negroes was substantially greater than that of the whites"(239), alarmed many white Southerners, and that in *Popular Science Monthly*, Dr. William Gilliam foresaw a "racial cataclysm," the rise of a "dark, swelling, muttering mass" of Negroes (240). Similarly, a Virginia historian predicted a "black peril," since "the blacks of the South will continue to expand numerically at an alarming rate"(244). Myths about the "remarkable fecundity of the African" also fueled racist panic about black population growth (24).

Just a few years later, however, census figures (of 1890) contradicted earlier results, revealing, as Frederickson notes, "that blacks were in fact increasing at a rate substantially below that of whites" and had "a very high death rate" (245–46). Yet the issue of racial competition continued to preoccupy white racist writers, who now eagerly reversed their former speculations. Frederickson has described how white supremacists of the late nineteenth and early twentieth centuries embraced a "Darwinian view" of race and species survival (231), and anticipated the ultimate demise of the American Negro—vanquished in an unequal contest for the "survival of the fittest" (247). According to Williamson, widespread belief in the destined extinction of the American Negro contributed to escalating racial oppression and violence against African Americans at the turn of the century: "If the blacks were a degenerating race with no future, the problem ceased to be one of how to prepare them for citizenship. . . . By appealing to a simplistic Darwinian or hereditarian formula, white Americans could make their crimes against humanity appear as contributions to the inevitable unfolding of biological destiny" (255). Indeed, many white supremacists of the period took it upon themselves to accelerate the progress of "biological destiny." Williamson has recorded that the closing years of the nineteenth century saw a "sudden and dramatic rise in the lynching of black men" (117), as well as an unprecedented mushrooming of one-sided race riots. Genocidal violence was accompanied by eugenics campaigns that targeted the "unfit" Negro sectors of the American population; in fact, some Southern racists offered the "proposal to sterilize all black females" as a solution to the race problem (214).

Genocidal violence, social Darwinism, and eugenics crusades undoubtedly had a profound impact upon black writers of the early twentieth century. Yet the recurring image of the endangered and devalued black child in literature of this period, central to such plays about lynching as Angelina Weld Grimké's *Rachel* and Georgia Douglas Johnson's *A Sunday Morning in the South*,[18] also emerges in tales of intraracial relationships, specifically in fictional portraits of "blue-veins" (light-skinned mulattoes who consciously separate themselves from Negro society as a whole). While Theodore Roosevelt and his followers during the early part of the century worried about blacks "outbreeding" whites,[19] black writers conversely deplored the calculated "breeding out" of blackness within light-skinned African-American families, whose dedication to the repression and containment of unruly "dark elements" disturbingly mirrors the racial obsessions of American white supremacists in the late nineteenth century.

The "credo" of "blue-veins," as Wallace Thurman describes it in *The Blacker the Berry,* clearly resembles the vision of racial annihilation painted by white "Darwinists" or eugenicists in the last decade of the nineteenth century. In 1893, white physician Dr. Eugene Rollins Corson foresaw a "process of fusion and assimilation" by which American "blackness" would ultimately disappear: "There will be a great loss of life, but there will be a Caucasianized element becoming larger and larger up to a certain point . . . where it will be hard to trace the alien blood." Other white "experts" of the period also hopefully predicted a "gradual whitening of the south," an obliteration of the Negro through "the dual process of elimination and absorption."[20] Similarly, the "blue-veins" described in *The Blacker the Berry* make "a conscious effort to eliminate the darker elements" in their families or social circles (29), and adopt the phrase "whiter and whiter every generation" as their "motto" (19). As Thurman explains, the goal of "breeding out" blackness necessitates judicious genetic screening of potential marriage partners: "It was found expedient [among light-skinned blacks] to exercise caution when it came to mating" (58).

Certainly, one might regard the "whiter and whiter" credo of Thurman's "blue-veins" not as a genocidal ideology, but as a sign of the mulatto's attempt to escape a dual identity, and to assimilate successfully into the larger society. What transforms Thurman's novel from a light mockery of the "colorstruck" black bourgeoisie into a chilling analysis of internalized "white" values among African Americans is the tragic role of the black-skinned protagonist Emma Lou—the "mistake" in her pale family's carefully constructed genetic plan. The "dark child" Emma Lou, the "alien member of the family" (22), recognizes her role as a symbol of disruption and disorder—unruly blackness—within a society striving to "guard against unwelcome and degenerating encroachments" (19): "[she] had been born into a semi-white world, surrounded by an all-white one, and those few dark elements that had forced their way in had . . . been shooed away" (13). Frequently "hidden away . . . on occasions when [her mother] was to have company" (221), the child Emma Lou soon decides that "there was no place in the world for a girl as black as she" (26). Emma Lou's family members associate whiteness with order and regulation, the successful working out of their generational scheme; blackness, on the other hand, signifies an intrusion of chaos into order, a dismantling of their master design. This family of "blue-veins," therefore, reflects the views of a much larger population: the white racists who view the elimination of blackness as "biological destiny," and who see "no place" in their national design for the black American.

Like Thurman's *The Blacker the Berry,* Eloise Bibb Thompson's "Masks" portrays a destructive intrafamilial campaign to eradicate the black "curse" in mulatto offspring. Describing the fatal obsession with color of the "quadroon" Julie, who screams and dies when presented with her dark newborn infant, "Masks" appears to burlesque "The Rushing In of Fools"—the club women's story in which a white mother dies of shock after giving birth to a black baby. For Julie, who marries the whitest man she can find (an "octoroon" as "fair as a lily") and who, as an expectant mother, resembles "an experimentalist in the matter of cross breeds, painfully nervous . . . over the outcome of a situation that she had been planning so long" (302), the blackness of her child represents a cataclysmic failure of calculation, the triumph of unpredictable and disruptive nature over eugenics. The baby's dark face— "identical with the one in the locket about her neck . . . the image of her chocolate-colored mother"—mocks Julie's campaign to efface unwelcome bloodlines and to conceal her own racial heritage. Unable to be safely hidden (like the mother's image inside the locket), Julie's child announces his ancestry to the world.

Tracing Julie's design from its inception in the mind of her grandfather (who wants to create a white "mask" that will disguise his own blackness) to its culmination in his granddaughter's elaborate genetic scheme and its fatal results, "Masks" demonstrates how the "blight" (302) of American racism is passed down from generation to generation. Inherited racial obsessions in "Masks" create literal madness: under the "baneful influence" of her grandfather Aristile during "her formative years," the young Julie—infected by the "half-crazed" notions of Aristile's "distorted mind" (301–302)—develops a hysteria about blackness that ultimately kills her. The ludicrous tale of Julie's death from shock not only parodies sensationalistic white-authored cautionary fables such as "The Rushing In of Fools," but also—more seriously— comments upon the diseased vision that transforms a new baby's face into a terrifying specter.

Jessie Fauset's *Comedy American Style,* like Thurman's *The Blacker the Berry* and Thompson's "Masks," ostensibly targets intraracial color prejudice, yet emerges as a disturbing portrait of American Negrophobia. In Fauset's novel, the light-skinned mulatto Olivia—who obsessively desires "white children" so that "the tenuous bonds holding her never so slightly to her group . . . [would be] perceptibly weakened" (29, 37)—is devastated by her delivery of a "bronze" third child, and sinks into a "black, though silent" rage after his birth. Named (before birth) for his mother, Oliver is Olivia's dark double, the visible evidence of a racial heritage she despises and denies. For Olivia, Oliver represents "shame," the "expression of her failure to be truly white" (205), and she consistently "contrive[s] not to be seen on the street with him" (42). Sent as a "tiny child, a baby" to "the house of first one grandparent and then another" (221), Oliver—like Emma Lou in *The Blacker the Berry*—represents the "mistake" in a mulatto mother's plan to produce white children, and is consequently banished.

Yet Olivia's Negrophobia is much more virulent and deep-seated than that of Emma Lou's mother; indeed, her racist musings sometimes resemble those of characters in Southern radicalist fiction. Convinced that "any union [with black people] mean[s] the introduction into the social order of something corrupt, repulsive" (206), Olivia affirms that she would rather see [her pale daughter] dead" than married to a black man—sentiments that echo those of the Thomas Dixon character, Tom Camp (from *The Leopard's Spots*), whose daughter is killed in an attempt to rescue her from the clutches of a black man: "There are things worse than death!" (quoted in Williamson, 143). Olivia also recalls another character from radicalist fiction—the maddened Helen in Robert Lee Durham's *The Call of the South,* who claws at herself (in Lady Macbeth fashion) after her black baby's birth, shrieking, "The poison of your [her mulatto husband's] blood is in my veins and will not come out! It is polluted, forever polluted!" Fauset's Olivia is similarly "frightened" to think "that within her veins, her arteries, her blood vessels, coursed enough black blood to produce a child with skin as shadowed as Oliver's," and she shrinks in horror from this evidence of "the black blood which she so despised" (205). Fearing the "taint" of blackness, the "corruption" of an American society infiltrated by "repulsive" elements, Olivia is clearly no mere "color snob" or "blue-vein," but a rabid Negrophobe—an ironic twin of Durham's mad Helen.

Yet why does Fauset, who dissects racism in *Comedy American Style* as a mental disorder—the "hateful," "ruthless," and "terrible obsession" that warps Olivia's character and estranges her from her family (144)—displace her indictment of white racism onto a "passing" mixed-race character? Although Fauset approaches a topic that, according to Toni Morrison, remains largely "avoided and unanalyzed" in American writings about race—"the effect of racist inflection on the subject"[21]—Olivia's mulatto identity calls into question her status as "subject" rather than "object" of racism; indeed, Olivia's personal experience of racial stigmatization as a child has shaped her own racist mentality, her desire to separate herself from Americans on the margin. Unfortunately, by examining the internalized "white" values of mulatto characters, writers such as Thurman, Thompson, and Fauset become vulnerable to charges that their "domestic" fiction remains fixated upon social distinctions within the African-American community—shirking the treatment of racial tensions in the larger society. However, the exclusionary blue-vein families in the works of these writers, functioning as microcosms of a racially divided America, clearly reflect a racial crisis of national dimensions. And by displacing the American race conflict onto the domestic arena, Thurman, Thompson, and Fauset perhaps circumvented the censorship (by nervous publishers) that threatened more direct and outspoken treatments of white racism during the early twentieth century—as the case of Walter White's controversial first novel illustrates. White's *The Fire in the Flint*—which "exposed the barbarity of [the] South . . . with scorching indignation," according to David Levering Lewis[22]—was originally considered too inflammatory for publication. After the long wrangle that finally resulted in the book's appearance in 1924, other Harlem Renaissance writers may have decided to err on the side of caution in their portrayals of racial turmoil.

Black writers who explored intraracial tensions or the psychological conflicts of African-American characters may have pacified would-be censors, but their indirect or ambiguous strategies for exposing racial strife inevitably led to misunderstandings of their intentions by black as well as white audiences. While Fauset has been criticized for an excessive preoccupation with color-consciousness among middle-class African Americans,[23] another Harlem Renaissance writer—Angelina Weld Grimké—was charged with race betrayal for her depiction (in *Rachel*) of an African-American woman who vows that she will never bring black children into the world. Clearly startled and offended when the play's black reviewers accused her of advocating race suicide, Grimké insisted that *Rachel* was directed "not primarily to the colored people, but to the whites." That one "sensitive, highly strung" character's sorrowful renunciation of motherhood within a racist society could be seen as an endorsement of genocide demonstrates how controversial and politicized the subject of African-American reproduction had become in the early decades of the twentieth century.[24]

For the "new Negro" of the twenties, the black baby was a beacon for the future, a sign of the strength and resilience of the African American—living proof that the race had survived both enslavement and the genocidal violence following Reconstruction. A metaphor not only for the endurance of a people deemed "unfit" by racial Darwinists at the turn of the century, the black baby also represented the newly emergent racial consciousness of the Harlem Renaissance. Gregory Holmes Singleton has pointed out that African-American poetry of the period is dense with references to "birth and rebirth" and with "themes of generation and regeneration"; indeed, "images of infants springing immediately from birth to join the struggle, and the concept of the race as the children of a new-born awareness are found throughout *The New Negro* (1925) and *The Book of American Negro Poetry* (1922)." [25] During an era in which the fictional black baby served as a symbol of survival and an affirmation of racial pride, it is perhaps not surprising that Rachel's tragic acknowledgment of her loss of faith in a hopeful future for her own black children was immediately misinterpreted.

In one of the most celebrated works of the Harlem Renaissance—Jean Toomer's *Cane*[26]—the black baby functions not merely as a metaphor for "new Negro" consciousness but also as a symbol of racial redemption. Indeed, Toomer transforms the dark child's "taint" into a cloak of destiny. If, on one hand, writers such as Thompson, Thurman, Fauset, and Grimké suggest that the black child in a white world remains marked irrevocably by racial alienation, Toomer, on the other hand, envisions a messianic role for the dark pariah. He portrays a racially divided American South that awaits the healing and regenerative touch of the black messiah (in "Esther") or the mixed-race "new American" (in "Becky"). For Toomer, who inverts racist associations of blackness with terror, disruption, or pollution, the dark child represents a regenerative vitality within a spiritless American culture. *Cane*'s "Esther" revises rather than mimics white-authored "dark child" tales: a black baby (who appears in a dream) emerges as a potential savior—an embodiment of an African-American heritage that Esther desires to recover, not repress. Similarly, in "Becky," a white woman's two mulatto sons, ostracized from the town, symbolize a defiant union of races, a crossing of a destructive divide. Describing *Cane* itself as "a spiritual form analogous to the fact of racial intermingling," Toomer prophesies that American society will be redeemed through "infusions" of blackness.[27]

As Cynthia Earl Kerman and Richard Eldridge have observed in their valuable biography of Toomer, the author's view that race crossings enrich American culture grew out of his tenaciously held faith that he himself—a product of a mixed racial heritage—was marked out for a spiritual mission on earth: "Something in me has always been convinced that I am a child of great destiny, that I have a star, that I am led on by it towards a great fulfillment. Nature in America experimented for three hundred years and with millions of blood crossings to produce one man" (quoted in Kerman and Eldridge, 65). The son of a light-skinned African-American father who "passed" when convenient and who abandoned the family shortly after Toomer's birth, the young writer often reimagined his origins. Although he sometimes glamorized his absent father, describing him as "part real, part legendary, a . . . portentous figure quite outside the ordinary run of life," he more often rejected the constraints of a particular familial lineage altogether, declaring that he was "fashioned on no antecedent, but . . . will be a prototype for those to come" (quoted in Kerman and Eldridge, 80). Toomer seemed to find a sense of orphanhood liberating, enabling him to cast himself as a man sent from God—the dark messiah.

Although Toomer's belief that he was without antecedents, a "man at large in the human world, preparing a new race," would increasingly lead him to claim a "supraracial" identity and to deplore a "dualistic" racial consciousness, *Cane* articulates his earlier notion of blackness as a vital and "robust" essence, now endangered by the absorption of the African American into the dominant society. Toomer foresees a time when "negritude" will have vanished in America: "As an entity, the race is loosing [*sic*] its body . . . if anything comes up now, pure Negro, it will be a swansong . . . The supreme fact of mechanical civilization is that you become part of it, or get sloughed off (under)." *Cane,* Toomer acknowledges, is imbued with "sadness derived from a sense of fading," of "futility to check solution."[28] Although the author refers in this passage to the loss of Negro folk culture within an urbanized America, he suggests in "Esther" that the race is literally "losing its body": the "chalk-white" Esther represents "solution," the bleaching-out of visible African roots through "amalgamation." Progressively wilting during the course of the narrative—becoming "listless," "weary," "beaten," and even "pale[r]" than she was as a child (25)—Esther is the vanquished Negro, destined for oblivion within white culture.

But the fading Esther struggles against dissolution by plotting to seduce—and become pregnant by—the "magnetically" black King Barlo, a vagrant preacher whose sermon celebrating the black American's African heritage enthralled her as a young girl. The "magnificent," "immense," "black-skinned" Barlo, who "assumes the outlines of his visioned African" (23), embodies a dynamic power that the "gray," "puny" Esther, whose "cheeks are flat and dead" (22), hopes to claim by bearing his child. In a dream vision, "she alone" rescues from flames a "black, singed, woolly, tobacco-juice baby" (24). Splattered with "scorched tobacco juice," a "saffron fluid" that a crowd of white men (in a sexually suggestive image) "squirt[s] just as fast as they can chew . . . gallons on top of gallons" (24), the baby is in danger of having his blackness diluted or "paled" (as Esther's visible African origins were similarly obscured). The dark child that Esther salvages from the genocidal flames, a "miraculous thing," brings her "joy" (24). Assuming the role of the "black madonna" painted on the courthouse wall after King Barlo's sermon, Esther views a union with Barlo—and the conception of a black baby—as an act of redemption, a means of restoring a lost racial vigor.

Esther's mission to recover her buried heritage and redeem her race clearly links her with the Old Testament queen whose name she shares. The biblical Esther, who changed her Hebrew name (Hadassah) and disguised her Jewish faith in order to become queen within the anti-Semitic Persian kingdom, proclaimed her true identity when the king's prime minister issued a decree calling for the destruction of Jews within the empire. By revealing her Jewish faith to the king, Queen Esther simultaneously recovered her heritage and saved her people. Toomer's Esther, like the biblical queen, approaches "King" Barlo with a similar mission: to reclaim her submerged African identity and to rescue her threatened race by conceiving a baby she imagines as the black messiah. Both Esthers view their missions as ordained—yet perilous— quests. In the Old Testament story, Queen Esther declares that she "will go unto the king, which is against the law, and if I perish, I perish" (Esther 4:17). Similarly, Toomer's Esther—filled with "purpose" and "resolution"—declares that "not [even] if it kills [her]" (26) will she allow her imagined place with Barlo to be usurped by others. However, although the biblical Esther crosses the forbidden boundary separating the King from his subjects and successfully completes her mission, Toomer's Esther remains balked on her side of the color divide separating the "near white" (24) mulatto from the "black-skinned" (22) Barlo. The reactions of Barlo and his companions to Esther's intrusion underscore her alienation from the black community: Barlo asks, "'What brought you here, lil milk-white gal?'" and admonishes, "'This aint th place fer y,'" while a "coarse woman" laughs at the "'gall'" of the "'dictie [higher-class] nigger'" (27).

Excluded from this circle of blackness, Esther herself quails before a world that appears frighteningly alien: the longed-for Barlo is suddenly "hideous" and "repulsive" in her eyes, and she "draws away" (27). Having scaled a long flight of stairs to reach Barlo, as daunting "as if she were mounting to some great height" (26), Esther has clearly embarked on a spiritually portentous mission; but her retreat from a union with the "visioned African" takes her "down" again, back into a world that she discovers has vanished into nothingness: "There is no air, no street, and the town has completely disappeared" (27). Unlike the biblical queen, Esther cannot reclaim her buried heritage; her unstable sense of identity consequently dissolves. The potential Madonna's "dream baby"—a black savior who would redeem a "fading" race—remains unconceived. Tellingly, "Blood-Burning Moon," a story that describes a black man burned to death by white townspeople, follows "Esther" in *Cane*—as if to reinforce the futility of Esther's dream of salvaging a threatened race from genocidal flames.

Transgressing a much more rigid boundary than the intraracial color line that Esther attempts to cross, a white woman in "Becky" has two sons by a black man and is "cast out" from her town. The community advertises Becky's liminal status by placing her in a rickety cabin at the literal border of the town, "the narrow strip of land between the railroad and the road." Yet the pariah Becky is also implicitly reverenced by both black and white townspeople, who secretly feed and shelter her, and give offerings in the form of "crumpled slips of paper scribbled with prayers" (7). By violating the miscegenation taboo, Becky assumes a role as spiritual martyr; the "poor-white crazy woman" (as the black people call her) endures exile for a potentially redemptive act—the bridging of a racial divide. "Becky" prefigures Toomer's later obsession with the creation of a "new order" through mixed-race unions; indeed, the writer envisioned his own marriage to the white Margery Latimer (who declared that her "stomach seems leaping with golden children, millions of them") as a "symbolic union for the creation of an American race." [29]

Like the biblical Rebekah—mother of twin sons Jacob and Esau, destined to become the progenitors, respectively, of the Israelites and the Edomites—Toomer's Becky bears in her womb mulatto sons who represent divided races, "two peoples, going their own ways from birth." [30] As the "ancestral mother of two nations," the New Testament's Rebekah nurtures both the dark-skinned Esau and the light-skinned Jacob; similarly, Becky symbolically reconciles two "nations" by caring for and raising children who simultaneously embody the black world and the white world: "White or colored? No one knew, and least of all themselves" (8). Both an outlaw and a mysterious, otherworldly figure (considered a "hant" by some, since "no one ever saw" her), Becky represents what George Hutchinson calls the "miscegenationist soul" so fascinating to Toomer: the "tabooed, denied, nearly unspoken spirit of a new conception." [31]

Exploring the origins of cultural conceptions of pollution and taboo, Mary Douglas has concluded that, in all societies, "dirt" represents "matter out of place . . . a set of ordered relations and a contravention of that order." Thus, "our pollution behavior is the reaction which condemns any object or idea likely to confuse or contradict cherished classifications." [32] As a "destruction of existing patterns," Becky's miscegenation within a rigidly segregated society becomes an act of defilement. However, as Douglas has further explained, most societies, while punishing transgression of boundaries, nevertheless hold the transgressors in awe: "To have been in the margins is to have been in contact with danger, to have been at a source of power" (96). Since contravention of order signifies "potentiality" as well as destruction, cultures "often sacralize the very unclean things which have been rejected with abhorrence" (159). Accordingly, the sign of "pollution" endows Becky with an aura of spiritual power, as the townspeople's offerings and prayers indicate. The "trembling of the ground" (6) upon which Becky's cabin (near the railroad tracks) stands evokes not only the "danger" of her liminal position, but also the mystical, implicitly sacred force that surrounds her. Embodying both meanings of taboo (the sacred and defiled), Becky serves as the potential herald of a new era.

Yet Becky's mission to reconcile the races by bearing "two nations" in her womb, like Esther's quest to become the black Madonna, is doomed to failure. Although the townspeople provide food for Becky and her sons, they cast out the children just as they earlier cast out the mother; the sons, "sullen and cunning," respond to this treatment by "shooting up two men and leaving town," thus repudiating both races: "Godam the white folks; godam the niggers" (8). When Becky's crumbling cabin falls down around her, the narrator of the story responds by running away; his companion Barlo similarly retreats, pausing only to throw his Bible into the rubble of the cabin. No one comes to retrieve Becky's body; it remains under the pile of rubble, and the Bible "flaps its leaves with an aimless rustle on her mound" (9). But the narrator's tale about Becky, related as a town legend, reveals that her hold over the townspeople is powerful even in death. Her "mound," undisturbed on the "islandized" ground that formed her place of exile (7), becomes a kind of temple, simultaneously sacred and profane: a reminder both of her transgression and her martyrdom. Just as Toomer inverts white authors' use of the "black baby" trope by depicting the "dark child" in "Esther" as a figure of redemption rather than of disruption, so does he turn white racist concepts of "pollution" inside out by suggesting that Becky's miscegenation and conception are acts of cleansing or healing. Like the womb of the biblical Rebekah, whose role as "ancestral mother" is prophesied before her sons' births, Becky's "sullied" womb becomes a sanctified place in which potential new tribes begin.

Providing a positive counter to the tragic or sardonic "dark child" tales of his contemporaries, Toomer's vision of potentially redemptive miscegenation in "Becky" prefigures late twentieth-century fiction that heralds the "hybrid" child as what Susan Gubar calls a "utopian icon of transracial consciousness." Gubar suggests that writers such as Marilyn Hacker, Jane Lazarre, Sherley Anne Williams, and Grace Paley, in portraying the "interdependence as well as the merging of races through the complicated two-in-oneness of the [white] mother/[black] child dyad," imagine a "panracial antidote to racism, an intersubjective solution to the violence of a racist past."[33] Patricia Williams similarly envisions the possibility of racial healing through radical race merging, wryly proposing "guerilla insemination" of the "symbolically sacred vessel of the white womb" as a way to "integrate this world from the inside out," to "shake up biological normativity." She asks, "What happens if it is no longer white male seed that has the prerogative of dropping noiselessly and invisibly into black wombs, swelling rank and complexifying identity? Instead, it will be disembodied black seed that will swell white bellies." The "clean containers of white wombs" will thus "bring the complication [of dark children] home to the guarded intimacy of white families, and into the madonna worship of the larger culture" (*Alchemy*, 188).

Unfortunately, Williams laments, "this won't work. We will end up with yet another generation of abandoned children, damaged in the manufacture, returned to the supplier" (188). In *Killing the Black Body: Race, Reproduction, and the Meaning of Liberty*, Dorothy Roberts echoes Williams's skepticism that mixed-race families, the "optimists' antidote to everything" (*Rooster's Egg*, 189), can dismantle destructive cultural ideologies. Certainly, Roberts contends, transracial adoption, although "painted as a catalyst for racial harmony," does not "threaten the supremacist code of white superiority [and] does nothing to diminish the devaluation of Black childbearing."[34] Indeed, within a society in which, as Williams charges, black babies are "dross," "worthless currency to adoption agencies," and "prayer[s] without answer" (*Alchemy*, 190), the image of the disowned or devalued dark child—first circulated in sensationalistic cautionary tales by white racists at the turn of the century, and then adopted by Harlem Renaissance writers as a means of parodying or indicting post-Reconstruction racial hysteria—still haunts the contemporary American landscape. The racial redemption that Toomer and his literary heirs prophesy remains, like Esther's dark messiah, an unrealized vision.

NOTES

1. Robert D. San Souci, *More Short and Shivery: Thirty Terrifying Tales* (New York: Delacorte Press, 1994), 134–38.
2. Patricia J. Williams, *The Alchemy of Race and Rights: Diary of a Law Professor* (Cambridge, Mass.: Harvard University Press, 1991), 189; hereafter, page numbers will be cited parenthetically in the text.
3. Patricia J. Williams, *The Rooster's Egg* (Cambridge, Mass.: Harvard University Press, 1995), 223; hereafter, page numbers will be cited parenthetically in the text.
4. See George Frederickson, *The Black Image in the White Mind: The Debate on Afro-American Character and Destiny, 1817–1914* (Middletown, Conn.: Wesleyan University Press, 1987); hereafter, page numbers will be cited parenthetically in the text. See also Winthrop Jordan, *White over Black: American Attitudes toward the Negro, 1550–1812*

(Chapel Hill: University of North Carolina Press, 1968); and Joel Williamson, *The Crucible of Race: Black-White Relations in the American South Since Emancipation* (New York: Oxford University Press, 1984); hereafter, page numbers will be cited parenthetically in the text.

5. Joel Williamson has noted that the last decade of the nineteenth century witnessed "the most awful display of interracial violence the South has yet experienced"; indeed, during the 1890s, "82 percent of the nation's lynchings took place in fourteen Southern states"; Williamson, *The Crucible*, 115–16.

6. According to Williamson, the "core" of the radical mentality was "the concept that Negroes, free from the restraining influences of slavery, were rapidly 'retrogressing' toward their natural state of bestiality." He explains that radicalism, which "appeared with dramatic suddenness in 1899 and swept powerfully through the South," was driven almost entirely by white Southerners' obsessive fears about Negro "assaults upon idealized Southern womanhood." Ibid., 111, 112, 116.

7. Judith Berzon, *Neither White nor Black: The Mulatto Character in American Fiction* (New York: New York University Press, 1978), 28; hereafter, page numbers will be cited parenthetically in the text.

8. Thomas Dixon, *The Leopard's Spots: A Romance of the White Man's Burden* (New York: Doubleday, Page, 1903), quoted in Berzon, *Neither White nor Black*, 34.

9. Ida B. Wells, *Crusade for Justice: The Autobiography of Ida B. Wells*, ed. Alfreda Duster (Chicago: University of Chicago Press, 1970), 270.

10. Robert Lee Durham; *The Call of the South* (Boston: L. C. Page, 1908), quoted in Berzon, *Neither White nor Black*, 43.

11. Gertrude Atherton, *Senator North* (New York: John Lane, 1900), 87.

12. Eloise Bibb Thompson, "Masks," *Opportunity* 5, no. 10 (1927): 300–302; hereafter, page numbers will be cited parenthetically in the text.

13. Wallace Thurman, *The Blacker the Berry* (New York: Arno Press, 1969), 22; hereafter, page numbers will be cited parenthetically in the text.

14. Jessie Fauset, *Comedy American Style* (New York: New York University Press, 1969); hereafter, page numbers will be cited parenthetically in the text.

15. Marita Bonner, *Frye Street and Environs: The Collected Works of Marita Bonner*, eds. Joyce Flynn and Joyce Occomy Stricklin (Boston: Beacon Press, 1987).

16. Hazel Carby, *Reconstructing Womanhood: The Emergence of the Afro-American Woman Novelist* (New York: Oxford University Press, 1987), 189.

17. Henry Clay Lewis, *Odd Leaves from the Life of a Louisiana Swamp Doctor* (Upper Saddle River, N. J.: Literature House, 1969).

18. See Angelina Weld Grimké, *Rachel: A Play in Three Acts* (College Park, Md.: McGrath, 1969); and Georgia Douglas Johnson, *A Sunday Morning in the South*, in *Black Female Playwrights: An Anthology of Plays before 1950*, ed. Kathy A. Perkins (Bloomington: Indiana University Press, 1989), 31–37.

19. As Gail Bederman documents, Roosevelt—fearful that the "less civilized races" were beginning to "outbreed" native-born white Americans—broadcast his alarm to the public, stating that "no race has any chance to win a great place unless it consists of good breeders," and calling for "willful procreative effort" on the part of the majority culture. See Bederman, *Manliness and Civilization: A Cultural History of Gender and Race in the United States, 1880–1917* (Chicago: University of Chicago Press, 1995), 201.

20. As Frederickson notes, the last decade of the nineteenth century "saw an unparalleled outburst of racist speculation on the impending disappearance of the American Negro. . . . Few who thus consigned an entire race to oblivion could conceal their satisfaction." Frederickson, *The Black Image*, 247–48, 257.

21. Toni Morrison, *Playing in the Dark: Whiteness and the American Literary Imagination* (Cambridge, Mass.: Harvard University Press, 1992), 11.

22. David Levering Lewis, *When Harlem Was in Vogue* (New York: Oxford University Press, 1989), 133.

23. For example, see Robert Bone's dismissive description of Fauset's fiction in *The Negro Novel in America* (New Haven, Conn.: Yale University Press, 1965), 101.

24. Grimké explains, "My purpose was to show how a refined, sensitive, highly-strung girl, a dreamer and an idealist, the strongest instinct in whose nature is to be a mother herself—how, I say, this girl would react to this force." Grimké, quoted in Perkins, ed., *Black Female Playwrights*, 9.

25. Gregory Holmes Singleton, "Birth, Rebirth, and the 'New Negro' of the 1920s," *Phylon* 43 (1982): 29–45.

26. Jean Toomer, *Cane,* ed. Darwin T. Turner (New York: W. W. Norton, 1988); hereafter, page numbers will be cited parenthetically in the text.

27. This description of *Cane* appears in a letter from Jean Toomer to Claude McKay composed during the summer of 1922; quoted in Cynthia Earl Kerman and Richard Eldridge, *The Lives of Jean Toomer. A Hunger for Wholeness* (Baton Rouge: Louisiana State University Press, 1989), 96; hereafter, page numbers will be cited parenthetically in the text.

28. Toomer to Waldo Frank, n.d. (late 1922 or early 1923), in *Cane*, 151.

29. Toomer and Latimer consciously cast themselves as martyrs to the cause of the new American race. Kerman and Eldridge acknowledge, "The view that they were combating an entire nation [by intermarrying] may seem extreme, but at times they must have felt so persecuted. They were receiving hate mail and calls." Kerman and Eldridge, *The Lives of Jean Toomer*, 203.

30. In *Genesis 12–50: A Commentary* (Cambridge, Mass.: Cambridge University Press, 1979), 121, Robert Davidson emphasizes that the biblical Esau and Jacob "are depicted not merely as individuals. They are the ancestors who give their names to two tribal groups."

31. George Hutchinson, "Jean Toomer and American Racial Discourse," *Texas Studies in Literature and Language* 35, no. 2 (1993): 242.

32. Mary Douglas, *Purity and Danger: An Analysis of Concepts of Pollution and Taboo* (London: Routledge and Kegan Paul, 1966), 35–36; hereafter, page numbers will be cited parenthetically in the text.

33. Susan Gubar, *Racechanges: White Skin, Black Face in American Culture* (New York: Oxford University Press, 1997), 230.

34. Dorothy Roberts, *Killing the Black Body: Race, Reproduction, and the Meaning of Liberty* (New York: Random House, 1997), 276. Roberts finds disturbing echoes of early twentieth-century racial politics in contemporary practices of "the new reproduction." She asks, "What does it mean that we live in a country in which white women disproportionately undergo expensive technologies to enable them to bear children, while Black women disproportionately undergo surgery that prevents them from being able to bear any?" Roberts maintains that the danger of such a disparity cannot be measured statistically: "With only 40,000 babies in the United States conceived through IVF since 1981, the racial disparity in its use will hardly alter the demographic constitution of the country. Rather, the harm occurs at the ideological level—the message it sends about the relative value of Blacks and whites in America" (285).

9 Lewis Hine's Family Romance

Richard S. Lowry

Lewis Hine's child labor photography occupies a particularly complex place in American cultural history. Consider, for example, the views on the cover of this volume and in figure 9.1: taken between 1910 and 1914, when Hine traveled the country as the photographer for the National Child Labor Committee (NCLC), they invoke a familiar version of his work. In photographs like these his children stand nearly isolated in a field of industrial labor, bearing witness to a machine culture that has grown beyond comprehension, as victims appealing unselfconsciously to our sympathy and inciting our outrage. It was Hine's mastery of this visual rhetoric that made such images so useful to the progressive reformers who put them to use advertising their causes. For instance, in Paul Kellogg's exhaustive 1907 sociological survey of industrial life in Pittsburgh, in such social reform magazines as *The Survey* and *Charities and Commons,* and in the countless publications and exhibitions sponsored by the NCLC, Hine's images were able to make vivid the human costs of social change. At the same time, their realism — made visible stylistically through their unambiguous framing of subjects who most often faced directly into the camera lens — signified an objectivity essential to the social scientific analyses and eventual reforms advocated by their sponsors. Hine's images revealed a truth that called for a pledge of reform on the part of the viewer, an action that would not only eventually right the wrong in the image — child labor — but harness the energies of modernity itself. In this way Hine's images have come to exemplify the deepest aspirations of progressive liberalism.[1]

9.1. Lewis Hine, Spinner in New England Mill, *1913, 1913; gelatin silver print, 12.6 x 10.1 cm. Courtesy of George Eastman House International Museum of Photography and Film.*

And yet, his photographs also partake of both an older, and today, more enduring, tradition of representation and action. After all, by 1910 Hine's rhetorical tactics were not new: Charles Dickens, following William Blake before him, had made the suffering of his young protagonists central to his fictional critiques of industrial England. The slumping posture and gaunt face of the glassworker, suggesting a fatigue beyond his years, recalls nothing more than the pathos of Oliver Twist's cry for "more, please." Just a decade before Hine had begun his serious work, Jacob Riis had included photographs of young "street arabs" in his popular magic lantern shows of the ravages of poverty in turn-of-the-century New York. The appeal of the children of Dickens, Riis, and Hine grew from their invocation, if only by negation, of the romantic child "discovered" in the eighteenth century by the likes of Jean-Jacques Rousseau and William Wordsworth, and celebrated in word and image by nineteenth-century American writers and artists. In Hine's case, the connection may not be obvious: his realism seems to distance his work from the deeply sentimental, and even sensuous, evocations of rosy cheeks, dimpled hands, and heavenly innocence that was so important to the Victorian mania for children.[2] Nonetheless, Hine's audiences would have framed the glassworker's suffering as much with the pastoral nostalgia of Mark Twain's Tom Sawyer and Winslow Homer's barefoot boys as with Dickens's Oliver Twist. The thin arms and rolled-up sleeves, the ill-fitting jumper, and the level gaze of the spinning girl would have echoed and negated the plump, wide-eyed appeal of the wildly popular print of John Everett Millais's painting of a little girl, *Cherry Ripe.*[3] Thus, undergirding the social fact of each photograph ("here is one who works at a dangerous job") was an intensely emotional culture of child love: the children in these images are all the more lovable by virtue of how unloved they are.

By making the child's body visible for inspection, Hine brought into powerful conjunction two discourses—public concerns of progressive reform and the personal, even intimate imaginings of modern childhood. Hine's children are wayward, vulnerable, neglected, even abused; they are also signs of social problems. They are at once objects of fantasy, lost or even "inner" children who must be saved to redeem their adult witnesses, and statistical bodies—facts marking a calculus of suffering that must be addressed by public policy. As such, his images thrust the sacred child of the late-Victorian bourgeois home into the glare of the public sphere as the object of social action. During the first decades of what had already been called "the century of the child," Hine's children stood at the crossroads of affect and public policy, making clear why historians have generally seen the child as the "theme" of the era's "progressive humanism."[4]

Animating the confluence of these two discourses of childhood was the powerful hold the family held on progressive America. It was, after all, the ideal domestic sphere, the haven from a heartless world, that served as the social correlative to the rural nostalgia of Twain and Homer, and the imaginative correlative for the absent love and nurture invoked by Hine's images. Referring to more (and less) than actual families, the family home was nonetheless also the institution that Hine and his contemporaries saw as best equipped to save the vulnerable and even dangerous child.[5] And yet, as was discussed at the White House Conference on the Care of Dependent Children in 1909, real families were often incapable, or unwilling, to give children the kind of moral guidance and physical well-being that the growing body of scientific experts on children saw as necessary to proper growth. As a result, reformers like Jane Addams, Florence Kelley, and Felix Adler began as early as the turn of the century to organize and lobby for the public aid to address what had once been understood as the most private of matters: the support of mothers and the care and raising of children. If the child represented the future of the republic, the new maternalists argued, then it was the obligation of the social body to step in as virtual parents—whether that be in the form of settlement houses like Hull House, or in federal government assistance.

Hine's children helped give Americans the visual vocabulary to confront and imagine the possibility of, and the strategies for, making the care and shaping not just of children but of all people the subject of public concern. On a larger historical scale, this new public attention marks the emergence in the United States of what Michel Foucault has called "governmentality," in which the state, for the sake of its own perpetuation, takes interest in the welfare of individuals.[6] This, of course, is a long way from the welfare state of today (Michael Katz has characterized this period as laying the origins for the "semiwelfare" state), but surely in the name of the child and in the model of the family we can see the emergence of a public, and a government, interested in what Jürgen Habermas has called the "formative functions" of the state.[7] In the effort, however, to reflect more clearly the cultural valence and social scale of Hine's work, I have chosen to call the affective technology of his images a "family romance," borrowing and inverting the meaning of Freud's phrase. Freud, after all, put the family at the core of the child's psyche; Hine and his peers put the child at the psychic center of an imagined family that included the domestic home, but reached out as well to constitute a public and finally a governmental parenting. On one hand, Hine drew on the historical tradition of children as discursive linchpins that held together the private world of family relations and the public arena of government: parents had to work to integrate future citizens into a world much like the one they inhabited.[8] On the other hand, Hine's images anticipate the curious and often debilitating discourse of contemporary childhood, in which the government and law increasingly intervene in our most intimate affairs to protect perpetually "at risk" children, a state of affairs which threatens to produce a society built on what Lauren Berlant has called, with only partial irony, "an infantile citizenship."[9] At stake, then, in this romance of the early twentieth century is how adults have come to use children (and other "dependent" adults), in the name of childhood, to imagine and legitimate specific social worlds.

Contemporary discussions of adult uses of children most often center on sexuality. James Kincaid has labeled the social logic of these concerns "the culture of child molesting," in which the sexual protection of vulnerable children tacitly legitimates their concerted sexualization.[10] Hine's images, I will argue, played a similar role during the early twentieth century, though more in the field of labor than sex. His images were used to protect children from the dehumanizing effects of rationalized labor (agricultural as well as industrial), but they also gave their viewers a visual vocabulary to humanize a reifying modernity. Mark Seltzer has argued for the centrality of what he calls "boyology" in turn-of-the-century America's effort to integrate nature and machine. If the physical development of boys' bodies represented nature at its purest, the subsequent training of them in such organizations as the Boy Scouts of America represented "the rewriting of . . . the natural body in the idiom of scientific management, systems of measurement and standardization, and the disciplines of the machine process." When Robert Baden-Powell described the Boy Scouts as "our character factory," he echoed his contemporaries, who understood the physical person, like the machine and its products, as "things that can be made." [11] Insofar as their bodies bear the marks of industrial domination, Hine's children are clearly being (un)made in his images. His children may have inversely recalled the robust nostalgia of *Tom Sawyer* and *Rebecca of Sunnybrook Farm,* but they also invited a highly critical medical gaze that would have seen figures like the glassblower as pathological (or even pathogenic), and the girl's level-eyed distrust suggestive of a dangerous precociousness. In short, in a phrase that took on more meaning during the span of Hine's career, the children were not "normal"—they deviated from the physical mean described with increasing precision by medical experts. If child labor was unhealthy, if it was inhuman, it was because Hine's photographs constructed in children's bodies a humanity formed by the rationalized environment that threatened them.

Human Documents

It is the quality of the humanity in Hine's work that has most caught the attention of critics. Early on his images were heralded simply as "human documents"; his self-consciously pedagogical and moral purpose was to explore, in words he used to describe later work, "The Human Side of the System." [12] Indeed, by many accounts, it was his success in documenting that humanity that earned his reputation during his lifetime and has given his photographs an abiding afterlife since his death in 1940 at the age of sixty-six. To be sure, Hine's "straightforward, clean technique" caught the eyes of the photographic historian Beaumont Newhall, as well as of photographers like Alfred Stieglitz, Berenice Abbott, and Mark Strand (who studied with Hine), and led to his belated "discovery" as an artistic fellow traveler in the ways of modernism. [13] And yet, all "technique" aside, it was his pictures' emotional punch that distinguished them for observers. The critic Elizabeth McCausland, the most vocal of Hine's late supporters, saw his images as "alive with warm, generous emotions"; they are, she wrote, filled with "the terror and pity of life." In his emotional immediacy Hine was for McCausland literally a missing link in a nascent history of American photography. In some ways he served for her as a kind of *idiot savant:* tinged with a late Victorian "humanitarianism," his pictures evinced a "union of form and content [that] must have been purely instinctive." His naive style thus bridged the gap between the unselfconscious pursuit of "purposive communication" by Matthew Brady, and the reflexive modernism of "straight photography" and contemporary documentary. [14] In 1989 Alan Trachtenberg, who has had a hand in sustaining

Hine's rediscovery during the last thirty years, seriously took up and expanded McCausland's historical argument in his book, *Reading American Photographs*. Hine does indeed turn back to Brady, argues Trachtenberg, by embracing his predecessor's ambitions to present to America a composite portrait of itself built of the myriad faces of its citizens. Hine, however, revises and broadens that vision by including in his portrait "working people, particularly manual laborers, particularly recent immigrants, and more particularly, working children." Hine's humanity thus gives us, in Trachtenberg's words, "a heightened, sympathetic awareness of the lives of others" that expands the reach of our sense of democratic obligations.[15]

In stressing the affective work of Hine's images, both McCausland and Trachtenberg usefully associate him with a powerful discourse of nineteenth-century humanitarianism that drew much of its power from an expressly sentimental practice that distinguished in particular our country's most trenchant discourse of reform—namely, that of antislavery.[16] Realized most memorably in Harriet Beecher Stowe's *Uncle Tom's Cabin,* such a form placed the suffering body of the slave at the center of what Thomas Laqueur has called a "humanitarian narrative." By detailing the pain of representative bodies on the auction block or at the whipping post, narratives like Stowe's built a rhetoric of compassion that encouraged readers and viewers alike to experiment with bridging social gulfs of race, class, gender, and age with a controlled but intense sentimental identification. But the humanitarian narrative did not stop there. By situating this affective bond within a larger moral account of evil and victimhood, such rhetoric sought to point directly toward the undertaking of some "ameliorative action"—the abolition of slavery, the relief of poverty, or the enactment of child-labor legislation.[17] The problem, of course was that in provoking this passion, both antislavery and child-labor narratives effectively "othered" or "pathologized" their subjects through their suffering. Indeed, this twin movement of alienation and compassion could easily enforce a social quiescence even as it provoked an affirming rush of sympathy in the viewer. Thus the popularity of sentimental reform rhetoric may well have had more to do with humanizing the audience, by calling forth ennobling sentiments of pity, than with helping the victims.

At issue in such a discourse, then, is the extent to which the affective intensity of sentimental reform—the purging drama of outrage, sympathy, and self-congratulation—encouraged a cultural myopia and a platitudinal self-indulgence in feeling humanized. For Newhall, McCausland, and Trachtenberg, Hine's images clearly transcend this messy emotionalism with their "clean," formal technique, and their "straightforward" commitment to the potential objectivity of the camera. What for McCausland makes the "terror" of Hine's pictures "more terrible," and thus what makes his humanity more trustworthy, are simply "the facts with which it is documented." [18] In the face of such truth, we cannot help but to act.

And yet, claims to objectivity have provoked more skeptical readings of Hine's images. Certainly most suspicious was Thomas Robinson Dawley, who, in *The Child That Toileth Not*—a challenge to what he saw as the inflated claims of industrial abuse put forward by the NCLC—included a photograph by Hine with the caption "How The Camera Lies." [19] The small boy in the picture, Dawley tells us, holding a cotton spindle alongside a bank of machines, was represented by Hine "as a child worker in the mill. The child never worked and the photograph was obtained by deception." In a sense, Dawley knew his man. In pursuit of what Hine called his "detective work" for the NCLC, he often did obtain his pictures on false pretenses, posing as a salesman of insurance, postcards, even Bibles, to gain access to factories that would have otherwise remained closed to him.[20] Knowing full well what he and his fellow operatives found in the field would be challenged, he checked his facts as carefully as he could—at times asking to see birth certificates and family Bibles. But working stealthily had its costs: often he could not confirm children's ages or what kind of work they did, or if they worked at all. Thus it may well be that the specific boy in the image had in fact never worked.

Yet for Dawley, and for us, the problem was not strictly one of inaccuracy. Dawley was right in mistrusting Hine's objectivity simply because Hine saw his mission in ideological terms: it was his job, Hine argued, to produce the "publicity and propaganda" needed to expose "in a visual way, the horrors of child labor." [21] Hine did at times chafe under the strictures of such work—in 1910 he voiced "grave doubts" about doing "another 'sneak'" in search of images—but in the end seemed to adopt, or at least adapt to, the reformist missions of his employers.[22] But the idea that disproving the facts behind one picture would compromise the impact of all of them misconstrues the purpose of his work. As Hine traveled the country photographing working-class life in Pittsburgh, or child labor from Rhode Island to Colorado to Louisiana, he served less to gather facts than to legitimate those gathered by his fellow social workers. In effect, he served as a publicist rather than as an investigator. This was certainly how Owen Lovejoy valued Hine's work when he was head of the NCLC. "The evils inherent in the system" of child labor, he wrote to Hine in 1938, "were intellectually but not emotionally recognized until your skill, earnestness, devotion, vision and artistic finesse focused the camera intelligently, sympathetically and effectively on social problems involved in American industry." Hine shared his employer's faith in the efficacy of his art as a "channel of publicity": as he argued, "a picture sympathetically interpreted" is a powerful "lever" for "social uplift." [23]

MAKING HUMAN JUNK

SMALL GIRLS AND BOYS WANTED

GOOD MATERIAL AT FIRST

High Wages

THE PROCESS

THE PRODUCT

No future and low wages   "Junk"

SHALL INDUSTRY BE ALLOWED TO PUT THIS COST ON SOCIETY?

9.2.. *Lewis Hine,* Making Human Junk. *National Child Labor Committee exhibition poster, photographs by Lewis Hine. Courtesy Library of Congress.*

This sense of mission gave him a peculiarly complex relationship to the social reality he sought to document, as Maren Stange has argued. Hine's willingness to put his material to instrumental use in the support of reform meant that what she calls the "flexible yet identifiable documentary style" of his pictures often served more to legitimate investigators' zeal "to discover and disclose social reality" than to initiate social action. The result was that, as it appeared in official reports, brochures, exhibits, and social work magazines, his work often "diminished the social and political presence of the very working people who were its subjects."[24] George Dimock sees this tendency most clearly manifested in the montage-like posters and storyboards Hine created from his own photographs: *Making Human Junk* (see fig. 9.2) reflects his practice of appropriating working children to his own ends—in effect, cutting them out of a complex social environment, as he does out of their pictures, to make ideological points (The tiny figure to the far left of the caption "THE PRODUCT" is the glassblower on the cover.) Such practice makes clear, Dimock argues, that "the child-labour photographs are used here to devalue rather than sacralize the child worker," transforming them into sociological types whose victimization melds into a sheer affectless and finally pathological "otherness" of the working class when visually measured by their distance from the world of subjective and material plenty that defines "normal" middle-class childhood.[25] As such, both critics locate Hine's humanism wholly within a liberal discourse of social knowledge, allied with corporate industry, the police, and a middle class anxious to consolidate its position in a world growing both more rationalized and more ethnically and racially complex.

If such critiques have the virtue of qualifying the more Whitmanian interpretations of Hine's humanist critics, they risk overdetermining the cultural politics of his images. After all, as Allan Sekula insists, as convincingly as Hine's common use of fully frontal poses employed "the 'language' of the body itself" to reference police lineups, medical studies, and other practices that associated sociological knowledge with social control, photography's meaning still remains a fundamentally "hybrid construction." Even the kind of "instrumental realism" Hine practiced yields to a certain indeterminacy, "a messy contingency" that emphasizes the particular, or "the circumstantial character of all that is photographed."[26] I would like to suggest that we take seriously the messy hybrid nature of Hine's children, and thus see his images as deploying the working-child's body as a site for the construction of a divergent and contradictory vision of the human. To be sure, in their dress, their ethnicity, their race, their class, and their occupations, Hine's children stand outside the frame of hegemonic vision. At the same time, this very otherness is rooted in their being children. As James Kincaid has put it, even as modern children are "alien, unknowable and not quite real," they are also "both inside us and distant from us, a repository of nostalgia and a hope for the future, weak and powerful, alluring and revolting."[27] Looking at children in effect represents a simultaneous act of self-othering and sympathetic outreach. It calls to the child in the adult and forces the adult to search the child for signs of a self; it is both instrumental and humanist.[28] Thus insofar as Hine's images participate in the discourses of progressive reform and rationalized humanity, they situate the campaign against child labor within the contradictory tendencies that have made the American child an honorary human.

In the Name of the Child

In the fall of 1918, months after the Great War had saved civilization, one Louise Graham summed up her argument in support of child labor reform in *Harper's Bazaar*. "Our civilization must march forward on the feet of little children, and as the child is war's weakest victim society must surround it with every care," she wrote. "But, after all, we cannot Americanize the child of foreign-born parents and make him one of us without drawing the parents, and particularly the mother, into our family circle. The destiny of a child is fixed by his home surroundings."[29] In a nutshell, Graham articulates the social importance of children: in the name of the child, and in the name of national, ethnic, and racial purity, society must form itself as a family, and offer children an extended home that will guarantee the future of civilization. She was not alone in putting children at the center of a national politics. While Hine traveled the country documenting labor, reformers worked assiduously to ensure that the nation could protect the "right to childhood."[30] Alexander McKelway put it this way in 1913, in his "Declaration of Dependence by the Children of America in Mines and Factories and Workshops Assembled": "[B]e it Resolved . . . That childhood is endowed with certain inherent and inalienable rights, among which are freedom from toil for daily bread; the right to play and to dream; the right to the normal sleep of the night season; the right to an education, that we may have equality of opportunity for developing all that there is in us of mind and heart."[31]

Such language of "rights" and "declaration" represents a decisive break with the nineteenth century, which for all of its celebration of childhood and concerted campaigns of "childsaving" saw children as decidedly private beings. However, the "child" animating such language had not walked onto the public stage fully formed; it had come to life gradually over the previous twenty years, as doctors, legal experts, and psychologists developed a composite portrait of what would come to be understood as "the whole child"— a being qualitatively different from adults in virtually every way. As early as the 1870s doctors had begun to attribute to children a unique biology, which in turn demanded an "anthropometry" that could establish means of growth and development against which children could be measured and diagnosed.[32] The medical tendency to see children as unique was reflected in the judicial system, where by 1906 there emerged in most of the country's urban areas juvenile courts that administered law based on a comprehensive understanding of a child's "condition." In essence, judges acted like doctors: in dealing with "troublesome" children, they sought to diagnose the quality of a defendant's childhood before administering developmentally appropriate sentences. To do this, they increasingly relied on the advice of pediatricians, educators, settlement-home officials, social workers, and psychologists, as well as the police, to assemble a holistic portrait of the child and the conditions under which it lived. On the basis of this report, children could be put on probation, sentenced to residential reform schools, or even taken permanently from their parents (who could themselves be convicted for contributing to the delinquency of a minor).[33]

New theories of developmental psychology contributed to, and were provoked by, this growing acceptance of children's unique condition. By far the most important figure was G. Stanley Hall, who in the 1890s posited a vision of childhood in which individualized development recapitulated Darwinian ages of evolution. And while his influence in intellectual circles waned by 1910, his popular presence was sustained well into the 1920s. In Hall's formulation, children went through a "savage" state before they could be "civilized." Parenting thus entailed less molding the child than managing this ontogenic evolution by providing a proper environment for its free expression. As John Dewey, an early admirer of Hall's, put it, "if we identify ourselves with the real instincts and needs of childhood, and ask only after its fullest assertion and growth, the discipline and information and culture of adult life shall all come in their due season."[34]

The new "whole" child constructed out of law, medicine, and psychology had a strong hand in shaping, and was in turn shaped by, the formation of a modern politics of maternalist reform. To the extent that it valued active parenting, the increasing emphasis of doctors and jurists on the importance of environment (and the consequent de-emphasis of heredity) to a child's well-being dovetailed well with Victorian sentimental domesticity and its reverence for the mother. At the same time, the emergence of childhood as a public concern offered women, poised to enter the public sphere themselves, an issue that was at once appropriately gendered and socially compelling. Indeed, if the child was the "theme" of the progressives, "motherhood," argues Molly Ladd-Taylor, "was a central organizing principle of Progressive-era politics inextricably tied to state-building and public policy."[35] As with childhood, however, the motherhood of Jane Addams, Florence Kelley, Lillian Wald, and Grace Abbott was not their mother's motherhood. Reformers like these emphasized a union of womanly instinct and scientific knowledge (and later, governmental support) as the key to developing children properly. This vision of "scientific motherhood" led to the organization in 1897 of the National Congress of Mothers, which became the Parents Teacher Association in 1908; it motivated Theodore Roosevelt in 1909 to hold the White House Congress on Children; and in 1912, it led Congress to establish the Children's Bureau in 1912—the first federal agency headed by women, and among the first federal initiatives devoted to the welfare of citizens.

Under the leadership of Julia Lathrop, a veteran of Chicago's Hull House, the Children's Bureau sought to establish itself as the preeminent agency of children and mothers. Its mission was to "investigate and report upon all matters pertaining to the welfare of children and child life, and . . . especially investigate the questions of infant mortality, the birth rate, physical degeneracy, orphanage, juvenile delinquency and juvenile courts, desertion and illegitimacy, dangerous occupations, accidents and diseases of the working classes, employment, accidents affecting children . . . and such other facts as have a bearing on the health, efficiency, and training of children."[36] The list suggests the vast range of sites in which children were now considered a public concern (as is also acknowledged by the support for the agency by the Daughters of the American Revolution, the American Prison Association, the Farmer's Education and Cooperative Union, and, of course, the NCLC): hospitals and doctors' offices, the workplace, schools, the home, and the courts. The list also lay the groundwork for the bureau's commitment to serving as a fact-finding and educational department grounded in the survey techniques of social science. Thus, one of its successes was the publication in 1914 of a guide for mothers, *Infant Care;* by 1921 there were more than a half million copies in circulation. Within ten years, the bureau issued over one hundred pamphlets, notices, flyers, and the like on child welfare.

Finally, while the list makes explicit that "the working classes" were to receive special attention, it leaves implicit that its definition of the problem, and its goal for reform, were grounded in the Anglo middle-class family. Spicy foods, English illiteracy, a lack of open spaces for play, and child labor all posed threats to the well-being of children—threats that were best met by bringing a child's life as much as was possible in line with that of the single-wage-earner, two-parent, well-housed family. This domestic unconscious guiding the inquiries and actions of the Children's Bureau aligned it with the class politics of the reform efforts and agencies with which Hine was involved. But at issue here is less the Children's Bureau's direct imposition of middle-class values on the working classes—the agency did not have the power or the money to pursue such a route—than the emergence, under the aegis of their outreach and publicity initiatives, of an "official" way of life built around the welfare of the child, a way of life legitimated by medicine, the courts, social science, and the government. With this, familial discourses emerged from a specific class context to the relative autonomy of the state and its institutions of welfare and knowledge. The "whole child" of the Children's Bureau helped to establish national guidelines for "normal" children, which in turn served as seismographs for registering any tremors of deviance in family or community behavior.

Priceless Children

One last comment on the congressional charge to the Children's Bureau: the language also suggests the extent to which child labor was both integral and not decisive to the social administration of the whole child. It was of course institutionally vital to the network of associations and institutions that governmentalized the child: Kelley and Wald, who first came up with the idea for such a bureau, as well as Addams, McKelway and Lovejoy were all important members of the NCLC and vital to the lobbying that helped the Children's Bureau bill through Congress. Nonetheless, on a broader level, it is important to understand the campaign against child labor as part of an effort to imagine, and to guarantee, the conditions for producing whole children, as well as a class-based initiative of labor reform. Child labor reform was part of a maternalist politics that sought to make the conditional outsourcing of the family in the name of the child an important social obligation. If mothers needed advice, help, and sometimes intervention to raise healthy children, fathers (and mothers) could expect the same "help" in placing their children in the work force. In the name of the "whole child," reformers sought to make the "whole family" a matter for public concern.

Even though the NCLC preceded the Children's Bureau, and operated independently of the government, the politics of the "whole child" lay close to the heart of the organization, as McKelway's "Declaration" makes clear. Taken together, the rights to "play" and "dream," and the attention to health of body, "mind and heart" posit a child different from adults, a child ultimately, as the declaration goes on to make clear, "helpless and dependent . . . [and] protected in the enjoyment of the rights of childhood."[37] McKelway's child represents what Viviana Zelizer has provocatively called "the priceless child:" no longer expected to work in support of the family (for those with enough income), the child came to be valued as "an exclusively emotional and affective asset [that] precluded instrumental or fiscal considerations."[38] It was this child that stood as the norm for child-labor reformers, and on whose behalf they set about establishing regulations. "OUR CREED," begins one NCLC poster in bold capitals above a medallion photograph of a mother and children striking a Madonna-like pose:

We Believe in Work
    Its Necessity and Dignity
We Believe in the Workers
    Through Them—Progress
We Believe in Education
We Believe in the Home
    Therefore We Would
Protect and Educate the Child of To-day
Train the Worker of To-morrow
    And Thus
Safeguard The Home[39]

"HOMEWORK [piece-work at home] DESTROYS FAMILY LIFE" trumpets another poster. "[It] allows unsupervised, greedy manufacturers and parents to make a mockery of childhood."[40]

The poster's connection between "greedy manufacturers and parents" aptly captures the familial politics of child labor reform by suggesting how out of touch the movement was with the conditions of labor that shaped much working class family life. The NCLC's local roots lay in the south, where reformers like Edgar Gardner Murphy in Alabama and McKelway in North Carolina had been struggling to establish state laws regulating work primarily in textile mills, and in New York, where similar attempts had been made to regulate factory and street trades.[41] As these regional efforts were brought together on a national front under the aegis of the NCLC, more trades were added for investigation and action: berry harvesting in New Jersey, Delaware, and Rhode Island, oyster canning in the Gulf coast states, glass factories and mining in Pennsylvania. Any work that paid, argued the NCLC and the Children's Bureau—any work that pulled children out of the home and prevented them from going to school—was harmful. Census findings seemed to tell a story of crisis on this front: the NCLC claimed that one million more children between the ages of ten and fifteen worked in 1900 than had in 1870. Most of this expansion, they argued, was due to increases in industrial labor. Labor statistics, however, suggest a somewhat different story. Whether or not we accept the number of one million, only sixteen percent of these workers were in what could be classified as industrial trades.[42] Work conditions varied widely: clerks and news carriers often worked part-time on their own, maybe with another job; others worked only seasonally with families. In many cases children who did work with families did so to contribute vital income; others accompanied parents as a form of makeshift daycare. Employers often counted on, and even advertised for, hiring entire families because it kept wages low and workforces stable.

Given the variability, and often the transience, of these conditions, it is understandable why, even as the Children's Bureau had succeeded with such public health initiatives as campaigns to reduce infant mortalities, both it and the NCLC were largely unsuccessful in establishing effective federal legislation regulating child labor.[43] Nor did they succeed in establishing strong enforcement of many state laws. Not only did manufacturers and local officials resist such efforts, working families and even the children whom such laws were supposed to protect saw the loss of possible income and autonomy as against their own interests.

Simply put, the conditions under which children worked, while often brutally exploitive, varied too widely to be easily legislated. More important, the expectations children and adults had toward work varied equally widely. Children of Italian families hired by *padrones* to work the berry fields in Delaware and New Jersey were expected to carry their weight (often literally) during the picking season, which was why they were pulled out of the last weeks of school in urban Philadelphia and Baltimore; moreover, many of them preferred the open air to the tenements of the city. Farm children were expected to spend hours on chores every day, with added seasonal duties, while they attended school as best they could. Girls often devoted equal time and energy to difficult, unpaid domestic labor. Even many mill children worked intermittently at jobs before returning to school or moving on. Those who did work full-time, often on night shifts, helped support their families when fathers could not work or when mothers stayed at home with younger children. Such contributions to family welfare, as well as the skills young workers learned on the job, could be a source of pride, an education many found more rewarding than school. In short, parents and children, as well as manufacturers, had many reasons to resist the enforcement of child labor laws, and few of these reasons had to do with "greed." This is not to argue that low wages and dangerous work conditions were not a problem: unions continued to organize and fight at times pitched battles against this exploitation. Rather, the family structure that adapted to, and in turn had to some extent shaped, work conditions in certain industries was more variable and resilient than the "official" family of the NCLC and the Children's Bureau. Children had economic *and* affective value to their families; they also commanded an agency within and without the family that to middle-class observers seemed dangerously precocious.[44]

Lewis Hine's Family Romance

In his public essays, field notes and reports, posters, and photography, Hine worked with a concept of the whole child and whole (official) family close at hand. That he personally could sacralize the mother/child bond is suggested by one of his few extant private images, of his wife and son in a Madonna-like pose, which itself echoes earlier images of immigrant groups taken on Ellis Island.[45] This tendency would account as well for his strong reaction to household piecework, which he saw as "one of the most iniquitous phases of child slavery"—witnessing it nearly drove him, he adds, "to hysterics."[46] Indeed, it is clear that laboring children attest in his images as much to the failure of family as they do to the monstrosity of work. These issues were certainly in Hine's mind while in the field. In an article published in *Survey* on oyster and shrimp canneries, Hine responded with outrage to a mother's pride in her child's capacity for work: "Can we call that motherhood? Compared with real maternity, it is a distorted perversion, a travesty."[47] Even more pointed is Hine's encounter with one Mr. Mitchell and his son in April, 1911. As Hine tells it in his field report, all but one of Mr. Mitchell's children are at work. As for Mr. Mitchell, "his occupation consisted in loafing around the corner-grocery, toting dinner to the children and lolling around the house and occasionally visiting the farm." He goes on: "His sanctimonious disquisition on his 'love for his family' was nauseating." Hine then exacts his revenge by taking a photograph of the man lounging on the porch of the store, "showing his favorite occupation, and also one of the youngsters deprived of his right to toil."[48]

Such impassioned outbreaks were in fact rare in Hine's reports, articles, and speeches; most often he wrote in a clipped, often ironic tone that stayed as close as possible to the facts he uncovered. Yet even this language reveals a very partial observer in contest with parents, local inspectors, employers, and even children, for the "truth" of child labor. Not only did he have to face down and outwit foremen, padrones, and owners to get sight of young workers, he then had to ascertain whether or not it was children he was observing. Birth certificates were rare, church records spotty, family Bibles and parental testimony unreliable. At Merrimac Mills in Huntsville, Alabama, Hine "succeeded in getting [photographing] a number of the youngsters, but the very youngest eluded me. Those I did get, when I asked ages, lied to me, as evidenced not only by my own observations but by the statements, often volunteered, of other boys." At Dallas Mills, also in Huntsville, "The very smallest fought shy of the camera. Some of the youngest boys were 12 years old, they said, but I knew better, and other boys said they were lying."[49]

As he invites his viewers to do with the photographs, when all documentation and context fails, Hine turns to observation of the body for his truth. Children below a certain size (often, his belt buckle) could not be twelve. People lie, but the child's body does not; it becomes for him the touchstone of truth for the "whole child." Thus, in their report from Delaware, Hine and his investigating team note that "the deadening monotony, close application, long hours, and absence of diversion" entailed in operating a can-capping machine "makes this form of work harmful and to be avoided by young children."[50] Time and again Hine and his colleagues note the bodily effects of work. "Fifteen pounds of pressure on the little hands!" writes one investigator about children carrying boxes of cranberries. "The strained position of the body of the child picking in the cranberry bog tells on the nervous system of the child. These little toilers all seemed stunted in growth and their mental development does not appear as high as normal children."[51] Hine even gathered handwriting samples of children's signatures to tell the story of their exploitation: their uncontrolled scrawls a poignant testimony as much to their bodily incompleteness as to their illiteracy.

The significance of this bodily truth becomes clear in his account of child labor practices in North Carolina, delivered at the NCLC annual meeting in 1915. "I found two little sisters spinning whose grandmother told me they were only six and seven years old," he related. "I found two boys under twelve whose hands had been mutilated in the mill. And I found any number of ten- and eleven-year-old children working an eleven-hour day (during the school term) at tasks involving eye strain and muscle strain. Is it any wonder, there- fore, that I found a whole family, mother and five children, the oldest of 17, of which not one could write his name?" [52] The abnormal strain of eye and muscle, the mutilation of hands: these flow naturally from families headed by matriarchs too weak to prevent six-year-old girls from working, and lead in- evitably to the wholesale illiteracy of families. Hovering behind this image is that of "normal children" (to quote the cranberry report) who grow physi- cally and develop mentally enough to write—"whole children" ensconced in "whole families." Those incapable families not only merited Hine's approba- tion, they justified his, and the NCLC's, intervention as the good parent who knows better. His weapon in this quest was his camera, which allowed him simultaneously to gather little children for virtual adoption, and publicly to expose miscreants like Mr. Mitchell.

This combativeness, however, describes only one scene of Hine's family romance. The Mr. Mitchells and lax grandmothers aside, even notwithstand- ing those "greedy" families who would subject their children to homework, the family that most attracted the attention of Hine's camera eye was the surrogate family of the workplace. Indeed, more often than castigating work- ing families, the collective weight of Hine's images tell stories of biological families degraded, splintered, and finally usurped by overbearing fathers and mechanized mothers associated with industry. Mr. Mitchell may loaf at the store, but the most insidious fathers are those foremen or "bosses" who seem to hold children hostage to the demands of labor.

This narrative dynamic is most clear in the numerous photographs Hine took of children with adults—photographs that place the children within complex and often rivalrous relationships between the adult subjects and the viewer/photographer. Indeed, there is a strong suggestion that in these images, as in the case with Mr. Mitchell, Hine used his photography as an explicit weapon in a paternal battle for custody of the children. This narra- tive is particularly visible in those images where children and adults pose in front of doorways to mills and workshops (see figs. 9.3 and 9.4). This common motif in Hine's work was born largely of necessity: when denied en- trance to a factory he often was forced to wait outside, at times for days, tak-

9.3. *Lewis Hine,* Gastonia, *N.C., Nov 1908. Courtesy Library of Congress.*

ing pictures of children coming and going.[53] His posed pictures thus mark
particularly rich moments of negotiation, complicity, and perhaps subter-
fuge between subjects, photographer, and viewer over issues of revelation
and concealment.

In figure 9.3, the triangle of the three men frames our view of the children
even as they use them to fence us out of the factory from whose doorway they
have emerged and through which they will pass. The cocky stance of the
young man on the right, echoed by the man at the door, suggests an arrogant
sense of ownership over the lint-covered boys. A similar dynamic operates in
figure 9.4, where the adult man's head rises above the girls in front. In the
deep background a brick and window wall again suggests a drama of access.
Of all the figures in both images only one—the small boy on the right—
smiles, and his is only half a smile. The girl in the center of figure 9.4, with
her tilted head and crossed arms, expresses a discomfort, perhaps impa-
tience, with the situation. The other girls and boys seem resigned to doing
what they are told or asked. As such, the confrontation between adults—
photographer, men, and viewers—unfolds across the bodies of the children.
The man behind the girls both asserts dominion and recedes into the blurry
background, a victim of Hine's depth of field; the cocky young man is cut off

9.4. Lewis Hine, Adolescents and Others in Payne/Cotton Mill, Macon GA. Girl on end with dropping eyelids has been helping there 1 Year, *1909; gelatin silver print, 4 5/16 x 6 1/2 in. Courtesy Milwaukee Art Museum, Gift of Robert Mann M1978.143.*

by the picture's frame. Are these evidence of Hine's part in the struggle for the children? And what about the children? Do they refuse the standard smile for the camera to hide an essential happiness—from us, or from the man behind them? Do they perform for Hine? The indeterminacy of these questions highlights the formality of the encounter between camera and workers. Hine and his audience are outsiders here; the group, however, is united with a host of intimacies, subjectivities, and experiences that are fundamentally familial in their privacy and intensity.

By progressive standards, of course, both groups are perverse families, knit together by economic need and instrumental use, and organized around the law of ownership rather than parental care. Most perverse is how "unchild-like" the children are: victims of this demonic domesticity, they suffer knowingly. Following this logic, factories, mines, workshops, and canneries serve, in many of Hine's images, as "homes" for these families, secret spaces of paternal transformation, where boys and girls, hidden from the sympathizing eye of reform, are molded into workers—or, into "HUMAN JUNK," as his best-known poster puts it (see fig. 9.2). Here, in a manner that recalls Herman Melville's story "The Tartarus of Maids," the factory appears as a demonic maternal machine, devouring childhood to produce a lifeless offspring that resembles nothing so much as zombies—not humanity, but the walking dead in children's bodies. They resemble less the muscular, drone-like workers of Fritz Lang's *Metropolis*—a subsequent fantasy of industrial re-production—than that primal figure of suffering Gothicism, Frankenstein's monster.

Hine's rhetoric of industrial reproduction and perverse family values was shared widely in the progressive press, where the incestuous devouring of children became a shorthand trope for the fears of the increasing social power of both industry and the exploited working class. Editorial cartoons pictured fat industrialists smiling over the depleted or degraded bodies of working children: "I really do love children" smirks one corpulent capitalist as they stumble past one of his factories.[54] Below another cartoon of a factory filling with children at one end and spewing crippled and sullen adults at the other, we are warned, under the headline, "Infamy of Child Labor in Facto-ries," that "[t]he child naturally looks to the parent for support, and when he is forced into labor and his earnings are taken from him for family use, the impressionable child mind becomes molded to the idea that labor is unre-quited and is a cruel injustice forced by wealthy employers. There the quick seed of Bolshevism is implanted."[55] The factory here digests, grinding "chil-dren's bones . . . into almighty dollars;" the factory also gives birth, once im-pregnated with Bolshevism, to living-dead malcontents whose bodies bear the harsh imprint of their abuse. If this cartoon takes the Gothicism implicit in Hine's child-labor images further than he himself did, it does suggest how widely shared was his concern that the industrial workplace was displacing the family as that place where children were raised.

Later in his life, when modernists had adopted him as their own, Hine re-called his days with the NCLC: "I was interested in bringing out the differ-ence between child labor (the negative, harmful aspects) and child work (that which gives training and educates). . . . There is a deal to be done with visu-alizing child labor today and the other kind of child work."[56] Hine's language here tells much of the story behind the progressive embrace of the "whole child": child labor is harmful, child work educates. Labor takes place in the industrial workplace, it destroys children by using their vitality as fuel, and leaves them as zombies. Work takes place in the extended family home, pre-serves childhood and encourages its energies, allowing children "naturally" to mature into adults. Thus, the role of photographic reform is to visualize the difference between labor and work, allowing the public to extend and rationalize the family space by making children conditional wards of the republic.

Hine himself kept this distinction clear in his mind. His well-known book for adolescent readers on the building of the Empire State Building, *Men At*

Work, like many of the photographs he took after his tenure at the NCLC, celebrated the expressive possibilities of bodies in harmony with machines and technology.[57] His photographs of schoolchildren at lab benches, or intent on miniature engineering projects, similarly imagined the constructive power of "work." The problem, of course, arises when we try to make the distinction: when *does* labor become work, or work labor? Marking that difference would not have been so important if industrial labor had not so threatened to assume all the powers of making people. But most important, it would not have seemed so pressing if the objects of both work and labor had not been children. In the name of the child, then, the threat of labor was met by schools, courts, and the government, supporting and taking on the role of the family in the making of children. Hine's work with the NCLC marks the moment when, in answer to that threat, the child displaced the worker as the image of the citizen, dislodging the republicanism that had stood at the heart of the national understanding of the public. It was Hine's romance, and remains ours today, that once in public, children could be "returned" to their "natural" family. It was his work to help locate that family not in the intimate spaces of nurseries and bedrooms of the domestic home, but in the halls of government, and in our nation's dreams of itself.

NOTES

1. Surveys of Hine's life and work include Judith Mara Gutman, *Lewis W. Hine and the American Social Conscience* (New York: Walker, 1967); Verna Posever Curtis and Stanley Mallach, *Photography and Reform: Lewis Hine and the National Child Labor Committee* (Milwaukee: Milwaukee Art Museum, 1984); and Lewis Hine, *America and Lewis Hine: Photographs, 1904–1940* (New York: Aperture Foundation, 1977).

2. On the Victorian infatuation with children, see James Kincaid, *Child-Loving: The Erotic Child And Victorian Culture* (New York: Routledge, 1992); Anne Higonnet, *Pictures of Innocence: The History and Crisis of Ideal Childhood* (London: Thames and Hudson, 1998); and Carolyn Steedman, *Strange Dislocations: Childhood and the Idea of Human Interiority, 1780–1930* (Cambridge, Mass.: Harvard University Press, 1995).

3. On the painterly child, see Sarah Burns, "Barefoot Boys and Other Country Children: Sentiment and Ideology in Nineteenth-Century American Art," *American Art Journal* 20, no. 1 (1989): 25–50.

4. "The century of the child" was coined in 1909 by the Swedish writer Ellen Key and is quoted in Kathleen W. Jones, *Taming the Troublesome Child: American Families, Child Guidance, and the Limits of Psychiatric Authority* (Cambridge, Mass.: Harvard University Press, 1999) 16. "Progressive humanism" is from Robert Wiebe, *The Search for Order* (New York: Hill and Wang, 1967), 169.

5. On the family, see Christopher Lasch, *Haven In A Heartless World: The Family Besieged* (New York: Basic Books, 1977); Stephanie Coontz, *The Way We Never Were: American Families and the Nostalgia Trap* (New York: Basic Books, 1992); Steven Mintz and Susan Kellogg, *Domestic Revolutions: A Social History Of American Family Life* (New York: Free

Press, 1988); and Eli Zaretsky, *Capitalism, The Family and Personal Life* (New York: Harper and Row, 1976).

6. Michel Foucault, "Technologies of the Self," in *Technologies of the Self: A Seminar with Michel Foucault,* ed. Luther H. Martin, Huck Gutman, and Patrick H. Hutton (Amherst: University of Massachusetts Press, 1988), 18–19.

7. Jürgen Habermas, *The Structural Transformation of the Public Sphere: An Inquiry into a Category of Bourgeois Society,* trans. Thomas Burger (Cambridge, Mass.: MIT University Press, 1991) 147ff; Michael B. Katz, *In the Shadow of the Poorhouse: A Social History of Welfare in America* (New York: Basic Books, 1986).

8. See Richard S. Lowry, "Domestic Interiors: Boyhood Nostalgia and Affective Labor in the Gilded Age," in *Inventing the Psychological: Toward a Cultural History of Emotional Life in America,* ed. Joel Pfister and Nancy Schnog (New Haven, Conn.: Yale University Press, 1998), 110–30.

9. Lauren Berlant, *The Queen of America Goes to Washington City: Essays on Sex and Citizenship* (Durham, N. C.: Duke University Press, 1997), 70ff, 97–123.

10. James R. Kincaid, *Erotic Innocence: The Culture of Child Molesting* (Durham, N. C.: Duke University Press, 1998).

11. Mark Seltzer, *Bodies and Machines* (New York: Routledge, 1992), 154, 153, 152.

12. Elizabeth McCausland, "Lewis W. Hine, Social Photographer," typescript, 5 September 1938, 4–5; in Elizabeth McCausland Papers, Documents Relating to Lewis Hine, Archives of American Art. Letter of Lewis Hine to Paul Kellogg, 20 June 1921, in *Photo Story: Selected Letters and Photographs of Lewis W. Hine,* ed. Daile Kaplan (Washington: Smithsonian Institution Press, 1992), 20.

13. Newhall used this phrase in a letter to Hine, February 1938, in Kaplan, ed., *Photo Story,* 107.

14. McCausland, "Social Photographer," 4.

15. Alan Trachtenberg, *Reading American Photographs: Images As History: Matthew Brady to Walker Evans* (New York: Hill and Wang, 1989), 166, 164, 199. See also his "Ever—the Human Document," in Hine, *America and Lewis Hine,* 118–37.

16. On sentimental culture, see Shirley Samuels, ed., *The Culture of Sentiment: Race, Gender, and Sentimentality in Nineteenth-Century America* (New York: Oxford University Press, 1992); and Laura Wexler, "Tender Violence: Literary Eavesdropping, Domestic Fiction, and Educational Reform," *Yale Journal of Criticism* 5, no. 1 (1991): 151–87.

17. Thomas W. Laqueur, "Bodies, Details, and the Humanitarian Narrative," in *The New Cultural History,* ed. Lynn Hunt (Berkeley and Los Angeles: University of California Press, 1989), 176.

18. McCausland, "Social Photographer," 5.

19. Thomas Robinson Dawley, *The Child That Toileth Not. The Story of a Government Investigation* (New York: Gracia, 1912); the image I discuss appears on page 113.

20. Lewis Hine, "Notes on Early Influences," typescript, n.d., 3, McCausland Papers.

21. Lewis Hine, "Biographical Notes" (1940), in Kaplan, *Photo Story,* 179.

22. Hine, "Notes on Early Influences," 3.

23. Owen Lovejoy to Lewis Hine, 21 July 1938, in Kaplan, *Photo Story,* 110; Lewis Hine, "Social Photography," in *Classic Essays on Photography,* ed. Alan Trachtenberg (New Haven, Conn.: Leete's Island Books, 1980), 111.

24. Maren Stange, *Symbols of Ideal Life: Social Documentary Photography in America, 1890–1950* (New York: Cambridge University Press, 1989), 65, 55.

25. George Dimock, "Children of the Mills: Re-Reading Lewis Hine's Child-Labour Photographs," *Oxford Art Journal* 16, no. 2 (1993): 49.

26. Allan Sekula, "The Traffic in Photographs," *Art Journal* 41, no. 1 (1981): 16; and "The Body and the Archive," *October* 39 (1986): 17.

27. Kincaid, *Erotic Innocence*, 53, 68.

28. On the culture of the "inner child," see Marilyn lvy, "Have You Seen Me? Recovering the Inner Child in Late Twentieth-Century America," in *Children and the Politics of Culture*, ed. Sharon Stephens (Princeton, N. J.: Princeton University Press, 1995), 79–104.

29. Louise Graham, "A Charter for Childhood," *Harper's Bazaar*, September 1918, 76.

30. The phrase is from Florence Kelley, *Some Ethical Gains through Legislation* (1905), quoted in Kriste Lindenmeyer, *"A Right to Childhood": The U.S. Children's Bureau and Child Welfare, 1912–46* (Urbana: University of Illinois Press, 1997), 1.

31. A. J. McKelway, "Declaration of Dependence by the Children of America," pamphlet (NCLC, 1910), National Child Labor Committee Collection, Library of Congress (hereafter, NCLC).

32. Bayard Holmes, "A Study of Child Growth: Being a Review of the Work of Dr. William Townsend Porter of St. Louis," *New York Medical Journal* 60 (1894): 420, quoted in Charles R. King, *Children's Health in America, A History* (New York: Twayne, 1993), 75.

33. On juvenile courts, see, Jones, *Troublesome Child*; Anthony Platt, *The Child Savers: The Invention of Delinquency* (Chicago: University of Chicago Press, 1969); and Joseph M. Hawes, *Children in Urban Society: Juvenile Delinquency in Nineteenth-Century America* (New York: Oxford University Press, 1971).

34. John Dewey, quoted in David I. Macleod, *The Age of the Child: Children in America, 1890–1920* (New York: Simon and Schuster/Macmillan, 1998), 25.

35. Molly Ladd-Taylor, *Mother-Work: Women, Child Welfare, and the State, 1890–1930* (Urbana: University of Illinois Press, 1994), 43. My subsequent discussion of child welfare owes much to Taylor's work.

36. Lindenmeyer, *"A Right to Childhood,"* 23.

37. McKelway, "Declaration."

38. Viviana A. Zelizer, *Pricing the Priceless Child: The Changing Social Value of Children* (New York: Basic Books, 1985).

39. "Our Creed," poster, n.d., NCLC Collection, Lewis Hine Photographs, #3522.

40. "Homework Destroys Family Life," poster, n.d., NCLC Collection, Lewis Hine Photographs, #3750.

41. Walter I. Trattner, *Crusade for the Children: A History of the National Child Labor Committee and Child Labor Reform in America* (Chicago: Quadrangle Books, 1970) remains the best account of the origins of the NCLC.

42. Macleod, *The Age of the Child*, 101–13, critically analyzes the NCLC's labor figures.

43. Congress did pass the Keating-Owens Bill in 1916, but it was quickly overturned by the Supreme Court as unconstitutional.

44. On family labor, see Jacqueline Dowd Hall, James Leloudis, Robert Korstad, Mary Murphy, Lu Ann Jones, and Christopher B. Daly, *Like a Family: The Making of a Southern Cotton Mill World* (Chapel Hill: University of North Carolina Press, 1987), 44–114; and Cindy Hahamovitch, *The Fruits Of Their Labor: Atlantic Coast Farmworkers and the Making Of Migrant Poverty, 1870–1945* (Chapel Hill: University of North Carolina Press, 1997) 14–67.

45. Dimock, "Children of the Mills," 49, discusses this image.

46. Lewis Hine, quoted in John R. Kemp, ed., *Lewis Hine: Photographs of Child Labor in the New South* (Jackson: University Press of Mississippi, 1986), 10.

47. Lewis Hine, "Baltimore to Biloxi and Back: The Child's Burden in Oyster and Shrimp Canneries," *The Survey*, 3 May 1913, 170, quoted in Dimock, "Children of the Mills," 47.

48. Lewis Hine, "Child Labor in the Cotton Mills of Mississippi, Photographic Investigation by Lewis W. Hine in April and May, 1911," 1, Box 3, NCLC Collection.

49. Lewis W. Hine, "Alabama Investigation," (August 1910) 1, Box 3, NCLC Collection.

50. Edward F. Brown and Lewis W. Hine, "Child Workers in the Fields and Canneries of Delaware," n.d. (1910): 6, Box 2, NCLC Collection.

51. Edward Fischer Brown, "Child Workers in the Cranberry Bogs," (1911): 17, Box 2, NCLC Collection.

52. Lewis Hine, quoted in Kemp, *Lewis Hine,* 18.

53. James Guimond, *American Photography and the American Dream* (Chapel Hill: University of North Carolina Press, 1991), 83–84, discusses this motif.

54. Newspaper cartoon, no citation, Box 48A, NCLC Collection.

55. Charles Grant Miller, "Infamy of Child Labor in Factories," New York *Christian Herald* (31 May 1919) n.p.; Box 48B, NCLC Collection.

56. Lewis Hine to Beaumont Newhall, 30 January 1938, in Kaplan, *Photo Story,* 106.

57. Peter Seixas discusses the relationship between Hine's earlier and later photography, in "Lewis Hine: From 'Social' to 'Interpretive' Photographer," *American Quarterly* 39, no. 3 (1987): 381–409. See also Dimock, "Children of the Mills," and Trachtenberg, *American Photographs.*

10 On Boyhood and Public Swimming

Sidney Kingsley's *Dead End*
and Representations of Underclass Street Kids
in American Cultural Production

Jeffrey Turner

This study sets out to explore a period of American history, the Great Depression, in which figures of childhood and youth would emerge as significant, sometimes ambiguous, cultural representations for adults in America. Indeed, the Depression was rife with images of youth. On the Broadway stage, representations of childhood played key roles in such plays as Jack Kirkland's adaptation of Erskine Caldwell's novel *Tobacco Road* and Eugene O'Neill's comedy *Ah, Wilderness!* (both 1933), Lillian Hellman's melodrama *The Children's Hour* (1934), Thornton Wilder's drama *Our Town* (1938), and Howard Lindsay and Russel Crouse's highly nostalgic adaptation of Clarence Day's memories of childhood, *Life with Father* (1939). On the big screen, such actors as Jackie Cooper, Judy Garland, Mickey Rooney, and Shirley Temple, as well as the kids in Hal Roach's *Our Gang* film shorts dominated Hollywood in the 1930s.[1] Additionally, children and youth were prominently displayed in Depression-era advertising campaigns; Works Project Administration photographs by Dorothea Lange, Margaret Bourke-White and Walker Evans; the popular and heavily reproduced illustrations of Norman Rockwell; works of literature like John Steinbeck's *The Red Pony* (first published in 1937); such comic book heroes as Little Orphan Annie (who debuted in 1924) and Batman's sidekick Robin (who made his first comic book appearance in 1939); and, finally, the media spectacles surrounding the 1932 kidnapping of Charles Lindbergh's two-year-old son as well as the birth and subsequent public display of the Dionne quintuplets in 1934.

In a period of great social and economic change, popular representations of childhood operated in the culture primarily as sites of innocence and purity, the promise of an optimistic future and/or the nostalgic evocation of a less complicated period of American history. This attempt to establish or fix a realm of innocence through the proliferation of youthful imagery—a strategy that hoped to simulate social stability through representations that might reflect the hopes and promises of a better future during a period of great anxiety and economic strife—only manages to mark 1930s America as vulnerable, calling into question the meanings of Depression-era representations of youth and innocence. In this essay I hope to explore these ideas by focusing on one of the most popular Depression-era plays to emerge on the Broadway stage, a work that introduced the "Dead End Kids" into the popular cultural imagination.

On the evening of October 28, 1935, Sidney Kingsley's *Dead End*, directed by the then twenty-nine-year-old Pulitzer Prize-winning playwright and produced and designed by Norman Bel Geddes, was set to open at the Belasco Theater on Broadway. Due to the show's controversial representations of childhood, the curtain was held and audience members were left to wonder whether *Dead End* would be allowed to go on. Historical evidence indicates that the Gerry Society (named after nineteenth-century child saver Elbridge Gerry, and also known as the New York Society for the Prevention of Cruelty to Children, or NYSPCC) had not yet determined whether to permit the thirteen boy actors, ranging in ages from ten to fifteen years old, to proceed with the evening's performance. In this essay I will discuss how the act of watching these boys on stage triggered a variety of Depression-era responses. Doing so provides the contemporary scholar a fine historical example of youth as a polymorphous category, as a commodity to be exchanged among producers, actors, directors, and audience members who paid to witness the spectacle of the "youthful" body on display.

Specifically, I argue that the representation of underclass immigrant boys on the Broadway stage functioned to mark the borders of white identity during a period of social instability. It is my contention that the boys' "nonwhite" bodies fell prey to a look that contained their power by rendering them erotic and, therefore, objects to be contemplated and controlled. A good example can be found in Stark Young's critical review of the play for *The New Republic*. Young describes the child actors in tacitly homoerotic terms, transforming these characters into potential objects of desire, noting that "where the boys clustered at their card game, the whole scene and, especially, the half-naked boyish bodies, were suffused with a kind of amethyst light in which the gleaming of the flesh was as realistic as Murillo."[2] Here Young ardently describes an intimate exchange shared by the boys in Kingsley's production, but he also articulates an intimacy shared among the boys on stage and the theater audience. What Young describes in his review verges on what scholar John Ellis has termed "fetishistic looking." For Ellis, fetishistic looking "is a gaze of longing, asking for the impossible abolition of distance that separates spectator and fiction." It also "implies the direct acknowledgment and participation of the object viewed."[3]

The display of the boys' bodies in various states of undress, their intense, often sexually aggressive bond of friendship dramatized in the play, and the young actors' willingness to commemorate their newfound status as Broadway stars (inviting the audience to revel in their comic antics and bad behavior) opens up potentially homoerotic readings of Kingsley's 1935 production, and such a reading is not so unusual, for the boys in *Dead End* can be directly linked to a number of homoerotic representations of adolescent male youth in American culture.

Homoeroticism, according to Allen Ellenzweig, is evoked when feelings of desire and/or affection between members of the same sex are released by a cultural text (drawings, paintings, poetry, prose, theatrical performance, sculpture, photography, sporting events, advertisements, film, television, and/or video imagery).[4] Such relations can exist openly within the text, lie submerged beneath the surface of a text, or emerge (as Stark Young's review of *Dead End* might suggest) in that relationship between a viewer/reader and the text. Expressions of homoeroticism in a work of art are not necessarily limited to the representation of physical or sexual activity but can be triggered by the full range of male or female bonding in settings best described as homosocial. Images of boys in Western culture have always contained erotic tension, and, as Camille Paglia has argued, the beautiful boy is considered "one of the west's great sexual personae."[5]

Dead End's preoccupation with erotically charged adolescent boys can be directly connected to late-nineteenth-century representations of childhood. As America underwent a transformation from a needs-based market economy to a desire-based market economy—what William Leach has termed the "democratization of desire"—the idea of childhood became complicated or problematized;[6] for it is during this period that the exalted, highly romantic image of childhood is "dirtied" by the forces of urbanization, industrialization, and the ever-encroaching hegemony of consumer capitalism. One need only look at the pictorialist school of photography, which emerged in Europe and the United States during the 1880s;[7] these artists (for example, American photographer Fred Holland Day) sought to follow artistic principles of painterly form and composition in their work and chose the nude adolescent male as one of their primary subjects. Thomas Eakins (1844–1916) was another popular, turn-of-the-century American artist who explored his fascination with male bodies through photography and paintings of nude male youth in Arcadian settings. Emmanuel Cooper has noted that Eakins, following the poetry of Walt Whitman, believed the openness of human relations and male friendship "could best be conveyed by careful study of the youthful and muscular naked body."[8] To this end he painted one of his most famous works, *Swimming (The Swimming Hole)* (1885).

Whitney Davis has argued that *Swimming* (and the available photographs of six boys—ages fourteen to twenty—that Eakins shot and developed as research for the painting) negotiates the boundaries between codes of decency and a nakedness that was captured (on film and canvas) solely to be stared at and admired (as opposed to serving a more formalistic or even spiritual aesthetic). The painting's homoerotic connotations, therefore, exist in tension with the dictates of social decorum, and Davis suggests that Eakins's work solicits a look necessary to frame the boys on the rock as objects of homoerotic desire. Davis's reading of the painting suggests that *Swimming* does not so much celebrate Whitmanesque egalitarianism as squash such chasteness in order to revel in the indecency—the uncivilized temerity—of naked, sexually charged boys at play in a natural setting far removed from the adult world of industrial progress.[9]

The American artist whose work holds the strongest connection to Kingsley's "Dead End Kids"—the boys in *Dead End* seem to have literally been lifted out of one of his paintings—is George Bellows (1882–1925), an urban realist and member of the ashcan school. The ashcan-school spirit was articulated by Bellows's mentor Robert Henri (1865–1929) who, as an instructor at the New York School of Art at the turn of the century, taught his students to reject the idealization of upper-class purity in favor of gritty, unedited scenes of city life among the working poor. The ashcan school (which included Henri, Bellows, George Luks, and William Glackens) was popular during the first-three decades of the twentieth century and challenged effete academy-trained artists with an aggressively masculine style. It was also known for narrowing the gap between "high art" and the "low art" of journalistic sketches and comic strips very popular at the time.

Bellows's well-known 1907 painting *Forty-two Kids* (see fig. 10.1) owes much to the proliferation of "kids" in comic strips from the 1890s (for example, the extremely popular Yellow Kid strips). In this painting, forty-two working-class boys in various states of undress swim in the Hudson River or wrestle and play upon a broken-down pier; the painting is similar in spirit and composition to Eakins's *Swimming*. In fact, Robert Hughes suggests Bel-

10.1. George Bellows, Forty-two Kids, *1907. Courtesy Corcoran Gallery of Art.*

lows's painting is a parody of Eakins's work, "exchanging Eakins's dignified Arcadian figures in their classic poses for a crowd of squirming, hopping bodies that reminded one hostile critic of "maggots." [10] Still, historian Sean Wilentz notes that Bellows's paintings—no matter how challenging in content and form—successfully manage not to alienate potential patrons among the bourgeoisie. Wilentz writes, "Radicals could see in Bellows's street kids what the Marxist John Spargo called the 'great vibrant passions' of the class riven metropolis. Middle-class Progressives could see the same figures as deprived little criminals, available for charity reform. And less politicized patrons could revel in a titillating sort of visual slumming, assuming that Bellows was *really* proclaiming the eternal innocence of youth and the age-old romance of poverty as a state of uncompromised authenticity." [11]

What about the painting's potential erotic content? Is it possible that Bellows's work provided an opportunity for the leisure class to reveal in a titillating sort of visual slumming (as Wilentz theorizes), eliciting looks that undermined the innocence of the boys and rendering them objects to be desired even as they are pitied? Although I suggest there is some erotic tension in the painting, other works by Bellows reveal how his representations of childhood and youth circulate with homoerotic potential. In a lithograph entitled *River-Front* (1923–24), Bellows stages a swarm of naked boys and men on a New York City riverbank, once again equating homoerotic sensuality

10.2. George Bellows, River-Front, *1923–24. Courtesy Amon Carter Museum.*

with public swimming (see fig. 10.2). In one corner a naked boy fondles him-self while another boy watches. In the center of the composition the body po-sitions of two boys in repose suggest sexual activity. Nearly every inch of the print is teaming with sexual urgency and the promise of release right down to the out-of-place and fully clothed upper-class gentleman in the lower left (top hat firmly in place) who is discovered by the viewer gazing upon a world of unfettered sensuality.

Contemporary social commentators often recognized how New York street kids were objectified either as sexual predators or bodies to be preyed upon. In one popular sociological study of a neighborhood on New York City's West Side, Ruth S. True, for example, suggests that the city streets cor-rupt children and unleash within them sexual yearnings and illicit desires. She writes,

> In common with other districts of the city the neighborhood has many sexual perverts, and these furnish an actual menace to the children. As infants, practically, the boys have heard the same stories repeated until they regard sexual matters as forbidden, of course,—and therefore, like smoking cigarettes and gambling, to be hidden from parents, police, or the authorities,—but with no sense of abhorrence. Knowledge of the methods of the perverts, on the other hand, leads to experimentation

among the boys, and to the many forms of perversion which in the end make the degenerate. Self-abuse is considered a common joke, and boys as young as seven and eight actually practice sodomy.[12]

The homoerotic attraction to youth that defines Bellows's paintings of New York City street kids swimming in the Hudson; Thomas Eakins's homosocial camaraderie at a rural swimming hole; or Fred Holland Day's photographs of nude immigrant boys can even be located in Norman Rockwell's popular 1921 *Saturday Evening Post* cover illustration *No Swimming*. Although the three boys in Rockwell's work are well shielded by items of clothing, this illustration is very much about the dangerous thrill of child nudity—the boys depicted are obviously running from some type of adult authority figure. This reading, of course, subverts the illustration's implied nostalgic "innocence." Such a thrill also exists in Sidney Kingsley's 1935 production of *Dead End*. The relationship among the young actors, whose good looks and charismatic personalities deemed them highly attractive, and the audiences attracted to these boys undermined Kingsley's social polemics and transformed *Dead End* into a voyeuristic spectacle of bodily display full of erotic potential.

Kingsley's 1935 melodrama depicts in graphic detail the tenement slums of Manhattan's Lower East Side in order to illustrate the consequences of environmental decay upon a group of young boys still innocent enough to dream of a better way of life. Revolving around these youthful street toughs, Kingsley's play takes place on a dead-end street and chronicles the emerging gentrification of Manhattan's lower-class neighborhoods, linking street crime with poverty and class conflict with the unequal distribution of wealth. Though no single character dominates the narrative, Kingsley's play is structured around the boys who swim in the East River and play along the river's edge (see fig. 10.3). In essence, the play depicts a group of children living at the margins of society, and it argues that to trample on the innocence of childhood is to assault one of the fundamental principles of American freedom.

As the curtain rises the stage directions reveal the boys to be "*swimming in the sewerage at the foot of the wharf, splashing about and enjoying it immensely.*"[13] Flinging gobs of river filth at each other, the boys physically communicate in forms of nonverbal yet vulgar gestures. When they speak, their words are hurled at each other in a rhythmic dialect of salacious street slang. Ranging in age from ten to sixteen, the boys trade insults and use sexually obscene language, smoke old cigarette butts, gamble, discuss the illicit pleasures of marijuana, cook potatoes over an illegal fire, and attack each other for want of anything better to do. Into their territory arrives Baby-Face Martin. A former street kid himself, Martin is a twenty-something gangster on the run from the cops for the murder of eight men. He has returned home, his face

10.3. Dead End *production photograph, 1935. Courtesy of Billy Rose Theatre Collection, the New York Public Library for the Performing Arts, Astor, Lenox and Tilden Foundations.*

reconstructed by plastic surgery, to see his mother and former girlfriend before he goes into permanent hiding.

The authorial voice of the play belongs to another grown-up street kid, Gimpty, a college-educated, would-be architect whose legs have been crippled by rickets. Gimpty is unemployed, frustrated by his surroundings, and involved in a futile relationship with a young woman who lives with a wealthy older man in a recently constructed luxury apartment building that towers over the dilapidated tenement houses. Both Martin and Gimpty seem to suggest the polemical outcome of growing up on the streets. As the kids plan, scheme, swim and survive, one cannot help but be reminded of Martin's descent into violent crime and Gimpty's inability to make positive social change despite escaping a life of misconduct through higher education.

As the action of the play moves toward a conclusion, Gimpty informs on Baby-Face (who dies in a climactic shootout) for the reward money needed to move his family out of the slums. Tommy, the leader of the gang of boys, is also ratted out by another boy and arrested by the police for attacking the father of a wealthy boy from the new building. In the end, Gimpty and Tommy's older sister Drina, a union organizer and social activist, seek out a lawyer for the teenage boy. Gimpty will use his "blood money" to save Tommy's life before it too is ruined, as was Baby-face Martin's, in reformatory school. Though this ending is hopeful, maybe even sentimentally naive, one is left unsure as to Tommy's future, and the future of all the boys barely existing at the "dead end" of the urban jungle.

The curtain did eventually rise that October evening in 1935 (supposedly Kingsley toned down some of the boy's obscenities to placate the authorities[14]), and *Dead End* would run for a very profitable 684 performances. In 1937 Samuel Goldwyn presented a successful film version of the stage play adapted by Lillian Hellman and directed by William Wyler, starring Humphrey Bogart and a cast of young actors, six of whom starred in the original Broadway production.[15]

For many the play was a powerful social text that generated a great amount of publicity for the plight of the urban poor during the Great Depression. Brenda Murphy argues that Kingsley's gritty, slice-of-life treatise on urban poverty, class struggle, and environmental determinism was "theatrical realism as [Emile] Zola described it."[16] Foregrounding representations of street youth as neglected innocents whose only options are crime, prison, and/or an early death, *Dead End,* for Murphy, seemed to cry out for audience members to enact social change. In fact, according to Kingsley scholar Nena Couch, "the stunning realism of *Dead End* confirmed Kingsley's commitment to writing plays that dug below the surface, not only to reveal social problems that many would have ignored, but to force society and government to address those problems."[17]

In the wake of *Dead End*'s popularity, the Boys' Clubs of America saw their financial contributions triple. One of play's biggest fans was first lady Eleanor Roosevelt, and due to her interest, *Dead End* became the first Broadway production to enact a command performance for the White House. Its success in the nation's capital lead President Franklin D. Roosevelt to appoint a government commission to study slum conditions in America's urban centers. Finally, Roosevelt ally Senator Robert Wagner proposed the first slum-clearance bill in the U.S. Congress, publicly crediting *Dead End* for inspiring the legislation.[18] To have accomplished such goals, Kingsley needed to have found an appropriate theatrical style of presentation to push his social polemics into the audience's face. Working collaboratively with his playwright-director, designer Norman Bel Geddes accomplished just that with his strikingly naturalistic stage setting.

Bel Geddes's setting complicates what theater scholar W. B. Worthen has termed the "rhetoric of realism." According to Worthen, the intent of stage realism is to erase theatricality in the name of a pictorial objectivity that governs both the acting style and the audience's reception of the event. Ideally, the audience (the assumed perspective for Worthen is always middle class) is cast as absent from the proceedings, observing the stage action from a safe distance. No matter what story the dramatic narrative may tell, the rhetoric of realism conceals "the audience's actual or figural role in the production of the 'problems' on stage."[19] To see and not be seen is the implied role of the audience in a work of stage realism, but Worthen argues that *Dead End*'s 1935 production design disrupted the realist paradigm to actively confront Broadway audiences and challenge them into acknowledging their "role" in the creation of urban slum neighborhoods. Thrusting the unfortunate inhabitants of this dead-end street literally into the orchestra seats, Bel Geddes's stage design unmasked "the privileged perspective of the spectator as a zone of privacy and illusionistic completion."[20]

If we take Worthen's reading at face value, one is led to question why, during a period of social and economic crisis, *Dead End*'s didacticism would attract such a large audience to become one of the most popular plays of the decade. This play should have offended its wealthy spectators, yet far from being outraged by what they saw, Broadway audiences were exhilarated by the controversial production. Theater scholar Sam Smiley offers one interpretation. He dismisses *Dead End*'s success due to "the results of an exaggerated emphasis on [its] theatrical, comic, and sensational aspects rather than [its] social content."[21] I would like to elaborate upon Smiley's interpretation and suggest *Dead End*'s popular appeal subverted Kingsley's effort to create a work of social propaganda; from this point of view the audience was not so much enraged as they were titillated by what they saw. It was the very conditions of poverty enacted on the stage—the spectacle of it—that attracted ticket buyers. Furthermore, the production offered multiple, often subversive, pleasures engendered by the display of these boys' bodies. Watching the "Dead End Kids" provided one of the most profound pleasures elicited by the production of Kingsley's play. The boys' polymorphous performativity was bound up in the pleasure they took in acting out and playing roles. These prepubescent and adolescent boys enthusiastically dramatized both innocence and deviance for their adult onlookers and in doing so challenged the belief that such categories can ever remain truly distinct, as some authorities contended.

Classified as "wholly objectionable" by the Catholic Archdiocese of New York City, *Dead End*'s representation of street urchins proved to be too hard for the New York theatergoing public to resist. There was something naughty going on at the Belasco Theater, and audiences wanted to discover for themselves exactly what that was. Indeed, in addition to Bel Geddes's set, most critics singled out the licentious performances of the boys onstage as reason enough to see the show. Therefore, critical reaction to the piece was mixed.

Although most were frustrated with the play's preachy sentimentality, the New York reviewers were unanimous in their celebration of the young boys who played the "Dead End Kids." *New York Times* critic Brooks Atkinson loved the young actors who transformed themselves into a "shrill, dirty, nervous and shrewd mob of boys." He went on to write, "Certainly the pitch of their voices has the piercing note of the tenement streets, and their water-skater running across the stage has the rhythm of half-naked pierhead swimmers."[22] Joseph Wood Krutch and Grenville Vernon also recognized the enormous contribution of the boys on stage. Vernon remarked that Kingsley's understanding of urchin street life on the East River waterfront was "positively uncanny. It is these children who make the play memorable."[23] Writing for the *Brooklyn Citizen,* Edgar Price colorfully summed up the 1935 production's central attraction, writing, "Street urchins play prominent parts. Your first glimpse of them leads you to believe that Mr. Geddes, with several assistants, lifted them bodily, dirt and all, from one of the streets along the lower East Side. However, a perusal of the program should convince you that they are not brats from the tenement and slum sections, but honest-to-goodness child actors. But program notes or no program notes, I still believe that they are street urchins. It seems to me no group of children could be so perfect in their portrayal of the various roles or be so filthy in body and mind unless they were accustomed to such an environment."[24]

In addition to their physical actions, the boys' language was also deemed offensive and therefore crudely appealing. Kelcey Allen, writing for *Women's Wear Daily,* agreed, further elevating the production's controversial status: "The vile words and oaths that ooze freely and naturally from the five or six tatterdemalions who squall and brawl upon the river bank will shock the nerves of the more cloistered folks of New York."[25] Of course, all this controversy could only heighten the audience's awareness of the play's "immoral" content, and, in the process, bolster ticket sales and name recognition.

Part of the appeal of the boy actors playing street kids in *Dead End* was their ability to both dramatize the gritty lives of impoverished youth and at the same time maintain their status as actors having a great time as the toast of the town. Indeed, both onstage and off these young actors openly celebrated the exhilarating freedoms of boy culture. Take, for example, a Sunday *New York Times* article written by A. V. Cookman, "A Reminder that Boys Will Be Boys: A Backstage Glimpse at Youngsters Who Perform in the Current *Dead End* is Proof of It." Declaring the boys the "reigning sensation" of Broadway, Cookman's entry into the boys' backstage inner-sanctum borders on fawning idolatry. The purpose of this article, I suspect, was to humanize the boys—to remind audiences that they were "just a bunch of noisy natural kids who happen to find themselves cast in a racy, colorful melodrama and have a lot of fun making the most of it."[26] The article also celebrates the boys' transgressive status as youth playing outside the boundaries of societal expectations. A short piece in the *New Yorker* exchanged Cookman's obsequiousness for ironic detachment, writing, "The boys were taking their pre-performance rest when we came in; they were sprawling about in their swimming trunks, reading, arguing, or (as God is our witness) playing chess. Billy Halop, who, as Tommy, has the juvenile lead, took charge of things and introduced us all around. Billy has *savoir-faire* and a father who shows you newspaper clippings. We talked briefly with Halop, Sr., and somehow got the idea that Billy was going to wind up in Hollywood."[27]

Another intriguing promotional device was a photograph distributed by Bel Geddes to area newspapers in which the boys—most of whom were costumed in the torn street clothes of their characters—are sitting down to a lesson in algebra. The tension between the boys' appearance and the formality of their teacher's presentation manages to evoke the boys' status as "normal," but the staged quality of the photograph disrupts the implied meaning and resists the restrictive world of the classroom in favor of the more playful and financially attractive theater space.

Both in character and offstage, these young actors' very presence celebrated a subculture where adult control gave way to the rough pleasures and hedonistic freedoms of boyhood. The "Dead End Kids" allowed audiences the opportunity to equivocate Depression-era anxiety and relate to the boys' ability to exist outside the boundaries of civilization and bureaucratic rule. The young actors on the Belasco stage were "performing" youth, and in so doing allowed their adult onlookers the opportunity to relish a period of life far removed from the crisis-addled world outside the theater walls. Audiences could revel in these boys' fragmented identities and their ability to transgress the socially coded and heavily codified world of masculinity in 1930s America.

It is no wonder that Kingsley provided for them a natural enemy in the character of Philip Griswald, the proper youngster who lives in the luxury apartment house and is described in Kingsley's stage directions as "*a well-dressed, delicate featured little boy*" (91). Philip (played in the 1935 production by Charles Bellin, whose blond hair and pale complexion was antithetical to the dark-haired, olive-complexioned boys who played the "Dead End Kids") is the perfect example of what literary critic Leslie Fiedler has termed the "Good Good Boy"—feminized, effete, well-ordered—a potent target for the kids on the street. The "Dead End Kids," using Fiedler's terminology, were "Good Bad Boys," unleashed and undisciplined.[28] Crude and unruly, these boys ran roughshod over their upper-class neighbors to attack the aristocratic culture that Kingsley indicates to be the cause of their misfortune.

Contrary to Fiedler's complete definition of the "Good Bad Boy," however, the "Dead End Kids" could never be described as "sexually as pure as any milky maiden."[29] These boys are sexually aggressive primitives; nevertheless, Kingsley's choice to focus upon the boys' bodily desires and bodily malfunctions ultimately renders them powerless. Their freedoms are seductive, but they must also be contained, and by the end of the dramatic action the boys' energies have been impoverished; their bodies are marked as vulnerable, and, therefore, weaker in spirit than the white, middle-class audience members who paid to watch them on the stage.

From its first moments, *Dead End* announced itself as a production fascinated by youthful bodies in action. The setting is a wharf over the East River. As the house lights went down, the audience could hear a gang of boys swimming in the filthy water just under the piles supporting the riverbank structure. Under the stage, the boys' bodies were sprayed with mineral oil to make it appear as if they were truly wet when rising out of the "water." Within minutes of their introduction, these boys maliciously turn on a Jewish boy, Milty, who is new to the neighborhood and interested in joining the gang. The initiation he receives is termed a "cockalizing," a pseudo-sexual ritual that Kingsley himself fondly remembers from his own childhood on the New York streets.[30]

This particular scene was quite vexing for producer Bel Geddes. In a note to the playwright dated August 27, 1935, he writes: "I believe your cockalizing scene will cause more troubles with the authorities than anything else and I don't believe you will get the kids to do it before an audience unembarrassed or natural."[31] The event is described in Kingsley's script as follows:

> *Suddenly* TOMMY *pushes* MILTY, *who stumbles backwards and trips over* ANGEL, *feet flying up. They all pounce on the prostrate boy, pin his arms and legs to the ground, unbutton his pants, pull up his shirt.*
> TOMMY. Gimme some a dat doit!
> SPIT *scoops up a handful of dirt: Heah! They rub it into* MILTY's *groin. He kicks and screams, hysterically laughing at the sensation. When he's through rubbing in the filth.* TOMMY *coughs up a huge wad of saliva and spits on* MILTY's *organ. Each of them spit, once round the circle.* (96)

Later, in the second act, the gang will attack Philip Griswald in a similar fashion. This second cockalizing, however, takes place in an offstage alleyway and is less playful and more vindictive in spirit—closer to a sexual assault than a ritual hazing. In Kingsley's production Philip reemerged onto the stage in tears, tucking in his shirt and zipping up his pants. The consequences of this attack will result in greater conflict for the boys, setting up Tommy to stab Philip's father with a penknife and eventually leading to Tommy's arrest and incarceration in the third act.

The open display of the boys' bodies in various states of undress (the published script calls for many of the boys to appear nude, though Bel Geddes quickly vetoed the idea), and the gangs' sexually aggressive roughhousing are not the only examples of bodily vulnerability or deviancy in Kingsley's text. Gimpty is disabled, his legs crippled due to an inadequate diet as a child. The gangster, Baby-Face Martin, has recently undergone plastic surgery in a futile effort to conceal his murderous past. One of the boys, nicknamed T. B., continually coughs up bloody phlegm. Martin's first love, Francey, is now a street whore rotting with venereal disease. Throughout the play vivid images of vulnerability and decay permeate the stage. In Bel Geddes's design, the luxury apartment building is never visible from the auditorium but exists outside the boundaries of the afflicted world of the stage. These choices determined how Broadway audiences of the 1930s would receive the inhabitants of this dead-end street, and it is not hard to argue that Kingsley's characters were easily read as representing an inferior social group marked as other than the white audience members who paid to watch the Broadway show.

To illustrate this point, one can turn to an advertisement for the Rogers Peet Company clothing stores that ran in the *Dead End* program as early as February 10, 1936, and as late as the May 24, 1937 edition. The ad copy read as follows:

Dead End
Dead End? Not here! Rather,
the open road to success via
good appearance. Smart and
authentic styling in clothing,
furnishings, hats and shoes.
The Best of everything
men and boys wear.

The ironies are not hard to follow. Clothes, according to cultural critic Richard Dyer, are the signs of wealth and status; "to be without them is to lose prestige."[32] As the Rogers Peet Company understood all too well, audience members attending a performance of *Dead End* were never going to end up like Kingsley's characters. The display of children's bodies in nothing more than torn bathing trunks or ripped denim trousers held close to the body by a piece of rope (not to mention the display of diseased bodies ravaged by tenement life) reflected a world outside the experience of those in the auditorium who could afford to shop at the Rogers Peet Company. The sexual deviancy and bodily vulnerability displayed on the Belasco stage served to reinforce the Broadway audience's sense of security, reminding them that unlike these street denizens, most white middle- and upper-class Americans had endured the worst of the Great Depression. They knew that they could still afford the "best of everything." As Dyer theorizes, the spirit of middle-class whiteness "could both master and transcend the white body, while the non-white soul was prey to the promptings and fallibilities of the body."[33]

The commodification and objectification of children and youth encompasses the entire history of American arts and letters. Since the first years of the new republic, the idea of America has been directly linked with images of the upstart child. Representations of youth have continually been tied to economic interests and issues of national identity in an effort to uphold a number of important American myths: innocence, individual autonomy, the centrality of the white subject, and the primacy of the patriarchal family system. Following the stock market crash of 1929, however, the proliferation of youthful representations in America undermined the perceived stability of the child figure, providing historians and scholars an opportunity to deconstruct these American myths and question the popular uses of such constructs. The need to fix the idea of innocence during a time of great anxiety reflects a national culture in conflict with itself, leading one to define the Great Depression, best expressed in the words of historian Lawrence W. Levine, "as a complex, ambivalent, disorderly period which gave witness to the force of cultural continuity even as it manifested signs of deep cultural change."[34]

In this study I have suggested that prominent child characters in Sidney Kingsley's *Dead End*—a highly successful, mainstream Broadway play produced in 1935 and subsequently released as a motion picture in 1937—functioned to reify the idea of innocence during a time of economic crisis. Their presence on the American stage served to bolster traditional hierarchical structures, in particular, white male authority. The fact that this essay has sought to read these representations as transgressive products of complex cultural forces—engaging issues of class, race, gender, and sexuality—does not negate the way these characters were initially conceived by playwrights, directors, and producers and received by their predominantly middle-class adult audiences.

One could argue the initial intent of *Dead End* was to draw attention to the urban American underclass, but the Broadway production was rendered by some to be ineffectual due to the production team's insistence upon sensationalizing their subject matter and emphasizing caricature over character. Representing the poor as an evening of theatrical spectacle provided privileged, white New Yorkers an unusual but popular evening of entertainment. Nevertheless, the representations of childhood at work in *Dead End* operated as a discursive strategy reinscribing traditional hierarchies of class, race, and gender as well as undermining the perceived authority of such structures. From this perspective, the youthful bodies at play in *Dead End* are revealed to be nothing more than empty signifiers, texts upon which adult audiences could write out their own fears and desires. But it is this instability, this fluidity of potentially conflicting interpretations, that functions to dismantle those dominant cultural hegemonies at work during 1930s America.

NOTES

1. Jackie Cooper (1921–) started his career in the *Our Gang* series, appeared in *The Champ* in 1931, and was nominated for an Academy Award for best actor that same year for his work in *Skippy.* Judy Garland (1922–1969) was immortalized in 1939 as Dorothy in Victor Fleming's musical film of L. Frank Baum's *The Wonderful Wizard of Oz.* That same year she was presented a special Academy Award. Garland costarred in many of the Andy Hardy films, as well as in Rodgers and Hart's *Babes in Arms.* Mickey Rooney (1921–) was the world's number one box office draw from 1939 to 1941. Awarded a special Academy Award in 1938, Rooney received his first nomination for best actor in 1939 for Busby Berkeley's film adaptation of *Babes in Arms.* He also played Tommy Miller in the 1935 film of Eugene O'Neill's *Ah, Wilderness!* and starred in numerous Andy Hardy films. Shirley Temple (1928–) was America's top box-office draw from 1935 to 1938. She was awarded a special Academy Award in 1934. For additional information see David Quinlan, *Illustrated Registry of Film Stars* (New York: Henry Holt, 1991).
2. Stark Young, "Dead End: 1: Mr. Norman Bel Geddes," review of *Dead End,* by Sidney Kingsley, *The New Republic,* 13 November 1935, 21.
3. John Ellis, *Visible Fiction: Cinema, Television, Video,* rev. ed. (London: Routledge, 1992), 47.
4. See Allen Ellenzweig, "Gay Images in Photography: Picturing the Homoerotic," *Out/Look* 3 (1990): 44–51.
5. Camille Paglia, *Sexual Personae: Art and Decadence from Nefertiti to Emily Dickinson* (New York: Vintage, 1990), 110.
6. See William Leach, *Land of Desire: Merchants, Power, and the Rise of a New American Culture* (New York: Vintage, 1993).
7. The pictorialists were initially led by British photographer Joseph William Gleeson White (1851–1898), an artist who took great interest in the primitive, romanticized muscularity of working-class boys. White and his contemporaries—photographers Frank Sutcliff (1853–1941) and Peter Henry Emerson (1856–1936) and painter Henry Scott Tuke (1858–1929)—were heavily influenced by the accomplished photographic form of a German expatriate living in Italy named Baron Wilhelm von Gloeden (1856–1931) who specialized in landscapes and nude studies of Sicilian boys. In 1893 White helped found the Linked Ring, a group organized in London to oppose the conservative policies of the Royal Photographic Society. Many international photographers were also members of this organization, including American Fred Holland Day (1864–1933). For further information and historical background see Emmanuel Cooper, *Fully Exposed: The Male Nude in Photography,* 2d ed. (London: Routledge, 1995), chaps. 8 and 9.

8. Ibid., 23.

9. See Whitney Davis, "Erotic Revision in Thomas Eakins's Narratives of Male Nudity," *Art History* 17 (1994): 301–41.

10. Robert Hughes, *American Visions: The Epic History of Art in America* (New York: Alfred A. Knopf, 1997), 332.

11. Sean Wilentz, "Low Life, High Art," *The New Republic*, 28 September 1992, 42.

12. Ruth S. True, *Boyhood and Lawlessness: The Neglected Girl* (New York: Survey Associates, 1914), 155.

13. Sidney Kingsley, *Dead End*, in *Sidney Kingsley: Five Prizewinning Plays*, ed. Nena Couch (Columbus: Ohio State University Press, 1995), 86; hereafter, page numbers will be cited parenthetically in the text.

14. In an item published in the *New York Times* two days after *Dead End's* opening, it is reported that Kingsley did make two or three "slight" alterations in his play to appease city officials; see "News of the Stage," *New York Times*, 31 October 1935, 17. Corroborating this information is a letter sent to Bel Geddes on 8 November 1935, written by NYSPCC general manager Ernest K. Coulter, which reads in part, "If we have been of any service in the way of getting lines out of the play which would undoubtedly have caused a storm of protest from persons particularly interested in child protection, we are very glad." Ernest K. Coulter to Norman Bel Geddes, 8 November 1935, The Norman Bel Geddes Theater Collection, Harry Ransom Humanities Research Center, Austin, Texas.

15. The boys eventually went on to great fame in a series of films about the exploits of the "Dead End Kids;" their enormous popularity lasted well into the 1950s. During that period more than seventy feature films were made that starred the boys as a group or in various combinations. In addition to the "Dead End Kids," these actors also appeared together on film as the "East Side Kids" and the "Bowery Boys."

16. Brenda Murphy, *American Realism and American Drama, 1880–1940* (Cambridge: Cambridge University Press, 1987), 149.

17. Nena Couch, introduction to Kingsley, *Five Prizewinning Plays*, xxi–xxii.

18. Sidney Kingsley, introduction to *Dead End*, in Kingsley, *Five Prizewinning Plays*, 81.

19. W. B. Worthen, *Modern Drama and the Rhetoric of Theatre* (Berkeley and Los Angeles: University of California Press, 1992), 28.

20. Ibid., 79.

21. Sam Smiley, *The Drama of Attack: Didactic Plays of the American Depression* (Columbia: University of Missouri Press, 1972), 85.

22. J. Brooks Atkinson, review of *Dead End*, by Sidney Kingsley, *New York Times*, 29 October 1935, 17.

23. Grenville Vernon, review of *Dead End*, by Sidney Kingsley, *Commonweal*, 8 November 1935, 48.

24. Edgar Price, review of *Dead End*, by Sidney Kingsley, *Brooklyn Citizen*, 29 October 1935, 5.

25. Kelcey Allen, review of *Dead End*, by Sidney Kingsley, *Women's Wear Daily*, 29 October 1935, 14.

26. A. V. Cookman, "A Reminder that Boys Will Be Boys: A Backstage Glimpse at Youngsters Who Perform in the Current *Dead End* is Proof of It," *New York Times*, 15 December 1935, sec. 11, p. 5.

27. "Toughies," *New Yorker*, 30 November 1935, 13–14.

28. See Leslie Fiedler, *Love and Death in the American Novel* (1966; reprint, with an introduction by Charles B. Harris, Normal, Ill.: Dalkey Archive Press, 1997).

29. Ibid., 270.

30. Kingsley, introduction to *Dead End*, 77.

31. Norman Bel Geddes to Sidney Kingsley, 27 August 1935, Bel Geddes Theater Collection.
32. Richard Dyer, *White* (London and New York: Routledge, 1997), 146.
33. Ibid., 23.
34. Lawrence W. Levine, "American Culture and the Great Depression," *Yale Review* 74 (1985): 213.

11 The Pedagogy of the Popular Front

"Progressive Parenting"
for a New Generation, 1918–1945

Julia Mickenberg

On January 12, 1936, the cover of the communist *Sunday Worker* showed a photograph of a father and daughter, sitting under a picture of Lenin, reading the *Daily Worker* together. The headline read, "A Paper for the Entire Family." Around this time, the *Worker* began publishing a "Woman's Page," and a "Junior America" page in its Sunday edition, and it began running a regular column, "Parents' Problems," by child expert Slava Dunn. Child rearing became a common subject of discussion in radical and Popular Front periodicals in the mid-1930s: the antifascist and prolabor *PM*, for instance, ran a parenting column by Dr. Benjamin Spock (as well as antifascist political cartoons by Dr. Seuss); *Woman Today*, the Popular Front version of the communist newspaper *Working Woman*, and the *Fraternal Outlook*, the magazine of the International Workers' Order, both added parenting columns to their pages in the late 1930s or 1940s.[1] People sympathetic to the labor movement opened family planning clinics, and Works Progress Administration nursery schools offered interracial parent-education programs that were attendant to the needs of working mothers.[2]

The heightened political consciousness characteristic of the 1930s filtered readily into child-rearing discourse, particularly as the spread of international fascism invited speculation on the origins of "the authoritarian personality" and discussions of the ways in which parents (and teachers) could best prepare children for the demands of living in a democratic society.[3] Examining the discourse around children's socialization as it was formulated by a progressive "formation"—of communists, independent radicals, and New Deal liberals—provides a window into the pedagogical function of the Popular Front, an antifascist coalition initiated by the American Communist Party in 1935 to counter the rise of fascism.[4] In other words, the Popular Front ideologies of antifascism, antiracism, prolaborism, democratic Americanism, and internationalism were translated not only into a set of expectations about raising children, but also into a willful attempt to shape the future through children.[5]

Progressive parenting (the term appears to have entered the popular lexicon in the 1920s) combined the developmental insights of Freudian psychology, the cultural relativism of anthropology, the child-centeredness and social consciousness of progressive education, the social-democratic discourse of antifascism, and, at least in some quarters, elements of revolutionary anticapitalism. In the mid- 1930s, as the Popular Front "structure of feeling" became part of a national, antifascist "common sense," a permissive and, increasingly, politicized model of parenting became part of the American mainstream. Moreover, as left-liberal cooperation ultimately became unsustainable by the late 1940s, children became the last common repository for the utopian hopes that had animated the radical and reformist activity of the 1930s. Although progressive parenting as a mainstream, politicized discourse would not survive the Cold War, its sentiments would be channeled into children's culture and would resurface in the liberation movements of the 1960s.

Although members of the 1960s New Left would scoff at claims that Dr. Spock's "permissive" parenting advice had created a generation without respect for authority, to the extent that Spock's popularity represented the institutionalization of progressive parenting, and to the extent that Spock himself identified with left-of-center politics, such accusations were not entirely off base.[6] Several scholars have suggested a link between the "democratic" or "permissive" ideology of parenting that developed in the late 1930s and 1940s and heightened concerns about authority and discipline that arose in reaction to fascism.[7] Likewise, recent studies of post-World War II race relations emphasize that a new liberal discourse on race, linked to antifascism, made racism un-American; this discourse probed early childhood experiences to discover the roots of the authoritarian, intolerant, and racist personality.[8] But the links in these discussions to discourse in the communist milieu are nearly invisible despite similarities in liberal and left-wing rhetoric, and despite shared personnel in media and institutions. For instance, some of the same individuals wrote for the left-wing *Fraternal Outlook* and for *Parents,* and the Child Study Association shared personnel with the Marxist Jefferson School of Social Science and the National Council on American Soviet

Friendship.[9] And, as I discuss elsewhere, some of the most popular writers of children's books in the mid-twentieth century were at some point in their lives close to the Communist Party.[10] This is *not* evidence of Soviet propaganda worming its way into something so basic as the nation's child rearing, but many educators and experts on child development did look to the Soviet Union for models in the 1920s and 1930s.[11] All of this *does* suggest that the Left, much more than scholars have acknowledged, helped to shape the national common sense vis-à-vis children in the mid-twentieth century. Even with the Cold War a thing of the past, McCarthyism has so scarred American public memory that it has become difficult to assess the impact of the communist Left on American culture and society in a clearheaded way. But the extent to which progressive coalition building centered upon children, and the real impact of a politicized parenting discourse, deserves examination. This essay charts the development of a leftist "progressive parenting" discourse, beginning in the 1920s, flowering in the 1930s and 1940s, and ultimately reflecting the extreme marginalization of communists and communist sympathizers by the 1950s.

While communists, socialists, anarchists and other radicals had consistently paid attention to children, operating schools, after-school programs, summer camps, and other educational and social programs, children assumed center stage in the communist milieu during the time of the Popular Front—that is, beginning in the mid-1930s.[12] Moreover, the approach to children in the rhetoric of the radical left changed with the Popular Front as the Communist Party dropped its revolutionary stance of the 1920s and early 1930s and sought to enter the American mainstream. As the party broadened its scope and claimed legitimacy in American revolutionary traditions, thousands of idealistic Americans in their twenties and thirties, many of them parents, joined the party and its affiliated organizations. To attract a broader following and to encourage coalition building with liberals, the party also began to devote more attention to private life and especially to "women's" issues. Columns on child rearing and child psychology in communist periodicals were part of this shift. Whereas earlier discussions on the subject of children had emphasized their suffering under capitalism and the need to involve both mothers and children in militant struggle, material geared toward both parents and children now reflected an interest in children's psychological as well as physical well-being.

The Popular Front's vital and sustained discourse around children combined the rhetoric of 1920s cultural radicals with that of political radicals like socialists and communists, also incorporating liberal theories of child development and education. According to writer Malcolm Cowley, "the idea of salvation by the child" was fundamental to the "doctrine" of a post-World

War I radical bohemia.[13] These cultural radicals and a new cadre of progressive educators identified children with hope, creativity, and innovation, and pursued the implications of psychoanalysis and recent educational theories for child rearing and development. They laid the greatest emphasis on giving children freedom to develop as individuals; they also assumed that adult institutions were corrupt, and that children were the basis for a new, more democratic, egalitarian and vibrant social order. As communists dropped their revolutionary rhetoric in the late 1930s and worked to create a broad antifascist coalition, they adopted and adapted the progressive parenting discourse that had begun to take shape in the 1920s, and they injected that discourse with a more explicit political component.

In the fall of 1926, *Progressive Education* carried an article by Dorothy Canfield Fisher on "How Children Educate Their Parents." This and other articles published in the journal that fall were subsequently collected and reprinted as a special issue, "The Progressive Parent." Essays in this collection spoke to a changed context for parenting and a new vision of childhood in the modern age. In essence, they suggested that parents trapped in the overmechanized grind of modern times could be liberated by their children, who could teach them a genuine feeling of selflessness and reconnect them with primal experiences so lacking in "civilized" societies. As Fisher put it, "we have so few strong, vital, primitive satisfactions left! The world seems bent on sterilizing all our older deeper impulses." Edward Yeomans's essay in the same collection, titled "Salvaging the Family," went beyond the question of personal regeneration to social regeneration, arguing that "the thing that has retarded human progress more than anything else [is] the inability of the divine strengths of childhood to carry over and through in spite of the establishment of civilizations, societies, religions and industries." According to Yeomans, "the organizers, the standardizers, the elder statesmen, the exploiters of all time, have never wanted that Child abroad, with its profound powers of love and forgetfulness of self, and insatiable curiosity and questioning and enormous capacity for disinterested work, for generosity and expression of beauty." Children, in other words, might hold the cure for "a sickness that threatens the spiritual life of the nation."[14]

Benzion Liber, a physician associated with the anarchist "modern school" movement, likewise insisted in his 1921 book *The Child and the Home: Essays on the Rational Upbringing of Children* that "the greatest obstacle to a better world is improper upbringing."[15] Liber's work established "permissivism" as the hallmark of progressive parenting decades before Spock. He argued that children should *never* be punished, for in disputes between children and adults, children were usually right. Although Liber believed most social institutions were corrupt, he rejected the idea of indoctrinating children with antiestablishment propaganda. Instead, Liber urged parents to give children freedom and the opportunity to think for themselves ("dogmatic radicals are not less unjust than dogmatic conservatives," he insisted). Truly rational, informed individuals would naturally question the contradictions inherent in the social order, he believed. Liber also maintained that false social distinctions might be wiped out if children could grow up without learning the racial, class, and gender prejudices that infected the older generation: "Just permit one generation of all white and black children of the South of the United States to frolic and romp together and refrain from telling them anything about the struggle that is going on or about the days of servitude and slave ownership; let them grow up with the sentiment gained personally from one another through direct contact, and the face of this great commonwealth is changed." Although many of Liber's ideas were obviously radical, he gained a relatively wide and sympathetic following.[16]

On the most basic level, Liber's assertion that children's upbringing could make or break the future was part of a wartime and post–World War I national consensus—not simply an understanding among those on the left—that linked national well-being to child welfare. What differentiated progressives and radicals from conservatives, and even from liberals, was the question of what constituted "proper" upbringing. In the 1920s, both traditionalists and progressives condemned the American family as a corrupt institution. Traditionalists argued that a lack of discipline and waning parental authority signaled the decline of society as a whole: psychologist John B. Watson, for example, criticized parents for their emotional excess and failure to instill children with proper habits and discipline. Progressives and radicals, on the other hand, believed that the rigidity of the American family could only lead to revolt among the young. The methods of child rearing and education that could best prepare a new generation to come of age in the modern era was the subject of heated debate, although most agreed that practices had to be altered in light of radically changed conditions.[17]

A growing number of radicals pinned their hopes for a new social order on the progressive school, which they believed might counter reactionary trends in public schooling. Agnes De Lima, for instance, argued that schools tended to destroy children's natural curiosity, delight, and engagement with the world around them. This problem was related to the fact that public school boards were invested in maintaining the status quo. In contrast, De Lima suggested that the freedom advocated by many of the new progressive schools was implicitly radical: "Some canny sleuth will discover that there is a direct connection between schools which set out deliberately to train children to think, and to develop creatively, and the radical movement." She pointed in particular to "those [schools] directed by people who have a vision of a new social order, and who believe that the way to prepare for it is to bring up a generation of free thinking, self-directing young people whose spontaneity, originality, and native curiosity have not been stifled nor confined within narrow grooves of conformity." [18]

Writing nearly twenty years later, Carleton Washburne, president of the Progressive Education Association, would argue that the tendency to associate "progressive" schools with "an atmosphere of radicalism" showed a false understanding of progressive education's true purpose. "Progressive education does not indoctrinate children with any particular solution to our problems," he insisted, "but instills in them a desire to examine all proposals, to get beneath propaganda and prejudice, to seek facts and reasons, and to think boldly. This is radicalism only in the best sense—getting at the roots of problems." [19] This central concern with creating socially conscious, independent thinkers characterized the discourse of progressive parenting as well as progressive education. As De Lima explicitly proclaimed and Washburne implicitly admitted, encouraging children to be informed and to think critically, were, in fact, radical propositions, which is why progressive education was so vehemently challenged by critics on the right. [20]

Implicit in much of the progressive-parenting discourse were Freudian and Marxist theories that became common coin in certain circles in the 1920s and 1930s. *The New Generation: The Intimate Problems of Modern Parents and Children,* a landmark collection published in 1930, typified the confluence of voices around the modern child. The book's editors, V. F. Calverton and Samuel D. Schmalhausen, collected thirty-three articles from a wide range of (mostly left-of-center) intellectuals, psychologists, literary figures, medical personnel and academics, including author Sherwood Anderson; Agnes De Lima; sexologist Havelock Ellis, proletarian philosopher, writer, and agitator Mike Gold, head of the Child Study Association Sidonie Gruenberg; poet and musician Alfred Kreymborg; Benzion Liber; anthropologists Bronislaw Malinowski and Margaret Mead; radical educator Scott Nearing; Bertrand Russell (who wrote an introduction to the book); and (conservative) behavioral psychologist John Watson. While varied in their disciplinary and political perspectives, contributors tended to be highly critical of existing family structures and modern educational systems; however, most were also hopeful about the liberatory potential of both psychology and education.

Calverton and Schmalhausen linked the "discovery of the child's personality" to broad-based hopes for a "new society—more humanistic than any of old, more creative and joyous and inspiring." Contributors to the book discussed how conditions might be brought about so that a humanized society would "fashion 'new parents for old'" and "make marvelously possible the child's coming of age." [21] Although the book's contributors and their articles represent a range of political positions that resist simple classification, as a collection they also represent a de facto coalition united by their hope for social regeneration, reform, or revolution through the child. The more radical commentators agreed that the family, at that time, was infected with the "quantitative mania" of the larger society and was in need of transformation. At minimum, the contributors all seemed to feel that parents needed to rethink their role. Were they fostering a "uterine-like," enclosed, self-complacent home life that kept family members from being concerned with larger social issues? Did children learn exploitation, greed, and "neurotic dependency" from their parents? [22]

If child-rearing manuals like Spock's would be criticized for having a middle-class bias, this collection (like Liber's own volume on child rearing), was conscious of the material and psychological costs of raising children in a family with limited means. T. Swann Harding, for example (echoing early-twentieth-century socialists like Ellen Key and John Spargo, but shifting emphasis from mothers to parents in general), concluded that the actual cost of bearing and raising children was so prohibitively high that working-class parents would soon decide to avoid parenthood altogether unless the state gave financial and medical support to all families. [23] Several contributors questioned Freudian psychology's emphasis on sexual pathos and repression and suggested that beyond material difficulties, working-class families were plagued by psychological problems arising from "the universal repression of common sense in the interest of an exploitative social order" [24]

For many commentators in *The New Generation,* the Soviets' programs for socializing children seemed to offer a model of balancing respect for children with the need to teach them particular values and behaviors. Arthur Wallace Calhoun, for example, argued that the Soviet Union's success in socializing children was the greatest testament to the power of psychology: the Soviet example seemed to prove that "if we chose to deal fairly with the child mind, we could in short order have an ideal world." [25] Calhoun's views reflected fairly widespread fascination with the Soviet Union in the 1920s and early 1930s, a fascination that extended well beyond the communist Left prior to the Cold War.

Mike Gold's essay "The Proletarian Child" most clearly reflected the Communist Party's discourse on children in the 1920s and early 1930s. Gold insisted that "the child" should not be discussed by psychologists and educational theorists as an abstraction, and that the class lines dividing children must be recognized in any theory of education that proclaimed to support the child's liberation: "The environment of poverty, and the compulsions of poverty, will always be more powerful than any school system in its effects on children," Gold proclaimed. Children who are hungry, who are forced to work in order to help feed their families, have a very different set of concerns from middle-class children, Gold argued. He believed that theorists of "the child" would have to address the cause of poverty itself, and then consider what it would mean to educate proletarian children in their best interest: "Shall they be taught to believe in trade unionism?" he asked. "In social revolution? In working class solidarity? Or are they to be taught on a basis of lies: that they too are to be college professors, lawyers and stockbrokers? This is the problem that every 'modern' educator has avoided until now: the economic status of the child, his class environment and future."[26]

In line with Gold's position, communist writing in the early 1930s on the subject of children—like Grace Hutchins's 1933 pamphlet, "Children under Capitalism," or like numerous articles in *Working Woman*—emphasized the misery of children living in capitalist countries and urged parents, especially mothers, to take an active role in combating "the poison of patriotism taught in the schools" by teaching children about class struggle.[27] Van Gosse has argued that the conditions of the Depression generated a discursive shift in communist rhetoric from male to female terrain as the entire working class—not simply male industrial workers—was suddenly mobilized. The struggle moved from shop floor to tenement and "from exploitation (you are making me a wage slave) to hunger (your system is starving our children)." Along with this shift, Gosse argues, communists turned for a "usable past" to the rhetoric of "the pre-World War I left of the Socialist Party (SP), the Industrial Workers of the World (IWW), and the larger milieu of radical labor from which the CPUSA sprang in 1919." This prewar Left "had consistently articulated a gender-conscious class politics focused on hunger, white slavery, and all the other evils of capitalist home-wrecking."[28] Articles published in the communist press in the early 1930s, especially in media geared toward women, detailed the condition of child laborers and praised mothers' activism on behalf of children. Publications directed toward children themselves—like *The New Pioneer*—urged boys and girls to become militant activists, to march in May Day parades, and to press for free school lunches, more playgrounds, and improved school facilities.[29]

While communists in the early 1930s may have found a usable past in the rhetoric of the pre-World War I Left, during the time of the Popular Front they turned to the liberatory rhetoric of the post-World War I "lyrical left." Thus *The New Generation* was a prescient marker of things to come, as it brought people of varying political persuasions into dialogue around issues that would become central to child-rearing discourse in the next two decades.

During the time of the Popular Front, in left-wing magazines and periodicals, child-related discourse ranged from explicitly political discussions (How do you discuss war or the labor movement with children? What can parents do to improve conditions in schools?) and imagery (cartoons depicting, for instance, Santa Claus giving children gas masks), to child-rearing columns that seem almost indistinguishable from mainstream advice in their emphasis on "understanding" the child's emotions. "Parent and Child" columns by Stella Chess, appearing in the *Fraternal Outlook* in the late 1940s, considered such subjects as "Respecting the Rights of Others," "Thumb Sucking," and "The First Day of School."[30] Several children's books recommended in the magazine had similar themes: *David's Bad Day* showed both children and parents how to cope with the trauma created for a child by the addition of a new sibling; *From Little Acorns* attempted to demystify reproduction and sexuality.[31] Although politics were muted in these sources, the very placement of such discussions within explicitly political magazines suggested that a seemingly personal matter like raising children was a political act. And, on the whole, child-rearing advice in left-wing outlets always made an implicit connection to the fact that a child's upbringing was tied to her ability to function in a social world.

Discussions and images of children had a similar function: commentary on schooling, child welfare, or inadequate social services for children; photographic images of crying children in Spain, of Harlem children living in poverty, or of children working in mines, canneries, and sweatshops or attending run-down schools suggested—individually and cumulatively—that *all* adults should be concerned with the physical health, welfare, and emotional security of *all* children. Likewise, critiques of American educational practices and children's media—including literature, film, comic books, and music—suggested that the *minds* of all children ought to be of common concern. Thus, progressive parenting was not only about raising one's own children with the right values and with physical and emotional security, but also about bringing up an entire generation and making the world better for all children.

The transformation of the newspaper *Working Woman* to the glossy magazine *Woman Today* in 1936 reflected the party's efforts to attract middle-class women, many of whom did not work outside the home. Child-rearing advice in *Woman Today* represented the new wisdom of progressive parenting: be attentive to your child's emotions, and teach your child to be socially conscious. Moreover, it reflected a more optimistic attitude about families: whereas in the early 1930s many radicals viewed the family, especially the middle-class family, as a malignant influence on the child, by the mid-1930s there was a greater sense that parents and children could cooperate—in conjunction with special organizations that served children—to nurture democratic consciousness and a commitment to the labor movement.

Like the articles in *Woman Today,* Slava Dunn's advice column in the *Sun-*

day Worker focused primarily on the child's mental and emotional development as they related to problems parents might have in disciplining their children. In one column, Dunn noted that many parents experience discipline problems with their children because they try too hard to control the child; that is, as Dunn put it, "they talk too much." According to Dunn, "there are dangers in constantly telling children what to do and what not to do. No one likes to be bossed—children no more than adults. Too much direction of every move the child makes can cause either rebellion against all possible requests and rules, or a lack of decision and initiative." Dunn insisted that in order to develop resourcefulness, initiative and judgment, children must be given responsibility and the opportunity to make choices.[32] Unlike Liber, Dunn displayed sympathy for parents' struggles. She noted that "often a parent who has a strong sense of inferiority takes it out on his children by bossing them, since this is his only way to feel important and superior to others. Such a parent needs help so that he can realize his own good points. He needs a boost from his mate or from some friend."[33]

Politics were basically undetectable in sources such as these, but occasionally they surfaced in vivid and sometimes comic ways. In May of 1936, for example, the *Sunday Worker* published a letter to Dunn that was said to be written by an almost-two-year-old named Poots. Poots told Dunn that although her parents rarely scolded her, and certainly never hit her, she *had* recently made Daddy very angry. Having been placed on "the little chair" for a while to do her business, Poots suddenly was seized with the desire to rifle through a drawer across the room, to see what might be in it. "Well," wrote Poots, "while I was busy with that, and Mother in the kitchen eating breakfast, I forgot I wasn't on the chair and made what they call a mess on the floor." Daddy thought that this time little Poots had earned herself a good spanking. But mother, who had just the night before read Dunn's article on "Backsliding Babies" in the *Sunday Worker*, thought differently and urged Daddy to refrain from giving Poots a whack on the behind. When Mother read Daddy the article over breakfast, he too changed his tune.

"Mother thinks it's pretty hard to know how to train a baby in a planless society," Poots noted sympathetically. "Are you training your children for capitalism? If so, it's just as well to make Brats out of them, so they will know how to be tough with the Bosses and Arbitration Boards. It's just as well to train them to lie—cleverly; not to believe what they read and hear. But," Poots declared in a gesture of optimism (and revolutionary zeal?), "Mother says we're putting our money on a Planned Society where a pro-social, cooperative attitude will be best. It's sort of puzzling what she means about putting money, because we're like most workers, I guess, and money's a thing there never seems to be enough of around this house to put on anything. And

I can't figure out yet what our planned society looks like, or where in the house we keep it. I guess I'll know when I grow up."[34] Poots made explicit what was implicit not only in most of Dunn's columns, but also in the numerous articles in Popular Front periodicals that emphasized the importance of attending to the child's emotional health, as well as her intellectual and physical health. Such concerns, along with a more permissive approach to discipline, were echoed in liberal discussions.

The economic and social crises of the 1930s, the rise of fascism, the threat of war, and widespread sympathy for the "forgotten man" had inspired educational reforms and a new outlook on parenting. All parents were now encouraged to apply a "spirit of criticism" to their child-rearing practices; more than teaching their children discipline and obedience, the new priority was to teach children "to think for themselves." Or put more forcefully, an educator writing for *Parents* in 1934 cited John Dewey's contention that "a chief end of education is to see the defects in existing social arrangements and to *take an active part* in bettering them."[35] A 1936 article in *Parents* noted "No longer, at least in America, may we exercise our arbitrary authority over youth, not with the same assurance of acceptance and continued love. . . . One may read this truth in any page of the cool objective studies of maladjustment made by modern sociologists and psychologists."[36]

Fascism, understood as all that "Americanism" was not, placed a burden on parents to enact, through their relations with their children, the democratic principles they claimed to embrace. An article appearing in *Parents* in November 1938 asked, "Are You a DICTATOR? You are on guard against dictatorship in politics, but what about the management of your own home? Are you training little goose-steppers there?"[37] The article told readers that rigid discipline was unsuited to democratic countries and homes. The popular parenting guide by Arnold Gesell and Frances Ilg, *Infant and Child in the Culture of Today*, contrasted models of parenting in a totalitarian "kultur" to those in a democracy, which "affirms the dignity of the person" and "favors reciprocity in parent-child relationships."[38] As democracy appeared threatened by fascism, home and school became bulwarks for building and maintaining democratic traditions.

The feeling of uncertainty and the social unrest characteristic of the age generated as well a growing emphasis on racial tolerance, which, psychologists and educators had come to believe, was something that, like prejudice, could be learned. "The soundest possible way to secure international peace is to kindle in our children a greater feeling of kinship with humanity at large," a writer for *Parents* noted in 1934.[39] Such concerns intensified as fascism began to spread through Europe and as war appeared imminent. Referring explicitly to German efforts to teach children racial hatred, *Parents* in 1938 noted that "the responsibility for bringing up children free from the poisons of prejudice and intolerance rests squarely on the shoulders of parents."[40] Racial prejudice was not just undesirable, it was now un-American.

Though many discussions, even those published in radical outlets, eschewed the outright ideological discourse in which Poots freely engaged, other child-related discourse in left-wing periodicals brought the concerns of working-class, ethnic, and minority parents to the forefront. Despite the Popular Front spirit of inclusivity and an attempt to build a broad-based progressive movement, those in the radical Left distrusted the dominant culture; an implicit and often explicit critique of liberal rhetoric and politics distinguished left from center in the discourse of progressive parenting. Repeatedly surfacing in the discourse was left-wing parents' concern that without a concerted effort on their part and on the part of the progressive community as whole, children would grow up with values unlike their own. Writing in *Woman Today* in 1936, Frances Liscomb asked, "Do you find that your children think it's queer when you go out on the picket line or take an active part in the labor movement?" Even children who rationally understood their parents' activism were bound to wonder why "in the funnies the strikers were always long-haired, wild-looking bearded men, shouting from soap boxes. In the movies none of the good people ever picketed." Parents wanting children to feel a sense of pride in their struggles find themselves "fighting a constant battle," Liscomb noted, "and often they do not realize the full extent of the forces which keep their children's interests foreign to their own."[41]

Left-wing groups ran an array of programs to help parents teach children not only about their values, but also about their ethnic and cultural heritage. Jewish *shules* offered after-school programs to teach Yiddish language and culture from a secular and "progressive" perspective. Similar programs were run in Ukrainian, Finnish, and Italian communities, many in connection with the International Workers' Order, which had a special program for children, the IWO Juniors. Likewise, a number of "junior unions" served children of union members. Such programs, like the summer camps and various cultural events sponsored by left-wing organizations, were vital elements of an alternative culture for children.[42] One of the major concerns of groups like the International Workers' Order was interethnic and interracial conflict; during World War II they worked to promote a general atmosphere of cooperation and peacefulness to counteract the violent atmosphere fostered by wartime.

The Second World War brought questions of children's physical and emotional security, as well as their ability to understand complex social issues, into sharp contrast. Even prior to American involvement in the war, the extent to which violence permeated American culture, and, in particular, children's culture (from toys to comic books to movies) was a source of distress to progressive parents. While children's war play was sometimes attributed to their need to act out violent fantasies or to compensate for inner fears and anxiety, more often such behavior was blamed on the violence that permeated American culture and, moreover, on the extent to which capitalism fostered such a culture of violence. For instance, a 1941 article in the *Fraternal Outlook* blamed boys' war play on the greed of "goggle-eyed" toy manufacturers, yellow journalists, and filmmakers who cared more about their own profits than about the tender young minds they were corrupting.[43] Perhaps the most difficult question for progressive parents was whether children should be taught to hate those who were German, Japanese, or Italian. For instance, an article in the *Fraternal Outlook* in 1943 asked "whether this might not lead to the same type of blind hatred, so methodically introduced to the children of fascist countries."[44]

Once the United States entered the war, emphasis on teaching racial tolerance, cooperation, and democracy became a staple of parenting advice and, even more so, of schooling; the intercultural education movement grew directly out of the desire to counter the racial ideology and authoritarianism characteristic of fascism.[45] Though never as openly political as communist magazines like the *Fraternal Outlook*, liberal commentary—in *Parents* magazine, or in books like Anna Wolf's *Our Children Face War*—reflected some of the same concerns. Articles in *Parents* debated the question of whether children (boys) ought to own guns; the Child Study Association tried to ease parents' concerns about war play, noting that "up to a certain point this is perfectly healthy—a real safety-valve."[46] In the late 1930s, several articles in *Parents* made strong statements against war,[47] and during the war, emphasis was placed on teaching the positive values of democracy, toleration, and cooperation. As to whether children should be taught to hate, Wolf declared that they should be taught to hate *fascism*, but not to hate all Germans, all Japanese or all Italians. "Hate can be a tricky emotion," she asserted. "[It] constricts the human spirit as often as it enspirits, especially if it is a hate that smoulders and lives on. Is this, perhaps, a war in which only something deeper and more enduringly passionate than hate will drive us forward to victory, and can make a peace that lasts?"[48]

Such sentiments appealed to members of the Popular Front Left. In the late 1930s and 1940s, books on education and parenting by liberal authors were reviewed and recommended in left-wing outlets like *New Masses* and *The Fraternal Outlook*. The Marxist Jefferson School of Social Science, which opened its doors in 1944, offered a course that year called Everyday Problems of Childhood and Family Life. The course bibliography included sixteen titles (all by liberal authors), among them *The Happy Family,* by John Levy and Ruth Monroe (1936); *We the Parents,* by Sidonie Gruenberg (1939; marked as "highly recommended"); *Your Child Meets the Outside World* (1941), by Elizabeth Boettiger (1941); *Infant and Child in the Culture of Today,* by Gesell and Ilg (1941; "especially recommended"); *The Parents' Manual,* by Anna Wolf (1941; also "highly recommended"); Wolf's *Our Children Face War* (1942); and pamphlets published by the Child Study Association including "Discipline: What Is It?" "What Makes a Good Home?" and "When Children Ask About Sex" (all "highly recommended").[49] Another course on Behavior and Development of the Pre-School Child listed many of the same books, but also included *Growing Up in New Guinea* by Margaret Mead (1930) and several sources on neuroses, psychoanalysis, and mental hygiene, reflecting a strong interest in both anthropology and psychoanalysis.[50]

One widely distributed booklet, which was on the Jefferson School of Social Science's reading list for a course on psychology, highlighted the need to teach racial tolerance during the war. *The Races of Mankind,* written by Columbia University anthropologists Ruth Benedict and Gene Weltfish, was first published in 1943 by the Public Affairs Committee, a liberal nonprofit educational committee. Used in U.S. Army orientation classes, the booklet went through two editions; it was made into an animated film in 1946, and then into a children's book, *In Henry's Backyard: The Races of Mankind,* in 1948.[51] Such emphasis on stamping out race hatred directly contributed to the *Brown vs. Topeka Board of Education* verdict in 1954. And as *Parents* magazine emphasized in the years following World War II, the threat of atomic warfare also heightened the need for children to play an active part in working for peace.[52]

Despite the popularity of *The Races of Mankind*'s message, however, efforts to teach children racial tolerance and the importance of peace became more infrequent in liberal circles by the early 1950s. Such efforts challenged the Cold War status quo by implicitly criticizing U.S. policy in the south and internationally. In schools, emphasis on teaching cooperation and understanding gave way to preparing children for war: civil defense films shown in schools, like the popular *Duck and Cover,* focused on what to do *when,* not *if,* an attack came, and school textbooks came to be filled with anti-Soviet and anticommunist propaganda. "Patriotic" organizations urged schools to ban books that criticized any aspect of the U.S. government, as well as books advocating socialism, communism, or "New Dealism."[53] In this context, *The Races of Mankind* became "subversive": by the early 1950s, it was banned and condemned for "creat[ing] racial antagonism."[54]

As the fate of *Races* would suggest, by the late 1940s and early 1950s, several factors combined to drive a wedge between independent progressives and their counterparts closer to the Communist Party milieu.[55] First, Soviet show trials and purges in the 1930s, the Soviets' alliance with the Nazis in 1939, and new evidence of Soviet espionage surfacing just after World War II all marked communists, who appeared to uncritically tout the Soviet line, as untrustworthy—indeed, as sinister allies in the eyes of many liberals. Second, the rise of McCarthyism forced many progressives and liberals to demonstrate their opposition to communists (with whom they had in years past cooperated). Third, the American Communist Party's increasingly secretive, hierarchical and undemocratic way of operating alienated many potential allies. And finally, the war's end and a period of unprecedented affluence precipitated a general movement among Americans away from left-wing politics.[56]

In 1951, as "atomic spies" Julius and Ethel Rosenberg awaited their fate in Sing Sing Prison, the campaign to save them focused on their soon-to-be orphaned children, taking every opportunity to show what good parents the Rosenbergs were. Indeed, in a gesture of love for her sons, from prison Ethel asked her lawyer to buy a copy of *The Races of Mankind* as a holiday gift for the boys;[57] she grasped the pamphlet's progressive message but failed to recognize that the gift would further mark her as "un-American." That same year, the Jefferson School of Social Science offered a seminar on "the ideological problems faced by children from progressive homes." At this meeting "parents complained that nowhere in school do their children get an honest interpretation of American history, and of the role played by Negro, Jewish and other peoples in building our country. Several told how their children, brought up in progressive homes, are confused and intimidated by the incessant anti-Communist and anti-Soviet propaganda they meet in school, comic books, over the radio and television."[58] Almost all discourse vis-à-vis children in the radical Left milieu indicated a sense of siege by the early 1950s, even as children emerged as the last remaining hope. "It has become so bad," one mother told the Jefferson School seminar, "that several progressive friends of mine have instructed their children, 'Whatever comes up in school, don't you open your mouth.'"[59]

Unlike courses offered at the Jefferson School in the mid-1940s, the instructor for a 1955 course on child development now recommended only books by Soviet authors; a student report comparing the teachings of the Soviet educator A. S. Makarenko to those of the liberal child expert Dorothy Baruch argued that the evil thoughts and improper behaviors that Baruch urged parents to react to through "understanding" would never even arise in a socialist society: "The job of the progressive parent is to wipe out the evil and violence which provokes such thoughts, rather than hoping such thoughts will disappear by expressing them."[60]

Although the 1950s actually brought heightened attention to children and families,[61] the original political implications of progressive parenting were muted. In mainstream discourse, progressive parenting boiled down to "accepting children" (to use David Riesman's phrasing); likewise, progressive education became "life adjustment" education, with courses on hygiene, dating, and other "practical" nonacademic subjects.[62] Meanwhile, those "progressive parents" still clinging to an idyllic vision of the Soviet Union tended to be sectarian in their views and were utterly isolated from the mainstream. But remnants of an antiorthodox progressive formation remained intact, even after Henry Wallace's failed presidential campaign in 1948. Perhaps the best evidence of that formation can be found in the children's literature and music of the 1950s and early 1960s: in Folkways and Young People's Records, and in books like *Harold and the Purple Crayon, Mary Jane, Swimmy,* and *Sylvester and the Magic Pebble,* as well as innumerable books of nonfiction.[63] Folksinger Pete Seeger and others—blacklisted from adult realms—turned to children, figuring that, as Seeger put it, "if we're going to save this world, we've got to reach the kids."[64] Carried by seeds in children's culture, the libratory, socially conscious values of progressive parenting would later be echoed in the discourse of the New Left. Young radicals—calling for "participatory democracy" and for "all power to the imagination"—challenged the social order, insisting that they were merely trying to reconcile the ideals they had been taught as children with the reality they saw around them.[65]

NOTES

1. The International Workers' Order, which had close ties to the American Communist Party, was an interethnic fraternal organization and mutual benefit society that also ran programs for families and children.

2. See "IWO Family Planning Clinic," *Fraternal Outlook,* May 1940, 29–30. On nursery schools see, for example, Marese Eliot, "Have You a Nursery in Your Town?" *Woman Today,* February 1937, 4–5, 30. On parent education see, for example, Marese Eliot, "Do You Understand Your Children?" *Woman Today,* May 1937, 12–13.

3. The term *authoritarian personality* comes from Theodor W. Adorno, but concerns he articulated in the 1950s were already widespread when *The Authoritarian Personality* was published in 1950. See Adorno, *The Authoritarian Personality* (New York: Harper, 1950).

4. On formations see Raymond Williams, *Marxism and Literature* (Oxford: Oxford University Press, 1977), 117.

5. On the Popular Front, see Michael Denning, *The Cultural Front: The Laboring of American Culture in the Twentieth Century* (New York: Verso, 1996), and Maurice Isserman, *Which Side Were You On?* (Urbana: University of Illinois Press, 1993). Less sympathetic interpretations include Harvey Klehr, *The Heyday of American Communism: The Depression Decade* (New York: Basic Books, 1984).

6. Spock himself was a *New Masses* subscriber in the 1930s and 1940s; he became an outspoken peace and antinuclear activist in the 1960s and 1970s. See Lynn Bloom, *Dr. Spock: Biography of a Conservative Radical* (Indianapolis: Bobbs-Merrill, 1972).

7. William Tuttle, "America's Children in an Era of War, Hot and Cold: The Holocaust, the Bomb, and Child Rearing in the 1940s," in *Rethinking Cold War Culture,* ed. James Gilbert and Peter Kuznick (Washington, D.C.: Smithsonian Institution Press, 1999), 14–34; William Graebner, "The Unstable World of Benjamin Spock: Social Engineering in a Democratic Culture, 1917–1950," *Journal of American History* 67 (1980): 612–29.

8. See, for example, Ruth Feldstein, *Motherhood in Black and White: Race and Sex in American Liberalism, 1930–1965* (Ithaca, N.Y.: Cornell University Press, 1999).

9. Sidonie Gruenberg, head of the Child Study Association and a respected author, also was involved with the Jefferson School of Social Science and with the National Council for American Soviet Friendship (NCASF). Benjamin Harris, " 'Don't Be Unconscious; Join Our Ranks': Psychology, Politics, and Communist Education," *Rethinking Marxism* 6 (1993): 68. Information on NCASF is at Tamiment Library, New York University. Papers of the Jefferson School of Social Science (in the Tamiment Library) and of the Child Study Association (at the University of Minnesota) indicate that Clara Ostrowsky, on the staff of the Child Study Association, was chair of the Children's Department at the Jefferson School and also ran the bookstore. Stella Chess, who had a regular column on parenting in *The Fraternal Outlook,* contributed occasionally to *Parents,* and Pearl S. Buck contributed to both *Parents* and *The New Masses.*

10. See Julia Mickenberg, *Seeds of Idealism: How Children's Books Linked the Old and New Left* (New York: Oxford University Press, forthcoming).

11. See, for example, John Dewey, *Impressions of Russia and the Revolutionary World* (1929; reprint New York: Teachers College, Columbia University, 1964); Vera Fediaevsky and Patty Smith Hill, *Nursery School and Parent Education in Soviet Russia* (New York: E. P. Dutton, 1936).

12. On the socialist education of children, see Kenneth Teitelbaum, *Schooling for Good Rebels: Socialist Education for Children in the United States,* 1900–1920 (Philadelphia: Temple University Press, 1993). On anarchist education of children, see Paul Avrich, *The Modern School Movement: Anarchism and Education in the United States* (Princeton, N.J.: Princeton University Press, 1980). On communist programs for children, see Paul Mishler, *Raising Reds: The Young Pioneers, Radical Summer Camps, and Communist Political Culture in the United States* (New York: Columbia University Press, 1999).

13. Malcolm Cowley, *Exile's Return: A Literary Odyssey of the 1920s* (New York: Viking Press, 1964), 60.

14. Dorothy Canfield Fisher, "How Children Educate Their Parents," 281, and Edward W. Yeomans, "Salvaging the Family," 284, in *The Progressive Parent* (Washington, D.C.: The Progressive Education Association, 1927), 279–88.

15. On Liber's involvement with the modern school movement, see Mishler, *Raising Reds,* 28. Benzion Liber, *The Child and the Home: Essays on the Rational Bringing-Up of Children,* 2d ed. (New York: Rational Living, 1923) 19–20.

16. Liber, *The Child,* 24–30, 74, 94, 97–98, 309. The book was published in an affordable paperback edition and received many favorable reviews not only from radical periodicals but also from mainstream news media including *The New Republic, The Survey,* the *Detroit News,* the *Minneapolis Tribune,* and the *New York World.* Reviews are cited on pp. 269–93 of the 1923 edition.

17. John B. Watson, *Psychological Care of Infant and Child* (New York: W. W. Norton, 1928).

18. Agnes De Lima, *Our Enemy the Child* (New York: The New Republic, 1925), 238.

19. Carleton Washburne, "What about Progressive Education?" *Parents,* June 1941, 34–35ff.

20. Progressive education was at the center of right-wing critiques of education during the Cold War. See, for example, Kitty Jones and Robert L. Olivier, *Progressive Education in REDucation* (Boston: Meador, 1956). The classic work on the history of progressive edu-

cation is Lawrence A. Cremin, *The Transformation of the School: Progressivism in American Education, 1876–1957* (New York: Alfred A. Knopf, 1961).

21. V. F. Calverton and Samuel D. Schmalhausen, preface to *The New Generation: The Intimate Problems of Modern Parents and Children*, ed. V. F. Calverton and Samuel D. Schmalhausen (New York: Macaulay, 1930), 11–13.
22. Samuel D. Schmalhausen, "Family Life: A Study in Pathology," 281–88; John B. Watson, "After the Family—What?" 55–73, in Calverton and Schmalhausen, eds., *The New Generation.*
23. T. Swann Harding, "What Price Parenthood?" in Calverton and Schmalhausen, eds., *The New Generation*, 355.
24. Arthur Wallace Calhoun, "The Child Mind As a Social Product," 85, and Schmalhausen, "Family Life," 355, in Calverton and Schmalhausen, eds., *The New Generation.*
25. Calhoun, "The Child Mind," 87.
26. Michael Gold, "The Proletarian Child," in Calverton and Schmalhausen, eds., *The New Generation*, 678, 679.
27. Grace Hutchins, *Children under Capitalism.* International Pamphlets vol. 33 (New York: International Publishers, 1933). "Women's Voice: Teach Children Truth about Patriotism—War," *Working Woman*, August 1933, 13.
28. Van Gosse, "To Organize in Every Neighborhood, in Every Home: The Gender Politics of American Communists between the Wars," *Radical History Review* 50 (1991): 112, 114.
29. See Mishler, *Raising Reds.* On the rhetoric of communist magazines directed toward children, see, for example, the inaugural issue of the *New Pioneer*, May 1931, 1–2.
30. Stella Chess, "Parent and Child," *Fraternal Outlook*, August–September 1948, 22; November 1948, 21; August–September 1949, 16.
31. Elsie McKean, *David's Bad Day* (New York: Shady Hill Press, 1949); Frances W. Butterfield, *From Little Acorns: The Story of Your Body* (New York: Renbayle House, 1951).
32. Slava Dunn, "Parents' Problems," *Sunday Worker*, February 2, 1936, 15.
33. Ibid.
34. "Poots' Prattles," *Sunday Worker*, 10 May 1936, 15.
35. Burton P. Fowler, "Encourage Your Children to Think for Themselves," *Parents*, May 1934, 23.
36. Hughes Mearns, "Education Isn't What It Used to Be," *Parents*, September 1936, 42.
37. James Lee Ellenwood, "Are You a Dictator?" *Parents*, November 1938, 16–17.
38. Arnold Gesell and Frances L. Ilg, *Infant and Child in the Culture of Today* (New York: Harper and Row, 1943), 10.
39. Rose Zeligs, "Teach Your Child Tolerance," *Parents*, August 1934, 15ff.
40. John Palmer Gavit, "Plain Talk About Race Prejudice," *Parents*, February 1938, 15ff. On early liberal efforts to teach children racial tolerance, see Diana Marcia Selig, "Cultural Gifts: American Liberals, Childhood, and the Origins of Multiculturalism, 1924–1939," Ph.D. diss., University of California-Berkeley, 2001.
41. Frances Lipscomb, "What Shall We Tell Our Children?" *Woman Today*, March 1937, 23–27.
42. For commentary on the experiences of children growing up in this milieu, see Judy Kaplan and Linn Shapiro, eds., *Red Diapers: Growing Up in the Communist Left* (Urbana: University of Illinois Press, 1998).
43. "Sidewalk Battle: While Men Die at War—and Kids Play at It, the Junior Section Continues to Serve I. W. O. Youngsters with a Constructive, Healthy Program with Constant Emphasis on Democracy and Peace," *Fraternal Outlook*, January 1941, 8–9.
44. "Not Hitler's Children: Scattered throughout America's Main City, Children Give Their Reactions to Hitler," *Fraternal Outlook*, June 1943, 8–9.

45. William Charles Beyer, "Searching for Common Ground, 1940–49: An American Literary Magazine and Its Related Movements in Education and Politics." Ph.D. diss., University of Minnesota, 1988. "Intercultural Education—A New Approach," *Common Ground*, Spring 1941, 116.

46. Bob Nichols, "Should a Boy Have a Gun?" *Parents*, October 1934, 26. Robert E. Simon and Mrs. Robert E. Simon, "Should a Boy Have a Gun?" *Parents*, October 1934, 27. Child Study Association, *Parents' Questions* (New York: Harper, 1942).

47. Agnes E. Benedict, "Youth Enlists for Peace," *Parents*, December 1938, 20–21ff. See also Florence Brewer Boeckel, "What Youth Thinks of War," *Parents*, May 1937, 26ff. *Parents* also spoke out against the suffering of children in Spain, see George J. Hecht, "Help Save the Children of Spain!" *Parents*, October 1937, 13.

48. Anna W. M. Wolf, *Our Children Face War* (Boston: Houghton Mifflin, 1943), 162, 171.

49. Bibliography from papers of the Jefferson School of Social Science, Tamiment Library, New York University. In Box #1, folder labeled "Psychology."

50. Ibid. See also Harris, "'Don't Be Unconscious.'"

51. The film, made with the support of the International Union of Automobile, Aerospace, and Agricultural Implement Workers of America, was directed by Robert Cannon and written by Phil Eastman, John Hubley, and Ring Lardner Jr. and distributed by the left-wing distribution company Brandon films. See also Ruth Benedict and Gene Weltfish, *In Henry's Backyard: The Races of Mankind* (New York: Henry Schuman, 1948).

52. Harriet Eager Davis, "Boys and Girls Are Working for Peace," *Parents*, July 1947, 30–31.

53. See National Council for American Education, "How Red Are the Schools? And How *You* Can Help Eradicate Socialism and Communism from the Schools and Colleges of America" (New York: National Council for American Education, 1950).

54. Testimony before the House Committee on Un-American Activities of Walter S. Steele (Washington, D.C.: Government Printing Office, 1947), 40–41.

55. Although communists tended to publicly identify themselves as *progressives* the term also was used as a contrast to more committed radicals. On the ideological distinctions between progressives, liberals, and communists see Judy Kutulas, *The Long War: The Intellectual People's Front and Anti-Stalinism, 1930–1940* (Durham, N.C.: Duke University Press, 1995).

56. For a useful discussion of the "liberal narrative" that characterized movement from youthful, utopian idealism in the 1930s to postwar, "mature realism," see Thomas Hill Schaub, introduction to *American Fiction in the Cold War* (Madison: University of Wisconsin Press, 1991). The extent of Soviet influence on rank-and-file members is a matter of hot dispute: recent findings in the Soviet archives show, for instance, that spying for the Soviet Union was more common than previously realized. See, for example, Harvey Klehr, John Earl Haynes, and Fridrikh Igorevich Firsov, *The Secret World of American Communism* (New Haven, Conn.: Yale University Press, 1995). On the other hand, some scholars have argued that while most Communist Party members were indeed misled by the Soviet Union, few of the rank and file were in fact strictly beholden to orders passed down from Moscow, and tended to have ambivalent and even creative relationships to policy. Even the Moscow documents can be interpreted not simply as incriminating evidence but as signs of the complexity of the communist movement. See, for example, James A. Miller, Susan D. Pennybacker, and Eve Rosenhaft, "Mother Ada Wright and the International Campaign to Free the Scottsboro Boys," *American Historical Review* 106 (2001): 387–430.

57. Ethel and Julius Rosenberg, in *Death House Letters of Julius and Ethel Rosenberg* (New York: Jero, 1953), 56.

58. "Parents Stress Ideological Needs of Children at Jefferson School Conference." Flier dated 5 February 1951. In papers of the Jefferson School of Social Science, Tamiment Library, New York University.

59. Ibid.

60. "Two Opposite Approaches to Discipline." Student report from a course on child development, May 1955. In papers of the Jefferson School of Social Science, Tamiment Library, New York University, folder labeled "Psychology." On the gradual purging of all Western theories of psychology from communist-associated forums, see Harris, "'Don't Be Unconscious.'"

61. Elaine Tyler May, *Homeward Bound: American Families in the Cold War Era* (New York: Basic Books, 1988).

62. See David Riesman, "Tootle: A Modern Cautionary Tale," in David Riesman with Nathan Glazer and Reuel Denney, *The Lonely Crowd* (New Haven, Conn.: Yale University Press, 1950), 107–11. On life-adjustment education, see Ronald Lora, "Education: Schools As Crucible in Cold War America," in *Reshaping America: Society and Institutions, 1945–1960*, ed. Robert H. Bremner and Gary W. Reichard (Columbus, Ohio: Ohio State University Press, 1982), 223–60.

63. On Young People's Records see David Bonner, *Revolutionizing Children's Records: The Young People's Records and Children's Record Guild Series, 1946–1977* (Lanham, Md.: Scarecrow Press, 2003).

64. Pete Seeger, interview with author, 2 December 1997, Cold Spring, New York.

65. James Miller, *Democracy Is in the Streets: From Port Huron to the Siege of Chicago* (1987; reprint Cambridge, Mass.: Harvard University Press, 1994), 7.

12 "Please Let Me Come Home"

Homesickness and Family Ties
at Early-Twentieth-Century Summer Camps

Leslie Paris

William Steckel's arrival at Adirondack Woodcraft Camp in 1939 was hardly propitious. "I was not the most enthusiastic twelve-year-old," he later recalled, and "the ride to camp was wet and gloomy for the 'new boys.'" In 1930, when ten-year-old Charlotte Goldstein lay in her Camp Wehaha bunk at night, she felt similarly melancholy. She missed her family and thought about her deceased mother. "I was a little lonely. You'd hear the trains at night. All in the big room there, ten of us girls." As Dick D. recalled of his arrival at Camp Dudley in 1921, "there was a slight drizzle making everything kind of gloomy in this new place and I was lonely, boy was I homesick." He knew, however, that his parents wanted him to benefit from camp, and so he "performed the first major prevarication that I can recall clearly and managed, through the tears, to produce my first letter home, which began (to use the idiom of the day): 'Dear Mother and Daddy, Camp Dudley is the berries, bush and all.'" [1]

Since the inception of summer camps in the late nineteenth century, proponents claimed that camping built character. [2] A foray into nature, they argued, would improve modern youth, who were at once pampered by urban conveniences, stressed and weakened by the pace of industrial life, and made prematurely sophisticated through their exposure to pool halls and motion pictures. Such children, faced with new challenges and opportunities, would become more resourceful and self-reliant. In 1904, Camp Idlewood, a private

12.1. "Wehaha girls," August 1926. Courtesy
Betty Jablon and Hyman Bogen.

camp for girls in New York State, claimed to teach "the science of right living,
how to be well, how to be strong, how to be beautiful."[3] The 1919 brochure
for Camp Wonposet, a Connecticut camp, promised similarly that "life in
a camp such as Camp Wonposet not only makes boys healthy and strong, but
develops their independence, resourcefulness, and strength of initiative."[4]
Indeed, at a moment when notions of intimate family life and the precious-
ness of children were ascendant, camps promised that nuclear families would
actually be ameliorated if they were temporary dismantled. As the 1916 brochure for White Mountain Camp, a private boys' camp in Maine, put the
matter, "The home—particularly in the city—no longer affords opportunities for boys to secure that physical, mental and moral training that our fathers got from participation in the manifold activities which were carried
on in the homes of our grandfathers."[5] Camp leaders, citing their own educational expertise and the importance of peer groups, insisted that they could
make better and happier children amid new (albeit short-term) "family"
arrangements.

For children, meanwhile, camp life represented an important rite of passage, often a first experience of community and self-reliance beyond the
physical boundaries of families and home neighborhoods. Yet as the stories
above suggest, the transition was not always effortless. Although camp activities were designed to foster intense communal identities, campers experienced rituals of incorporation in divergent ways. Camps may have been
"total institutions" of sorts, to use sociologist Erving Goffman's phrase, but

children attended them for limited periods of time, and they had other experiences against which to measure, and sometimes to resist, camp worlds.[6] Homesickness was emblematic of the difficulty that many children experienced in moving from one mode of life to another.

This paper considers how children, their parents, and camp staff imagined and negotiated camp "family," homesickness, and children's resistance to adult plans more generally. The problem of homesickness, I suggest, offers historians of childhood a unique lens through which to consider the intergenerational production of children's culture and experience: that is to say, adults' attempts to create cohesive communities for their young charges, and the processes through which children came to understand themselves as members of new communities. Communal affiliation was a fluid process, not a fait accompli; the mechanism of camper self-identification was complex; and the meanings attendant to the experience were mutable. We know that childhood is, by its nature, a time of change and self-discovery. The question of camp homesickness allows us to focus on these changes, while considering identification and resistance more broadly.

The Making of (Homesick) Campers

In the late nineteenth century, camps were the province of a few "muscular Christians" who, yearning nostalgically for robust preindustrial pasts, aimed to introduce elite Protestant boys to the physical and moral reinvigoration of "natural" spaces. At the turn of the twentieth century, about twenty-five private camps served elite boys, while a few hundred organizational camps run by youth groups, settlement houses, and charities catered to middle- and working-class boys.[7] Within the first few decades of the twentieth century, camping would grow from an experimental practice to a mainstay of mass culture. By 1930, between three and four thousand summer camps enrolled millions of boys and girls of all kinds: recent immigrants and the social elite; the children of radicals and conservatives; Protestants, Jews and Catholics; and children of all races.[8] Still, the rise of camping affected some children more than others. Children from the urban northeast were far more likely to attend summer camps than their counterparts in other regions; in an era of segregated camping, few camps served African Americans; boys were more often sent away to camp than were girls; middle-class parents had more options than did their working-class counterparts; and some ethnic groups took to camping with more enthusiasm than did others.

From the beginning, then, camps were sites of social consolidation, where children of similar backgrounds could form a cooperative cultural life away from other influences.[9] Parents usually chose (or, in the case of working-class families, had available to them) camps that reflected their own class, race, and religious identity. The directors of middle-class camps, for instance, usually built up their enrollments by soliciting their neighbors, their students, or the children of their friends. Organizational camps, including those run by the Young Men's Christian Association (YMCA), the Girl Scouts of the U.S.A., and settlement houses, drew on already-existing urban or suburban clienteles.[10] Most early-twentieth-century camps were further segregated by gender. As a result of such distinctions, most campers actually encountered more homogeneous social worlds than the ones they had left behind.[11]

While it was not unusual for a child to depart for camp along with a local friend or sibling, camp life was never simply an extension of life at home. Although camps, to a significant extent, reflected their mostly urban constituencies, these leisure institutions created new routines and proposed new social identities. Such work often began prior to children's arrival at camp. In the 1920s, before the working-class children attending Life Camps stepped onto the train in New York City, these boys had already "become" members of various Native American tribes, while the girls were initiated into groups named after indigenous trees and birds.[12] Meanwhile, Eleanor Deming, director of the elite Camp Mirimachi, asked the returning campers to begin the process of making community by writing to the new girls, enclosing a photo and asking for one in return; when the girls met at the train station en route to camp, they already knew one another by sight.[13] The process of initiation continued on the voyage to camp, as children traveled, both physically and metaphorically, away from the ordinary spaces of their homes. Everyday camp rules and routines were not yet fully in play, but new campers, whether learning camp songs or talking excitedly among themselves, were already congregants in a shared culture.

Once at camp, the pace of such initiations increased. When in 1927, the New York City boys arrived at the Young Men's Hebrew Association's (YMHA) Surprise Lake Camp, they were immediately thrust into a stimulating pace that precluded much free time, either for reflection or for moping. Reaching the camp at lunchtime, they ate their first meal together at long communal tables in the dining hall. Each boy was then assigned to a tent group. Within the larger camp "family," campers generally lived in units of about six to twelve children, homogeneous by age and always divided along gender lines. Each unit followed a program of activities together, under the supervision of their counselors. These adults (who were often significantly younger than campers' own parents) provided near-but-not-quite-parental supervision: leading activities, monitoring cleanliness and bedtimes, and sleeping in the same tent or cabin. At many camps, the staff were known as Aunt or Uncle

So-and-So, while the youngest children were under the care of an official "Camp Mother." In addition to joining these more intimate groups, new campers developed a relationship with the camp at large, and even with the nation: after their swimming tests, the Surprise Lake tent units rejoined for dinner and a campfire, and a ceremonial lowering of the U.S. flag.[14] This fairly typical series of initiations offered up communal identity at a variety of levels.

Yet despite camps' many efforts to provide a range of structures of allegiance and community, not all children came to recognize the camp "family" as loving and supportive. One lonely adolescent girl at Camp Boiberek, a New York camp that emphasized Yiddish and Jewish culture, spent time wandering around the camp by herself, alienated from her peers, and counting the days until she would be released from her misery. "Just 1½ weeks more and I'm going home," she wrote to her parents in 1933. "It will be swell. . . Mom, please let me come home a week before the camp." For this camper, camp had become a kind of torment. "I'm not getting along well with the girls," she explained.[15]

Early-twentieth-century camps differed in the degree of regimentation they espoused; some kept children busy at activities scheduled down to the quarter hour, while others embraced principles of camper autonomy and free play. But they held in common the belief that homesick children needed to throw themselves into camp life. In July 1927, the Surprise Lake Camp newspaper gave the following advice to its campers: "If you find you are becoming homesick it means that you are not active enough and you are not a good mixer. The remedy is simple, play more games with other boys and mix with them and you will be just like the other campers." A decade later, at the end of the camp season, the paper publicly credited one Ned Weiss, "who made a sensational jump from a typical homesick case to splendid camper. Good work, Ned."[16] Camps made space for the difficulty of adjustment, and interpellated children as active partners in their own transformation. Getting over homesickness, camp staff explained, was part of growing up. In the meantime, those who felt sad were to keep busy until the feeling passed.

Children's loneliness and alienation tended to be most severe during the first few hours or days of camp, when everything seemed new and unsure, or at particularly quiet moments, such as while lying in bed at night. These feelings were often most acute for younger campers (most camps served children between the ages of eight and sixteen, but some took children as young as five or six years of age) and for those who had never before been away from home. Suddenly, the regular social order had been reoriented. With this in mind, camp staff made a special point of welcoming and showing interest in those children who seemed bewildered by the transition from home. As William

Steckel noted, the morning after his arrival at camp "The man called 'Chief' stopped a skinny kid with steel-rimmed glasses [himself] and said 'Hi, Billy, how are you doing?' He actually knew my name on the first day." [17] Herman Beckman, director of Camp Dudley, a YMCA camp in New York, was reputed for knowing his campers, not only by name but by number (each Dudley camper, from 1885 onward, had been assigned his own number, in ascending order) and hometown. For many "new boys," Beckman's personal interest "filled the gap which made you feel being away from home was not so bad and Camp Dudley was a good place to be," as one camper later recalled. [18]

Such personal attention convinced many homesick children to stay on at camp. If, in the mid-1930s, a homesick boy at the New York Children's Aid Society camp asked to go home, "Doc," the camp leader, would give his consent, but would ask the boy in question to wait for the next train. In the meantime, "Doc" would bring the boy along with him on a contrived trip that involved visiting nearby horses, or eating an ice cream cone; comforted, the boy would then decide to stay. [19] In 1940, one Surprise Lake counselor took a more direct approach to such distress. In his diary, Bill. S. noted several encounters with Eddie, a camper who, at the beginning of the summer, was clearly unhappy. The counselor "persuaded him to try licking his case of loneliness." The next day, Eddie, according to Bill, "seem[ed] happy" and had decided to stay. [20] Because homesickness was in part a response to the particular conditions of camp life, it tended to abate when children felt a connection to caring and capable adults. Conversely, those campers who had encounters with inexperienced or uncaring counselors were more likely to experience homesickness. In the spring of 1941, many experienced counselors broke their contracts with Surprise Lake Camp in order to take better-paying jobs in the wartime economy. The camp director speculated that the immaturity of the counselors he was later able to recruit was to blame for a serious bout of homesickness among the boys that summer. As the counselors became more experienced, the boys' anxiety abated. [21] In this sense, homesickness operated as a kind of barometer of communal joy and dissatisfaction.

Homesickness also emerged, unsurprisingly, as a response to unpleasant camp experiences. In July 1933, one boy wrote to his mother that the other boys were ruining his vacation at Camp Boiberek. "I wan't [sic] you to either take me home or send me to another camp at the end of the month," he pleaded, explaining that his fellow campers treated him as their inferior, had ripped up his bathing suit, and frequently used water pistols to wet his shirts. "I don't enjoy any of the meals because the boys are always goading me if you know what that means," he concluded. [22] This letter prompted his parents to write to the camp, enclosing their son's letter and asking for more information. In 1940, the mother of another Boiberek camper responded similarly to a letter begging her to "Please take me home very soon because I don't like the camp counslier [*sic*] especially [*sic*] the counslier. He hits me and accouses [*sic*] me of doing things that I didn't do. Please take me home. Please take me home. Please write to me. Your loving son." As the mother explained to camp director Leibush Lerher, "I would like you to investigate but without [the son and the counselor] knowing that I wrote to you. The thing that I wonder about most is the *hitting*."[23]

While parents speculated about the events that had precipitated their children's unhappiness, camp staff tended to blame parents when campers were discontented or difficult. These troubles, many camping proponents argued, resulted from damaging family environments—an extrinsic factor—rather than camp programs themselves. As one camp counselor bluntly put the case, "Most of the problem cases in a boys camp can be traced directly to the home, severe as that indictment may sound."[24] Boys' camps, which frequently posited themselves as alternatives to the overly feminized home, were particularly likely to blame mothers for overindulging and overprotecting their sons, and to imagine that possessive mothers resisted sending their children away from home.[25] Joseph Lieberman, who in the 1920s directed the innovative coeducational Pioneer Youth Camp, noted with disdain that one of his campers, a twelve-year-old boy, had been doted on by his mother: "During her first visit she fawned on him, petting and hugging him, inquiring after all his needs, repacked his valise, remade his bed."[26] As Lieberman implied, such parents would only have themselves to blame if their children subsequently became homesick.

From the staff's perspective, homesickness was most likely to reemerge when parents visited their children. The arrival of relatives threw into question the "family" structure of camp life, and the authority of the staff to set and to enforce their own rules. Although many parents and children eagerly awaited such visits, their reunions sometimes led to dissatisfaction or culminated in tearful farewells. The magazine *Parents* instructed its mainly middle-class readership in the arts of camp adjustment: making a graceful goodbye to one's children at home, writing often during the first week, staying away for at least two weeks, and keeping the child in camp when visiting.[27] This social contract was not, however, always maintained; despite having selected the camp in question, not all parents were willing or able to delegate responsibility and control. In 1924, one Surprise Lake Camp counselor reported in exasperation that "in all frankness, it may be said that if the parents had not visited the camp there would have been less homesickness. There was only a little homesickness but that little can be directly traced to parents who came to camp and asked their children if they would not like to go home with them."[28] Our Lady of Lourdes Camp, serving Catholic girls in New York, explained in 1939 that parents could only visit on the third Sunday of each month, and that they were not allowed to stay over at camp or take meals with the children. "Frankly," the camp's brochure explained, "we must confess that in our experience frequent visits from relatives and friends invariably have the effect of making the children discontented."[29]

Some parents pushed their children to be more independent, or saw camps as conveniences freeing them to enjoy their own vacations; others were more ambivalent about this short-term separation. Asking children if they would like to come home was one of several ways in which parents chafed against camps' assertion of familial authority and attachment, tested their child's loyalty, or tried to reassert the primacy of their own family bond. A few parents acted out in more dangerous or disturbing ways: arriving at camp without prior notification or taking boats out from the dock without permission. More frequently, the parental challenge operated on a subtler register; for example, while many camps explicitly forbade parents from sending food packages to their children, some parents simply could not resist this means of demonstrating their affection. "I am sure," one frustrated girls' camp director wrote to parents in 1930, "I can . . . regard the packages that have come simply as an oversight on your part, and not an attempt to undermine the morale of the camp."[30] In other words, the desire to reunite the family on its original terms, or at least to reassert its privileges, was shared by some parents as well as by children. In 1930, the mother of a boy attending Camp Waziyatah in Maine wrote to the camp's director, "I certainly have missed my baby. I had no idea two months could possibly be so long," while another described herself and her husband as having been "two neurotic, lonesome parents" while their son attended this camp in 1929.[31] In the early twentieth century, although the camp industry was expanding rapidly, relatively few parents had themselves attended summer camps as children. Many parents, like their children, were new to this ritualized separation. For doting parents, many of whom only received short postcards from their busy children, the successful acclimatization to camp life signaled their progeny's growing independence: necessary, but somewhat bittersweet.

In response to parents' own ambivalence, and to ensure that children had time to become comfortable within their new communities, many two-month camps explicitly barred parents from visiting their children during the first two weeks of the season. Meanwhile, they worked to create cohesive communities, which required for their success a cultural as well as physical divide between campers and all "outsiders" (including parents). "We're dressed up for the visitors," one boys' camp song explained in 1934,

> The parental inquisitors, that
> Snoop around on Wednesdays and Sundays.
> Because no people come around,
> We generally bum around on
> Saturdays, Tuesdays, Thursdays, Fridays, Mondays.[32]

Parental visits, the song suggested, intruded upon the privileges of camp life. Increasing numbers of camps began to restrict parents to official weekend "visiting days," though none denied parents the fundamental right to see their children at some point during the season.

If parents were outsiders, they were also clients who had to be treated with care. They could, if they wished, pull their children from camp at any moment, or damage a camp's reputation upon their return home. On the other hand, parental visits represented opportunities for camps to consolidate intergenerational goodwill by showcasing their varied activities, good food, and beautiful terrain. Parents were often invited to sports days, pageants, and final banquets, special events at which their children's achievements were celebrated. Moreover, for the owners of full-season private camps, the desire to keep parental disruptions at a distance was in tension with the real financial possibilities these visitors represented. The practice of lodging parents or offering them meals, for a fee, represented an important secondary source of income. In the industry journal *Camper and Hiker,* director Belle Lowenstein of New York's Camp Valcour explained to her peers in 1927 that "it is for the good of the child that we don't want promiscuous visiting" but added that "financially we are the losers by this [policy], as money can be made by the parents' visits."[33] In practice, however, weekly visits occurred only where a camp was reasonably proximate to the family home. Campers spending nine weeks at an Adirondack or Maine camp, for example, might expect to receive one extended visit at mid-season, during which time their New York- or Boston-based parents might stay at a nearby resort and visit regularly. Campers within a few hours' drive of a major city might see their parents more regularly, but those who attended two-week organizational camp sessions might not receive any visitors at all.

Camps' claims about disruptive parents must be read in light of the complex ways in which adult authority was negotiated within camp settings. The ideal camp "family," which would somehow both respect and bypass parents' rights, was not easily achieved, nor were questions of autonomy, loyalty, and attachment readily resolved. Children who were sensitive to competing adult claims for attachment and authority were caught in the middle. Their homesickness was engendered not only by their own fears and anxieties, but also by those of the adults around them.

In 1939, Alan Lurie was six years old when he first attended summer camp. When his father came to visit him, the unhappy boy tearfully begged to be taken home. Despite this show of emotion, his father refused. The next year, however, when Alan asked to go to a different camp, his wishes were respected.[34] Harriet S. was more unusual in that she successfully pleaded her case. She attended Camp Ta-Go-La in New York for only three weeks, during which time her family was staying at an area resort: "I missed my mother and all the rest of the family especially since I knew they were nearby. The camp was beautiful but I found excuses to want to leave saying the food was bad and they make you clean the bunk." With the active support of her grandmother, Harriet left camp and joined her family at their hotel.[35] Because many camps charged parents by the month, some homesick children hoped to leave early, at no extra cost to their families. One unhappy boy, upon hearing that his parents had already paid for the rest of the summer, cried bitterly because he realized that he would have to stay on.[36]

Although boys were just as likely as girls to experience homesickness, some onlookers decried any sign of weakness as unmanly. In 1943, when a ten-year-old boy attending Camp Dudley wrote to his mother that he was homesick and wanted to come home, she replied that he would better enjoy camp when he came to know his cabinmates and participated in a greater number of camp activities. In the meantime, she explained, he must learn to hide his feelings. "Don't let anybody know you are homesick," she said, "and enter in as many things as you can and you won't have time to be homesick. Men never show their feelings like this and you would be a '*SISSY*' if you came home. Buck up and be a sport and the answer is YOU CAN *NOT* COME HOME, so you must make the best of it. If you don't enter in things, the boys will not like you and it will then be even harder for you."[37] The general exhortation to "buck up and be a sport" was not, however, limited to boys, nor was it a universal practice; many younger boys, especially, found sympathy and advocacy when they shared their distress.

Because camp life was supposed to be a character-building experience, and homesickness was, by all accounts, a temporary phase, even those parents who were sympathetic to their children's misery usually kept them at camp, no matter how hard their children begged to come home. But from the perspective of the most disconsolate campers, leaving camp was the only real solution. One Boiberek camper wrote a postcard to his mother in late July 1936, begging her, "Please come for me as soon as you can. If by August 2, you are not here I think I will run home. If you come and stay here with me I'll stay. But please come as soon as you can." The situation did not improve, and a letter then followed that read, "Please come for me because I'll get very sick for you. Mother I've changed my mind, if you do not come for me in 5 days I'll go alone home without my trunk. In this case I'll be home maybe August 20. I mean it mother. Please don't let everybody read this letter. When I come home I'll never again go to a camp." Despite the piteous tone of these messages, the boy's parents did not relent. Instead, they turned to the camp director for professional advice, explaining that. "We are just lost for words to express our sorrow and would like to know what you would advise." [38]

Although parents and staff did what they could, the ability of most campers to overcome homesickness ultimately attested to their own resiliency and determination. In 1934, on her first day at the Central Jewish Institute's Camp Cejwin, New Yorker Mitzi Brainin was miserable, but the feeling, she later recalled, passed swiftly: "I cried myself to sleep during rest hour and after that I don't recall being homesick for even 5 minutes." [39] Although intense while it lasted, her loneliness was fleeting. All three of the campers I cited at the beginning of this essay grew to enjoy their respective camps, and each came to see homesickness as a phase they had undergone during the transition to camp life, even as a kind of strengthening ordeal. Alan Lurie, the boy who had begged his father to take him home, had by the age of eight become a seasoned veteran of three summer camps. As he explained in the pages of the Surprise Lake Camp newspaper, "You Get Used to All Kinds of Things." [40]

Most campers did exactly that. Generally speaking, camps were successful in soliciting new identities and allegiances. These recreational venues would become, for millions, central sites of pleasure and identification. Many campers adopted special camp-only nicknames—at Camp Andree, a Girl Scout camp for adolescents, one group of campers took on the monikers Van, Scotty, Ditt, Mugs, and Chippy—that attested to their new insider status, their distance from ordinary life, and their active participation in making camps special spaces of personal transformation. [41] These nicknames also ritualized new ways of thinking about family and kinship outside of traditional bounds. Having converted to camp membership, many of the same children who had cried on arrival would weep even harder on their departure. For happy campers, camps were by no means fictive families, even if they were temporary ones.

Indeed, for most campers, the prospect of being sent home midseason was a threat rather than an aspiration. At Camp Dudley, one eleven-year-old boy was expelled in 1940 after a month of what the staff described as selfishness and fits of temper. They had first tried moving the boy into a new cabin group, but when he continued to act out, the camp director wrote to the boy's father in New York City, telling him to meet his son at Grand Central Station in two days' time.[42] Similarly, Rose Schwartz was sent home from Camp We-haha, the institutional camp of the Manhattan Hebrew Orphan Asylum, after she was discovered smoking.[43] In 1924, the nurse at Camp Andree told three teenage girls who were, in her opinion, "hysterical," that anyone with such attacks was not fit for camp life, and that they would be sent home if they continued. All three campers soon quieted down.[44]

Usually, the staff response to troubled or rule-breaking children was not so draconian. At one private camp in New York, the most common method of discipline was the removal of privileges. Unlike schools or juvenile deten-tion centers, within which children sometimes experienced forcible coercion, camps attempted more subtle methods of control: peer pressure, one-on-one talks, punishments, and, at the limit, expulsion from the community. Camps also offered campers various safe outlets through which to vent dissatisfac-tion. Camp culture was rife with parody and pranks, which allowed, within limits, for critiques of camp authorities and everyday practices. Such events as Topsy-Turvy Day, when campers took on some of the responsibilities of staff and the counselors played at being irresponsible babies, stood between official and unofficial camp culture.[45] Campers who short-sheeted beds, sat-irized their counselors at "talent nights," or dropped their sleeping coun-selors into lakes may have imagined that they were challenging authority, but such acts actually left the social contract intact, enhancing community life rather than contesting it. Within limits, staff supported what they interpreted as signs of children's growth and independence. The staff at Camp Norge, the Fresh Air Camp of the Norwegian Lutheran Welfare Association, pretended not to notice that some of the boys had established "secret" huts in the woods. In point of fact, the staff privately supported this practice.[46]

Children did not usually rebel openly against camp authority, but, as the case of homesickness suggests, neither did they always conform to staff expectations. Along the spectrum, homesickness was one of the milder and more acceptable forms of resistance to camp life. Children sometimes sur-reptitiously smoked cigarettes, sneaked out of their bunks after "lights out" to kiss on the baseball field, hit their bunkmates, stole from one another, and pushed other campers underwater at the lake. By comparison, homesickness was akin to bedwetting, a sometimes annoying and troublesome but rela-tively involuntary form of resistance to camp expectations, and one that af-fected younger children disproportionately. Those campers who remained homesick or who wet their beds were not "bad," they were simply imperfect citizens. Yet homesickness was sometimes a factor in more explicitly antag-onistic forms of behavior. In 1940, after one camper was reprimanded for climbing a tree, he did exactly the same thing again five minutes later in full sight of his counselor. The boy then denied having done so. The counselor concluded that this homesick boy was deliberately transgressing camp policies in hopes of being sent home.[47]

The particular ways in which campers misbehaved expose a central tension within the camping movement. These institutions presented themselves as spaces of adventure and independence, while promising to regulate and monitor their young charges. They wanted campers to remain children, but to become better ones; to act more grown up, but not so grown up as to smoke or to leave the camp's grounds. And yet, despite the fact that the clients of a particular camp more often than not came from families of a single class, religion, and racial background, they experienced the "inside" of camp in individual, shifting and unequal ways. Even the most homogeneous peer groups did not respond identically to becoming campers. Unhappy campers, like anxious parents, challenged camps' claim to represent a kind of near-parental authority. Although camps were grounded in unequal relations, and adults controlled much of what campers did, the case of homesickness suggests that both staff and parents were at times hard-pressed to secure campers' consent.

The inability and sometimes unwillingness of homesick children to adapt to camp represented a form of refusal on a different register than juvenile delinquency or so-called problem girls.[48] While other scholars have shed light on adult institutions shaping the lives of supposedly deviant children, camps show the more ordinary, mundane ways in which children found themselves unable to meet adult expectations. But although dissent was a feature of camp life, it was not the primary or overwhelming feature. Campers sometimes allowed disaffection to be seen, or refused to play by some of the camp rules, but they generally fulfilled their major obligations nonetheless. Adults, meanwhile, saw campers as clients to be pleased; in the new child-centered marketplace, of which camps were an important part, dissatisfied children could complain to their parents and never return.[49] Thus, camps required for their success goodwill and intergenerational negotiation. If camps were important adult-run institutions of social instruction, ideology and indoctrination, where communal values were reinforced and new forms of association were nurtured, they were also, if imperfectly, spaces of children's own culture and desire.

Children's homesickness, precisely because it was so often transient, usefully highlights both the mutability of children's identities and the complexities of their relations with adults and with one another. While camps represented themselves as ideal communities, campers were able to integrate themselves into this vision to different and changing degrees. Like Charlotte Goldstein, some were lonesome at night and happy during the day. Like Alan Lurie, others were homesick one year and perfectly content the next. As children explored new forms of independence and of interdependence with others, their perceptions of camp varied. Many were successfully incorporated into the camp community, and came to see its rules and structures not only as natural and desirable, but as their own.

NOTES

1. William Steckel, quoted in *Remembering Woodcraft by Campers and Councilors over Fifty Years*, ed. Elizabeth Chisholm Abbott (Old Forge, N.Y.: Adirondack Woodcraft Camps, 1975), 49; Charlotte Cohn (nee Goldstein), interview with the author, New York City, 13 May 1999. Dick D. to Willie, 10 March 1977, in "Memories: Tents to Cabins"; Camp Dudley, Westport, New York (hereafter CD).

2. On the early camping movement, see Eleanor Eells, *Eleanor Eells' History of Organized Camping: The First One Hundred Years* (Martinsville, Indiana: American Camping Association, 1986); Jenna Weissman Joselit with Karen S. Mittelman, *A Worthy Use of Summer: Jewish Summer Camping in America* (Philadelphia: National Museum of American Jewish History, 1993); Philip Deloria, *Playing Indian* (New Haven, Conn.: Yale University Press, 1998); Robert H. MacDonald, *Sons of the Empire: The Frontier and the Boy Scout Movement, 1890–1918* (Toronto: University of Toronto Press, 1993); and Leslie Paris, "Children's Nature: Summer Camps in New York State, 1919–1941" (Ph.D. diss., University of Michigan, 2000). On nature, tradition, and antimodernism see Peter J. Schmitt, *Back to Nature: The Arcadian Myth in Urban America* (New York: Oxford University Press, 1969); T. J. Jackson Lears, *No Place of Grace: Antimodernism and the Transformation of American Culture, 1880–1920* (New York: Pantheon, 1981); and Michael Kammen, *Mystic Chords of Memory: The Transformation of Tradition in American Culture* (New York: Vintage Books, 1991).

3. "Camp Idlewood, Lake Oscawana, New York" (1904), uncataloged camp brochures, n.c. 1, New York Public Library (hereafter NYPL).

4. "Camp Wonposet" (1919), n.c. 7, NYPL.

5. "White Mountain Camp, for Boys and Young Men" (1916), n.c. 3, NYPL.

6. Erving Goffman, *The Presentation of Everyday Life* (Garden City, N.Y.: Doubleday Anchor, 1959); see also Jay Mechling, "Children's Folklore in Residential Institutions: Summer Camps, Boarding Schools, Hospitals, and Custodial Facilities," in *Children's Folklore: A Source Book,* ed. Brian Sutton-Smith, Jay Mechling, and Thomas W. Johnson (New York: Garland, 1995), chap. 13. While Goffman's work is useful for exploring the process of institutional regimentation and meaning making in intentional communities, I would argue that not all "total institutions" function in the same way; camps were intended as spaces of pleasure, and were thus radically different from the almost complete subjugation that Goffman describes in the insane asylum. See Erving Goffman, *Asylums: Essays on the Social Situation of Mental Patients and other Inmates* (Garden City, N.Y.: Anchor, 1961).

7. Porter Sargent, "An Historical Retrospect of the Summer Camp," in *A Handbook of Summer Camps* (Boston: Porter Sargent, 1928), 18–27.

8. Porter Sargent, *Handbook of Summer Camps* (Boston: Porter Sargent, 1933), 117. "Children First," *Camp Life* 4, no. 6 (1932): 1. Because many camps did not affiliate with regional or national organizations, contemporaries could only estimate the industry's strength.

9. Randal K. Tillery makes this point in regard to contemporary summer camps in "Touring Arcadia: Elements of Discursive Simulation and Cultural Struggle at a Children's Summer Camp," *Cultural Anthropology* 7, no. 3 (1992): 374–88.

10. On the sorting of urban publics into camping publics, see Leslie Paris, "A Home Though Away from Home: Brooklyn Jews and Interwar Children's Summer Camps" in *Jews of Brooklyn,* ed. Ilana Abramovitch and Séan Galvin (Boston: University Press of New England, 2001), 242–49.

11. Like Cindy S. Aron, I see vacationing as inherently different from much urban leisure, tending to reinforce rather than to diminish social distinctions; see Aron, *Working at Play: A History of Vacations in the United States* (New York: Oxford University Press, 1999), 222.

12. Lloyd Burgess Sharp, "Education and the Summer Camp: An Experiment," in *Contributions to Education* no. 390 (New York: Teachers College, Columbia University, 1930), 56–57.

13. This camp policy is described in *Camping* 1, no. 2 (1926): 10.

14. Max Oppenheimer, "Report of the Work Done at Surprise Lake Camp during the Summer of 1927" and "S. L. C. Reports, Summer Camp, 1905–1938"; 92nd Street YMHA, New York City (hereafter YMHA).

15. Letter to Mr. Lehrer, dated 8/24/33, folder 65, Institute for Jewish Research, Center for Jewish History, New York City (hereafter IJR). This collection contains a good number of letters from homesick campers, forwarded from parents to the camp director and subsequently kept on file at the camp; this does not imply that Boiberek had an abnormally high percentage of unhappy campers.

16. "Surprise Lake Camp Echoes, 1914–1934," 16 July 1927; "Surprise Lake Camp Echoes, Oct. 1936, Sept. 1938," 1 September 1937, YMHA.

17. Steckel, *Remembering Woodcraft*, 49.

18. Eugene du Pont Cowlin to W. J. Schmidt, 19 January 1976, CD.

19. Bob Noto, interview with the author, New York City, 1 April 1999.

20. Bill S., "Day Book, Permanents, 1940," in "Daily Programs 1940," YMHA.

21. "Surprise Lake Camp, 41st Season, Report, 1941," 2, 11, in Surprise Lake Reports, 1939–1943, YMHA.

22. J. to Mom, 19 July 1933, folder 65, IJR.

23. F. to N., postmarked 28 July 1940; N. to Mr. Lehrer, 30 July 1940, folder 108, IJR.

24. Orrell A. York, "A Study of Educational and Recreational Advantages of Boys' Summer Camps" (M.A. thesis, New York State College for Teachers; 1939), 31; Adirondack Museum, Blue Mountain Lake, New York.

25. For example, as Nat Holman, director of New York's Camp Scatico for boys, argued, mothers were averse to sending away their children for the first time. "Camps, they'll tell you, are all very good but their child is too young, or having never been away from home is particularly attached to the mother, or any one of a million and one alibis advanced by the mother in her attempts to keep her child with her." See Holman, "What I Think of Camping," *Camping World* 1, no. 1 (1935): 9.

26. Joseph Lieberman, *Creative Camping: A Coeducational Experiment in Personality Development and Social Living; Being the Record of Six Summers of the National Experimental Camp of Pioneer Youth of America* (New York: Association Press, 1931), 181.

27. "A Parent's Part in Camping," *Parents* 11, no. 6 (1936): 7. Note that these kinds of instruc-

tions anticipate and imply a middle- or upper-class camp that continues all summer long; these wealthier clients were *Parents'* audience.

28. "Report—Season 1924 Permanent Division," in "Report of the Temporary Junior Division, Season of 1924," YMHA.
29. "Our Lady of Lourdes Camp Association" (1939) n.c.1, NYPL.
30. Cornelia Amster to parents, 14 July 1930, Camp Che-Na-Wah, Minerva, New York.
31. Letters to Bertha Gruenberg, 21 August 1930 and early September 1929, in folder, "CW: Letters of Appreciation, 1926–36," box 2, Bertha Gruenberg Collection, Schlesinger Library, Radcliffe Institute, Harvard University.
32. Brant Lake Camp song from the "revusical" *Fair Enough* (1934), Brant Lake Camp, Brant Lake, New York.
33. *Camper and Hiker* 1, no. 3 (1928): 27; NYPL.
34. "Surprise Lake Echoes, 1940–1942," 10 July 1941, YMHA.
35. Harriet Silver to author, 10 July 1999.
36. L. C. to Mr. Kneff, 28 July 1941; folder 116, IJR.
37. Letter, C. B. to her son, July 1943, in camper reports, CD.
38. Postcard, G. to R., postmarked 24 July 1936; G. to Mother, n.d., from Bunk 8; R to Director, 25 July 1936; folder 78, IJR.
39. Mitzi Alper (nee Brainin) to author, 23 June 1999.
40. "Surprise Lake Echoes, 1940–1942," 10 July 1941, YMHA.
41. "Canoe Trip—1937," in Camp Andree reports 1937, Girl Scouts of the U.S.A., New York City (hereafter GSUSA).
42. File on H., camper reports, CD.
43. Rose Schwartz, interview by Rose Miller, 18 January 1987, 22, in the William E. Wiener Oral History Library of the American Jewish Committee, Dorot Jewish Division, NYPL.
44. See "Health Report, Camp Andree, 1924," in Camp Andree reports 1924, GSUSA.
45. See Leslie Paris, "The Adventures of Peanut and Bo: Summer Camps and Early-Twentieth-Century American Girlhood," *Journal of Women's History* 12, no. 4 (2001): 47–76.
46. Brooklyn Eagle camp file, Camp Norge, 18 August 1941, Brooklyn Collection, Brooklyn Public Library. On the early history of this camp, founded by a Norwegian-American minister in 1915, see the camp file, 25 July 1952.
47. "Second Period Reports, 1940," YMHA.
48. See, for example, Mary Odem, *Delinquent Daughters: Protecting and Policing Adolescent Female Sexuality in the United States, 1885–1920* (Chapel Hill: University of North Carolina Press, 1995).
49. On early-twentieth-century children and consumerism, see, for instance, Miriam Formanek-Brunell, *Made to Play House: Dolls and the Commercialization of American Girlhood, 1830–1930* (New Haven, Conn.: Yale University Press, 1993); Lisa Jacobson, "Raising Consumers: Children, Childrearing, and the American Mass Market, 1890–1940" (Ph.D. diss., UCLA, 1997); and Gary Cross, *Kids' Stuff: Toys and the Changing World of American Childhood* (Cambridge, Mass.: Harvard University Press, 1997).

13 Transformative Terrains

Korean Adoptees and the Social Constructions of an American Childhood

Catherine Ceniza Choy and Gregory Paul Choy

"I have adopted Korean radar, I'm sure of it. Perhaps all adopted Koreans have it built inside. We come battery equipped once we're shipped over by plane."[1] In her narrative "China," from the groundbreaking 1997 anthology *Seeds from a Silent Tree*, Korean adoptee Kari Smalkoski writes that, on one occasion, her "adopted Korean radar" directs her attention to three adopted Korean children and their parents in a car parked next to hers. She observes, "The father has features of Norwegian and German ancestry. He could be anyone's father growing up in the suburbs of Minneapolis, cleaning a garage, mowing a lawn, going fishing, watching football on Monday evenings, barbecuing on the grill in the summertime. His daughter does not look like anyone's daughter growing up in the suburbs of Minneapolis. Everything about this father/daughter relationship appears normal."[2]

One might sense a contradiction in Smalkoski's narrative because immediately following an expression of explicit abnormality—"His daughter does not look like anyone's daughter growing up in the suburbs of Minneapolis"—she writes that "everything about this father/daughter relationship appears normal." However, these two sentences, lacking a transitional word or a conjunction that might subordinate or coordinate one remark to the other, reflect the dichotomous nature of contrasts in the cultural psyches of the authors who pen many of the entries in *Seeds from a Silent Tree*. These contrasts of normal/abnormal, American/Korean, white/yellow stem from the ongoing troubled relationship between the visible foreignness of the Asian body and the unique racialization of Korean adoptees in the United States. Their distinctive upbringing—having been raised by primarily white adoptive parents, retaining limited, if any, memories and knowledge of Korea and their birth families, feeling white, and yet seen as Asian in the United States—creates a racialized double consciousness that situates their American identity in tension with their Korean roots.

In many of the entries in *Seeds from a Silent Tree,* the authors confront the difficulty of overcoming the U.S. racialization of the Asian body as un-American and inferior, despite the prominent U.S. role in international and cross-racial adoption in the second half of the twentieth century. Smalkoski illuminates these contrasts and the difficulty of overcoming them by pointing out that although the "behavior" of this father/daughter relationship "appears normal," what interrupts their quotidian life is the visuality of their relationship to outside observers. Racialized differences written on their bodies socially construct the physical and cultural boundaries of who counts (as well as who does not) as normal, Minnesotan, and American. The normalcy of the father is assumed in his whiteness, and that whiteness limns a series of practices that demarcate his Americanness, citizenship, and nationality. It gives him cache into the "practices" (cleaning a garage, mowing, fishing, watching football, barbecuing) that enable him to be abstracted into what Lauren Berlant has called the "National Symbolic," the "tangled cluster" of political and cultural spaces that bind Americans together.[3] It allows him to become an integral part of the American family, assumed to be a white, heterosexual, monogamous middle-class domestic arrangement that has historically separated Americans from "others."[4] Thus, his "Norwegian and German ancestry" enables him to be "anyone's father" in the suburbs of Minneapolis, while his adopted Korean daughter is unable to be "anyone's daughter."

Smalkoski's narrative also illustrates the ways in which the dynamics of the racialization of Korean adoptees take place in relation to gender and sexuality. She elicits the sexual awkwardness of the relationship between the white father and his Korean adopted daughter as the daughter matures. Smalkoski continues to write that "however, when she is my age, society, even Minnesota society with all its adopted Koreans, will not find them so normal looking. When she is much older and her father says to her in public, 'Anna, this way, hon,' when she falls behind him, they simply will not appear so normal."[5] Smalkoski implies that the general U.S. public will interpret this visual image of the adult "Asian" woman with an adult white "American" man as a sexual relationship tinged with the exoticism and degradation that accompanies racial stereotypes. Thus, Smalkoski's observation that "they simply will

not appear so normal" refers to the pervasiveness of some of the most powerful "controlling images" of Asian women in the United States.[6] In relation
to the adult white American male, Anna may be seen as his prostitute or mail-
order bride, not as his daughter.

This essay analyzes the intersecting themes of race, nation, and the body
in the mixed-genre, fiction, poetry, and autobiographical narratives of Korean adoptees in the United States recently published in *Seeds from a Silent
Tree*, edited by Tonya Bishoff and Jo Rankin. It highlights the ways in which
these Korean adoptees' narratives confront the racialized assumptions of an
"American childhood" and critique the assimilationist and nationalist fantasies of U.S. liberalism most recently promoted by scholars such as David
Hollinger who use transracial adoption as the celebratory signal of the end
of the significance of race in U.S. culture.[7] The Korean adoptee contributors'
awareness of cultural contradictions in a supposedly racially tolerant, multicultural American society creates longing for a different vision of plural childhoods, homes, and identities that span racial and geographical borders. These
pluralistic visions of their Korean American childhoods directly acknowledge
(as opposed to ignore, belittle, or deny) the hypocritical pervasiveness of U.S.
racialist and nationalist assumptions regarding citizenship and family. In doing so, we argue that while these narratives expose the limits of current racial
categories such as "Asian American," they also challenge the current romanticization and celebration of racial mixing and hybridity embodied in mixed
race and transracial adoptee populations by presenting a more critical view
of U.S. liberal ideologies.

Toward a Qualitative Analysis of Intercountry, Transracial Adoption

Since the end of the Korean War, the adoption of Korean children has truly
been a global phenomenon. Between 1958 and 1990, families in Western nations adopted approximately 130,000 Korean children. While France and
Sweden are among the major receiving countries of Korean adoptees, the
United States has been the top receiving country of Korean children, adopting over 50 percent (approximately 80,000) of this world total.[8] Although
American families have adopted children from all over the world, Korean
children have dominated the numbers of orphans receiving U.S. immigrant
visas through the late 1990s.[9]

The origins of this phenomenon can be partly traced to the emergence of
the sentimental discourse of familial love without national boundaries, which
became popular in the United States during the Cold War. In her thought-
provoking essay on adoption and the Cold War commitment to Asia, Chris-

tina Klein analyzes international, cross-racial adoption advertisements and the popular film *South Pacific,* arguing that this sentimental discourse constructed a national identity that "figured Americans as protectors of Asia while denying any imperial ambitions."[10] While Klein's study reflects the important insights on international adoption that can be gleaned from a cultural studies and historical perspective, most of the secondary literature focuses on the contemporary medical, legal, and social-service-oriented problems associated with this phenomenon. Although many of these studies on international adoption include Korean adoptees, they lump them together with Eastern European adoptees, eliding the racialized differences among these groups.

Furthermore, while some studies have addressed Korean adoptees' racial and ethnic formations in the United States, they are primarily informed by quantitative methodologies of social science, which attempt statistically to measure Korean adoptees' and their adoptive families' perceptions of self-esteem and racial and ethnic identity. Based on their statistical findings, most of these studies conclude that Korean adoptee children and teenagers have high levels of self-esteem and strong attachments to their adoptive families. For example, in his 1975–76 study of 406 Korean children between the ages of twelve and seventeen who had been adopted by American families, Dong Soo Kim concluded, "The study shows that adopted Korean children tend to progress very well in all areas of their lives, indicating no special problems in their overall, long-term adjustment. Their self-concept was remarkably similar to that of other American teenagers (represented by a norm group in a standard scale with an impressively positive self-esteem)."[11] Complementing Kim's findings, Rita Simon and Howard Altstein more recently concluded, in their study of 124 white American families throughout the United States who adopted 168 Korean children in the late 1960s and 1970s, that most adoptees viewed their experiences positively. According to the majority of adoptees, the race of their parents did not matter and they would recommend transracial adoption.[12]

In these studies, Korean adoptee children and adolescents emerge as a new model minority, curious (as opposed to angry or hostile) about racial difference but ultimately thriving in the process of assimilation. As Mike Mullen concluded in his study of Korean adoptee children, "Not one of the informants expressed regret or anger about being adopted; curiosity was the more common response when the adoptees' affinity with whites was called into question. Korean children who have been adopted by white families have a fairly distinct identity development process and diverge from a more traditional minority identity development approach."[13] The reference to the divergence from a "more traditional minority identity development approach" is reminiscent of the popularization of the Japanese-American model minority in the late 1960s and early 1970s, which portrayed Japanese-American families as "successful" American minorities in contrast to African Americans and other racialized groups.

However, although the conclusions from these quantitative studies suggest that the racial conflicts among Korean adoptees, their white adoptive parents, and dominant white American culture are relatively insignificant, some of their findings also point to the need for a qualitative analysis of Korean adoptees' experiences regarding racism and identity formation. For example, although Dong Soo Kim concluded that Korean adoptees' self-concept "was remarkably similar to that of other American teenagers," he added that "both sexes of adopted Korean children appeared to be extremely concerned with their physical appearance, complaining of their small stature, dark skin, flat noses, short legs, and so on. With this kind of negative body image, they tend to reject their own racial background."[14] These disparate findings indicate that Kim does not consider racial identity and difference to be significant factors in the "self-concept" of Korean adoptees, and suggest the need for qualitative analyses that confront these contradictions about race, identity, and the body in the United States.

The Face of Race

Korean adoptees' anxiety about their body image is historically rooted in intersecting early-twentieth-century beliefs about corporeal and cultural assimilation. In *Asian/American: Historical Crossings of a Racial Frontier,* David Palumbo-Liu analyzed the ways in which the migrant body served as an index of assimilation in the United States. For example, in 1907, Congress created an immigration commission that reported that immigrants' bodies were being physically transformed the longer they stayed in America. The head shapes of European Jews and Italians purportedly changed into a more uniform American head shape. Palumbo-Liu argues that in U.S. history, "the sign of race can best be seen on the face," which has historically demarcated essential differences between groups.[15] These differences physically as well as culturally distinguish "Asians" from "Americans" and inform the racialized exclusion of Americans of Asian descent from U.S. cultural citizenship throughout the twentieth century, with the World War II internment of approximately 120,000 Japanese Americans (two-thirds of whom were born in the United States) as one of this exclusion's most egregious examples. Thus, despite the U.S. economic incorporation and exploitation of Asian-American labor from the building of the transcontinental railroad by Chinese male laborers in the second half of the nineteenth century to the alleviation of critical nursing-care shortages by predominantly Filipino women in the second half of the twentieth century, this cultural exclusion haunts Asian Americans across class, gender, and ethnic lines.

What distinguishes Korean adoptees from other Asian Americans, however, is not their labor in the U.S. economy, but rather their "consumption" by white adoptive families in the United States. However, despite having been raised in white adoptive families, many of the Korean adoptee authors emphasize the ways in which the racialized foreignness inscribed on their bodies, and in particular their faces, negate their Americanness. Lacking the normative facial features of "Americans," Korean adoptees become physically and culturally marked as un-American. For example, in "New Beginnings," Sherilyn Cockroft reflects on the ways in which her facial differences prevented her from having a "normal" American childhood: "I have always had an idea of what normality was—to have parents who were not divorced, to live within a certain range of income, to listen to pop music, to go to football games, to go to college, and finally to get married and give my children a 'normal' childhood." [16] Yet it is a somatic, not a socioeconomic or heterosexist, barrier that she is unable to cross. Cockroft continues, "However, I didn't have a 'normal' childhood. Not that I had a bad childhood, but I always felt different and inferior. . . . Even going to the mall, people would sometimes stare at me because I looked different. On one occasion in my early teens, I remember an innocent child said to me, 'How come your face is so flat?' Even though the child asked an innocent question, I felt very uncomfortable with my appearance." [17]

Thomas Park Clement recalls a similar, though more physically abusive, childhood experience while waiting for his mother on a street corner: "Two boys a little older than me came up and shoved me to the ground and kicked me over and over saying, 'Hey chink, where'd you get those funny eyes?'" [18] This racialized incident is not an isolated one. In junior high school, Thomas encounters a boy named Red who approaches him, another boy, and three girls. "Hanging around girls was a new thing," Thomas recalls, but he was "feeling okay" about himself. However, Thomas continues, "[Red] pressed his hands to each side of his temples and pulled back which made his eyes look a little more like mine. . . . He called me a 'Chink' and left laughing with his friends." [19] Red's racial taunts emphasized by the physical contortion of his face leads Thomas to confront his own physical differences inscribed on his face: "That night I began to practice in front of the bathroom mirror. . . . I looked at my eyes and opened them as wide as I could stand without them hurting. I used my fingers. I looked at them closely in the mirror where my nose was almost touching the mirror. Yes, Red was right. They did not look like his."[20] Given this context of racialized taunting and abuse in his American childhood, the title of Clement's piece, "The Unforgotten War," is ambiguous, perhaps purposely so. What war has he not forgotten: the Korean War that resulted in his being a street orphan, or the one he fights as a Korean adoptee in America? The very existence of Korean adoptees is a ramification of war, so the "moments" Clement recalls become points on a continuum of a "war" that is not only unforgotten but, as a result of his very remembrances, continues on.

The Child in the Mirror

The confirmation of racialized physical otherness through one's reflection in the mirror and the inability of typically American behavior to overcome the stigma of racial difference are overlapping and recurring themes in *Seeds from a Silent Tree*. As in pieces by Wayne A. Berry (Oh, Ji Soo), Mi Ok Song Bruining, Thomas Park Clement, Young Hee, Ellwyn Kauffman, Rebecca Smith, and others, the reflection of their Korean faces evokes an experience of disjointedness. The mirror, or the reflection therein, is a site for recognizing racial difference because of what it both signifies and denies to its onlooker. The Korean face, the "yellow" face that stares back at its possessor, denies abstraction into the National Symbolic, divesting all hope of being defined / inscribed as American by dint of doing things American. Berry (Oh, Ji Soo), in "Completing My Puzzle . . ." recalls, "As a child, being called names like: *chink, Chinaman, rice paddy*, etc. and watching classmates pull up the corners of their eyes to mimic me only strengthened my actions to be as American as much as I could be."[21] However, his reflection in the mirror reminds him that his "American" actions are unable to transform his face into a normative American one, thus preventing him from becoming American psychologically as well as physically: "As comfortable as I pretended to be though, I could not deny the fact that I was Korean. I was always reminded of this when I looked in the mirror or paged through family photo albums, and saw my jet black hair in comparison to my mother and two sisters' red hair."[22]

The consistent jeers, racial slurs, and quizzical looks (mainly from white children and adolescents) lead some Korean adoptees to internalize the belief that the body authenticates national and cultural identities. And this somatic association with Korea in particular and Asia in general is not a source of pride (a corporeal bridge that links the "best of both worlds"), but rather of frustration, self-hatred, and shame. As Rebecca Smith remembers, "Growing up in a large Swedish community in the Midwest introduced me to the first criteria of what was considered the norm. Fair skin and blond hair were the standards I measured myself against. Honestly, I had no idea I didn't fit that description unless I saw my reflection in the mirror. I thought of myself as Caucasian. What a shock to find out that I wasn't. . . . At the age of four, I discovered that being different was not the same as being special. Being taunted and teased by my peers was a rude awakening to how different I really was." [23] Mi Ok Song Bruining links this physical insecurity to psychological turmoil, writing, "I was convinced I was going insane because I felt so inauthentic. I did not feel white, as I had been raised. I did not feel Asian, as I clearly looked and was. . . . Adolescence is traumatic enough without being targeted for being racially different, culturally identified as 'alien' & looking like no one else—peer, child, or adult. I was stared at, harassed, bullied, called names, insulted, threatened & verbally abused by other kids—younger & older—on a daily basis—on the school bus, in school, stores, restaurants, & many other public places in Rhode Island." [24] According to Young Hee, the mirror's revelation of her nonwhiteness leads to self-hatred: "I used to believe I was white. . . . Theoretically I was white, my family is white, the community I grew up in was white. . . . However, my image staring back at me in the mirror betrayed such a belief. There I saw it, the rude and awful truth . . . slanted-hooded eyes, non-existent eyelashes, 'yellow' skin, short legs, and long torso. I hated myself, this betrayal, being given such a look without any knowledge of where it came from." [25] And, for Ellwyn Kauffman, this reflection is a constant, shameful reminder of his otherness: "I was ashamed of my ethnicity. All my friends were white. My parents were white. Who was this Korean in the mirror? The mirror was the inescapable reminder of where I had come from." [26]

The statements—"I thought of myself as Caucasian," "I was convinced I was going insane because I felt so inauthentic," "I used to believe I was white"—speak to a racial schizophrenia familiar to Asian-American studies and other ethnic studies scholars. The "schizophrenia" is what Kim, Simon and Altstein, Mullen, and other social scientists attempt to quantify (and inadvertently attempt to gloss over and resolve) in their studies of Korean adoptee "self-concept" or "identity development." It is a "condition" of living on, or in, a yellow/white racial binary, and an Asian/American cultural and national binary. The Asian-American subject finds herself pushed and pulled in too many contradictory ways by straddling the line. The push and pull of this condition is exemplified in two short poems by Jo Rankin and David Miller, respectively, and tellingly titled "Exchange" and "Tightrope." [27] In "Exchange," Rankin opens with the image of a seemingly irreconcilable cultural divide: "Born unto two / Realities, two cultures: too different." This cultural divide is inextricably linked to national borders: "Crying silent tears while attempting to / Exchange American branches for / Korean roots." For

David Miller, the tightrope represents the psychological as well as cultural and national lines that he straddles and balances with caution:

Walking a tightrope
Pulled on both sides
Korea
America
For if I fall either way
I lose a part of me.

In an essay on the problematic nature of rehabilitative representation in ethnic literature, critic Sau-ling Cynthia Wong accuses Chinese-American writers Frank Chin and Amy Tan of respecularizing the very Chinatown exotica that their narratives set out to debunk. Both writers, claims Wong, "end up producing works . . . in which the ethnic subject's gaze betrays an apparently inextricable influence from the dominant culture." [28] Wong's criticism describes a familiar dilemma among writers who foreground race in their work—namely, how do ethnic writers illuminate the inscriptedness of race within a national culture without respecularizing its exotica "by so strenuously drawing attention to the process of othering, by making outraged protest and strident refusal the central project of [their] characters"? [29]

While outraged protest and strident refusal might not specifically describe the general tone of the pieces in *Seeds from a Silent Tree* (though they certainly apply in some of them), the spectacle of race and racism in many of the pieces take on those "exhibitionist" aspects of identity that Wong bemoans in Chin and Tan. Indeed, racial difference is the artifact upon which the contradictions of national creed are so apparent, and that artifact is nowhere more apparent than in the metaphor of the Asian face staring back from the mirror. The "Korean face" in the mirror is, to the personae in *Seeds from a Silent Tree*, the synecdoche for the nonwhite body, the foreign nation, the undesirable and unassimilable alien.

While many of the entries in the anthology border on what are by now considered hackneyed expressions of racialized identity in Asian-American literature—either/or, inside/outside, white/nonwhite binaries; encounters with racists and fetishists; and quotidian orientalism—what is interesting and unique about *Seeds from a Silent Tree* is that few, if any, of the writers consider themselves as writing from the perspective of "Asian America." None of the authors self-identifies as Asian American in the autobiographical notes included in the anthology. Rather, the reference is to being an adopted Korean. Given that uniqueness within the context of Asian-American identity, and also given that this is the most widely disseminated anthology of its kind, the very process of respecularization that Wong critiques in Chin and Tan becomes central to *Seeds from a Silent Tree*. The process is given warrant by the situated and shared irony of the authors' experiences: they were born Korean, but were raised by primarily white Americans in small, rural areas or suburbs.

Reading the Mirror

The unique American childhood of Korean adoptees casts a different perspective on the metaphor of the Asian face staring back from the mirror. While the scholarly contributions of Asian-American studies and other ethnic studies scholars render the cultural meanings of this racialized face (i.e., not white, not American) seemingly obvious, for adopted Koreans, the face in the mirror is also a touchstone of memory—for some, literally—of a place they once called home. For example, in Zoli Seuk Kim Hall's "Him, Her, and I," the narrator stands "at the front door of a missing memory with no forwarding address." [30] However, the mirror enables her to see her Korean mother's "brown black head." She concludes,

> as if it has always been like this
> the self of the present watching
> her find pieces of her selves, inside the puzzle
> of that mirror, gleaming back into her life.

In this anthology the concept of home is distinct from previous conceptions of home in Asian-American literature. Traditional concepts of "home" are metaphorical or imagined places located somewhere in America's past, or within a dreary American ethos of romance.[31] They are based on a trope of longing and desire constructed on the legislative promise of the American creed (such as the right to the "pursuit of happiness") and therefore contingent upon an insinuation of U.S. nationalism. By contrast, in *Seeds from a Silent Tree*, concepts of home are split into two very real places: Korea and America. Although Korea and America figure as metaphorical and imagined places as well, the tangible existence of these two places inspires many of the pieces in the section "Reunions," which focuses on adopted Koreans' physical as well as emotional journeys back to Korea in order to search for their birth mother(land).

In their 1973 preface to *Aiiieeeee!* (the groundbreaking anthology of Asian-American literature published at the height of the Asian-American movement), editors Frank Chin, Jeffrey Paul Chan, Lawson Fusao Inada, and

Shawn Hsu Wong harshly criticized the belief that Asian Americans were either Asian or American (white), or measurably both. According to them, being either/or was a myth and having a dual personality was an "equally goofy concept," since, in their conception of prototypes, Asian Americans got their "China and Japan from the radio, off the silver screen, from television, out of comic books, from the pushers of white American culture that pictured the yellow man as something that when wounded, sad, or angry, or swearing, or wondering whined, shouted, or screamed 'aiiieeeee!'"[32] Their strident denial that an Asian/American double consciousness could ever exist applies in the case of the adopted Korean, but not in the way they might have imagined.

Some of the writers in *Seeds from a Silent Tree* were too young at the time to be able to recall now in retrospect the concrete details of their lives in the orphanages of Korea; others recall in vivid detail their childhood spent there. Thus, whereas Chin, Chan, Inada, and Wong claim that there is no discrete "Asian" side to Asian-American identity, for those in *Seeds from a Silent Tree* the two experiences are simply too incompatible to exist simultaneously in the same mind—or even, as Tonya Bishoff's poem "Unnamed Blood" describes, the same lifetime.[33] According to the poem's narrator, "I am thinking / there is more than / a singular / birth place time date." The narrator's travel by plane to the adoptive country marks another birthing process that psychologically and physically attempts to erase the first lifetime:

I was squeezed through the opening
of a powerful steel bird
that carried me far away,
and with each mile,
I felt the needle
tear the thread
through the moist flesh
of my lips
and with each mile,
the thread pulled
tauter and tauter
till I could no longer call
for Omoni
I could barely moan—and eventually
I became silent,
and the silence spread
throughout my blood
and seeped
into my bones

as the bird thrust me
into soft, white fleshy arms
and the afterbirth
poured through my eyes
surrounding me in a
pool of salty
death

This incommensurate condition compels the search for beginnings in Korea, reflected in the first section of the anthology, "Roots Remembered and
Imagined," and is given fuller development in the middle sections, "Trans-
plantations" and "Reunions." The search for the authors' Korean origins is
both psychological and physical—some of the narrators retrieve memories
of their early childhoods in Korean orphanages, whereas others write about
physically returning to Korea. Searching for their Korean "side" should not
be interpreted as a form of false racialized consciousness in which Korean
adoptees psychologically and physically return to Korea because they internalize that they can only be Asian or measurably half Asian after living in the
United States. Rather, this psychological and physical journey that so many
of the authors allude to speaks to a collective form of resistance to the tri-
umphalist historical narratives about U.S. military involvement in Asia that
emphasize U.S. benevolence over imperial ambitions, and about U.S. immigration that emphasize color-blind assimilation over racial exclusion. Such
propagandist narratives have silenced many Korean adoptees in the public
record through their overwhelmingly positive focus on the white families
that graciously welcome Korean children and, in doing so, rescue them from
abject states of poverty, ignorance, and disease in Korea. However, in *Seeds
from a Silent Tree,* the Korean adoptee contributors present alternative narratives about their "welcome" in the United States. In "Dear Luuk," Kari Ruth
points to their troubling commodification and exploitation: "I have heard
parents commenting that adopting Korean children is an enriching cultural
experience and that other adults should do the same. Those parents must
not understand that the price they paid for us was insignificant to the price
we pay to fit into their world. . . . Now we're told that our cultural displacement has a purpose—multiculturalism. . . . I guess someone forgot to ask us
if we wanted to be American's diversity mascots."[34]

We can trace the "movement" of the works in *Seeds from a Silent Tree* by
analyzing the ways in which the speakers "read" their own conditions. The
pieces are written overwhelmingly in the first person, and though there are
no explicit literary categories distinguishing fictive works from the nonfic-
tive, many of the pieces reflect personal experiences. In a sense, then, one can

think of the writers of the anthology as readers of their own identity. Such an approach allows for a kind of reader-response analysis not of the readers of the anthology, but of the personae within the pieces reading race and nation on their own faces. To return to the familiar trope of the face in the mirror, what does an interrogation of those scenes yield in terms of how nation is being "read" or conceived of by the respective speaker?

Norman Holland offers a psychoanalytical paradigm for the ways readers engage texts and the world around them. In his 1985 work *The I,* he goes so far as to offer a substitution for the verb *reading* that he feels more accurately describes the way humans engage the written word. A successful reading encounter, Holland claims, involves the engagement of our defenses, expectations, and fantasies, all of which lead to a resultant transformation. These qualities essentially define the way we read the world to such an extent that the verb *reading* could be replaced by the acronym DEFTing:

> In effect, DEFTing suggests that we live in a psychological version of our basic adaptation as mammals. The body temperature of a fish simply equals the temperature of its water. We, however, have evolved beyond the cold-blooded animals. We create inside our bodies, in our blood, the warm, nourishing sea the fish finds outside. Psychologically, we create an inner environment of symbols. Then we live in a delicate tension between our inner and outer world of symbols.
>
> We are active human beings precisely because there is a difference between the heterogeneous, constantly changing outer world and the more homogenous, more constant world within. In acting we accept that difference, for example, the separateness and absence registered by language, but we try to DEFT it away. We try to make absence presence. . . . We live in a feedback or deconstruction which requires difference for us to (try but not quite manage to) render difference into sameness.[35]

Trying to make "absence presence" is, according to its editors, what compelled the creation of the anthology. "*Seeds from a Silent Tree* emerged from absence searching for presence," writes coeditor Bishoff in the first line of the introduction.[36] While Holland might only have marginally been thinking of its application to racial identity, DEFTing offers multiple ways to analyze the metaphor of the "readers reading" (to play off of the title of Holland's more famous work) in *Seeds from a Silent Tree.* DEFTing is synonymous, Holland implies, with taking action—or rather, it is a kind of action that for the purposes of analyzing the contributions to *Seeds from a Silent Tree* denotes agency. What immobilizes the narrators, as they stare into the mirror in a seemingly eternalized moment of antinarcissist obsession, is the inability to reconcile the disparate readings of their reflection. "So we are created by the culture and codes around us, yet we create what we are created by," writes Holland.[37] The metaphor of the mirror can be read as an endless loop of inseparable yet irreconcilable difference in which the viewer, the narrator looking into the mirror, stands in shock of what the "culture and codes" have made of the viewed, the reflection. The space between viewer and reflection is symbolic, and begs a reading itself as a kind of racially and nationalistically charged habitational space. The way out of that loop, Holland contends, is through a transformative experience that essentially changes not just the conception of our own self-identities, but, subsequent to that change, the parameters of cultural contact itself. It is a transformation wrought by the reader—in the case of *Seeds from a Silent Tree*, the author—who in effect, reconstructs and redefines his cultural space. It is a movement from a state—or space—of abjectness to one of agency.

To be inextricably bound in a political space initiated by a reading experience assumes that one enters that experience, as Holland claims, with defenses, expectations, and fantasies already formed, and informed, by political, cultural, and—something Berlant and Holland do not explicitly consider, but which obtains in a reading of *Seeds from a Silent Tree*—racial constructs. There is an enormous gap in the anthology between the eventuality of inscription into the National Symbolic and the centrifugal, racialized forces that disrupt that inscription—a madness that is always impending, if not actualized. Thus, in Lee Herrick's poem "Jap" from the final section, "Seeds of Resolution," the narrator finds himself at a seemingly ordinary gas station on a seemingly ordinary day:

> pumping gas at the am pm
> It is a normal afternoon in the valley
> like all afternoons in the valley,
> split between modern duty
> and the desire of something better.
> We are in the same world.[38]

The seemingly ordinary quality of this situation is powerfully disrupted, however, when the narrator observes another driver at the station mouthing racial epithets at him, constructing the racialized difference that excludes the narrator from existing in the "same world" as the racist perpetrator:

> what you don't realize
> is that I see you

in your red anger . . . your vomit words,
like swords,
hurled at me: *god damn jap*
I look down at my chest
my almond eyes open wide
breath sputtering
blood dripping.
I pull it from just beside my heart
and I still stand.
This is where racism begins
in the throat
at the station
in the heart of valley afternoons.[39]

Imagine, the narrator (like many others in *Seeds from a Silent Tree*) demands, the existential panic of always being seen before you are seen. The narrator's madness is manifested in fantasies of how he might respond to this form of everyday racism:

I imagine
instead of thrusting this bloody sword
into you and killing us both off
slowly, I whisper to you: *I am not god*
I am not damned
and I am not Japanese.[40]

Using Holland's concept of DEFting, what then is the resulting transformation (assuming that is the end result of a reading experience) as the Korean adoptee writers "read" their defenses, expectations, and fantasies? To act implies mobility and the agency to reshape one's sense of space. The transformation required for the narrators in *Seeds from a Silent Tree* to be "active human beings," to coin Holland's generic term, occurs in the transcendence of the abject space of the metaphorical and literal mirror. At the conclusion of "Jap," we witness this mobility, reconstruction of space, and transcendence as the narrator with his "almond eyes open wide" views the wounds and scars that racism has inflicted upon him, and confronts his desires for vengeance as he approaches the racist perpetrator in order to "drop the sword and feel / my chest, stronger / and I imagine a space / with no swords / and / no constellations."

We can read the space of the mirror, then, as an arena where representation, rehabilitation, and recuperation of identity are in countenance. In her

1996 *Immigrant Acts: On Asian American Cultural Politics*, Lisa Lowe conceptualizes that space of recuperation as the emergence of Asian-American culture, "an alternative cultural site and the place where the contradictions of immigrant history are read, performed, and critiqued."[41] The emergent narratives surrounding the space of recuperation close the distance "from the terrain of national culture," which has historically and judicially alienated Asian Americans.[42] For many of the Korean adoptee writers in *Seeds from a Silent Tree*, their "American" childhood experiences have made them profoundly and painfully aware of the distance separating them from the terrains of two national cultures, those of both the United States and Korea.

Thus, Su Niles's narrative "Obstacles and Challenges," in the final section of the anthology, opens with her individual struggles, which she links with the collective struggles of other adopted Koreans: "This has been my most difficult challenge: To overcome the effects of a turbulent childhood . . . because I was Korean in an all-white family, I fought the feelings of isolation and loneliness. Other adoptees have similar stories to share."[43] As the piece continues, the narrator relates that she is "compelled to assimilate all that [she] can about Korea and what being Korean means" but laments that she will never be "wholly Korean." Despite the dehumanizing and demoralizing obstacles and challenges that emerge because "the world sees [her] as a Color," Niles recuperates the narrator's American and Korean identities through the act of writing. "I walk in this skin. And in this skin, I am any American," she writes, challenging the observation in Kari Smalkoski's narrative, which opened this essay, that the adopted Korean daughter "did not look like anyone's daughter growing up in the suburbs of Minneapolis."[44] Yet in her final paragraph Niles writes, "Through the years of understanding the impact of inter-country adoption on myself and other adoptees, I have finally come to accept these things: I am Korean. I will always be Korean."[45]

As the Korean adoptee writers in *Seeds from a Silent Tree* read, perform, and critique the contradictions of their migrant histories, they simultaneously join and transform Asian-American cultural terrains. Their stories poignantly remind us of the importance of confronting these past and present contradictions if we are ever to transcend them.

NOTES

1. Kari Smalkoski, "China," in *Seeds from a Silent Tree: An Anthology by Korean Adoptees*, ed. Tonya Bishoff and Jo Rankin (San Diego: Pandal Press, 1997), 73.
2. Ibid., 73–74.

3. Lauren Berlant, *The Anatomy of National Fantasy* (Chicago: University of Chicago Press, 1991), 4–5.

4. See Louise Michele Newman, *White Women's Rights: The Racial Origins of Feminism in the United States* (New York: Oxford University Press, 1999).

5. Smalkoski, "China," 74.

6. For an analysis of "controlling images" and their relationship to the economic and social oppression of subordinate groups, see Patricia Hill Collins, *Black Feminist Thought: Knowledge, Consciousness, and the Politics of Empowerment* (Boston: Unwin Hyman, 1990).

7. David A. Hollinger, *Postethnic America: Beyond Multiculturalism* (New York: Basic Books, 1995), 117.

8. A/K/A World, "Korean Adoptees: Statistics," A/K/A World, online at <http://akaworld .org/Koreanstat.html>.

9. U.S. Department of State, Office of Children's Issues, "Immigrant Visas Issued to Orphans Coming to the U.S.," online at <http://travel.state.gov/orphan_numbers.html>.

10. Christina Klein, "Family Ties and Political Obligation: The Discourse of Adoption and the Cold War Commitment to Asia," in *Cold War Constructions: the Political Culture of United States Imperialism, 1945–1966,* ed. Christian G. Appy (Amherst: University of Massachusetts Press, 2000), 38.

11. Dong Soo Kim, "Intercountry Adoptions: A Study of Self-Concept of Adolescent Korean Children Who Were Adopted by American Families," (Ph.D. diss., University of Chicago, 1976), 56, cited in Rita J. Simon and Howard Alstein, *Adoption across Borders: Serving the Children in Transracial and Intercountry Adoptions* (Lanham, Md.: Rowman and Littlefield, 2000), 86.

12. Simon and Alstein, *Adoption across Borders,* 100–104.

13. Mike Mullen, "Identity Development of Korean Adoptees," in *Reviewing Asian America: Locating Diversity,* ed. Wendy L. Ng, Soo-Young Chin, James S. Moy, and Gary Y. Okihiro (Pullman: Washington State University Press, 1995), 73–74.

14. Kim, "Intercountry Adoptions, 56, cited in Simon and Alstein, *Adoption across Borders,* 87.

15. David Palumbo-Liu, *Asian/American: Historical Crossings of a Racial Frontier* (Stanford, Calif.: Stanford University Press, 1999), 87.

16. Sherilyn Cockroft, "New Beginnings," in Bishoff and Rankin, *Seeds from a Silent Tree,* 16.

17. Ibid.

18. Thomas Park Clement, "The Unforgotten War," in Bishoff and Rankin, *Seeds from a Silent Tree,* 29.

19. Ibid., 30.

20. Ibid.

21. Wayne A. Berry (Oh, Ji Soo), "Completing My Puzzle . . ." in Bishoff and Rankin, *Seeds from a Silent Tree,* 121.

22. Ibid.

23. Rebecca Smith, "Unconventional Seoul," in Bishoff and Rankin, *Seeds from a Silent Tree,* 106.

24. Mi Ok Song Bruining, "A Few Words From Another Left-Handed Adopted Korean Lesbian," in Bishoff and Rankin, *Seeds from a Silent Tree,* 66.

25. Young Hee, "Laurel," in Bishoff and Rankin, *Seeds from a Silent Tree,* 86.

26. Ellwyn Kauffman, "Bulgogi," in Bishoff and Rankin, *Seeds from a Silent Tree,* 46.

27. Jo Rankin, "Exchange," in Bishoff and Rankin, *Seeds from a Silent Tree,* 93; and David Miller, "Tightrope," in Bishoff and Rankin, *Seeds from a Silent Tree,* 107.

28. Sau-Ling Cynthia Wong, "Ethnic Subject, Ethnic Sign, and the Difficulty of Rehabilita-

tive Representation: Chinatown in Some Works of Chinese American Fiction," *Yearbook of English Studies* 24 (1994): 258.

29. Ibid.

30. Zoli Seuk Kim Hall, "Him, Her, I," in Bishoff and Rankin, *Seeds from a Silent Tree*, 36.

31. Notable examples include Carlos Bulosan, *America Is in the Heart* (New York: Harcourt, 1946); Monica Sone, *Nisei Daughter* (Boston: Little, Brown, 1953); John Okada, *No-No Boy* (Seattle: University of Washington Press, 1995); and Shawn Wong, *Homebase* (New York: Plume, 1979).

32. Preface to *Aiiieeeee! An Anthology of Asian American Writers*, ed. Frank Chin, Jeffrey Paul Chan, Lawson Fusao Inada, and Shawn Hsu Wong (New York: Mentor, 1991), xii.

33. Tonya Bishoff, "Unnamed Blood," in Bishoff and Rankin, *Seeds from a Silent Tree*, 37–38.

34. Kari Ruth, "Dear Luuk," in Bishoff and Rankin, *Seeds from a Silent Tree*, 144.

35. Norman Holland, *The I* (New Haven, Conn.: Yale University Press, 1985), 105–6.

36. Tonya Bishoff, introduction to Bishoff and Rankin, *Seeds from a Silent Tree*, 1.

37. Holland, *The I*, 105.

38. Lee Herrick, "Jap," in Bishoff and Rankin, *Seeds from a Silent Tree*, 161.

39. Ibid., 161–62.

40. Ibid., 162.

41. Lisa Lowe, *Immigrant Acts: On Asian American Cultural Politics* (Durham, N.C.: Duke University Press, 1996), ix–x.

42. Ibid., ix.

43. Su Niles, "Obstacles and Challenges," in Bishoff and Rankin, *Seeds from a Silent Tree*, 152.

44. Ibid., 153.

45. Ibid., 154.

14 Reel Origins

Multiculturalism, History, and the American Children's Movie

Manuel M. Martín-Rodríguez

It is time to recognize that the true tutors of our children are not school-teachers or university professors but filmmakers, advertising executives and pop culture purveyors. Disney does more than Duke, Spielberg outweighs Stanford, MTV trumps MIT.

—BENJAMIN R. BARBER,

QUOTED IN HENRY A. GIROUX, *THE MOUSE THAT ROARED*

No sane person would now look to Hollywood movies for the truth of contemporary social practice.

—CATHERINE BELSEY, *SHAKESPEARE AND THE LOSS OF EDEN*

This essay explores the tension expressed in the juxtaposition of the two epigraphs above: on the one hand, the fact that the entertainment industry has become the de facto teacher of the American child in more ways than one; and on the other, the lack of control that society as a whole (and children in particular) have over the educational legitimacy of products coming out of the major studios in Hollywood. My interest, in this sense, is to explore the ways in which two of those culture purveyors cited by Benjamin Barber—Disney and Spielberg (the latter through the DreamWorks SKG production company)—have become history teachers by producing and releasing historical or historically situated films like *Pocahontas* (Disney, 1995), *The Road to El Dorado* (Dream-Works, 2000), and *The Emperor's New Groove* (Disney, 2000). In particular, these three feature films share an interest in exploring pre-European America: the latter at an unspecified time before the arrival of the first Europeans; the former two at the historical juncture of the encounter between indigenous and European civilizations.

The coincidence of a relatively large number of historical children's movies in such a brief period of time forces us to inquire about the reasons for the studios' current interest in exploring the American past.[1] What would make Disney and DreamWorks look back to the distant American past at the turn of the twenty-first century? Also, what is the American child like at the turn of the twenty-first century, and why would the studios *want* to teach that child American history, and how? These questions are closely interrelated, as I will explore in detail below, since the answer to the latter sheds much light on the former.

The "American child" remains, of course, a critical construct, much in the sense observed by Carolyn Steedman about "the child" in general, who writes, "My experience, of actually working with children, has made me aware of the split that exists between children and 'the child.' Both history and many psychologies tell us . . . that 'the child' is a construct: that beyond a bit of anatomy and physiology, and perhaps the order of language acquisition, there is not much there that isn't a matter of adult construction, adult projection." [2] As a population group, on the other hand, American children resist now more than ever the consolidation of their differences into a one-size-fits-all critical or conceptual construct, regardless of how refined it might be. For my purposes here, the difference to which Steedman calls attention is essential because the population group that American children presently compose is multicultural, multilingual, multiethnic, and multiracial in unprecedented proportions.[3] The "American child," however, remains a singular, necessarily reductionist concept to be constructed from adult projections, so much so that, even if we were to conceive the American child as a *multicultural* American child this constructed multiculturalism could never describe the real difference experienced by real American children who belong to one or more ethnic and cultural minority groups. And yet, for the mass media, including the film industry, the task of addressing actual American children largely hinges upon such an envisioned constructed commonality that the notion of the American child represents.

This is a point worth keeping in mind when approaching the three movies that I will analyze, as well as other "ethnic" children's films recently released by the Hollywood studios, including the Disney films *Aladdin* (1992), *The Hunchback of Notre Dame* (1996), *Hercules* (1997), and *Mulan* (1998); and— to a lesser extent—*The Little Mermaid* (1989), *Beauty and the Beast* (1991), and *The Lion King* (1994).[4] The "ethnicity" of these movies is limited to (some of) their characters and does not extend to their producers and writers nor even to the films' intended audience, which is an ethnically undefined "multicultural" construct (or, as Guillermo Gómez-Peña would phrase it, a "culti-multural" discourse of sameness under the guise of difference, that I prefer to call "*mall*ticulturalism," since it organizes cultural differences as an uncritical display for the consumption of the curious, much in the same way in which a mall arranges its retail space).[5] That is, the films do not function so much as an overture to particular ethnic groups in the audience as they do a reinforcement of societal values about those very same groups. This should be apparent from the fact that some of these movies have been received with harsh criticism from individuals and collectives belonging to the ethnic groups represented.[6] It has also been reflected in criticism by scholars who point out the many stereotypes that plague virtually all of the motion pictures mentioned above. In that sense, while the films do indeed reflect a societal interest in questions of race and ethnicity in the United States,[7] their treatment of ethnicity itself results in something akin to what Ella Shohat (in a slightly different context), has interpreted as a process of marginalization by conceiving ethnicity as a "deviation" from the norm of mainstream America. "The disciplinary assumption that some films are 'ethnic' whereas others are not is ultimately based on the view that certain groups are ethnic whereas others are not," she writes. "The marginalization of 'ethnicity' reflects the imaginary of the dominant group which envisions itself as the 'universal' or the 'essential' American nation, and thus somehow 'beyond' or 'above' ethnicity. The very word *ethnic,* then, reflects a peripheralizing strategy premised on an implicit contrast of 'norm' and 'other,' much as the term *minority* often carries with it an implication of minor, lesser, or subaltern."[8]

Because of this foregrounding of ethnicity from a dominant position, and despite the participation of "ethnic" actors and actresses playing the voices of many of the characters involved in these films, the movies themselves remain what Michel de Certeau has called "heterologies"—that is, discourses on the other "built upon a division between the body of knowledge that utters a discourse and the mute body that nourishes it."[9] In fact, while allowing the ethnic actors to voice over the lines of a previously written script, these motion pictures retain tight control of all utterances, paradoxically rendering silent the ethnic other that they profess to represent through the spoken word, and reserving for themselves the role of an ethnographer or "a translator of otherness," as Ana M. López suggests is the case in films for adult audiences.[10] No matter how much ethnicity may have been emphasized in recent films, the "ethnic" still remains an other in Hollywood's children's movies, the object of fascination and repulsion at the same time, much along the lines of what Homi K. Bhabha has identified as an "ambivalence that gives the colonial stereotype its currency: ensures its repeatability in changing historical and discursive conjunctures; informs its strategies of individuation and marginalization; produces that effect of probabilistic truth and predictability which, for the stereotype, must always be an *excess* of what can be empirically proved or logically construed."[11] Bhabha's understanding of contradictory representation, on which I rely throughout this essay, allows the critic to move beyond a more simple understanding of the stereotype in order to engage in an exploration of the pleasure/anxiety tension implicit in Hollywood's recent heterological children's films. In what follows, I explore how this ambivalence works in the retelling of history and ethnicity to the turn of the century American child.

My analysis of three films here follows the order in which they were released. In itself, I believe that the sequence they form is of significance, as they start closer to home (the arrival of the Anglo-American to lands that later became the United States—in *Pocahontas*), move farther away in time and space (to ancient Mexico and the arrival of the Spanish—in *The Road to El Dorado*), and even farther in time and space (to the pre-Hispanic Inca empire—in *The Emperor's New Groove*). While I am not suggesting that this particular ordering is the result of a deliberate plan, I would like to argue that it is nonetheless indicative of a common rhetorical strategy used to depict the other (particularly the Hispanic other) as foreign and far removed from the United States. American children watching these films in movie theaters or in their video formats have thus followed a path that has taken them (and the "natives") farther and farther away from the present-day United States in a sort of symbolical deportation. One could choose to reverse the order for the sake of analysis, following the films' own temporality rather than that of their release dates, but this approach most likely does not represent the order in which most American children have actually watched these movies.

This Land is Your Land: Pocahontas,
Imperial Expansion, and the Politics of Body/Language

Loosely based on the life of its historical namesake, *Pocahontas* (Disney, 1995) is also a primordial example of Hollywood's alleged new sensitivity toward the Native American, translated to the realm of children's entertainment.[12] In this respect, Eleanor Byrne and Martin McQuillan have called attention to the fact that, like all "new beginnings," this shift in the representation of the American Indian required "a new myth of foundation (reading that possessive both ways)," a role that *Pocahontas* was meant to play.[13] One should not overlook, however, the fact that just a year earlier, Disney had released the megahit *The Lion King (1994),* a deeply racist movie that may be read as a filmic commentary on the African-American experience, on the Latino experience, or (perhaps more accurately) on both. Neither should one forget that before *The Lion King, Aladdin* (1992) and *The Little Mermaid* (1989) had indulged in the by-now-habitual stereotyping of Arabic and Caribbean peoples, respectively.[14] Therefore, a pattern of engaging issues of ethnicity was already visible by the time of the release of *Pocahontas,* forcing us to consider what is different in the case of this latter film vis-à-vis the others I have mentioned.

What makes *Pocahontas* different from its predecessors is precisely the fact that it deals with a people whose origins cannot be traced to anywhere else but what is today the United States of America. Geographical displacement is easily achieved in the other films, but it is not an option in *Pocahontas.* In *The Lion King,* for instance, the hyenas live in a shadowy place across the border; Aladdin, in turn, inhabits a fictitious—yet very recognizable—Oriental(ized) country; and Sebastian (the heavily accented crab in *The Little Mermaid*) reminds the viewer of the Caribbean with his pronunciation. The Algonquin Indians, however, were already here when John Smith and John Ratcliffe arrived.

Of equal importance is the fact that American children in *Pocahontas*'s audience would normally have a context in which to situate the movie they are watching. Through family and school, American children are taught every year about the Pilgrim "forefathers" and their first encounter with the friendly "Indians." Many of these same children would have, no doubt, either dressed as Pilgrims or as "Indians" at some point in their lives before seeing the movie, normally as part of school plays and the like. Watching the filmic Pocahontas give John Smith corn (instead of the gold he seeks) would immediately be understood by even the youngest in the audience within the Thanksgiving narrative context. The "bad guys" on each side (Ratcliffe and Kokoum) may incite their companions to war, but the good Indian and the good conqueror know that there is a way to come together as friendly peoples.

As a matter of fact, *Pocahontas* goes to great lengths to erase the traumatic traces of violence in the displacement and eventual genocidal decimation of the Native American, and in this fact resides the first of its many historical shortcomings. While fighting occupies a considerable portion of the film, it is always overshadowed by the attempts to find peaceful resolution to conflicts and by the desire to portray the natives as willing to allow the newcomers to claim their land as their own.[15] In this sense, *Pocahontas* should be read against the context of a series of narratives of land dispossession and repossession, including Walter Prescott Webb's famous history *The Texas Rangers: A Century of Frontier Defense,* in which the author unintentionally highlights the complexity of ownership when he analyzes the so-called Indian problem, writing, "From the above sketch of the Indian situation in Texas during the early part of the nineteenth century, it should be apparent that the first permanent settlers—Anglo-Americans from the United States—would find a complicated and troublesome Indian problem to resolve before they could hold *their* land in peace."[16] In his attempt to make the Native Americans and the Hispanic/Mexican residents look like tourists *avant la lettre,* Webb is eventually betrayed by grammar: should we read "their" above as applying to the "Indians" or to the "Anglo-Americans"? While the context leaves no doubt about what Webb means, language destabilizes meaning, as the above quote clearly suggests.

This destabilizing property of language is emphasized in actual documents written from the point of view of the colonized (the "Indian"), in which we find a very different picture of how language functions as a site of struggle rather than as a point of encounter. One of the most striking texts in this sense is the Andean drama *Tragedia del fin de Atahualpa,* from which I take this scene involving the future Inca Sairi Tupac, the Spanish captain Francisco Pizarro, and his indigenous interpreter Felipillo, to illustrate my point:

> SAIRI TUPAC
> Barbudo adversario, hombre rojo
> ¿por qué tan sólo a mi señor,
> a mi Inca le andas buscando? . . .
> Antes de que se levante
> ésta su clava de oro . . .
> piérdete, regresa a tu tierra
> barbudo enemigo, hombre rojo.
> PIZARRO
> (sólo mueve los labios)
> SAIRI TUPAC
> Hombre rojo que ardes como el fuego
> y en la quijada llevas densa lana,

me resulta imposible comprender tu extraño lenguaje
    PIZARRO
(mueve los labios)
    FELIPILLO
Sairi Tupac, inca que manda,
este rubio señor te dice:
"¿Qué necedades vienes a decirme,
pobre salvaje? Me es imposible
comprender tu obscuro idioma." [17]

As I have suggested elsewhere, language is clearly used in this scene to demarcate cultural and social opposition by rendering Pizarro incomprehensible and thus silencing him onstage. Furthermore, by stressing the impossibility of communication without an interpreter, the text also casts a shadow over linguistic practices that supported colonialism, such as the famous *requerimiento,* a formula used by the Spaniards to claim ownership of the lands they encountered.[18]

In *Pocahontas,* Disney not only shows that it has learned its (historical) grammar lesson but also goes a step further by precisely making language a subject of the movie. Yet *Pocahontas* does away with the translator (and even with ambiguity) by suggesting that only an understanding heart is needed to communicate with the European other. In one of the most dramatic scenes in the film, John Smith and Pocahontas meet for the first time after spying each other from afar. While the natives have been speaking English up to this point in the movie for the benefit of the viewer (with some Algonquin language words thrown in for "authenticity"), the scriptwriters decided to foreground linguistic difference at this particular point. Oddly enough, after listening to Pocahontas in perfect English for a good number of minutes, the viewer is now made to realize that she does not know how to speak English. Thus, when John Smith addresses Pocahontas in his language, she replies in Algonquin, which makes Smith conclude she has not understood a word he has said. In a sense, we are back at the scene between Sairi Tupac and Francisco Pizarro, only there is no Felipillo in sight. At this point, however, magic comes to the rescue as Pocahontas remembers her wise Grandmother Willow's song (played as background music during this scene). In the song, the elder assures Pocahontas that if she listens with her heart she will understand. To the viewer's (and even John Smith's) amazement, Pocahontas tells Smith her name in a full, albeit hesitant, English sentence.

This cumbersome linguistic moment serves to reaffirm a set of stereotypical images that associate the primitive other with magic and instinct (as op-

MANUEL M. MARTÍN-RODRÍGUEZ

posed to European rationality), while at the same time portraying conquest and colonization as a willingness on the native's part to cooperate with the process by becoming Europeanized (by embracing the newly arrived's language). By thus displacing the native's center of gravity from the language-processing brain and the language-articulating mouth to the heart and the ear, the native becomes an emotional, passive figure. Needless to say, this is "Distory" at its best, reinforcing the ideological myths of colonialism,[19] a position not too far removed from that of fifteenth-century grammarian Elio Antonio de Nebrija, who wrote—in the first Castilian grammar, published the very same year Columbus arrived in the Americas—about language as a tool for imperial expansion.

Traditional gender roles are also invoked in this scene to further depict the process of imperial advance as one involving love between the soon to be subaltern and the occupying European power. The visual referent employed by Disney to that effect is that of engagement or wedding, as the hand of the European man reaches out to hold the woman native's hand. In thus accepting the foreign language and the foreign body, Pocahontas becomes a willing, subordinate extension of the new authorities in terms that are rather familiar for imperial discourses, in which the ethnic other is frequently portrayed as a female body of desire, thus sublimating war into the fiction of a love conquest (even if the historical Pocahontas was never engaged to Smith). In this gesture, older members of the audience will no doubt recognize the conventional motif of the erotic conquest of the female ethnic other as a metonym for the fictional ideologeme of conquest as the loving coming together of peoples. Mexico had its Malinche, and the United States (of Disney) now has its Pocahontas.

Fictionalized history is but one side of the Disney story in *Pocahontas*. The other is constituted by that which is not said.[20] The film ends with Smith and Ratcliffe being shipped back to Great Britain, one in bed (wounded) and the other in chains (as a prisoner). This physical withdrawal of the two main characters in the British camp is a misleading clue for the audience, suggesting a false ending in which the British would somehow withdraw from the Americas except for a small contingent left behind at their hurriedly constructed fort. The strategy is consistent with previous Disney practices of portraying historical events as moments in the past that have no bearing on the present. In this way, the natives of *Pocahontas* can indeed belong to the conventional category of the "noble savage," first popularized in the eighteenth century, while having nothing to do with present-day Native Americans from reservations across the country (and particularly those interested in land retribution). For children in the audience, these natives may no longer be the "injuns" in *Peter Pan,* as Byrne and McQuillan have noted, but they certainly are not the real flesh-and-bone Native Americans of the late twentieth century, either.

Happily Ever Before: Hispanics Causing Panic

DreamWorks' *The Road to El Dorado* (2000) tells the story of the arrival of the Spaniards in Mexico in 1519, even if it deals with a fabled rather than an actual city. While one would expect Hernán Cortés (the historical leader of the Spanish expedition) to play an important role in this film, Cortés is in fact relegated to a minor part as a dark presence toward the beginning and then again toward the end of this feature film. Cortés's obsession—finding gold—is equated with Ratcliffe's in *Pocahontas;* but because he stays outside of El Dorado, his influence on the plot is minimal. In his stead, Miguel and Tulio (two accidental/occidental "tourists"[21]) end up representing the colonizing enterprise in the DreamWorks version. In contrast to Cortés, Miguel and Tulio are two likable roguish characters who try to make as much as they can of their situation without any master plan. Their lot, as main characters, is to be mistakenly taken for gods by the natives (as real-life Spaniards were), and to encounter Chel, the filmic equivalent of Malintzín (in history, Cortés's interpreter and lover). In the end, however, and contrary to all historical fact, Miguel and Tulio help the Doradans seal off their city to prevent the entrance of Cortés and his army.[22]

In *El Dorado,* a geographical dislocation accompanies the temporal displacement toward the past already seen in *Pocahontas,* as the audience is asked to transport itself to sixteenth-century Mexico and (briefly) Spain. As in the case of *Pocahontas,* no connection is made between the historical peoples represented in the film and their descendants today, thus suggesting a rupture in the historical continuum and portraying the past as a static moment paradoxically somehow outside time.[23] In failing to make any connections between early Mexicans and their descendants today (many of whom have probably watched this film), *El Dorado* engages in an ideologically laden commentary about the present as much as it strives to re-create the past. In particular, in a filmic context already saturated with negative messages about Hispanics and/as immigrants, *El Dorado*—posing as a potential tribute to the Latino historical heritage—can be read instead as a visual equivalent of the xenophobic "go back to where you came from."

The depiction of the indigenous peoples of Mexico in *El Dorado* is in accordance with earlier stereotypes about Mexicans (and Latinos in general) that are deeply rooted in U.S. popular culture. Gone is the *gravitas* of the Native Americans in *Pocahontas,* as are their physical strength and fitness: these ancient Mexicans, with the exception of the priest and the ball players, are either obese and fond of feasts and music (as is Chief Tannabok) or weak, feeble citizens abused by the soldiers for violating a curfew. Most of the natives in *El Dorado* are childish and naive, perhaps following the example of their leader, who is fond of practical jokes and silliness in general. They are also deceitful, reinforcing earlier cinematic stereotypes about the treacherous Mexicans [24]: on one occasion, they are told by Chief Tannabok to smile at the "gods" as if they meant it.

Equally absent in *El Dorado* are love and wisdom from the female other, as Chel is clearly no Pocahontas. Inspired, as mentioned, in the historical character of Malintzin, Chel is the Spaniards' best ally in El Dorado. However, her motivations are not of the high kind that attracted Pocahontas to John Smith in the Disney film. Rather, from the very beginning she constructs their relationship as *business,* as she discusses her take of the loot with Miguel and Tulio. Like Pocahontas, Chel is sexualized, but what in Pocahontas was a statuesque physical beauty (accompanied by a dignified demureness) becomes a lascivious behavior in the shorter and chubbier Chel. Like any other hot-blooded Hollywood Latina, Chel is aggressive and more than slightly businesslike in her sexuality, using her body to cement an alliance with the European male (Tulio, in this case).

A third disturbing element in the presentation of the ancient Mexicans is the film's portrayal of religion. Through the evil, black magician Tzekel Kan, the native religion is depicted as barbaric (through the high priest's obsession for human sacrifice) and threatening to the state (suggesting several times an attempt on Tzekel Kan's part to seize power through religious fanaticism). In this regard, the movie is much closer to the present moment of reception than it is to the historical moment; U.S. anxiety about "evil" clerical regimes (particularly, these days, in the Arab world) surfaces quite clearly in *El Dorado* as one of its songs literally speaks of "all those prayers and all those *salaams*" as a source of danger. In this context, it is remarkable that the film manages to avoid any reference (visual or otherwise) to Catholicism: there are no priests accompanying the Spaniards, no crosses anywhere, and no religious interest on the part of the Europeans.

Another relevant difference between *El Dorado* and *Pocahontas* resides in their treatment of the Europeans. Of course, the need to define *European* becomes important, as Hollywood does not treat all Europeans equally. Southern Europeans, for one, have seldom participated in the positive traits reserved for Anglo-Saxon and other northern Europeans, and so the Spaniards in *El Dorado* are subject to a process of stereotyping as consistent as that characterizing the ancient Mexicans. Cortés is a dark, menacing force, significantly more ominous and brutal than the more refined Ratcliffe in *Pocahontas*. Furthermore, whereas in *Pocahontas* Ratcliffe is made a prisoner and sent back to England (thus suggesting an end to the abuses against the natives and the beginning of a just European rule), at the end of *El Dorado* the ominous Cortés marches through the jungle, missing El Dorado but on his way, no doubt, to brutalizing the natives elsewhere. On the other hand, Miguel and Tulio—while somewhat endearing—are clearly no match for John Smith in his heroism and high sense of altruistic justice (nor can their looks equal his).

Spain itself, furthermore, is subjected to a barrage of stereotypical images at the beginning of the film, with the portrait of street life in an unidentified (and therefore assumed by the viewer to be representative) southern port city. There we find our soon-to-be heroes (who, in truth, are somewhat closer to Spanish literature's pícaro than to proper heroic figures) gambling, serenading "señoritas" with a guitar, pretending to defend their "honor" with quickly drawn swords, and (already!) running in front of the bulls through the streets of the city as onlookers occasionally shout "¡Olé!" (as do spectators later on, when the Spaniards play a game of pelota with the Mexicans). The only people working in DreamWorks' Spain are the soldiers and those loading Cortés's ships; otherwise, the country seems to live in a permanent state of merry entertainment for which the streets are the main stage.

Considering that DreamWorks chose to use a character based on Cortés's translator, one would expect language to play an important role in this film, but *El Dorado* is rather disappointing in this respect. Everybody speaks English from the very beginning and there is never a linguistic misunderstanding between the characters. The only noticeable linguistic aspect in this film is the fact that Miguel and Tulio speak Spanish with an accent. Clearly, DreamWorks did not think it was important to have the Spaniards sound like Spaniards, as these roles went to Kenneth Branagh (Miguel) and Kevin Kline (Tulio). In fact, Hispanic actors were only used for the voices of the Doradans.[25]

What does take place in *El Dorado* is a great deal of cultural translation, as Chel has to repeatedly explain to the Spaniards the meaning of certain beliefs, practices, and ceremonies. This cultural difference is essential for my reading of the movie. By unbalancing the power equilibrium in El Dorado society (due to their ignorance of protocols and practices), the Spaniards become the source of terror for the common Doradans. In accepting their role as "gods," for instance, they bolster Tzekel Kan's power, which results in a constant death threat for innocent citizens. In their later siding with Chief Tannabok (enacting, in this case, a favorite divide-and-conquer tactic of the real life Cortés), they also cause much fright and danger for the population of the city, as Tzekel Kan assumes certain powers as the religious leader—and therefore representative of the gods—that result in the curfewing and the brutalizing of the denizens of El Dorado. Only at the very end of the film do these peculiar Hispanics stop causing panic in El Dorado—just as a new Spaniard arrives in an attempt to take their place.

Embedded in this exploration of cultural difference and hegemony is a narrative of colonialist economy that further strengthens the fiction of a good conqueror. This fiction largely rests on the familiar noble savage myth. Other than Tzekel Kan (who is nonetheless presented as an aberration hated by everyone else), the natives are a people living happily before the arrival of the Spaniards. In the song that introduces the film, their land is referred to as a paradise created by the gods a thousand years ago. Because of their paradisiacal location and existence, the Doradans (with the exception of Chel, the only principle female character) are portrayed as absolutely uninterested in worldly possessions and, in particular, in gold. In fact, when the newly arrived Spaniards demand a tribute other than human sacrifices, the natives are happy to give them all the golden objects stored in the temple, a considerable treasure that, in Tulio and Miguel's own words, will make them richer than the king of Spain. Ariel Dorfman and Armand Mattelart have analyzed the connotations of this peculiar type of economic transaction, a common occurrence in children's entertainment forms dealing with the other, in their classic study, *How to Read Donald Duck*.[26] First of all, Dorfman and Mattelart, who concentrate on Disney's comics, notice the common occurrence in those comics of a treasure that "is to be found in the Third World, and is magically pointed out by some ancient map," as is the case as well in *El Dorado*. More importantly, Dorfman and Mattelart notice that in surrendering his treasure to the newly arrived, "[t]he native is relieved of something he would never have thought of using for himself or as a means of exchange."[27]

This fiction of the willing surrender of the native's richness is one of the most cherished myths of neocolonialism. As such, it is always tied to the motif of the "first-world" savior who comes to the natives' "rescue" rather than try to convert them into political and economical subordinates. In *El Dorado*, the map that Miguel and Tulio win by playing with loaded dice brings them to the fabled city, where they are welcomed and greeted by childlike, friendly natives who make them their gods (even if almost everyone knows they are fake). They are offered the gold, which they plan to take back to Spain in a ship constructed by the natives. At this point and in this context, the movie makes its final statement about history. On the one hand, Miguel and Tulio, the fictional Spaniards, are allowed to play the role of the gold-deserving white saviors, as they first rid the city of the evil Tzekel Kan, and then prevent the entrance of Cortés (led by Tzekel Kan) into El Dorado. On the other hand, Cortés, the historical Spaniard, is denied contact with the natives, thus allowing history to stop. Without Cortés, there is no war, conquest, miscegenation, or present-day Mexicans. In this way DreamWorks—like Disney with *Pocahontas*—manages to cut the historical lines of communication between the past and the present while posing its product as a historical film. By creating a happily-ever-before (the Spaniards came) fiction of Mexico, the natives are reduced to an ahistorical people, much in the way in which the Native Americans are in *Pocahontas*. Dorfman and Mattelart describe a similar rhetorical movement of erasure in the Disney comics. They write, "The seizure of marginal peoples and their transformation into a lost purity, which cannot be understood apart from an advanced capitalist society, are ideological manifestations of its economic-cultural system. For these peoples exist in reality, both in the dependent countries and as racial minorities . . . within the U.S. itself." [28]

One is left to wonder what the biggest concern of DreamWorks' pseudo-historical enterprise really is. Is it Hispanics causing panic with their arrival in paradisiacal ancient Mexico, or Hispanics as an ethnic minority (soon to be the largest minority when this film was released) causing panic among neonativists in the 1990s United States?

Past(oral) Settings: Groovy Natives Meet the Cuzco Clan

Disney's *The Emperor's New Groove* (2000) takes the viewer farther back in time and space than the previous two films I discussed. While not a historical movie in itself, *The Emperor's New Groove* is historically situated in the pre-Hispanic Inca empire. Because of this, and because it continues the trend set by *Pocahontas* and *El Dorado,* I include it in this essay about history in recent children's movies, although my analysis will be necessarily shorter in this case. Like its predecessors, *The Emperor's New Groove* is marked by the way in which it speaks to both historical and present time. In this latter sense, the film supports itself in the context of conservative efforts to reduce the size and the role of the federal government (by dealing with a capricious central ruler who threatens local control of resources), as well as in the context of President Bill Clinton's 1999 "lands legacy" initiative, which was designed to acquire (or develop) land in 110 parks and historic locations in forty states, and which met with the opposition of conservative groups, including the Competitive Enterprise Institute, by foregrounding the issue of land appropriation by the central power.

The plot revolves around whimsical and all-powerful emperor Kuzco and his desire to build a new summer residence for himself (Kuzcotopia) atop a hill on the countryside. In order to do so, he must destroy an existing village, an action he is prepared to take as absolute ruler. In the meantime, however, his just-fired advisor (Yzma) transforms him into a llama with the aid of her magical powers. The transformed emperor spends most of the film with Pacha, a resident of the village he intends to destroy. Pacha, rather submissively, helps the emperor to go back to the palace and get the antidote needed to become human again. In the end, the transformed Kuzco finds a way to relocate Kuzcotopia, thus sparing Pacha's village.

As a heterological film, *The Emperor's New Groove* is the least inclusive of the three movies. Even though all of its characters belong to the same world (the Inca empire in ancient Peru), not a single Quechua or Hispanic actor was hired to play the voices in this film (needless to say, no Quechua or Hispanics are involved in significant roles in the direction, production, or even the musical score of the film). Ethnic/cultural conflict is not part of this film (as was the case with the other two films), since all characters are supposed to belong to the same ethnic group.[29] However, difference is marked throughout the film in terms of class and gender: the peasant Pacha's facial traits, for instance, are clearly identifiable as indigenous, as opposed to those of the characters from the capital city (nameless in the movie, but clearly the Incas' own capital, Cuzco);[30] Yzma, in her part as the evil female character, is depicted as an extremely thin and shriveled old lady, in accordance with similar grotesque characterizations of the female villain in earlier Disney films.[31]

In its relation to ancient history, *The Emperor's New Groove* continues developing the theme of the existence of a bucolic society prior to the "arrival of civilization" already seen in *El Dorado*. The natives are a happy people who live a mostly carefree existence in their remote hilltop villages. Family scenes at Pacha's home are used to further reinforce this image. Contrary to the norm in most previous Disney films, Pacha's family is portrayed as a complete unit in which none of the natural parents are absent or dead. Moreover, his ancestors are said to have lived in that particular village for the last six generations, and continuity is visually suggested by the fact that Pacha's wife is pregnant with a third child. Domesticity is indeed the trope associated with happiness in *The Emperor's New Groove:* the good female—as opposed to the wicked Yzma's—stays home and takes care of the house and children. Even when she is indignant, Pacha's wife finds a way to calm herself by washing one thing or another.[32] Were it not for the meddling interference of the Cuzco rulers, Pacha and his family would be happy living as their ancestors did.

Considering that the action in *The Emperor's New Groove* predates the arrival of the Europeans explored in *Pocahontas* and *El Dorado,* the pastoral setting of this film is to be understood within the "noble savage" frame of reference already analyzed above. In fact, this 2000 film is uncannily close to the examples from 1960s Disney comics—many of them set in the Inca (thinly disguised as Inca-Blinca) empire as well—in which Dorfman and Mattelart found how the myth of the childish noble savage functioned to validate a most cherished fantasy of the technological revolution. They write, "Moral: one can continue living in the city as long as there remains an ultimate refuge in the country; and as long as there survives the reality and idea of a noble savage. . . . The technological revolution is primed by the periodic return to the tribe, as long as it keeps its figleaf or loincloth [or poncho!] on."[33]

The fact that Kuzcotopia is going to be built after all can thus be interpreted as reaffirming the possibility of the natural man's coexistence with the technological amusement park, a line of thinking that may turn out to reflect Disney's own position in Florida, or even comment on Disney's troubles with its once-projected history theme park in Virginia.[34] In any case, in constructing the image of the ethnic other (regardless of whether she inhabits the city or the countryside) as a child driven by either the uncontrollable desire to have fun (Kuzco) or by an almost blind sense of obedience (Pacha), Disney follows a well-established tradition employed as a covert justification for the colonial enterprise. Chicana poet and essayist Pat Mora is one of many to react to such ideologically biased images when she notices how "this country often views us as either fiery, and thus less than rational, less than intellectual; or as docile, and thus less than effective, less than assertive."[35] The playful native, caught in a picturesque past she cannot escape, appears to be just waiting for the foreign civilizing power to bring progress and technology to her land.

More important for my purposes here, the construction of such an Arcadian locale and the lack of historical continuity also function in *The Emperor's New Groove* as a counternarrative to the stories of poverty, war, and deprivation that force present-day Latin-American immigrants to come to the United States.[36] After the film, mainstream viewers would have no way of comprehending the reasons for Latin-American immigration to the United States, but would rather be left with a paradisiacal image of the countries (inexplicably) left behind by the immigrants, frozen in a time before conflict. Unlike more politicized features such as Gregory Nava's independent film *El Norte* (1983), in which the Central American "paradise" is shattered by civil war, *The Emperor's New Groove* indulges in an atemporal myth in which the worst that can happen is to be the victim of black magic and thus turned into an animal in order to be taught a lesson. This is what happens to the city- and refinement-loving Kuzco, who is turned into the most rural of the Peruvian animals, the llama, as punishment for his urban insensitivity. The wicked, powerful, and independent Yzma, in turn, is transformed into the most domestic of the animals, a cat, and she is therefore domesticated and brought back to what should have been her gender-determined role in a peaceful and patriarchal society. But, if a lesson is learned (as it is for Kuzco), one recovers a playful self and will continue to enjoy an ahistorical existence free of pathos.

The rather obvious moral of the story resembles that of *Pocahontas* and, to a lesser extent, *The Road to El Dorado*: we can all live together in harmony so long as we accept our predestined roles in society. These include the native as a docile friend of the conqueror, the peasant as a submissive servant of the compassionate authority (whom the former regenerates through his kindness and simplicity), the woman as an obedient companion of the patriarch.

Class (and Ethnicity) Dismissed!

It is time now to return to the question I posed at the beginning of this essay. Why history? Why now? And to what American child is it being taught? Because of the increasingly multicultural face of the United States, Disney and DreamWorks are confronted with the problem of reaching children from cultures that have been the object of one-sided depictions for decades. They also need to reach Anglo-American children whose daily contact with youngsters from other ethnic groups makes those other cultures better known to them and much more nuanced than their earlier depiction in film, television, and fiction would reveal. Simple stereotypes are no longer acceptable, and the studios have responded with creating ambivalent pictures in which a high dose of cultural idiosyncrasy meets with a familiar, reassuring context that reinforces mainstream values and incorporates those foreign elements into nonthreatening conventional formulas.

At the same time, because adults are responsible for making these films and because adults are a large segment of their audience as well,[37] these films are built into a complex matrix of social referents that may be perceived by certain groups in the audience while they are entirely missed by others. As such, mainstream anxiety about racial and ethnic unrest are clearly part of the context for these films. *Pocahontas,* the earliest of the three, stresses its message of unity against the backdrop of the O. J. Simpson trial and subsequent strife; *The Road to El Dorado* and *The Emperor's New Groove* need to be read against the background of neonativist reaction to Latin-American immigration to the United States and, in particular, to the erosion of benefits and services for undocumented and even legal immigrants in this country.[38]

With this perspective in mind, we can begin to answer why Disney and

DreamWorks are interested in all of a sudden teaching American history to the American child. First, by eliminating, altering, and embellishing episodes of the past, they can construct a utopian vision of American history, one in which Native Americans were not decimated; Spaniards never conquered most of America nor participated in the process of *mestizaje* [miscegenation] that most distinguishes the Latin-American and Latino populations today; and in which the natives lived simple, lazy lives in harmony with nature. In addition, by eliminating any lines of continuity between the (depicted) past and the (lived) present, these films avoid engaging in a meaningful exploration of difference; rather, difference is portrayed as a thing of the past, a museum piece of sorts that the ethnographical movie offers the viewer for his voyeuristic consumption.[39] The resulting product is an ideologically loaded version of America's history (of a "reel" more than a "real" origin), in which the role reserved to non-European peoples is that of willingly facilitating the newcomers' imperial project or staying out of their way. Through temporal and geographical distance, furthermore, the American other is ironically kept out of U.S. history, as he inhabits only the past and/or a remote land without connections to that from where the (U.S.) viewer watches.

Reel history serves, therefore, to "correct" and reframe historical processes for the consumption and education of a heterogeneous group (American children and their parents) that is nonetheless invited to assume a homogenizing position (the "American child" or parent), conceived of as a "universal" group "beyond ethnicity." As such, reel history is a regressive strategy aimed to recreate and at the same time reduce the fear of social disintegration through the fiction of a *mall*ticultural coexistence of difference. Actual American children exposed to these history lessons may or may not recognize them as such.[40] They may, of course, construct alternative, more complex messages from their own enjoyment of the movies, possibly identifying with characters such as Chel, Tzekel Kan, or Yzma in ways not likely intended by the movies' narratives and visual imageries. Stuart Hall's ideas on the encoding and decoding of media messages indeed suggest that emancipatory readings can supersede preferred interpretation.[41] While much research on actual audiences is still needed to confirm possible alternative decodings of these films, my partial and anecdotal evidence indicates that minority children are definitely not comfortable identifying with characters supposedly from their own ethnic groups in these movies. Probably recognizing the commodification of ethnicity that the films involve, minority viewers find themselves in a contradictory position since, as members of distinct cultural groups, they cannot embrace the privileged normative position from which their ethnicity and their cultures are gazed upon in these heterological films. Yet because of the "ethnic" content of the films, and because of the "cultural authority

MANUEL M. MARTÍN-RODRÍGUEZ

and legitimacy" of the cultural purveyors involved,[42] minority children are invited and expected to recognize the *reel* experience as a *real* one.

In this context, (re)inserting the multicultural history of America into the school and the family curriculum seems to be the only alternative in order to provide American children with the kind of cultural literacy that would allow them to negotiate a more inclusive, more diverse, and better-constructed definition of what it means to be an American child when watching these and similar movies. Perhaps it is time for Duke, Stanford, MIT, and the local school district to start fighting back.

NOTES

The subtitle for the second section of this essay—"Hispanics Causing Panic"—is taken from Kid Frost's album *Hispanic Causing Panic* (Virgin Records America, 1-91377).

1. Throughout this essay, I use the term *American* to refer to both Latin and Anglo America unless the context restricts this meaning. My use of the term *American child*, however, is restricted to issues pertaining to children in the United States.

2. Carolyn Steedman, *Past Tenses: Essays on Writing, Autobiography and History* (London: Rivers Oram, 1992), 194.

3. The 2000 U.S. Census reports a population of roughly 281 million for the United States, approximately 28.5 percent of which is under nineteen years of age. The Census also identifies 12.3 percent of the population as black or African American, 12.5 percent as Latino (regardless of race), roughly 1 percent as Native American, 3.6 percent as Asian, and 5.5 percent as "other" race. Given these figures, and the fact that at least the African-American and the Latino populations are younger in age than the other groups, it is easy to sense the diversity of American children in the twenty-first century. See the U.S. Census, online at <http://www.census.gov/Press-Release/www/2001/tables/dp_us_2000.PDF>.

4. As I have suggested elsewhere, ethnic issues are part of an allegorical subtext in *The Lion King*, in which the border conflict between the lions and the hyenas can also be read as a metaphor for the current situation along the U.S.- Mexico border. See Manuel M. Martín-Rodríguez, "Hyenas in the Pride Lands: Latinos/as and Immigration in Disney's *The Lion King*," *Aztlán* 25, no. 1 (2000): 47–66. The most exhaustive treatment of ethnicity in Disney's films is found in Eleanor Byrne and Martin McQuillan, *Deconstructing Disney* (London: Pluto, 1999).

5. Gómez-Peña's critique of cosmetic multiculturalism is best summarized in the following quote: "Like the United Colors of Benetton ads, a utopian discourse of sameness helps to erase all unpleasant stories. The message becomes a refried colonial idea: if we merely hold hands and dance the mambo together, we can effectively abolish ideology, sexual and cultural politics, and class differences." See Gómez-Peña, *Warrior for Gringostroika* (Saint Paul: Greywolf, 1993), 57. I am suggesting that recent "ethnic" children's movies tend to likewise erase all meaningful differences by decontextualizing difference. Ramona Fernandez has also made explicit the critique of Disney's treatment of cultural difference as an object of mass/mall consumption. "Ordinarily," she writes, "Disney grossly distorts culture differences, homogenizing them into a happy culti-multural mix from which every alien element emerges Mickey-clean and ready for shopping mall consumption."

See Fernandez, "Pachuko Mickey," in *From Mouse to Mermaid: The Politics of Film, Gender, and Culture*, ed. Elizabeth Bell, Lynda Haas, and Laura Sells (Bloomington: Indiana University Press, 1995), 242. Not coincidentally, the publicity campaign for *Pocahontas* began, on 3 February 1995, with a twenty-four-city mall display. For further details on the campaign, see Gary Edgerton and Kathy Merlock Jackson, "Redesigning Pocahontas: Disney, the 'White Man's Indian,' and the Marketing of Dreams," *Journal of Popular Film and Television* 24, no. 2 (1996): 92.

6. For further information on Arab-American protest against *Aladdin*, see Janet Wasko, *Understanding Disney: The Manufacture of Fantasy* (Cambridge: Polity Press, 2001), 140–41; for *The Lion King*, see Martín-Rodríguez, "Hyenas," 50–52.

7. Byrne and McQuillan, in *Deconstructing Disney*, 215, draw a clear connection between the films and their social climate: "[T]he most recent Disney films have appeared to be actively engaging with questions of race, racism, ethnic cleansing and tolerance of cultural difference, marked by the climate of liberal social politics ushered in by the Clinton era. In the period immediately following his inauguration as President in 1993, from 1994 to 1996 Disney produced three films which signaled that bad old Disney would be purged and a new agenda for approaching race and national identity might emerge."

8. Ella Shohat, "Ethnicities-in-Relation: Toward a Multicultural Reading of American Cinema," in *Unspeakable Images: Ethnicity and the American Cinema*, ed. Lester D. Friedman (Urbana: University of Illinois Press, 1991), 215.

9. Michel De Certeau, *The Writing of History*, trans. Tom Conley (New York: Columbia University Press, 1988), 3.

10. Ana M. López, "Are All Latins from Manhattan? Hollywood, Ethnography, and Cultural Colonialism," in Friedman, ed., *Unspeakable Images*, 406.

11. Homi K. Bhabha, *The Location of Culture* (London: Routledge, 1994), 66.

12. Robert Burgoyne explores the shift in the treatment of Native Americans in recent films for adult audiences, from a position "providing the principal terms of otherness—savagism, infantilism, cannibalism, madness—against which the nation-state has historically defined itself," to "agents of a powerful counternarrative of nation, [and] bearers of an alternative historical consciousness." See Burgoyne, *Film Nation: Hollywood Looks at U.S. History* (Minneapolis: University of Minnesota Press, 1997), 40. For an assessment of how the Disney film relates to Pocahontas's life and history see Byrne and McQuillan, *Deconstructing Disney*, 113–16; Janet Wasko, *Understanding Disney*, 141–42; and Edgerton and Jackson, "Redesigning Pocahantas," 95–97.

13. Byrne and McQuillan, *Deconstructing Disney*, 111. The authors further illustrate the shift by comparing *Pocahontas*'s Native Americans with the "injuns" in *Peter Pan* (105–6). Given Disney's ability to reinvent itself without changing much of its formula over time, the notion of "new beginning" should be taken with a grain of salt, however. During World War II, for instance, Disney had already "reinvented" itself along the lines of the Good Neighbor Policy, thus attempting to adopt a new sensitivity toward Latin America(ns). In the words of Julianne Burton, "[Disney's 1945] *The Three Caballeros* also lays claim to considerable significance because it, and the related set of documentary travelogues, animated cartoons and live-action/animation combinations which led up to it, are the product of a concerted effort to expiate the past sins of North American cultural chauvinism, to replace hollow and hackneyed stereotypes with representations of Latin Americans ostensibly rendered on their own terms." See Burton, "Don (Juanito) Duck and the Imperial-Patriarchal Unconscious: Disney Studios, the Good Neighbor Policy, and the Packaging of Latin America," in *Nationalisms and Sexualities*, ed. Andrew Parker, Mary Russo, Doris Sommer, and Patricia Yaeger (New York: Routledge, 1992), 25. The fact

that the good neighbor's goodwill was later replaced by newer and reformulated stereotypes suggests that "new beginnings" are not necessarily permanent shifts in direction.

14. Byrne and McQuillan notice the connection with the Persian Gulf War and the crude mixture of "the Ayatollah and Saddam Hussein" that constitutes the evil character Jaffar, "encoded by the familiar marks of Western racism, wearing black clerical robes and a 'sinister' Islamic moustache and goatee." See Byrne and McQuillan, *Deconstructing Disney*, 74, 76. For an assessment of ethnic stereotyping in *The Little Mermaid*, see Patrick D. Murphy, "'The Whole Wide World Was Scrubbed Clean': The Androcentric Animation of Denatured Disney," in Bell, Haas, and Sells, eds., *From Mouse to Mermaid*, 125–36.

15. At the end of the film, in fact—after Pocahontas has persuaded her people to follow the path of love, not war—the wounded Smith receives a visit from Chief Powhatan, who addresses him as a brother and tells him he is always welcome among them.

16. Walter Prescott Webb, *The Texas Rangers: A Century of Frontier Defense*, 2d ed. (Austin: University of Texas Press, 1965), 7; emphasis added.

17. In translation:

> SAIRI TUPAC
> Bearded enemy, ruddy man,
> Why are you looking for
> my Lord, the Inca?
> . . . Before He raises
> his golden club . . .
> get lost, return to your land
> bearded enemy, ruddy man.
>   PIZARRO
> (only moves his lips)
>   SAIRI TUPAC
> Ruddy man, you who burn like fire
> you with the thick wool on your jaw,
> I cannot understand your strange language.
>   PIZARRO
> (moves his lips)
>   FELIPILLO
> Sairi Tupac, Lord in command,
> this blond man is saying:
> "Poor savage wretch,
> What is that foolishness?
> I cannot understand
> your confusing language."

Tragedia del fin de Atahualpa, in Miguel Leó Portilla, *El reverso de la Conquista: Relaciones aztecas, mayas e incas* (Mexico City: Joaquín Mortiz, 1985), 171–72; my translation.

18. Manuel M. Martín-Rodríguez, "'A Net Made of Holes': Toward a Cultural History of Chicano Literature," *Modern Language Quarterly* 62, no. 1 (2001): 1–18.

19. *Distory* is the term proposed by Stephen M. Fjellman to describe "Disney's Norman Rockwell view of history . . . designed to soothe park visitors" by tapping into "people's nostalgic need for a false history" by rewriting the historical account and/or by leaving only "the parts that 'should have happened.'" See Fjellman, *Vinyl Leaves: Walt Disney World and America* (Boulder, Colo.: Westview, 1992). I am appropriating Fjellman's term

for my analysis of film since I believe it is useful to describe the experience of "mainstream people" watching recent historical movies for children.

20. Historical erasure is, according to Mike Wallace, Disney's ultimate signature in dealing with the American past. See his "Mickey Mouse History: Portraying the Past at Disney World," *Radical History Review* 32 (1985): 33–57. For an analysis of how historical "silences" work in Disney's theme parks see Fjellman, *Vinyl Leaves*, 106ff.

21. Since Miguel and Tulio end up in Cortés's ship (and thus in El Dorado) as accidental stowaways, I am borrowing this pun from Marjorie Garber, "The Occidental Tourist: *M. Butterfly* and the Scandal of Transvestism," in Parker et al., eds., *Nationalisms and Sexualities* (New York: Routledge, 1992), 121–46.

22. In this respect, the movie clearly distorts historical facts by playing with the figures of two shipwrecked Spaniards who lived for a while with the Mayans. One of them, Jerónimo de Aguilar, joined Cortés's troops and served him as a translator (as the initial link between Malintzín and Cortés). The other Spaniard, Gonzalo Guerrero, married a noble Mayan woman and decided to stay with his new people. While in the movie Miguel toys with the idea of staying in El Dorado (albeit as a god, not as a husband), he ends up leaving with Tulio and Chel. The natives in this film are not identified as Mayan, but their physiognomy and their location suggest that they are. At the entrance of the tunnel leading to El Dorado, however, two prominent Olmec heads are visible—perhaps the remnants of that older civilization, perhaps a decorative effect added by the illustrators.

23. *El Dorado*'s strategy, in this sense, contrasts with material for children produced in Mexico around the same time. Francisco Trujillo's *La conquista para niños,* for instance, allows children to transport themselves to the past and back to the present, as it explores "tantos acontecimientos [que] dieron pie para que, tras una gran violencia, surgiera una nueva nación marcada por el mestizaje [so many events that led to, after much violence, the creation of a new miscegenated nation]." See Trujillo, *La conquista para niños* (Mexico City: Selector, 2001), back cover; my translation.

24. One of the first analyses of these stereotypes is found in Arthur G. Pettit, *Images of the Mexican American in Fiction and Film* (College Station: Texas A&M University Press, 1980), esp. chap. 2.

25. Rosie Perez is the voice of Chel, and Edward James Olmos the voice of Chief Tannabok. Armand Assante, an actor of mixed Italian and Irish descent often called upon to play Hispanic characters, is the voice of Tzekel Kan; Cortés's voice is that of Jim Cummings. Interestingly, this situation almost mimics El Teatro Campesino's 1968 play *La conquista de México [The Conquest of Mexico]*, written by Luis Valdez, in which the Chicano theater group had the Spaniards speaking English and the Mexicans speaking Spanish. Yet what was in the Chicano play a clever technique to make a linguistic/political commentary that equated the Spaniard's conquest of Mexico with the Anglo-American takeover of the U.S. Southwest seems to be here nothing but a poor casting decision. See Luis Valdez, *La conquista de México,* in *Early Works* (Houston: Arte Público, 1990).

26. Ariel Dorfman and Armand Mattelart, *How to Read Donald Duck: Imperialist Ideology in the Disney Comic,* trans. David Kunzle (New York: International General, 1991, 4th printing; orig. Spanish ed., 1971). While this book remains the best (and almost the only) known Latin American-based response to Disney's ideological project, resistance to the Disneyfication of Latin America has a longer, more varied trajectory, including the anti-Disney campaign of Peruvian poet Alejandro Romualdo and others. On Romualdo, see Winston Orrillo, "Un cuarto de siglo de la denuncia: Alejandro Romualdo arremete contra las tiras cómicas," in *La pedagogia reaccionaria de Walt Disney (y otros ensayos),* ed. Winston Orillo (Lima: Causachun, 1981), 105–10.

27. Dorfman and Mattelart, *How to Read Donald Duck,* 61, 49. The Doradans, in fact, are de-

picted as equally happy throwing the gold to Xibalba, a divinized whirlpool at the bottom of the main temple.

28. Ibid., 96–97.

29. A certain degree of what Albert Memmi called "the mark of the plural," the fact that "[t]he colonized is never characterized in an individual manner," is visible here in the homogenization of various communities and nations into a single entity. Stereotypical images of "the Mexican" are employed in this film to characterize the Incas (e.g., when Yzma is made to wear a Mexican *charro* hat at a restaurant's birthday celebration, and when children in Pacha's village play with a piñata to the rhythm of Mexican music). See Memmi, *The Colonizer and the Colonized* (London: Souvenir Press, 1974), 85.

30. The depiction of the city's surroundings leaves no doubt about this identification. Incidentally, some of the architectural design is somewhat reminiscent of that of Fritz Lang's *Metropolis,* thus emphasizing the connection between city and power.

31. As Janet Wasko notes, "Disney heroines are *always* beautiful, shapely, and often sexually attractive, while female villains are typically ugly and either extremely thin (Cruella) or grossly fat (Ursula), thus perpetuating norms of physical beauty prevalent in mainstream American culture." See Wasko, *Understanding Disney,* 116. The somewhat orientalized yet mainstream beauty of Pacha's wife confirms this stereotype.

32. Disney's emphasis on family life in this film can be read as a manifestation of the electoral debate about family values during the most recent presidential campaign. The family-life trope is so firmly established in this film that traditionally hidden winks to gay and lesbian members of the audience are actually made explicit here. As Pacha and Kuzco—the latter still a llama but disguised as an ugly woman—eat at a roadside restaurant, Pacha attempts to fool the waitress by telling her that they are on their honeymoon, to which the waitress retorts by blessing them for coming out in public. On Disney and gay issues, see Sean Griffin, *Tinker Belles and Evil Queens: The Walt Disney Company from the Inside Out* (New York: New York University Press, 2000); and Julianne Burton, "Don (Juanito) Duck," 21–41.

33. Dorfmann and Mattelart, *How to Read Donald Duck,* 93.

34. For a summary of that project's troubles, see William F. Van Wert, "Disney World and Posthistory," *Cultural Critique* 32 (1995–96): 187–214.

35. Pat Mora, *Nepantla: Essays from the Land in the Middle* (Albuquerque: University of New Mexico Press, 1993), 58.

36. In this sense, I disagree with Gilbert Adair, for whom "Disney's fable of an Arcadian American history wrecked by incursions from the Old World is obviously a means of allaying a bad conscience, while voicing xenophobic resentments about corrupt Europeans." See Adair, quoted in Edgerton and Jackson, "Redesigning Pocahontas," 97.

37. For a description of how Disney's products cut across different age groups, see Wasko, *Deconstructing Disney,* 185.

38. For an assessment of this context, see Juan F. Perea, ed., *Immigrants Out! The New Nativism and the Anti-Immigrant Impulse in the United States* (New York: New York University Press, 1997).

39. In *Reel to Real: Race, Sex, and Class at the Movies* (New York: Routledge, 1996), 223, bell hooks calls attention to "this current trend in producing colorful ethnicity for the white consumer appetite" and the ensuing commodification of blackness. I claim that these movies continue that trend, expanding the reach of the appropriation of ethnicity and targeting young viewers.

40. That actual European children have succumbed to a similar process of Disneyfication of their own history is the main thesis of Matteo Sanfilippo, for whom "Non è quindi sorprendente che i bambini italiani credano al Medioevo secondo Walt Disney, dato anche

che raramente famiglie e scuola spiegano loro criteri di verosimiglianza storica ispirati ai monumenti nelle nostre cittè [it is not surprising therefore that Italian children would believe the Disney version of the Middle Ages, since neither school nor family tend to explain their historical verisimilitude criteria inspired in the monuments in our cities]." See Sanfilippo, *Il Medioevo secondo Walt Disney: Come l'America ha reinventato l'Età di Mezzo* (Roma: Castelvecchi, 1993), 92; my translation.

41. See Stuart Hall, "Encoding and Decoding," in *Culture, Media, Language,* ed. Stuart Hall, Dorothy Hobson, Andrew Lowe, and Paul Willis (London: Hutchinson, 1980), 128–38.

42. The quoted text is from Henry A. Giroux, *The Mouse That Roared: Disney and the End of Innocence* (Lanham, Md.: Rowman and Littlefield, 1999), 84.

NOTES ON CONTRIBUTORS

GILLIAN BROWN is professor of English at the University of Utah. She is the author of *Consent of the Governed: The Lockean Legacy in Early American Literature* (Harvard University Press, 2001) and *Domestic Individualism: Imagining Self in Nineteenth-Century America* (University of California Press, 1990). She is currently at work on a manuscript tentatively titled *The Rise of Children's Literature.*

CATHERINE CENIZA CHOY, assistant professor of American studies at the University of Minnesota Twin Cities, is the author of *Empire of Care: Nursing and Migration in Filipino American History* (forthcoming, Duke University Press). Her current research focuses on the history of the adoption of Asian children in the United States.

GREGORY PAUL CHOY is assistant professor of English at the University of St. Thomas in St. Paul, where he teaches courses in critical reading and writing, contemporary American literature, and Asian-American literature. His scholarly work has focused on concepts of space and place in selected works of Asian-American literature.

LAURA DAWKINS is assistant professor of American literature at Murray State University, where she teaches African-American literature and gender studies. She is currently working on a book, *A Story To Pass On: The Tradition of "Activist Mothering" in African-American Women's Literature.*

MELANIE DAWSON teaches at the College of William and Mary and has recently published on Edith Wharton, Charlotte Perkins Gilman, and Henry James. With Susan Harris Smith, she edited *The American 1890s: A Cultural Reader* (Duke University Press, 2000). Her current project, titled *Spectacles of Agency: Home Entertainment and the Inscription of Middle-Class Identity, 1850–1920,* explores the leisure practices of nineteenth-century adults and the cultural work that represented and formed a modern middle-class consciousness.

LESLEY GINSBERG is an assistant professor in the Department of English at the University of Colorado, Colorado Springs. She has published articles on Nathaniel Hawthorne, Edgar Allan Poe, nineteenth-century American children's literature, and the American Gothic, and is completing a manuscript tentatively titled *The ABCs of the American Renaissance.*

KELLY HAGER is assistant professor of English at Simmons College, where she teaches Victorian literature and children's literature. She has published on Dickens's *David Copperfield* and is completing a manuscript about the failed-marriage plot and its intersection with the legalization of divorce.

CAROLINE F. LEVANDER is associate professor of English at Rice University. The author of *Voices of the Nation: Women and Public Speech in Nineteenth-Century American Literature and Culture* (Cambridge University Press, 1998), she is currently at work on a book, tentatively titled *Cradling Liberty: The Child and the Racial Politics of U.S. Culture.*

RICHARD LOWRY is associate professor of American studies and English at the College of William and Mary. He is author of *"Littery Man": Mark Twain and Modern Authorship* (Oxford University Press, 1996), as well as articles on nineteenth-century boyhood and subjectivity, and photography. The essay included in this volume is part of a larger project on family, publicity, and subjectivity.

MANUEL M. MARTÍN-RODRÍGUEZ is associate professor and director of Hispanic studies at Texas A&M University. His publications include *Rolando Hinojosa y su "cronicón" chicano* (Universidad de Sevilla, 1993), and essays in the *Handbook of Hispanic Cultures in the United States,* the *Cambridge History of Latin American Literature,* and the journals *Bilingual Review, Modern Language Quarterly,* and *Aztlán,* among others.

MICHELLE A. MASSÉ is associate professor of English at Louisiana State University. She is the author of *In the Name of Love: Women, Masochism, and the Gothic* (Cornell University Press, 1992), and essays on psychoanalysis, feminism, and fiction. She is currently working on a project about Louisa

May Alcott and the formation of feminist canons. Massé is the editor of the Feminist Theory and Criticism series from the State University of New York Press.

JULIA MICKENBERG is assistant professor of American studies at the University of Texas at Austin. Her book, *Seeds of Idealism: How Children's Books Linked the Old and New Left,* is forthcoming from Oxford University Press.

LESLIE PARIS is assistant professor of history at the University of British Columbia in Vancouver, Canada. She is currently completing a book on the early history of American children's summer camps, which is forthcoming from New York University Press.

KAREN SÁNCHEZ-EPPLER is professor of American studies and English at Amherst College. The author of *Touching Liberty: Abolition, Feminism and the Politics of the Body* (University of California Press, 1993), she is currently at work on a book tentatively titled *Rearing a Nation: Childhood and Social Formation in Nineteenth-Century America.*

CAROL J. SINGLEY is associate professor of English and a fellow in the Center for Childhood Studies at Rutgers University, Camden. She is the author of *Edith Wharton: Matters of Mind and Spirit* (Cambridge University Press, 1995); editor of three books on Wharton; and coeditor of two volumes of critical essays, on feminist theory and Calvinism in the modern era. She is currently completing a book about adoption in American literature and culture.

JANE F. THRAILKILL is an assistant professor of English at the University of North Carolina, Chapel Hill. She has published essays in the journals *American Literature* and *English Literary History,* and is currently completing a manuscript on therapeutic realism in nineteenth-century American fiction.

JEFFREY TURNER teaches in the Department of Theater Arts and Communication Studies at Hamline University. He has been involved with the Saratoga International Theater Institute and received his Ph.D. in theater from the University of Colorado, Boulder.

INDEX

Abbott, Berenice, 188

Abbott, Grace, 194

Abbott, Jacob C., *Rollo* books, 19, 37 n. 17

Abbott, John S. C., *The Mother at Home*, 94

abolition, images and rhetoric of, 85–89, 91–93, 95–98, 101, 103 n. 17, 105 n. 43. *See also* slavery

Abraham, Nicolas, and Maria Torok, 161; *The Wolf Man's Magic Word*, 158, 165 nn. 15, 20

absorption: objects and interests of, 15, 16, 17, 18, 19–20, 23, 36 nn. 4, 5; pleasurable, 21–22; of children, 23–24, 26–27, 29, 35, 36

Adams, W. H. Davenport, *Woman's Work and Worth in Girlhood, Maidenhood, and Wifehood*, 74

Addams, Jane, 186, 194, 196

Adler, Felix, 186

Adoption: placing out, 53–58; and sentimentalism, 264–65; and transracial, 10, 181, 263, 264–65. *See also* Korean adoptees

Adorno, Theodor, 17, 241 n. 3; *The Authoritarian Personality*, 241 n. 3

Alcott, Amos Bronson, 41

Alcott, Louisa May, 6, 7, 108, 110, 121, 126 n. 13

  Eight Cousins, 108, 126 n. 14

  Little Women 18, 20, 25, 28, 29, 75–76, 84 n. 49, 107–8, 109, 110, 111–15, 117, 121, 123, 126 n. 14

  "Our Little Newsboy," 44

  Rose in Bloom, 108, 110, 112–13, 116–18, 120

Alden, Isabella, *Pansy* books, 112

Aldrich, Thomas Bailey, *The Story of a Bad Boy*, 37 n. 17

Alger, Horatio, 6, 19, 32, 39 n. 52, 46–48, 49, 61 n. 21

  Fame and Fortune, 47

  Ragged Dick books, 20, 32, 39 n. 51, 46, 47

  Struggling Upward, 32, 39 n. 51

  Young Outlaw, The, 45, 49, 60 n. 13

Allen, Kelcey, 218

American Prison Association, 195

Anderson, Alexander, 86, 88 fig. 4.3, 96

Anderson, Sherwood, 151, 231

Ariès, Philippe, 3–4, 5, 65, 73; *Centuries of Childhood*, 3

Armstrong, Nancy, 64

Ashcan school, 211

Atherton, Gertrude, *Senator North*, 169

Norton, Caroline, "Bingen on the Rhine," 111

Obholzer, Karin, 160; *The Wolf Man,* 157, 161
Ostrowsky, Clara, 242 n. 9
otherness, 9, 152, 192, 269, 282–83, 286–87, 294, 296, 298 n. 12
Our Young Folks (children's magazine), 37 n. 17

Paglia, Camille, 210
Paine, Thomas, 4
Palumbo-Liu, David, *Asian/American,* 266
Pankejeff, Sergei ("Wolf Man"), 8, 149, 151, 154–62, 165 nn. 15, 18, 19, 20, 166 nn. 23, 25; "My Recollections of Sigmund Freud," 157
Parents magazine, 227, 236–37, 238, 239, 242 n. 9, 244 n. 47, 252, 261 n. 27
Parley's magazine, 97, 98
Paulding, James Kirke, 105 n. 43
Peabody, Elizabeth, 19, 23
Peck, George W., *Peck's Bad Boy,* 37 n. 17
Phillips, Adam, 29–30, 39 n. 50
photography: child-labor 9, 184–92, 198–204; WPA, 208; Linked Ring, 223 n. 7; pictorialist school of, 210–11, 223 n. 7; and progressive images of children, 234
Plato, 15; *Republic,* 14
play, 6, 7, 13–36, 41, 48, 51–52, 56–57, 84 n. 50, 150, 196; games and toys, 37 n. 37, 38 n. 45, 39 n. 47, 48–49, 58, 65, 66–67, 68–71, 156; and gender, 24–27, 57, 58, 63–74, 76, 80, 81 n. 12, 82 n. 19, 83 n. 48, 84 n. 49; and identity, 54, 58; war, 238
PM magazine, 226
popular fiction, 112, 121; nineteenth-century, 15–19, 36; and race, 167–81
Popular Front, 237, 238; and pedagogical function, 226–41
Popular Science Monthly, 171
Porter, Jane, *Scottish Chiefs* and *Thaddeus of Warsaw,* 127 n. 22
Price, Edgar, 218
Progressive Education magazine, 229
Progressive Education Association, 231
progressive movement, 244 n. 55; and parenting, 226–41; 92, 194. *See also* Popular Front; Communist Party

psychic trauma, 140–43, 144 n. 7, 147 n. 31
psychoanalysis, 150–62, 163 n. 7, 165 nn. 19, 20, 274; and Popular Front, 239. *See also* Freud, Sigmund, and Freudianism

race: and "black baby" tales, 8, 167–81; consciousness, 8–9, 17, 262, 264, 265, 270, 273; and devaluation, 168, 172, 174, 176, 180, 181; exclusion because of, 266–67, 273, 275; and miscegenation, 168–70, 172–81, 183 n. 29; and progressive attitude, 236–37, 238, 239; relations, 170–71, 175, 176, 227; and respecularization, 268–71, 274, 276; and slavery, 85–102, 189; stereotypes, 168, 262–263, 282, 283, 284, 286–87, 288–90, 298 n. 12, 298 n. 13, 301 n. 29
Rankin, Jo, "Exchange," 269–70
reading and reading lists, 7, 106–24, 125 n. 7, 146 n. 23, 147 n. 30; and DEFTing, 274–75, 276; literacy, 110, 200; Marxist bibliography, 238; and taste, 110, 111, 112–13, 116, 117, 119–20, 121; and trauma, 143. *See also* canon, literary; child: discipline of
realism: in children's fiction, 23; literary, 144 n. 7, 147 n. 29, 151, 244 n. 56; in photography, 184–204; on stage, 216–17; and trauma, 8, 128–30, 131–35, 141, 144, 148 n. 33
Rebekah (biblical), 179, 180
reform, 41–58, 189, 192–98, 203, 212
Reiner, Jacqueline, 3
Remarks on Children's Play, 7, 66–68
representation: of children, 16, 19, 23, 208, 209, 210; contradictory, 283; of girlhood, 64; of ethnics in children's films, 284, 285, 287–89, 292, 298 n. 13, 301 n. 29; in play, 6; of slavery, 85–102; and trauma, 129, 130, 133, 137, 138–39; 143, 146 nn. 23, 26; of underclass boys, 209–223; of violence against children in media, 133
Richardson, H. D., *Holiday Sports and Pastimes for Boys,* 71
Riesman, David, 241
Riis, Jacob, 185
Roach, Hal, *Our Gang* film shorts, 208
Robert Merry's Museum (children's magazine), 24–25, 90, 97–98